INTERNATIONAL LIBRARY OF NEGRO LIFE AND HISTORY

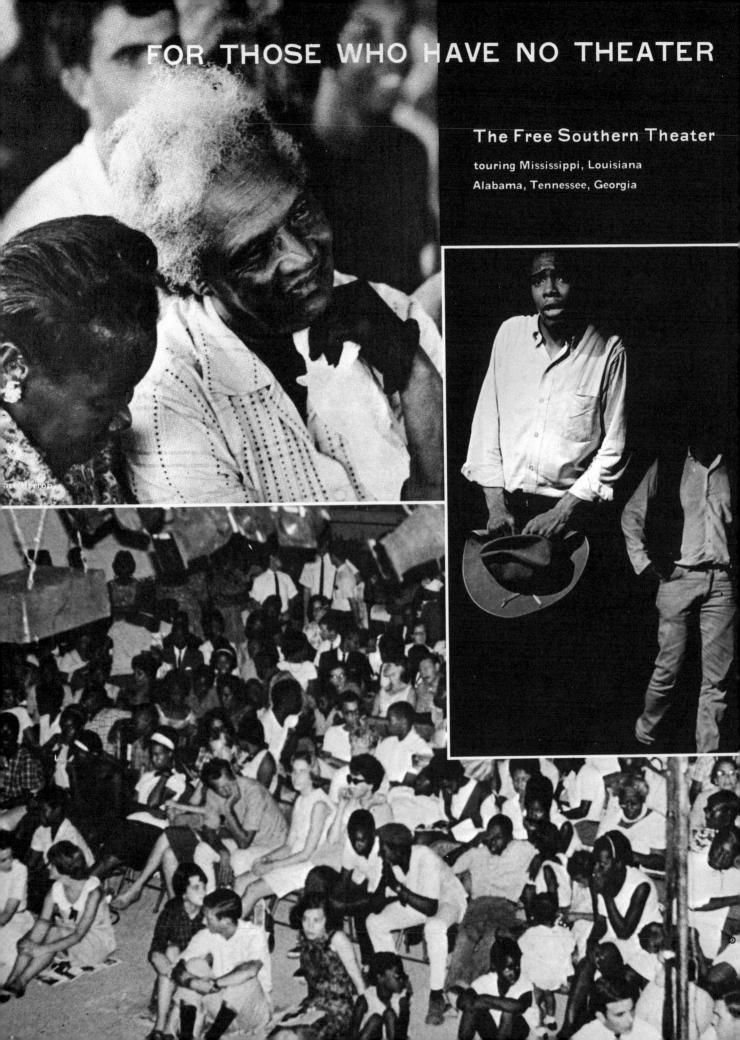

FOR THOSE WHO HAVE NO THEATER

The Free Southern Theater

touring Mississippi, Louisiana
Alabama, Tennessee, Georgia

INTERNATIONAL LIBRARY OF

NEGRO LIFE

AND HISTORY

ANTHOLOGY
OF THE AMERICAN NEGRO
IN THE THEATRE

A Critical Approach

Compiled and Edited with an Introduction by

LINDSAY PATTERSON, *comp.*

PUBLISHERS COMPANY, INC., NEW YORK, WASHINGTON, LONDON

under the auspices of
THE ASSOCIATION FOR THE STUDY OF NEGRO LIFE AND HISTORY

13

For

LANGSTON HUGHES

Editor-in-Chief, CHARLES H. WESLEY

Research Editor, PATRICIA W. ROMERO

Production Editor, ALLAN S. KULLEN

Art Director, ARCHIE MIDDLETON

Copy Editor, MARY NEELY ELDRIDGE

Editorial Coordinator, EMILY EVERSHED

THE EXECUTIVE COUNCIL OF
THE ASSOCIATION FOR THE STUDY OF NEGRO LIFE AND HISTORY

Preface

THE Association for the Study of Negro Life and History joins with Publishers Company, Inc., in presenting this new series of volumes which treat in detail the cultural and historical backgrounds of Negro Americans. This Association, a pioneer in the area of Negro History, was founded in Chicago on September 9, 1915, by Dr. Carter G. Woodson, who remained its director of research and publications until his death in 1950.

In 1916 Dr. Woodson began publishing the quarterly *Journal of Negro History*. In 1924 Negro History Week was launched, and since that time it has continued on an annual basis in the month of February, falling between the birth dates of Abraham Lincoln and Frederick Douglass. The *Negro History Bulletin* was first published in 1926 to serve both schools and families by making available to them little-known facts about Negro life and history.

During the fifty years of its existence, the Association for the Study of Negro Life and History has supported many publications dealing with the contributions of Negro Americans to the growth and development of this country. Dr. Woodson wrote several books which have served as standard texts in schools throughout the nation; and as a result of his scholarship and dedication others became interested in disseminating factual studies which would put the Negro in true perspective in American history.

With this fact in mind, we gratefully acknowledge the contributions of these previous scholars, which have aided us in the preparation of this *International Library of Negro Life and History*. Our grateful acknowledgment is also expressed to Charles W. Lockyer, president of Publishers Company, Inc., whose challenging approach has made possible this library.

Though each of the ten volumes in this set can stand as an autonomous unit, and although each author has brought his own interpretation to the area with which he is dealing, together these books form a comprehensive picture of the Negro experience in America. The three history volumes give a factual record of a people who were brought from Africa in chains and who today are struggling to cast off the last vestiges of these bonds. The anthologies covering music, art, the theatre and literature provide a detailed account of the black American's contributions to these fields—including those contributions which are largely forgotten today. Achievement in the sports world is covered in another volume. The volume on the Negro in medicine is a history of the black American's struggle for equality as a medical practitioner and as a patient. The selected Negro leaders in the biography book represent the contributions and achievements of many times their number. Lastly, the documentary history sums up the above-mentioned material in the words of men and women who were themselves a part of black history.

CHARLES H. WESLEY

Washington, D.C.

Editor's Note

I WISH to thank the following people for assistance in compiling this book: Allan Kullen for his splendid mechanical services; Emily Evershed for her more than excellent editing, which at all times was resourceful and astute; Raoul Abdul and Phil Petrie for their helpful suggestions on inclusion of material; Clinton Wilder for his reading of the galleys and his recommendations; Mrs. Jean B. Hutson of the Schomburg Collection of the New York Public Library, and her staff, Bruce Bates, Elizabeth Myers, Cora Eubanks, Ernest Kaiser, Richard Waters and Nancy Jessen, for their cheerful assistance; Mary Eldridge and Hedda Garza for their impeccable editorial sense; Henry Kier and Milton Meltzer; and Langston Hughes for use of his archives and facilities.

LINDSAY PATTERSON

New York City
January, 1967

Acknowledgments

WE are grateful for permission to use the following material in this book.

"One Hundred Years of Negro Entertainment," by Allan Morrison, published in *Ebony* magazine, September 1963. Copyright 1963, by *Ebony* magazine. Reprinted by permission of the author.

"Goodbye, Mister Bones: The Emergence of Negro Themes and Characters in American Drama," by Gerald Bradley, published in *Drama Critique,* Spring 1964. Copyright 1964, by the National Catholic Theatre Conference. Reprinted by permission of *Drama Critique.*

"The Negro and the American Stage," by Alain Locke. Copyright 1926, by Alain Locke. Reprinted by permission of the author's estate.

"The Drama of Negro Life," by Montgomery Gregory. Copyright 1925, by Montgomery Gregory. Reprinted by permission of the author.

"The Gift of Laughter," by Jessie Fauset. Copyright 1925, by Jessie Fauset. Reprinted by permission of the author's estate.

"Musical Comedy," from *Negro Musicians and Their Music,* by Maud Cuney-Hare. Copyright © 1936, by the Associated Publishers, Inc. Reprinted by permission of the Associated Publishers.

"Clorindy, the Origin of the Cakewalk," by Will Marion Cook. Copyright 1947, by Dr. Mercer Cook. Reprinted by permission of Dr. Mercer Cook.

"The Negro Playwright on Broadway," by Raoul Abdul, adapted from a lecture delivered May 27, 1954, at the Countee Cullen Branch Library, New York City. Reprinted by permission of the author.

"The Negro Dramatist's Image of the Uni- verse, 1920–1960," by Darwin T. Turner, published in the *CLA Journal,* September 1960. Copyright 1960, by the *CLA Journal.* Reprinted by permission of the *CLA Journal.*

"A Woman Playwright Speaks Her Mind," by Alice Childress, published in *Freedomways,* Winter 1966. Copyright 1966, by *Freedomways.* Reprinted by permission of *Freedomways.*

"American Theater: For Whites Only?" by Douglas Turner Ward, published in the *New York Times,* August 14, 1966. Copyright 1966, by the *New York Times.* Reprinted by permission of the author and his agent, Gilbert Parker.

"How I Became a Playwright," by Garland Anderson, published in *Everyman* (London), May 1928. Copyright 1928, by Garland Anderson. Reprinted by permission of the author's estate.

The Chip Woman's Fortune, by Willis Richardson. Copyright 1923, by Willis Richardson. Reprinted by permission of the author.

"The Federal Theatre," by Sterling A. Brown, from the *Myrdal–Carnegie Study,* 1940. Copyright 1940, by the Carnegie Foundation. Reprinted by permission of the author.

"Karamu," from *Any Place but Here,* by Arna Bontemps and Jack Conroy (originally published as *They Seek a City*). Copyright © 1945, 1966, by Arna Bontemps and Jack Conroy. Reprinted by permission of Hill and Wang, Inc.

"The Free Southern Theater: An Evaluation," by Tom Dent, published in *Freedomways,* Winter 1966. Copyright 1966, by *Freedomways.* Reprinted by permission of *Freedomways.*

"The Negro Actor Attempts Legitimate," by Sterling A. Brown, from the *Myrdal–Carne-*

Table of Contents

Introduction

IT IS a surprising state of affairs—in view of the Negro's contribution to the arts in this country—that so little on the Negro in the theatre exists in book form. There is virtually nothing of consequence about the Negro in dance; and there is very little about his performance in films, save two volumes published in England two decades ago and almost unobtainable here. It is hard to understand why this is true, since the Negro, to date, has gained his greatest equality in American life through the arts.

This anthology is an attempt to fill this gap, though it is by no means the definitive work on the Negro in the theatre, but rather a critical record of his achievements, which are many, and his lack of opportunity, which is considerable.

One tends to think of the theatre as being one of the most liberal institutions in America; but the fact is, the theatre has broken little new ground for the Negro since the late 1800's, when he displaced the blackfaced white minstrels on stage. Today the theatre continues, by and large, to reflect the stereotype of the Negro of yesteryear. Should the theatre mirror our times? Or should it set the pace?

This has been a hotly debated issue among producers and should be a primary concern of playwrights. Many producers, however, cite the economic hazards of the theatre, and its spiraling costs, as a basis for their reluctance to chance the unfamiliar, the step which might "offend" the public. This might be a valid argument were it not for the rec-ord, which plainly shows the financial successes of such potentially "offensive" offerings as *Jamaica, Golden Boy, No Strings, The Owl and the Pussycat* and *The Great White Hope*. Producers, I think, have grossly underestimated the intelligence and tolerance of their audiences. From my own knowledge of the theatre, it seems to me that the public will patronize any show that is entertaining and stimulating, regardless of its racial content.

What are possible solutions? Afro-American theatres? Most of the authors included in this volume see a need for such theatres. Will this also solve the employment problem of the Negro actor? Not totally, of course; but it will, at this point—and more importantly—give the young Negro playwright an opportunity to experiment. At present, he has few facilities in which to see his plays performed, and therefore he has few arenas in which to develop and mature as a dramatist.

If theatrical producers underestimate the intelligence and tolerance of their audiences, then movie producers seemingly are unwilling to make any estimation at all. Hollywood is still virtually the dream factory of fifty years ago, when it could safely portray the Negro as a handkerchief-head darky. Now, in the face of opposition, it has chosen to make just a few tepid attempts to deal with the black man and his problems. A few independent producers have shown real courage, it is true, but Hollywood—to put it mildly—remains hypocritical. For all the liberal attitudes expressed by white stars and producers,

one is hard put to discover any extensive change of approach in their movie-making. Groups of Hollywood luminaries do not hesitate to charter jet liners at a moment's notice to attend freedom rallies in the most rabid strongholds of racism, but their movies remain steadfastly lily-white. These are people who, in many cases, head their own production companies; and yet, where their voices would be most effective, they are curiously silent.

Ironically, the most complete gain for the Negro in the theatre has been in the almost total desegregation of movie houses and legitimate theatres. But behind the footlights, mere token concessions have been made to integration.

It is interesting and noteworthy that none of the articles in this volume appears dated. Alain Locke's "The Negro and the American Stage" (1926) seems as contemporary as Woodie King, Jr.'s, "Problems Facing Negro Actors" (1966). We know that progress has been made. How much? Time, seemingly, has not been a reliable indicator.

LINDSAY PATTERSON

New York City
January, 1969

In the Beginning

ONE HUNDRED YEARS OF NEGRO ENTERTAINMENT
by Allan Morrison

GOODBYE, MISTER BONES
by Gerald Bradley

THE NEGRO AND THE AMERICAN STAGE
by Alain Locke

THE DRAMA OF NEGRO LIFE
by Montgomery Gregory

THE GIFT OF LAUGHTER
by Jessie Fauset

MUSICAL COMEDY
by Maud Cuney-Hare

CLORINDY, THE ORIGIN OF THE CAKEWALK
by Will Marion Cook

Ira Aldridge

One Hundred Years of Negro Entertainment

by Allan Morrison

IT IS ONE of the supreme ironies of history that the Negro, whose folklore furnished the authentic core of popular culture in the United States and shaped its growth, should have had to fight against odds and obstacles to make his contribution to the performing arts and to express his talent. The vitality of the Negro's influence on American music, dance and drama has been irresistible, its impact profound and lasting.

The last 100 years has seen great improvements in the condition and status of the Negro entertainer. Starting as a figure of ridicule, a comic type and an object of the white man's amusement, he has slowly moved to a position of dignity and even protest and struggle. Serving his apprenticeship in minstrel companies, he acquired professional polish in musical comedies and finally emerged as a creative performer of more than one dimension. Out of the ranks of Negro entertainers came musicians, composers, comedians and creators of songs and dances.

Before slavery ended, the Negro had started to permeate popular music and eventually dominated it. Negro slaves provided the music of the plantations, entertaining for their masters who sat on the Big Porch of the manse. For nearly 100 years this servant-master relationship of Negro performers to white audiences continued in various forms. The early Negro entertainers had to withstand derision and contempt and were never allowed

to forget that they came from a people of bondage.

A decade before the Emancipation Proclamation was issued free Negroes in New York were allowed to see the stage version of *Uncle Tom's Cabin* but in segregated seats. The play was performed by an all-white cast. But long before that Negroes had been performing on stages. In 1821 the African Company of Negro actors was formed in New York and presented their plays at the African Grove in Greenwich Village. October 27, 1821, the following snide announcement appeared in the New York *National Advocate*: "The gentlemen of color announce another play at their pantheon, corner of Bleecker and Mercer Streets on Monday evening. . . . They have graciously made a partition at the back of the house, for the accommodation of the whites."

Whites attended the African Company's performances but often to jeer and shout insulting words at the actors. Because of a succession of incidents provoked by rowdies, the authorities closed down the theater. About this same period came Ira Aldridge who inspired and vitalized Negro acting and actors during and long after a remarkable career which ended in 1867 with his death in Lodz, Poland. Grandson of an African chief, Aldridge was the first of a long line of Negro artists who emigrated to Europe to find outlets for their talent and an acceptance impossible in their native land. Aldridge overcame initial resist-

ance in England to become one of the most celebrated Shakespearean actors of his day. Othello was his greatest role, but his total achievement was to prove that a black man was capable of classic performance by the highest standards of white men.

Early archives of U. S. entertainment reveal that Negro performers were eager a century or more ago to demonstrate that they, too, wished to make a witness for freedom. The Luca family, one of the pioneer Negro musical troupes of America during the pre-minstrelsy era, performed at the anniversary celebration of the Anti-Slavery Society in New York in 1853. When the Civil War began, many Negro entertainers in the North joined their free racial brothers in vocal support of the Union and its war aims. Many volunteered for military service against the Confederacy or took part in the ceaseless agitation for freedom.

The issuance of the Emancipation Proclamation occurred when minstrelsy was moving from the plantation, where it began, to the professional stages of the country. It was developed into an authentic American art by the freedmen who entered show business after slavery. The earliest minstrels were former slaves or freedmen who escaped or migrated to the non-slavery states. Negro minstrel stars like James Bohee of the Bohee Brothers and James Bland gave command performances to European monarchs and one gave banjo lessons to an English king. Minstrelsy marked the beginning of Negro participation in the American theater. Most of these early minstrels barnstormed the country from their headquarters in New York where they were the nucleus of New York's first black bohemian circles. A few of these minstrels were frustrated classical actors who had read Shakespeare's plays and knew parts from other classics. They instinctively rebelled against the indignities of burnt-cork min-

strelsy and nourished a passionate yearning to play classic tragedy.

By the time Negro minstrels entered show business on a substantial scale in the late 1860's, the pattern of minstrelsy had been set by white minstrels who borrowed from the songs and dances of the slave performers and exploited this material commercially. The Negro professional minstrels conformed to the pattern, blackening their faces, but at the same time bringing new freshness and vitality to the minstrel stage. Minstrelsy left a damaging imprint on entertainment in the United States because it caricatured Negro life and pictured the Negro as an irresponsible, grinning, banjo-playing and dancing type devoid of dignity and depth.

Though minstrelsy was a distasteful way stop along the road to dignity, it had its value. Negro minstrel companies like the Original Georgia Minstrels and Howard's Novelty Minstrels were training grounds for performers who were able to move on to the next phase of theatrical life. But terrible damage had been done to the image of the Negro entertainer: he had been forced to don a mask decreed by white society. "The American white man was determined to have his fun out of the Negro," observes Professor Sterling Brown in an analysis of the social role of minstrelsy. For nearly a century, Negro entertainers strove to rid themselves of the stigma symbolized by the mask they had to wear.

The color bar in the theater prevented Negroes from being cast in white productions until 1877, and not until 1879 was the first genuinely Negro Topsy seen in the play *Uncle Tom's Cabin.* The blackface tradition received a shattering blow in the 1890's with the production of *The Creole Show,* which for the first time glamorized the Negro girl and opened a pathway to a series of epochal all-Negro musical comedies. *The Octoroons,* which followed this show in 1895, was billed as a "musical farce," but made history be-

cause for the first time Negro females were used as principal performers. This was a rich period for the Negro entertainer, the years of the cakewalk and the "coon songs," of the Jonah man and the beginnings of ragtime. Spirituals began to be appreciated as serious music. It was also a time when the Negro began to reject the blackface caricature of himself and to exhibit a capacity for playwriting and musical composition.

The break with the minstrel tradition was further widened in the 1898-99 theatrical season when the musical *A Trip to Coontown,* written by the legendary Bob Cole, was presented in New York. It was the first show to be produced and stage-managed by Negroes and based on a script which had structure and continuity. Though still stereotypical in style, this show was revolutionary in technique and moved Negro entertainment another step away from minstrelsy.

By 1890, the federal census reported a total of 1,490 Negro "actors and showmen" in the U.S., none of whom were appearing in legitimate dramatic productions. The 1910 census showed that the total number of professional entertainers had risen to 3,088, most of whom were employed in all-Negro musicals.

Meanwhile, the Negro comic art had been entwined with controversy since the 1890's when Ernest Hogan, Bob Cole and Williams and Walker threw the Broadway theater into an uproar with their antics. Hogan wrote the smash song hit, "All Coons Look Alike to Me," which earned him considerable royalties but troubled his conscience in later years. He was attacked for writing a song which reinforced white prejudice against Negroes, but like some Negro entertainers of his generation and type defended what he did by pointing out that the song helped make work and money for destitute performers. However weak this argument was, it must be remembered that it was society which demanded that the Negro in entertainment should work in a racially-degrading idiom.

Many a Negro entertainer has amused the white man at the price of heartbreak and loss of dignity. Bert Williams, one of the true titans of U.S. show business, was touched with genius, but, like so many of his colored brethren who had to play the buffoon for the white man, he had a secret longing to perform in serious drama outside of burnt cork. For ten years, Williams was a star of *The Ziegfeld Follies,* and his triumphs there made him a brilliant and colorful figure of modern America. He brought to the theater of his time a unique excitement. Dead at the early age of 46 in 1922, he had blazed a trail for the Negro performer from the minstrel stage to the legitimate theater, and had unlocked doors which for a century had excluded colored performers from white shows. Williams is a pivotal figure in the onward movement of the Negro entertainer because by his charm and talent he did much to conquer prejudice and to overcome hostility to mixed casts. Technically, he refined the art of Negro comedy by replacing crudity with finesse and drollery. His subtlety and superb presence made white audiences laugh from their bellies, but offstage he was a sober, serious and unhappy man imprisoned by the bars of prejudice.

During the New York race riots of 1900 Negro entertainers became focal figures and targets of the wrath of white mobs seeking black victims. At the height of these disturbances, cries were heard "get Ernest Hogan and Williams and Walker, and Cole and Johnson." These were the names of famous Negroes in show business whom the crowds knew and regarded as symbols of the Negro community. Hogan, who had opened in a show at the old Winter Garden Theater, and George Walker narrowly escaped injury at the hands of anti-Negro mobs. When race relations deteriorated, Negro progress in the entertaining

arts slowed down, indicating a direct connection between the Negro's status as a citizen and his freedom to express himself artistically. During the decade of 1890-1899, 1,665 Negroes were lynched in the U. S. For the Negro population the picture was grim; for the Negro entertainer the outlook was dark and discouraging.

After 1910 the Negro entertainer made his impact felt largely through spectacular musical shows in which the teams of Williams and Walker and Cole and Johnson starred. Then a number of Negro stock companies were organized which stimulated theatrical activity in the larger Northern cities. The most important of these, the Lafayette Players of Harlem, presented creditable versions of plays that had been produced on Broadway with white casts. The Lafayette Players disbanded in the late 1920's, but not before it had produced one great star, Charles Gilpin. Gilpin and Paul Robeson, then a fledgling actor fresh out of Rutgers and Columbia, were responsible for major break-throughs for the Negro in the theater of that time. Gilpin's electrifying performance in the lead role of *The Emperor Jones* by Eugene O'Neill was the most distinguished event of the 1920 season, while Robeson was projected into dubious fame by his role in *All God's Chillun Got Wings,* the controversial O'Neill play about interracial marriage. O'Neill displayed courage in daring to write about this taboo theme, but partly conformed to the mores of the day by making his white woman heroine go insane under the pressures of miscegenation.

Show Boat, first presented on Broadway in 1927, helped to demolish other taboos on the use of Negroes in the theater. Dignified and full-dimensional portrayal of Negro character was a long time coming to the American theater. *Porgy,* the play, introduced a new approach to Negro character by white playwrights. Though imperfect in treatment and redolent of the old romantic conception of the Negro, *Porgy and Bess* and *The Green Pastures* were commercial milestones for the Negro theatrical performer. The Federal Theater of the depression days further helped to erase racial barriers by giving Negro actors and performers opportunities in its productions. For the first time under its program, Negro actors received serious professional training. By the beginning of World War II the hoary and false idea that the Negro was a born actor who did not require training had been discarded.

World War II unleashed forces of change that altered the position of the Negro actor and performer, and changed the attitudes of producers, writers and directors on the use of Negroes and racial themes. Traditional casting of Negroes in servant roles without depth diminished. The Negro began to be cast more as a human being.

But Broadway on the whole dragged its feet in realistic portrayal and democratic casting of Negroes. The 1943 production of *Othello* starring Paul Robeson was a landmark because for the first time a Negro played the title role on Broadway. It had taken a century to achieve even this concession, but it reflected a change in the theatrical climate of the times. When the late Canada Lee acted the part of Daniel de Bosola in whiteface in *The Duchess of Malfi* in 1946, Boston drama critic Eliot Norton wrote: "Mr. Lee's performance . . . seemed to prove the point at issue, that a colored actor can portray credibly a white role, just as white actors, for generations, have personated people of the other race."

Actors Equity Association, the professional actors union, has in recent years advocated non-racial casting of Negroes. In 1959 the Association called upon "all responsible creative elements of the theater arts to grant freedom of choice . . . to cast aside preconceptions regarding the casting of Negro artists . . . to extend their scope and participation in

SECOND SERIES
OLD DAN EMMIT'S
ORIGINAL
BANJO MELODIES
NEVER BEFORE PUBLISHED

SONGS IN

DAR HE GOES, DATS HIM!
MY OLD DAD.
CORNFIELD GREEN.
SCHOOLMASTER ABROAD.
DE OLD BANJO.
BLUE TAIL FLY.
ROCK SUSANDER.

THIS SERIES.

POMPY O'SMASH.
LEDDER BREECHES.
DE BANJO NIGGER.
DE WILD GOOSE NATION.
BACK ACTION SPRING.
WALK JAW BONE.

Mr. D. D. EMMIT.

AS SUNG BY HIM WITH UNPRECEDNTED SUCCESS,
AT THE THEATRES & CONCERTS, BOTH IN EUROPE & AMERICA.

BOSTON, PUBLISHED AT KEITH'S MUSIC PUBLISHING HOUSE 67 & 69 COURT ST.
Where may be found every description of Negro Songs.

LITH. OF E.W. BOUVÉ BOSTON.

Price 25 cts. nett

Entered according to act of congress in the year 1844 Chas H. Keith in the clerks office of the district Court of Massachusetts.

all types of roles . . . in all the forms of American entertainment." Actors Equity in 1948 forbade its members to perform in Washington, D.C., theaters practicing discrimination, and in 1962 wrote into the contract negotiated with theater owners the following clause which is now included in every legitimate theater booking contract throughout the country: "The actor shall not be required to perform in any theater or other place of performance where discrimination is practiced because of race, color or creed against any actor or against any patron as to admission or seating in such theater or other place of performance." The Ethnic Minorities Committee of Actors Equity conferred in June with representatives of the Society of Stage Directors and Choreographers in an effort to bring about greater use of Negro performers and to encourage playwrights to include in their plays appropriate and dignified parts for performers from the Negro and other ethnic groups.

Only last June the American Guild of Variety Artists, which has jurisdiction over night club, vaudeville and circus entertainers, urged its 15,000 members not to appear at places of entertainment which discriminate, but has not yet translated this with a specific prohibition in a union contract. Jim Crow in entertainment is now exceedingly unfashionable, but little more than a decade ago most Negro performers were frequently making the humiliating compromise of appearing where their own people were barred from seeing them. Josephine Baker, who began as an end girl in the chorus lines of such hit Negro musicals of the early 1920's as *Shuffle Along* and *Chocolate Dandies,* returned from European expatriation in 1951 to strike an important blow at the color bar in entertainment. She insisted on a no-discrimination clause in her contracts with clubs and embarked on a colorful crusade against bias which made powerful enemies for her but earned her new millions of admirers.

Broadway, Hollywood and the vast television industry have been reluctant to keep pace with changing interracial relations or to heed the just demands of the Negro for fuller participation and fairer portrayals. The question of how far the entertainment media have mirrored the Negro's progress and included him adequately goes to the root of the position of the Negro performer today. Integration in the performing arts is moving all too slowly, but the tempo has recently accelerated and there are other encouraging indicators of change. Now, as 100 years ago, the Negro's place in the entertainment arts reflects his progress and status in the larger society of which he is a part, is, in fact, inseparable from it.

Negro entertainers have been assaulted and insulted by segregationists and racists. In the South, mixed shows arouse the fury of extreme racists like New Orleans political boss and arch-segregationist Leander Perez who in 1956 showed his displeasure when Ted Lewis did his celebrated *Me and My Shadow* number at the Roosevelt Hotel by throwing bread and a tray on the floor. Lewis was performing with Elroy Pace, his Negro "shadow."

The great Bill Robinson reached the summit of show business but endured many humiliations during his ascent. Sarah Vaughan, at the crest of her fame, was pelted with tomatoes in a Chicago theater. Nat Cole was the victim of a vicious onstage attack by members of the White Citizens Councils while appearing before a segregated audience in his hometown of Birmingham, Ala., in 1956. The attack on Cole was preceded by a gathering of his assailants at the back of the theater and the muttered exhortation, "Let's get that nigger!" Cole drew severe criticism for agreeing to perform before segregated Southern audiences and for declining an invitation from NAACP's Roy Wilkins to join the developing

crusade against racism, though he later became a life member of the Association. Besides Cole, the NAACP Life Membership roster includes such entertainers as Lena Horne, Sammy Davis, Jr., Fats Domino, Johnny Mathis, Duke Ellington, Count Basie, Harry Belafonte, Chuck Berry, Al Hibbler, Mahalia Jackson, Louis Jordan, Jonah Jones, Joe Williams, Clyde McPhatter and Marian Anderson.

The courage shown by protesting Negro thousands in direct-action campaigns in the South has inspired artists like Lena Horne, Dick Gregory and Al Hibbler to publicly participate in the national Negro upheaval for full freedom. They have carried the fight into such segregation strongholds as Jackson, Miss., and Birmingham. Gregory has been beaten and imprisoned.

Mahalia Jackson coordinated a mammoth Southern Christian Leadership Conference benefit program in Chicago which raised nearly $40,000 for the civil rights cause. Johnny Mathis pledged to give the NAACP and SCLC $20,000 in fees from performances in New York and Chicago. The militant temper of today's Negro entertainers is shown in their appearances at the numerous benefit shows being staged around the country and their pledges of financial contributions.

During the much-publicized meeting in New York last June, between Attorney General Robert F. Kennedy and a group of Negro intellectuals and performers, Harry Belafonte and Lena Horne surprised the President's brother with the vigor and clarity with which they articulated the cardinal demands of Negro Americans. "Individual human rights— the God-given dignity of man. That's all we're fighting for," Belafonte thundered.

The Negro entertainer of old usually had been forced to sell his wares to prejudiced audiences, to use a racial idiom and, even more damaging psychologically, to be a racial buffoon rather than a human being. The goals of the Negro entertainer of 1963 are essentially the same as those sought by his predecessor during the past century: to be judged strictly on talent, to discard undignified identities and stereotypes and to demand and assert his own humanity.

The story of the Negro in the entertainment arts has been one of growing affirmation of manhood and citizenship. His final goal will not be reached until his story cannot be isolated from the larger panorama of American entertainment as a whole and when he can make his contribution as an individual actor, singer, dramatist and citizen. One hundred years ago most roads were closed to the full unfettered expression of the Negro performer's talent. Today the way is open as never before.

— 1963

Bert Williams and George Walker were pivotal figures in the Negro's gradual acceptance into the world of show business.

Josephine Baker, who began her career as an end girl
in the chorus lines of such hit Negro musicals of
the early Twenties as *Shuffle Along* and *Chocolate
Dandies,* returned from European expatriation in 1951
to strike an important blow at the color bar
in entertainment.

Although acknowledged as the greatest entertainer
in his field, Bill Robinson often suffered the same
racial humiliations as the Negro in the street.

GARRICK THEATRE

LEE SHUBERT and JOHN CRAIG..............Lessees

FIRE NOTICE

Look around NOW and choose the nearest Exit to your seat. In case of fire walk (not run) to THAT Exit. Do not try to beat your neighbor to the street.
ROBERT ADAMSON Fire Commissioner.

WEEK BEGINNING MONDAY EVENING, APRIL 23, 1917.
Matinees Wednesday and Saturday

MRS. HAPGOOD Presents

THREE PLAYS

By RIDGELY TORRENCE

Under the Direction of
ROBERT EDMOND JONES

THE RIDER OF DREAMS

A COMEDY

Cast of Characters

Lucy Sparrow .... Blanche Deas
Booker Sparrow .... Joseph Butt
Madison Sparrow .... Opal Cooper
Dr. Williams .... Alexander Rogers

GRANNY MAUMEE

A TRAGEDY

Cast of Characters

Granny Maumee .... Marie Jackson-Stuart
Pearl .... Fannie Tarkington
Sapphie .... Blanche Deas

PROGRAM CONTINUED ON SECOND PAGE FOLLOWING

PROGRAM CONTINUED

*SIMON THE CYRENIAN

A PASSION INTERLUDE

"And as they led Him away they laid hold upon one Simon, a Cyrenian— and on him they laid the cross that he might bear it after Jesus."—Luke 23, 26.

Cast of Characters

Procula .... Inez Clough
Drusus .... Andrew Bishop
Acté, Princess of Egypt............................Lottie Gray
Battus .... Theodore Roosevelt Bolin
Simon .... John T. Butler
Pilate .... Alexander Rogers
Barrabas .... Jesse Shipp
The Mocker with the Crown of Thorns................Robert Atkin
The Mocker with the Scarlet Robe................Thomas William
Egyptian Herald .... Frederick Slade
Centurion .... Andrew Bishop
Longinus .... Ralph Hernandez
Soldiers........................... { Jervis Wilson / Earl Taylor / Lisle Berridge }
Attendants to Procula...................... { Thomas William / Jerome Osborne, Jr. }
Attendants to Acté........................ { Olga Hamilton / Dorothy Hampton / Samuel Tobias }

Scene—The Garden of Pilate's House at Jerusalem.
Time—The Day of Jesus' Crucifixion.

(Mr. Bishop appears by arrangement with the Lafayette Stock Company)

*(Although Cyrene was in Northern Africa, the wall paintings in the vast Cyrenian tombs depict black people instead of brown. The Jesus' cross-bearer was a black man, as the early Renaissance painters represented him, is a fact that holds a certain suggestion bearing upon a phase of modern society.)

Costumes and scenery designed by Robert Edmond Jones.
Scenery executed by Dodge and Castle and Lee Lash Studios.
Lighting by William Pennington.
Costumes by Mrs E. A. Logan.
Properties from C. W. Miller; Sied'e Studios.

EXECUTIVE STAFF

Business Manager ....Lawrence J. Anhalt
General Representative ....Mrs. James W. Johnson
Press Representative ....Hiram K. Moderwell
Supervisor of Music...................J. Rosamund Johnson
Chief Electrician .... John Horohan
Assistant Electrician .... John Brennan
Carpenter .... John Ellis
Master of Properties .... John Ahearn
Stage Manager .... Jesse Shipp

J. T. Brym, Conductor.
Orchestra, Members of the Clef Club.
Choral Director, William C. Elkins.

MUSICAL PROGRAM

Singing Overture
First Intermission
Characteristic Negro Songs
Second Intermission
Negro Spirituals

(Note:—"Walk Together Children," sung before the rise of the curtain on the play is an old Negro spiritual developed by J. Rosamund Johnson.)

Goodbye, Mister Bones

The Emergence of Negro Themes and Characters in American Drama

by Gerald Bradley

IN THE beginning there was the darkie, chirping "Yassuh" and "Nosuh" and "Ahse gwine down to de sprink house 'n' ead me some waddemelon." He was not new when Harriet Beecher Stowe's novel *Uncle Tom's Cabin* became a play. He shuffled on the American stage in 1798 as Ralpho, a character in Robert Munford's *The Candidates,* and has been around, on stage and in print, ever since. There must have been a reason for him —comic relief, no doubt—and a basis in fact for his speech and actions. Perhaps the old slaves did dance and skip and, in trying to combine their various tribal tongues with the graciously developing mouth-full-of-grits English of the White Southerner, did say "gwine" and did pronounce some g's as k's. Not all did, of course; but then, not all Irishmen say "Wurra, wurra" and "Soints presarve us," although one would have a hard time proving it if he were to use American plays and novels as historical evidence.

The stage Irishman has almost disappeared, just as in society he has almost melted into the American mass. So, too, it may be hoped, have the "Mamma-mia" Italian and the "Oy, vey" Jew. The stage Negro, however, has not been assimilated—at least, not nearly so completely. But then, he has not yet melted into society, either. Although he may no longer be Ralpho or Mr. Bones or Rastus, he is seldom more than a combination of Uncle Tom and Mammy, principally because the Negro is still usually written about by white playwrights and because there was from the first, as a result of segregation, a lack of contact between true Negro life and literate society. Where the Negro is concerned, his treatment in drama has paralleled his treatment in society.

I am concerned to show the development of Negro themes and the treatment of the Negro character in American drama in the quarter-century from 1893 to 1917—years when the American drama as a whole was coming to maturity. It was during this period that the minstrel show stereotypes of the Negro race began to crumble, along with other easy generalizations about racial and national groups, opening the way for the plays of Eugene O'Neill, Paul Green, Marc Connelly, DuBose and Dorothy Heyward and their contemporaries; and it was during this period that the first "New Negroes" were growing to maturity—people like W. E. B. Du Bois, Bert Williams and Paul Laurence Dunbar, who would in turn lead to the second wave of New Negroes, such as Alain Locke, Paul Robeson

and Countee Cullen. I think the Negro's emergence on stage as a human being came primarily from his emigration to the North, where he was able to achieve an education of sorts and establish himself in previously all-white fields; and, secondarily, from the white writers' growing realization of this new phenomenon.

In 1899 there was produced James A. Herne's *The Reverend Griffith Davenport*—the major post-bellum play dealing with a real Negro theme. Earlier, several anti-slavery plays of the 1850's had had Negro themes, including the many adaptations of *Uncle Tom's Cabin* and Mrs. Stowe's other novel, *Dred*, Mrs. J. C. Swayze's *Ossawattomie Brown*, J. T. Trowbridge's *Neighbor Jackwood*, several plays by the Negro playwright William Wells Brown, and Dion Boucicault's *The Octoroon*. These all appeared in the ten years before the War Between the States. In quality, they were flagrant melodrama, with *Uncle Tom's Cabin* and *The Octoroon* the best of the lot. William Wells Brown's plays were notable only for being probably the first by an American Negro. They included *Experience or How to Give a Northern Man a Backbone* and *Escape, or a Leap to Freedom*, which Sterling A. Brown in *The Negro Caravan* described as bad "even for nineteenth century drama." These plays were not produced; they were read at Abolitionist meetings.

Slavery was certainly a valid Negro theme in drama, but the ante-bellum writers distorted it by treating it only as a matter of white conscience rather than of a people's shameful degradation: it was not that those enslaved were worthy of a better fate, but that their enslavers were godless cads. I prefer to choose Herne's *The Reverend Griffith Davenport* as a starting-point for Negro themes in drama, despite the fact that the theme is secondary, since it is really about slavery and the Negro's

condition under that system, as it seemed to one looking backward from 1899.

But it was the first attempt in forty years—since *The Octoroon*, in fact—to deal seriously with a Negro theme. It shows us different aspects of slavery and gives us meatier characters. As a white slaveholder who detests slavery, Davenport must decide whether his slaves are better off in bondage or as freedmen. Herne shows the lazy, contented plantation life of Davenport's slaves, their pride in "family," their dislike of freedmen " 'thout no fam'ly nor nothin' "; as well as the plight of slaves under stricter and more brutal masters; for example, the slave Sampson stabs himself to death in the Davenport living-room, rather than endure life with his own master after having been caught in an attempted escape. Knowing he cannot keep his slaves and his self-respect, Davenport must either sell them or free them. Nobly—since all heroes then were noble—he frees them. This action, along with his vote for Lincoln, alienates his Virginia neighbors. Davenport and his family are forced to flee. Later, returning to Virginia as a scout for the Union Army, he is captured. He is finally reunited with his loving but pro-slavery wife on the old plantation, " 'thout no slaves nor nothin'."

The story had little immediacy thirty-four years after the end of the Civil War, but it contained a Negro theme of some import, because the turn of the century found the Negro at the lowest point of his life since the Emancipation. The power and freedom of Reconstruction days had been all but dissipated, and racial incidents were occurring frequently both in the North and the South—an upsurge of lynchings in the South and the New York race riot of 1901 being examples in point. The main situation is, significantly, that of a man torn between his beliefs and his culture, who chooses to fight the good fight and comes out a winner. It is a re-examination of the evils of slavery, the thematic pur-

pose of which is to point out that—no matter what—things are better now, in 1899.

Probably the first play of the period to deal solely with a Negro theme was *Caleb, the Degenerate,* written by a Negro, Joseph S. Cotter, Sr., and published in 1903 in Louisville. A moral lesson on the dangers of depravity, its purpose was to influence officials of Tuskegee Institute to concentrate on practical training, rather than book learning. Although written in a terribly inept blank verse, it is perhaps the closest thing to a folk play ever turned out in the United States; by which I mean, it is obviously written by a member of the "folk" with the purpose of influencing the "folk" to act in a certain manner. That its "folk" element is hidden behind a blank-verse form is less of a handicap to it than is, say, Paul Green's removal from the "folk"—educationally, economically and physically—during the time he was writing the main body of his "folk" plays.

Like William Wells Brown's plays, however, *Caleb* was never staged; it was read at meetings. In its incidents and dialogue it is frequently laughable, and perhaps it is well that it was left unproduced. Near the end of the play, for example, Olivia, a poor but industrious colored girl, is sent to Boston to get money for her foster father's industrial arts school. She returns with $100,000, explaining that "Chance threw me with a group of millionaires" who believed in her cause. Cotter stressed industrial arts, avoidance of politics, the benefits of hard work, and the idea that the Negro was now American, not African.

The Rev. Thomas Dixon's *The Clansman* is the third play to deal with a Negro theme. It appeared in 1905, adapted by the playwright from his novel of the same name (as was D. W. Griffith's film *Birth of a Nation*) and another of his novels, *The Leopard's Spots.* An apologia for the formation of the Ku Klux Klan during the Reconstruction, it is not badly written, compared to much else from the

period; but it was, and is, certainly controversial. The portrayal of the former Southern white aristocracy's oppression at the hands of freed Negroes, carpetbaggers and rednecks is extreme—so extreme, in fact, that an ardent integrationist and his daughter are converted to the Klan's cause by the hero of the play, a noble chap who organizes the local Klavern and routs the villainous oppressors. At one point, when interracial marriage is almost forced by law, Dixon has one of his characters comment on the "grip of a black beast's claws on a white girl's throat." The "black beast" is the lieutenant-governor, a Negro who is attracted to the integrationist's daughter. Not only did *The Clansman* have as its apparent aim the justification of the Klan, which was then hanging many Negroes, but it also shared the limitation of Herne's play, in that its Negro theme was not pertinent to the Negro.

The fourth play to deal with Negro themes, and perhaps the best play to appear before the work of Ridgely Torrence, is Edward Sheldon's *The Nigger,* first produced in 1909 at the New Theatre, New York City. Sheldon's hero Philip Morrow, aristocratic and successful, is a Southern politician of the early 1900's. He had first been elected to office as sheriff on his promise to "keep the niggers in their place." Now, as governor, he is confronted with violent race-riots which he believes are incited by too much bad whiskey. Morrow is urging a Prohibition law when a cousin, an unscrupulous distiller whom such a law would bankrupt, tells him that his grandmother was a beautiful quadroon and threatens, if Morrow continues his Prohibition drive, to disclose the fact to the world and ruin him. Beaten either way, Morrow decides to renounce his governorship and to devote his life to aiding his fellow Negroes in the state.

Sterling Brown contended that *The Nigger* was "certainly far removed from Negro life,"

WINTER GARDEN

TO-NIGHT AND EVERY NIGHT

Will be performed, a new play, in five acts, illustrative of AMERICAN CHARACTER AMERICAN SCENES and SOUTHERN HOMES, called the

OCTOROON

Or Life in Louisiana.

The scene is laid in the Delta of the Mississippi River, on the Plantation of Terrebonne. The time—the present day.

CHARACTERS.

Mrs. Peyton, of Terrebonne Plantation, in the Attakapas, widow of the late Judge Peyton .... Mrs. Blake

George Peyton, her nephew, educated in Europe, and just returned home. .... Mr. A. H. Davenport

Jacob McCloskey, formerly overseer of Terrebonne, but now owner of one half of the estate .... Mr. T. B. Johnston

Salem Scudder, a Yankee from Massachusetts, now overseer of Terrebonne, great on improvements and inventions, once a photographic operator, and been a little of everything generally .... Mr. J. Jefferson

Pete, an "ole uncle," once the late Judge's body servant, but now "too ole to work, sa" .... Mr. G. Jamieson

(His first appearance in New York for many years)

Zoe, an Octoroon girl, free, the natural child of the late Judge by a Quadroon slave .... Mrs. J. H. Allen

Sunnyside, a planter, neighbor and old friend of the Peytons. .... Mr. G. Holland

Dora Sunnyside, his only daughter and heiress, a Southern Belle .... Mrs. Stoddart

Lafourche, a rich Planter .... Mr. Stoddart

Wah-no-tee, an Indian Chief, of the Lepan Tribe .... Mr. Pearson

Paul, a yellow boy, a favorite of the late Judge's, and so allowed to do much as he likes .... Miss Burke

Ratts, Mate of the Magnolia steamer .... Mr. Harrison

Colonel Poindexter, an Auctioneer and slave salesman .... Mr. Russell

Jules Thibodeaux, a young creole Planter .... Miss H. Secor

Caillou, an Overseer .... Mr. Peck

Jackson, a Planter .... Mr. Tree

Claiborne, the auctioneer's Clerk .... Mr. Ponisi

Grace, a yellow girl, a slave .... Miss Gimber

Solon, a grief boy slave .... Mr. [illegible]

Dido, the cook, a slave .... Mrs. Dunn

Mrs. Claiborne .... Miss Clinton

Minnie, a Quadroon slave .... Miss Walters

Planters, Slaves, Deck Hands and Ladies.

SCENE OF THE FIRST ACT.

The PLANTATION of TERREBONNE.

A Southern home under a Southern sun. The little darkies, "dem's wuss dan Skeeters." Pete, the old servant. George Peyton just arrived home. A Paris lion in a canebreak. Madame Peyton and the patriarchal home. The good old Judge. Salem Scudder's description of Zoe, the Octoroon. The two overseers. A confession The strange relation and affection existing between Madam Peyton and her husband's natural daughter. Plantation life. Southern waste and Northern thrift. Zoe, the Octoroon. The arrival of Sunnyside and Dora. Dora Sunnyside a portrait. George cannot understand the social position of Zoe. McCloskey arrives. The hard customer. Paul, the yellow boy, and Wah-no-tee, the Indian hunter. The strange affection between the savage and the boy slave, companions in the Swamp hunt. Paul and the Indian start across the Red Cedar Swamp for the United States mail. Border United States mail delivery. The foreclosure on Terrebonne. The plantation to be sold. The last hope of recovering the estate. The Judge's desk. McCloskey's love for the Octoroon. "I cannot marry you, but I can make you mistress of the richest estate in Louisiana." The two overseers review the state of things. The live oak and the creeper. Two live Yankees, or diamond cut diamond. Scudder's confession of his love for Zoe. McCloskey discovers the free papers of Zoe. The judgment. The dark hope. The resolve.

ACT THE SECOND.

THE LANDING ON THE ATCHAFALAYA.

The Lumber Shed.

Scudder returns to his old trade and takes a photograph. Paul wants his picture took. Pete brings terrible news. Zoe confirms it. George's declaration of his love. "He does not know what I am." The "eighth blood." McCloskey's resolve. Wah-no-tee and Paul. The apparatus at work. The daguerreotype portrait. Paul takes his own likeness, assisted by the Indian The savage's fear for the machine. Thinks it a deadly weapon. Paul sits for his portrait. The attack. The murder. The letter and the flight. "Terrebonne will be sold, and Zoe will be mine." The revenge of the Indian, and his grief for Paul.

ACT THE THIRD.

THE PARLOR AND HALL AT TERREBONNE.

Preparations for the sale. McCloskey claims the pound of flesh. The slaves are to be sold. Pete on the stump. His address to his "cullerd brudders." Darkie enthusiasm.

THE SLAVE SALE.

Ratts, the mate of the Magnolia Grace, the yellow girl, and her children. "Buy me, mas'r?" Pete on the stand. His indignation at going cheap. No. 4—The Octoroon girl, Zoe. Consternation of the slaves. McCloskey bids. The assault by George. Bowie knives and revolvers. Dora's revenge on Zoe, who has taken away her lover. The sale of the Octoroon

ACT THE FOURTH.

THE BOILER DECK OF THE MAGNOLIA

THE LANDING AND THE WOODPILE.

Roll on the cotton bales. Take her guards under. She is freighted down into the solid mud, and can't float. No matter, "Wood up; hang on to the safety valve; she'll crawl off on her paddles." Alarm! The Indian comes. Wah-no-tee, the murderer of Paul. Seizure of the savage. Popular fury. Lynch him! Lynch him! Scudder protects him. Paul's grave discovered, and the missing mail bags brought to light. Evidence strong.

THE LYNCH TRIAL.

Counsellor Scudder defends the Indian. Scudder on Lynch. A new witness arrives very unexpectedly. An alteration of the entertainments for that evening. Scudder on McCloskey. Improved and corrected Edition. McCloskey in a fix. The verdict and the seizure of the prisoner. McCloskey's escape.

THE SHED ON FIRE.

Cut the ropes. Back her out. Clear away. The criminal away. His Indian destiny pursues him.

The Destruction of the Steamer Magnolia by Fire

ACT THE FIFTH.

Scene First.—The Negro Quarter—Night.

Zoe seeks her old nurse, Dido. The old Obi Doctress. The drink that cures the Red Fever. The night after the sale. Life is so beautiful to one so young.

Scene Second.—The Cane Brake—Sunrise.

McCloskey out of danger. His flight through the swamps. His escape. The dusky shadow of death behind him. The Indian on the war path. The pursuit. The human bloodhound.

Scene Third.—The Red Cedar Swamp.

Scudder and Pete on their road home. The alarm. What's that in the bush, "A Bar or a runaway Nigger." The man hunt. The wolf run down at last. The Indian and his victim. Save me from the scalping knife of the savage. Judge Scudder's revision of the lynch verdict. His decision. Pete's petition. Scudder relents. His protection of the white man.

Scene Fourth, and Last.

The parlor at Terrebonne again. Zoe's adieu to her home before she leaves it for the house of her new master. The glass of water. The arrival of scudder. The joyful news. Pete in a bad way. Zoe's freedom. Free at last.

THE OCTOROON GOES HOME

THE VISION OF THE LANDING.

LITTLE PAUL'S GRAVE.

McCloskey appeals to the highest tribunal. The last that was seen of the Indian Wah-no-tee.

During the winter season the doors will open at 6¾. The entertainments will commence at 7½. Families bringing children are informed that the entertainments conclude before 10½ o'clock.

On Saturday, December 31st, for the convenience of persons living at a distance,

A GRAND MATINEE.

THE OCTOROON will be given with all its splendid cast. **Doors open at half-past Twelve. Curtain will rise at half-past One.**

HERALD PRINT.

National Theatre!

Formerly the Chatham, in Chatham street, near Roosevelt.

Sole Lessee, Proprietor, and Manager .... A. H. PURDY

First and Second Dress Circles and Upper Boxes .... 25 Cents
Orchestra Arm Chairs .... 50 Cents
Parquette for Colored Persons .... 25 Cents
Exclusive Private Boxes .... $5 ; One Person to Private Box $1

Doors open at 7, curtain will rise at quarter before 8 o'clock, precisely.

Unprecedented! Twelfth Week of the Grand Drama.

The immense success attending the representation of the great Moral Drama of UNCLE TOM'S CABIN has induced the Manager to announce it for Every Evening during the month of October. The Youthful Wonder,

LITTLE CORDELIA HOWARD

Appearing in her original character of the Gentle Eva,

MR. J. J. PRIOR — MR. LINGARD

As George Harris — As Uncle Tom.

MR. G. L. FOX,

As Phenias Fletcher.

MR. J. B. HOWE,

From the London Theatres, as St. Claire,

Together with

THE FULL NATIONAL COMPANY

Thursday Evening, Oct. 6th, 1853,

And Every Night (Sundays excepted,) during October,

The New and Wonderfully Successful Dramatic Version of

UNCLE TOM'S CABIN

Or, Life among the Lowly.

DRAMATISED FROM

MRS. HARRIET BEECHER STOWE'S

World renowned work by G. L. Aiken Esq.

IN SIX ACTS

Eight Tableaus & Thirty Scenes,

EMBRACING THE WHOLE WORK,

In which will be introduced the original songs, composed and written expressly for this piece by G. C. Howard, entitled

TO LITTLE EVA IN HEAVEN, and UNCLE TOM'S RELIGION.

Published by Oliver Ditson, Boston, and for sale by Perry & Co., Firth and Pond, and all the principal Music Stores in New York.

LITTLE CORDELIA HOWARD,

In her Original Character of EVA, as performed by her over TWO HUNDRED NIGHTS.

MR. J. J. PRIOR as . . . George Harris

Uncle Tom, the faithful Slave .... Mr. J. Lingard

George Harris a Fugitive .... J. J. Prior

Gumpton Cute, the Yankee .... H. Stone

Phenias Fletcher, the Kentuckian .... G. W. L. Fox

St. Claire, the Southern Gentleman .... J. B. Howe

Legree, the Pirate Slave dealer .... N. B. Clark

Mr. Wilson, the Quaker .... Toulmin

Deacon Perry .... L. Fox

Marks, the Lawyer .... Herbert

Old Shelby, the insolvent Planter .... Rose

George Shelby, the son .... Mr. Blake

Tom Loker, the Slave hunter .... G. Lingard

Haley, the Slave Trader .... Mack

Sambo, the Slave of Legree .... Mack

Jumbo, the Slave driver .... McDonnell

Alf Mas, the Slave purchaser .... Daymond

Skeggs, the Auctioneer .... Lyons

Adolph, the Master's man .... Mitchell

Waiter, the smart man .... Cline

Doctor, the last visitor .... Smith

Harry, the child of the fugitive .... Mast. Murray

Slaves, Planters, Citizens, &c

EVA, the flower of the South .... LITTLE CORDELIA HOWARD

Topsy, the Girl that never was born .... Mrs. Mack

Aunt Ophelia, the Vermonter .... Mrs Bradshaw

Eliza, the fugitive wife .... Mrs. W. G. Jones

Cassy, the distracted .... Mrs. Bannister

Emeline, the Quadroon Slave .... Miss Barber

Marie St Claire, the victim of custom .... Miss Landers

Chloe, the wife of Uncle Tom .... Mrs. Lingard

Female Slaves, &c.

The Play is beautifully interspersed with **Singing and Dancing.**

Song, Old Folks at Home, words and Music by E. P. Christy, Esq .... Uncle Tom
Dance and Song .... Topsy
To Little Eva in Heaven, words and music by G. C. Howard .... St. Claire
Uncle Tom's Religion, words and music by G. C. Howard .... Uncle Tom

TABLEAUS IN THE DRAMA.

1st. THE ESCAPE OF ELIZA.
2nd. THE TRAPPERS ENTRAPPED.
3rd. THE FREEMAN'S DEFENCE.
4th. DEATH OF LITTLE EVA.
5th. THE LAST OF St. CLARE.
6th. TOPSY BUTTING THE YANKEE.
7th. CASSY HELPING UNCLE TOM.
8th. DEATH OF UNCLE TOM.

NOTICE.---The Ladies and Gentleman will please remain seated until the **Curtain Descends,** that every effect may be given to the **Last Grand Tableaus.**

N. B. The performance will conclude at Eleven o'clock Every Evening

In preparation and will be produced, when an opportunity presents itself, "**The Key to Uncle Tom's Cabin,**" by G. L. Aiken, Esq. **Little Katy, or the Hot Corn Girl,** by C. W. Taylor, Esq **Paridise Lost,** by C. W. Taylor, Esq., all of which have been secured by Copyright in the Southern District of New York.

but I defend its place in the list of plays with Negro themes on the basis of its effects, as indicated by this quotation from "The Ten Dramatic Shocks of the Century" (*Cosmopolitan,* 1949):

> . . . nearly 40 years before Sinclair Lewis' *Kingsblood Royal* [this play] treated of Negro blood in a man supposedly white, and of his love for a woman of pure Caucasian blood. The theme at the time was theatrically sensational and induced qualms in the audience. . . . Adding to the general shock was the dialogue presenting the acquiescent Southern attitude toward lynching.

There's the key: lynching. It was the first time that a playwright of any stature had faced the contemporary problem of mob murder—on the slightest whim—of any poor chap not prudent or sanitary enough to have been born white. However romantic Sheldon may have been in his dramaturgy, his acceptance of lynching as a valid subject for drama falls in line with his *Salvation Nell* of a year earlier, and with some of his later plays such as *The Boss,* and points to him as perhaps America's first social playwright.

On March 30, 1914, Thomas Heywood's *A Woman Killed with Kindness* was staged at a special matinee at the Lyceum, New York City. To complete the bill, the Stage Society presented Ridgely Torrence's Negro folk tragedy, *Granny Maumee,* at the urging of Dorothy Donnelly, who played the title role, and of Emilie Hapgood. Heywood's play elicited either indifference or hearty dislike from the critics; but, according to Edith J. R. Isaacs in *The Negro in the American Theatre,* the modern play attracted their "keen interest as dramatic pioneering which deserved the heartiest encouragement."

A Negro of royal African blood, Granny Maumee is proud of her race and full of hatred for white people. When her granddaughter returns to the cabin with a child fathered by the grandson of one of her son's murderers, Granny invokes "ancient magic curses upon the man who has wrought her family this last

unbearable injury." But Granny Maumee has lived too long in a Christian world: the spirit of forgiveness overcomes the voodoo, and, as she submits to its power, she dies. The play is not tragedy, nor is it folk—if we define folk plays as those arising from the people, rather than from onlookers such as Paul Green or J. M. Synge. But it is an exciting, stageworthy play, the importance of its thematic material lying in its interest in the folk —in the thoughts and emotions of the three Negro women it involves; that is, in the Negro as a human being.

The same spirit is to be found in *Rachel,* a tract play written by Angelina Grimke (a Negro poet, not the abolitionist of the 1850's) for propaganda purposes of the National Association for the Advancement of Colored People. First produced March 3, 1916, by the N.A.A.C.P. Drama Committee in Washington, D.C., it later played at the Neighborhood Playhouse in New York, and in Cambridge, Mass. *Rachel* is about a young colored woman in a Northern city who loves children so much that she refuses to marry, because her children would be mistreated, victimized and despised simply because of the color of their skin. Its dialogue is stilted and didactic, but the play has merit on the basis of its theme and characters.

On April 5, 1917, at the Garden Theatre in New York, the Hapgood Players revived *Granny Maumee* along with two other plays by Torrence—*The Rider of Dreams* and *Simon the Cyrenian.* The latter is less a play than a religious pageant; the former, a pleasant little comedy about a hard-working woman's efforts to buy a house. Again, Torrence's interest centers in his people. Negro themes in drama are now developed: human beings facing human problems in a human way. The door is opened to the future—to, for example, *A Raisin in the Sun*; but it will take many years, and some regressions, to step through that doorway.

* * * * * *

A long history of stereotypes, usually comic, preceded and accompanied the emergence of Negro *character* in American drama, which may be dated from 1893 when Clay M. Greene and Joseph R. Grismer wrote *The New South.* As Sterling Brown said of the Comic Negro in the preceding era, "By 1850, the chicken-stealing, watermelon-eating, razor-wielding, bombastic, comical 'darky' had become a stage convention." This convention was followed, in the anti-slavery plays, by the Heroic or Nobly-Forgiving Black or Contented Slave (Mammy), and that most hapless of heroines, the beautiful Octoroon. The latter was by then commonly regarded as a beautiful woman rather than a racial mutant. Of her treatment in Boucicault's play, Brown said: "The whole desire of her life is to find a white lover, and then go down, accompanied by slow music, to a tragic end." (It is interesting that, when Boucicault's melodrama was staged in London, its ending was both happy and acceptable: the beautiful octoroon Zoe's white lover married her.)

These character-types were scarcely one remove from the black-face minstrel shows. They existed in a world that was like a bowl either of peaches-and-cream or of tear-tasting gruel. If they wished anything from life, it was only a piece of watermelon or the opportunity to be nice to their white folks—in several ways. The stage Negro never became seriously angry; he never imparted any emotion beyond laughter or helpless pity. He persisted, not only because American drama itself was so late in reaching artistic maturity, but also because in life the Negro lacked contact with the whole of society; and that lack of contact, let me stress, was reciprocal.

With *The New South,* progress of a sort was made by introducing a fourth stereotype —that of the Brute Negro—in the character of Sampson, a murderer. James A. Herne, the playwright mentioned above, played

Sampson; and, according to A. H. Quinn in *A History of American Drama,* "in a powerful scene represented the growing effect of fear in a Negro's mind" long before Eugene O'Neill wrote *The Emperor Jones.* Quinn suggests that its success prompted Herne to adapt Helen H. Gardner's novel, *An Unofficial Patriot,* into the play already discussed, *The Reverend Griffith Davenport,* using the Brute Negro type in it along with a variety of other Negro characters. In contrast, Joseph S. Cotter, Sr., used none of the usual Negro stereotypes in *Caleb, the Degenerate*; but his use of blank verse and his excesses in glorifying and damning his people reveal them as puppets, instead of created characters. The Brute Negro reappeared in *The Clansman,* but this time he was the lieutenant-governor and a prime reason for creating the Ku Klux Klan.

The first real breakaway from various types of plantation Negroes in a popular play occurred in 1909, with the production of Eugene Walter's *The Easiest Way.* Walter specified that Annie, the heroine's maid, "must not in any way represent the traditional smiling colored girl or 'mammy' of the South"; rather, she is "cunning, crafty, heartless, surly, sullen. . . ." Annie was the first depiction of the Northern urban Negro—mother to *Rachel* and to Jim Harris in *All God's Chillun,* and grandmother to Bigger Thomas and Walter Lee Younger.

We may exclude from consideration as a Negro character Philip Morrow, the governor in Edward Sheldon's *The Nigger,* especially since his "blood" is only one-sixteenth "tainted." But Sheldon created two other Negro characters who manage to go beyond the stereotypes: Mammy Jinny, Morrow's nurse, and her sister Belle, who is Morrow's grandmother and whom we know only through a very well-written letter which Morrow reads aloud during the action and which reveals the true story of his father's birth. Sheldon also

went beyond the Brute Negro in portraying Jinny's grandson Joe, who is hunted down and lynched because he raped a white girl. Joe becomes as much of a human being as white playwrights were permitting in those days.

Even though they speak like propaganda tracts, Rachel and her family in Miss Grimke's *Rachel* are all believable people. There are subtle shadings of thought and emotion that suggest naturalism and manage to surmount the dialogue. In fact, it is the people of *Rachel, The Rider of Dreams* and *Granny Maumee* who are the first real Negroes—that is, characters entirely divorced from the over-blown caricatures of the late Victorian stage. Sterling Brown said: "It is the way of drama to heighten reality, but in plays of Negro life, the heightening is greater than usual"; and this is true of characters in the other plays, if they are not rendered remote, like Granny Maumee or the characters in *Simon the Cyrenian*. The closest Ridgely Torrence came to using a conventional Negro stereotype in his three plays is in the character of Madison Sparrow in *The Rider of Dreams*. He might be considered a Comic Negro, addicted to gin and watermelon, crap games, chicken-stealing, and the rest; but Torrence gives him dimension in his dreams and drives, so that he becomes a real—if slightly romanticized—person.

Despite their brief run, Torrence's plays had a strong and lasting effect on the American theatre. Indeed, James Weldon Johnson said in *Black Manhattan* that their production was . . .

> the most important single event in the entire history of the Negro in the American theatre. . . . The stereotype traditions regarding the Negro's histrionic limitations were smashed. It was the first time anywhere in the United States for Negroes in the dramatic theatre to command the serious attention of the critics and of the general press and public.

Edith Isaacs underscores their historic importance by noting that they provided work for Negro actors, technicians and other stage-workers; they gave impetus to later writers, like Eugene O'Neill who used Negro actresses in *The Moon of the Caribbees* (1918); and they made welcome Negro theatregoers, heretofore limited to Harlem reproductions of Broadway and Shakespearean plays. In rating the top ten performances of 1917, George Jean Nathan included Opal Cooper (Madison Sparrow in *The Rider of Dreams*) among the men, and Inez Clough (Procula in *Simon the Cyrenian*) among the women. Not a bad record, considering that they were perhaps the first Negro dramatic actors to appear on Broadway, or even within whistling distance of it.

From the first, the white writer has been at a disadvantage in depicting the Negro. The greatest weakness of Harriet Beecher Stowe was her lack of knowledge of slaves and slavery, says J. C. Furnas in *Goodbye to Uncle Tom*; and playwrights of the period under discussion seemed to have known just as little as she did about Negroes. I can find no evidence that Edward Sheldon, for instance, ever traveled south of Chicago or New York before writing *The Nigger*. Cotter and Miss Grimke were Negroes, and their knowledge of Negroes is evident in their work. Torrence, a native of Xenia, Ohio—a sort of Penn Station on the Underground Railway, populated by many slaves and owners—doubtless knew Negroes and perhaps even some ex-slaves, to judge by his familiarity with the subject-matter as reflected in his plays.

Yet Torrence was an outsider; so, too, were Eugene O'Neill, DuBose and Dorothy Heyward, Paul Green and other white writers of Negro life. Despite the various Brotherhood sermons one is exposed to, there is a difference —general enough to be called a racial difference—between white and Negro people on similar social strata. Perhaps it is only a difference in attitude, a matter of environment

rather than heredity; but it is what makes the writing of Lorraine Hansberry and Langston Hughes ring truer, when they handle Negro themes, than similar writings by white playwrights. This is not a matter of racial superiority, one way or another; nor is it a question of dramaturgic skill, but of knowledge of subject-matter. The Negro playwright, seeing his characters from the inside, so to speak, can better avoid the stereotype and create Negro characters that have particularity as Negroes and complexity as human beings. If the Negro playwright has the dramaturgic skill to create three-dimensional characters, these creations will begin to point to Everyman—universal, generalized mankind; and their portraiture, gaining authenticity from the playwright's intimate knowledge of the colored man, can transcend color and point to the whole of humanity. It can do so because this knowledge enables him always to see the Negro as a human being.

—1964

JOHN GRAHAM TRIED BY A NEGRO JURY
A THRILLING AND ACCURATE REPRODUCTION OF A HISTORICAL SCENE

The Negro and the American Stage

by Alain Locke

IN THE appraisal of the possible contribution of the Negro to the American theatre, there are those who find the greatest promise in the rising drama of Negro life. And there are others who see possibilities of a deeper, though subtler, influence upon what is after all more vital, the technical aspects of the arts of the theatre. Certainly to date (1926) the Negro influence upon American drama has been negligible. Whereas even under the handicaps of second-hand exploitation and restriction to the popular amusement stage, the Negro actor has considerably influenced our stage and its arts. One would do well to imagine, therefore, what might happen if the art of the Negro actor should really become artistically lifted and liberated. Transpose the possible resources of Negro song and dance and pantomime to the serious stage, envisage an American drama under the galvanizing stimulus of a rich transfusion of essential folk-arts and you may anticipate what I mean. A race of actors can revolutionize the drama quite as definitely and perhaps more vitally than a coterie of dramatists. The roots of drama are after all action and emotion, and our modern drama, for all its frantic experimentation, is an essentially anaemic drama, a something of gestures and symbols and ideas and not overflowing with the vital stuff of which drama was originally made and to which it must return for its rejuvenation, cycle after cycle.

Primarily the Negro brings to the drama the gift of a temperament, not the gift of a tradition. Time out of mind he has been rated as a "natural-born actor" without any appreciation of what that statement, if true, really means. Often it is intended as a disparaging estimate of the Negro's limitations, a recognition of his restriction to the interpretative as distinguished from the creative aspect of drama, a confinement, in terms of a second order of talent, to the status of the mimic and the clown. But a comprehending mind knows that the very life of the drama is in dramatic instinct and emotion, that drama begins and ends in mimicry, and that its creative force is in the last analysis the interpretative passion. Welcome then as is the emergence of the Negro playwright and the drama of Negro life, the promise of the most vital contribution of the Negro to the theatre lies, in my opinion, in the deep and unemancipated resources of the Negro actor, and the folk arts of which he is as yet only a blind and hampered exponent. Dramatic spontaneity, the free use of the body and the voice as direct instruments of feeling, a control of body plastique that opens up the narrow diaphragm of fashionable acting and enlarges the conventional mannerisms of the stage—these are indisputably strong points of Negro acting. Many a Negro vaudevillian has a greater store of them than finished masters of the polite theatre. And especially in the dawn of

the "synthetic theatre" with the singing, dancing actor and the plastic stage, the versatile gifts of the Negro actor seem peculiarly promising and significant.

Unfortunately it is the richest vein of Negro dramatic talent which is under the heaviest artistic impediments and pressure. The art of the Negro actor has had to struggle up out of the shambles of minstrelsy and make slow headway against very fixed limitations of popular taste. Farce, buffoonery and pathos have until recently almost completely overlaid the folk comedy and folk tragedy of a dramatically endowed and circumstanced people. These gifts must be liberated. I do not narrowly think of this development merely as the extension of the freedom of the American stage to the Negro actor, although this must naturally come about as a condition of it, but as a contribution to the technical idioms and resources of the entire American theatre.

To see this rising influence one must of course look over the formal horizons. From the vantage of the advanced theatre, there is already a significant arc to be seen. In the sensational successes of *The Emperor Jones* and *All God's Chillun Got Wings* there have been two components, the fine craftsmanship and clairvoyant genius of O'Neill and the unique acting gifts of Charles Gilpin and Paul Robeson. From the earlier revelation of the emotional power of the Negro actor by Opal Cooper and Inez Clough in the Ridgely Torrence plays in 1916 to the recent half-successful experiments of Raymond O'Neill's Ethiopian Art Theatre and the National Ethiopian Art Theatre of New York, with Evelyn Preer, Rose McClendon, Sidney Kirkpatrick, Charles Olden, Francis Corbie and others, an advanced section of the American public has become acquainted with the possibilities of the Negro in serious dramatic interpretation. But the real mine of Negro dramatic art and talent is still in the sub-soil of the vaudeville

stage, gleaming through its slag and dross in the unmistakably great dramatic gifts of a Bert Williams, a Florence Mills or a Bill Robinson. Give Bojangles Robinson or George Stamper, pantomimic dancers of genius, an artistic libretto, score and setting; give Josephine Baker, Eddie Rector, Abbie Mitchell or Ethel Waters a dignified medium, and they would be more than a sensation, they would be artistic revelations. Pantomime, that most essential and elemental of the dramatic arts, is a natural *forte* of the Negro actor, and the use of the body and voice and facile control of posture and rhythm are almost as noteworthy in our average as in our exceptional artists. When it comes to pure registration of the emotions, I question whether any body of actors, unless it be the Russians, can so completely be fear or joy or nonchalance or grief.

With his uncanny instinct for the theatre, Max Reinhardt saw these possibilities instantly under the tawdry trappings of such musical comedies as *Eliza, Shuffle Along* and *Runnin' Wild,* which were in vogue the season of his first visit to New York. "It is intriguing, very intriguing," he told me, "these Negro shows that I have seen. But remember, not as achievements, not as things in themselves artistic, but in their possibilities, their tremendous artistic possibilities. They are most modern, most American, most expressionistic. They are highly original in spite of obvious triteness, and artistic in spite of superficial crudeness. To me they reveal new possibilities of technique in drama, and if I should ever try to do anything American, I would build it on these things."

We didn't enthuse—my friend Charles Johnson of *Opportunity* and myself, who were interviewing Mr. Reinhardt. What Negro who stands for culture with the hectic stress of a social problem weighing on the minds of an over-serious minority could be expected to enthuse. *Eliza, Shuffle Along, Runnin'*

Wild! We had come to discuss the possibilities of serious Negro drama, of the art-drama, if you please. Surely Director Reinhardt was a victim of that distortion of perspective to which one is so liable in a foreign land. But then, the stage is not a foreign land to Max Reinhardt; he has the instinct of the theatre, a genius that knows what is vital there. We didn't outwardly protest, but raised a brow already too elevated perhaps and shrugged the shoulder that carries the proverbial racial chip.

Herr Reinhardt read the gestures swiftly. "Ah, yes—I see. You view these plays for what they are, and you are right; I view them for what they will become, and I am more than right. I see their future. Why? Well, the drama must turn at every period of fresh creative development to an aspect which has been previously subordinated or neglected, and in this day of ours, we come back to the most primitive and the most basic aspect of drama for a new starting point, a fresh development and revival of the art—and that aspect is pantomime, the use of the body to portray story and emotion. And your people have that art—almost as a special genius. At present it is prostituted to farce, to trite comedy—but the technique is there, and I have never seen more wonderful possibilities. Yes, I should like to do something with it."

With the New Russian Theatre experimenting with the "dynamic ballet" and Meyerhold's improvising or creative actor, with Max Reinhardt's own recently founded International Pantomime Society inaugurated at the last Salzburg festival, with the entire new theatre agog over "mass drama," there is at least some serious significance to the statement that the Negro theatre has great artistic potentialities. What is of utmost importance to drama now is to control the primitive language of the art, and to retrieve some of the basic control which the sophisticated and conventionalized theatre has lost. It is more important to know how to cry, sob and laugh, stare and startle than to learn how to smile, grimace, arch and wink. And more important to know how to move vigorously and with rhythmic sweep than to pirouette and posture. An actor and a folk art controlling the symbolism of the primary emotions has the modern stage as a province ripe for an early and easy conquest. Commenting on the work of the players of the Ethiopian Art Theatre, discerning critics noticed "the freshness and vigor of their emotional responses, their spontaneity and intensity of mood, their freedom from intellectual and artistic obsessions." And almost every review of Gilpin's or Robeson's acting has spoken of it as beyond the calculated niceties, a force of direct and overwhelming emotional projection. It is this sense of something dramatic to the core that flows movingly in the blood rather than merely along the nerves of conscious effort that we speak of as the racial endowment of the Negro actor. For however few individuals there may be who possess it in high degree, it is racial in the sense of being a characteristic folk capability, a heritage latent at least in a rather unique group experience.

Without invoking the obvious analogies of the contemporary Irish and the Russian drama, we can see in this emotional endowment great resources for the theatre. In terms of the prevalent trend for the development of serious Negro drama, we may expect these resources to be cultivated and claimed as the working capital of the Negro Theatre. They are. But just as definitely, too, are they the general property and assets of the American Theatre at large, once the barriers of discrimination are broken through. These barriers are slowly breaking down both on the legitimate stage and in the popular drama, but the great handicap, as Carl Van Vechten so keenly points out in his *Prescription for the Negro Theatre,* is blind imitation with the Negro and with Broadway, stagnant conven-

tionalism. Negro dramatic art must not only be liberated from external handicap and disparagement, but from its internal and often self-imposed limitations. It must more and more have the courage to be original, to break with established dramatic convention of all sorts. It must have the courage to develop its own idiom, to pour itself into new molds; in short, to be creatively experimental. From what quarter this impetus will come we cannot quite predict; it may come from the Negro theatre or from some sudden acceptance of the American stage, from the art-theatre or from the commercial theatre, from an American source, or first, as so many artistic emancipations seem to have come, from the more liberal patronage and recognition of the European stage. But this much is certain—the material awaits a great exploiting genius.

One can scarcely think of a complete development of dramatic art by the Negro without some significant artistic reexpression of African life and the traditions associated with it. This may seem a far cry from the conditions and moods of modern New York and Chicago and the Negro's rapid and feverish assimilation of all things American. But art establishes its contacts in strange ways. The emotional elements of Negro art are choked by the conventions of the contemporary stage; they call for freer, more plastic material. They have, of course, no mysterious affinity with African themes or scenes, but they do have for any life that is more primitive and poetic in substance. So, if, as seems already apparent, the more sophisticated race consciousness of the Negro should move back over the trail of his group tradition to an interest in things African, the natural affinities of the material and the art will complete the circuit and they will most electrically combine. Especially with its inherent color and emotionalism, its freedom from body-hampering dress, its odd and tragic and mysterious overtones, African life and themes, apart from

any sentimental attachment, offer a wonderfully new field and province for dramatic treatment. Here both the Negro actor and dramatist can move freely in a world of elemental beauty, with all the decorative elements that a poetic emotional temperament could wish. No recent playgoer with the spell of Brutus Jones in the forest underbrush still upon his imagination will need much persuasion about this.

More and more the art of the Negro actor will seek its materials in the rich native soil of Negro life, and not in the threadbare tradition of the Caucasian stage. In the discipline of art playing upon his own material, the Negro has much to gain. Art must serve Negro life as well as Negro talent serve art. And no art is more capable of this service than drama. Indeed the surest sign of a folk renascence seems to be a dramatic flowering. Somehow the release of such self-expression always accompanies or heralds cultural and social maturity. I feel that soon this aspect of the race genius may come to its classic age of expression. Obviously, though, it has not yet come. For our dramatic expression is still too restricted, self-conscious and imitative.

When our serious drama shall become as naive and spontaneous as our drama of fun and laughter, and that in turn genuinely representative of the folk spirit which it is now forced to travesty, a point of classic development will have been reached. It is fascinating to speculate upon what riotously new and startling drama may come from this. Dramatic maturings are notably sudden. Usually from the popular sub-soil something shoots up to a rapid artistic flowering. Of course, this does not have to recur with the American Negro. But a peasant folk art pouring out from under a generation-long repression is the likeliest soil known for a dramatic renascence. And the supporters and exponents of Negro drama do not expect their folk temperament to prove the barren exception.

—1927

The Drama of Negro Life

by Montgomery Gregory

PRESIDENT-EMERITUS Charles William Eliot of Harvard University expressed the inspiring thought that America should not be a "melting-pot" for the diverse races gathered on her soil but that each race should maintain its essential integrity and contribute its own special and peculiar gift to our composite civilization: not a "melting-pot" but a symphony where each instrument contributes its particular quality of music to an ensemble of harmonious sounds. Whatever else the Negro may offer as his part, there is already the general recognition that his folk-music, born of the pangs and sorrows of slavery, has made America and the world his eternal debtor. The same racial characteristics that are responsible for this music are destined to express themselves with similar excellence in the kindred art of drama. The recent notable successes of Negro actors and of plays of Negro life on Broadway point to vast potentialities in this field. Eugene O'Neill, who more than any other person has dignified and popularized Negro drama, gives testimony to the possibilities of the future development of Negro drama as follows: "I believe as strongly as you do that the gifts the Negro can—and will—bring to our native drama are invaluable ones. The possibilities are limitless and to a dramatist open up new and intriguing opportunities."

Before considering contemporary interest in Negro drama, it will be well to discover its historical background. William Shakespeare was the first dramatist to appreciate the "intriguing opportunities" in the life of the darker races; and in his master-tragedy *Othello,* he has given us the stellar role of the Moor in a study of the effect of jealousy upon a nature of simple and overpowering emotion. So great an embarrassment has this "Black-a-moor" been to the Anglo-Saxon stage that the "supreme tragedy of English drama" has suffered a distinct unpopularity, and its chief interpreters have been compelled to give a bleached and an adulterated presentation of the black commander of the Venetian army. Thus O'Neill had an excellent precedent for his *Emperor Jones.*

The example of Shakespeare was not followed by his immediate successors. In fact, a character of sable hue does not appear in the pages of English literature until a century later when Aphra Behn wrote that sentimental romance, *Oronooko,* portraying the unhappy lot of a noble Negro prince in captivity. This tearful tragedy had numerous imitators in both fiction and drama, an example of the latter being the *Black Doctor,* written by Thomas Archer and published in London in 1847. It was not long after this publication that London and the continent were treated to an extraordinary phenomenon—the appearance of a Maryland Negro in *Othello* and other Shakespearean roles in the royal theaters. Ira Aldridge is thus the first Negro to

Charles S. Gilpin, the most distinguished product of the Lafayette Players of Harlem, attained national prominence through his electrifying portrayal of the lead in Eugene O'Neill's *The Emperor Jones*.

Paul Robeson as Othello.

SAM S. SHUBERT THEATRE

CENTRAL THEATRES LEASING & CONSTRUCTION CO.

EMERGENCY NOTICE: In the event of an alert, remain in your seats. A competent staff has been trained for this emergency. Keep calm. You will receive information and instructions from the stage.   F. H. La GUARDIA, Mayor

FIRE NOTICE: The exit indicated by a red light and sign nearest to the seat you occupy is the shortest route to the street. In the event of fire please do not run—WALK TO THAT EXIT.
         Patrick Walsh, Fire Commissioner
         and Chief of Department

It is urged for the comfort and safety of all, that theatre patrons refrain from lighting matches in this theatre.

THE · PLAYBILL · A · WEEKLY · PUBLICATION · OF · PLAYBILL · INCORPORATED

Week beginning Sunday, October 24, 1943   •   Matinees Thursday and Saturday

THE THEATRE GUILD

Administration: LAWRENCE LANGNER and THERESA HELBURN

presents

PAUL ROBESON

in

The Margaret Webster Production of

OTHELLO

by

William Shakespeare

with

JOSE FERRER   UTA HAGEN
MARGARET WEBSTER   JAMES MONKS

Production Designed and Lighted by
ROBERT EDMOND JONES

Music Composed by Tom Bennett

Associate Producer
JOHN HAGGOTT

surmount the bars of race prejudice and to receive recognition on the legitimate English-speaking stage.

Up until the Civil War, then, there was but meager interest in the drama of the African or Negro in England, and practically none in the United States. That great sectional conflict aroused a tremendous sentimental interest in the black population of the South and gave us Harriet Beecher Stowe's *Uncle Tom's Cabin,* which also enjoyed a wide popularity as a drama. *The Octoroon,* written on the same pattern, soon followed on the American stage. These works mark the first instance where an attempt is made to present to the American public in a realistic manner the authentic life of the Negro. They accustomed the theater-goer to the appearance of a number of Negro characters (played by blacked-face white actors) on the stage, and this fact was in itself a distinct gain for Negro drama.

Although *Uncle Tom's Cabin* passed into obscurity, "Topsy" survived. She was blissfully ignorant of any ancestors, but she has given us a fearful progeny. With her, popular dramatic interest in the Negro changed from serious moralistic drama to the comic phase. We cannot say that as yet the public taste has generally recovered from this descent from sentimentalism to grotesque comedy, and from that in turn to farce, mimicry and sheer burlesque. The earliest expression of Topsy's baneful influence is to be found in the minstrels made famous by the Callenders, Lew Dockstader, and Primrose and West. These comedians, made up into grotesque caricatures of the Negro race, fixed in the public taste a dramatic stereotype of the race that has been almost fatal to a sincere and authentic Negro drama. The earliest Negro shows were either imitations of these minstrels or slight variations from them. In fact, the average play of Negro life today, whether employing white or black actors, reeks with this pernicious influence.

It was not until 1895 that the Negro attempted to break with the minstrel tradition, when John W. Isham formed *The Octoroons,* a musical show. Minor variety and vaudeville efforts followed, but the first all-Negro comedy to receive Broadway notice was Williams and Walker's *In Dahomey,* which played at the Forty-sixth Street Theatre for several weeks. Williams and Walker, Cole and Johnson, S. H. Dudley, and Ernest Hogan now presented a succession of shows in which the Negro still appeared in caricature but which offered some compensation by the introduction of a slight plot and much excellent music and dancing. Such shows as *Abyssinia, Rufus Rastus, Bandana Land,* and *Mr. Lode of Koal,* are still familiar names to the theater-goers between 1900 and 1910. During the latter year "Bert" Williams' inimitable genius was fully recognized, and from then until his death he was an idol of the American public. It may not be amiss to state that it was Williams' ambition to appear in a higher type of drama, and David Belasco states in the introduction to *The Son of Laughter,* a biography of "Bert" Williams by Margaret Rowland, that his death probably prevented him from appearing under his direction as a star. Negro drama will always be indebted to the genius of this great comedian and appreciative of the fact that by breaking into *The Follies* "Bert" Williams unlocked the doors of the American theater to later Negro artists.

The reader will probably be familiar with the extraordinary successes of the latest Negro musical comedies, *Shuffle Along, Runnin' Wild,* and *From Dixie to Broadway,* and with the names of their stars—Sissle and Blake, Miller and Lyles, and Florence Mills. In many respects these shows represent notable advances over the musical shows that preceded them, yet fundamentally they carry on the old minstrel tradition. Ludwig Lewisohn, the eminent New York critic, thus evaluates their work: "Much of this activity, granting

talent and energy, is of slight interest; much of it always strikes me as an actual imitation of the white 'blacked-face' comedian—an imitation from the Negro's point of view of a caricature of himself. All of these things have little or no value as art, as an expression of either the Negro individual or the Negro race." Yet in all justice it should be said that these shows have given a large number of talented Negroes their only opportunity for dramatic expression and have resulted in the development of much stage ability. "Bert" Williams and Florence Mills are examples of dramatic geniuses who have elevated their work in these productions to the highest art. Certainly historically these musical shows are a significant element in the groping of the Negro for dramatic expression, and who knows but that they may be the genesis for an important development of our drama in the future?

Serious Negro drama is a matter of recent growth and still is in its infancy. It is in this field of legitimate drama that the Negro must achieve success if he is to win real recognition in the onward sweep of American drama. The year 1910 may be said to mark the first significant step in this direction, for it witnessed the production with a distinguished cast, including Guy Bates Post and Annie Russell, at the New Theatre in New York City, of Edward Sheldon's *The Nigger* (later called *The Governor*), a somewhat melodramatic treatment of the tragedy of racial admixture in the South. It marks the first sincere attempt to sound the depths of our racial experience for modern drama. A more sympathetic and poetic utilization of this dramatic material appears a few years later in the composition of three one-act plays (*Granny Maumee, The Rider of Dreams,* and *Simon the Cyrenian*), by Ridgely Torrence. Of equal importance was the artistic staging of these plays with a cast of talented Negro actors by Sheldon, Mrs. Norman Hapgood, and others. The

venture was a pleasing artistic success, and but for the intervention of the World War might have resulted in the establishment of a permanent Negro Little Theatre in New York City. Not only had the public been impressed with the artistic value of such plays, but it also had been given its first demonstration of the ability of the Negro actor in other than burlesque parts. Opal Cooper especially won the plaudits of the critics, and, like John the Baptist, he proved to be only the forerunner of one who was to touch the peaks of histrionic accomplishments.

Then by a *tour-de-force* of genius—for the histrionic ability of Charles Gilpin has been as effective as the dramatic genius of Eugene O'Neill—the serious play of Negro life broke through to public favor and critical recognition. Overnight this weird psychological study of race experience was hailed as a dramatic masterpiece and an unknown Negro was selected by the Drama League as one of the ten foremost actors on the American stage. In any further development of Negro drama, *The Emperor Jones,* written by O'Neill, interpreted by Gilpin, and produced by the Provincetown Players, will tower as a beacon-light of inspiration. It marks the breakwater plunge of Negro drama into the main stream of American drama.

In 1923 Raymond O'Neill assembled a noteworthy group of Negro actors in Chicago and formed the "Ethiopian Art Theatre." Following successful presentation there he launched his interesting theater on Broadway. Whereas Torrence started out with several original race plays, O'Neill attempted the adaptation of Oscar Wilde's *Salome* and Shakespeare's *Comedy of Errors.* His chief success was the production of *The Chip Woman's Fortune,* a one-act race play by the young Negro dramatist Willis Richardson. The acting of Evelyn Preer, the Kirkpatricks, Olden and Solomon Bruce was equal to the best tradition of the American theater—but

even great acting could not atone for an unwise selection of plays. This untimely collapse of a most promising enterprise should hold a valuable lesson for other promoters of Negro drama.

Since these passing successes of the Negro on the regular stage, there have been several hopeful experiments in the Little Theatre and educational fields, with larger likelihood of permanent results. At Howard University, in Washington, D.C., the writer, with the enthusiastic co-operation of Marie Moore-Forrest, Cleon Throckmorton, Alain Leroy Locke and the University officials, undertook to establish on an enduring basis the foundations of Negro drama through the institution of a dramatic laboratory where Negro youth might receive sound training in the arts of the theater. The composition of original race plays formed the pivotal element in the project. The Howard Players have given ample evidence of having the same significance for Negro drama that the erstwhile "47 Workshop" at Harvard University and the North Carolina University Players have had for American drama in general. Atlanta University, Hampton Institute, and Tuskegee Institute have been making commendable efforts in the same direction. In Harlem, the Negro quarter of New York City, Anne Wolter has associated with her an excellent corps of dramatic workers in the conduct of "The Ethiopian Art Theatre School."

Finally, mention must be made of two young Negro actors who have been maintaining the same high standard of artistic performance as established by Gilpin. Paul Robeson has succeeded to the rôle of *The Emperor Jones,* and has appeared in the leading part in O'Neill's latest Negro drama, *All God's Chillun Got Wings.* Eugene Corbie has likewise given a creditable performance as the "Witch Doctor" in *Cape Smoke.* Thus a sufficient demonstration has been made that Gilpin's achievement was not merely a comet-flare across the dramatic horizon but a trustworthy sign of the histrionic gift of his race.

The past and present of Negro drama lies revealed before us. It is seen that the popular musical comedies with their unfortunate minstrel inheritance have been responsible for a fateful misrepresentation of Negro life. However, the efforts toward the development of a sincere and artistic drama have not been altogether in vain. O'Neill and Torrence have shown that the ambitious dramatist has a rich and virgin El Dorado in the racial experiences of black folk. As the spirituals have risen from the folk-life of the race, so too will there develop out of the same treasure-trove a worthy contribution to a native American drama. The annual prizes now being offered through the vision of Charles S. Johnson of *Opportunity* magazine and of W. E. B. Du Bois and Jessie Fauset of *Crisis* magazine for original racial expression in the various literary forms are acting as a splendid stimulus to Negro writers to begin the adequate expression of their race life.

Our ideal is a national Negro Theater where the Negro playwright, musician, actor, dancer, and artist in concert shall fashion a drama that will merit the respect and admiration of America. Such an institution must come from the Negro himself, as he alone can truly express the soul of his people. The race must surrender that childish self-consciousness that refuses to face the facts of its own life in the arts but prefers the blandishments of flatterers, who render all efforts at true artistic expression a laughing-stock by adorning their characters with the gaudy gowns of cheap romance. However disagreeable the fact may be in some quarters, the only avenue of genuine achievement in American drama for the Negro lies in the development of the rich veins of folk-tradition of the past and in

the portrayal of the authentic life of the Negro masses of today. The older leadership still clings to the false gods of servile reflection of the more or less unfamiliar life of an alien race. The "New Negro," still few in number, places his faith in the potentialities of his own people—he believes that the black man has no reason to be ashamed of himself, but that in the divine plan he too has a worthy and honorable destiny.

The hope of Negro drama is the establishment of numerous small groups of Negro players throughout the country who shall simply and devotedly interpret the life that is familiar to them for the sheer joy of artistic expression.

— 1925

The Gift of Laughter

by Jessie Fauset

THE BLACK man bringing gifts, and particularly the gift of laughter, to the American stage is easily the most anomalous, the most inscrutable figure of the century. All about him and within himself stalks the conviction that like the Irish, the Russian and the Magyar he has some peculiar offering which shall contain the very essence of the drama. Yet the medium through which this unique and intensely dramatic gift might be offered has been so befogged and misted by popular preconception that the great gift, though divined, is as yet not clearly seen.

Popular preconception in this instance refers to the pressure of white opinion by which the American Negro is surrounded and by which his true character is almost submerged. For years the Caucasian in America has persisted in dragging to the limelight merely one aspect of Negro characteristics, by which the whole race has been glimpsed, through which it has been judged. The colored man who finally succeeds in impressing any considerable number of whites with the truth that he does not conform to these measurements is regarded as the striking exception proving an unshakable rule. The medium then through which the black actor has been presented to the world has been that of the "funny man" of America. Ever since those far-off times directly after the Civil War when white men and colored men too, blacking their faces, presented the antics of plantation hands under the caption of "Georgia Minstrels" and the like, the edict has gone forth that the black man on the stage must be an end-man.

In passing one pauses to wonder if this picture of the black American as a living comic supplement has not been painted in order to camouflage the real feeling and knowledge of his white compatriot. Certainly the plight of the slaves under even the mildest of masters could never have been one to awaken laughter. And no genuinely thinking person, no really astute observer, looking at the Negro in modern American life, could find his condition even now a first aid to laughter. That condition may be variously deemed hopeless, remarkable, admirable, inspiring, depressing; it can never be dubbed merely amusing.

* * * * * *

It was the colored actor who gave the first impetus away from this buffoonery. The task was not an easy one. For years the Negro was no great frequenter of the theater. And no matter how keenly he felt the insincerity in the presentation of his kind, no matter how ridiculous and palpable a caricature such a presentation might be, the Negro auditor with the helplessness of the minority was powerless to demand something better and truer. Artist and audience alike were in the grip of the minstrel formula. It was at this point in the eighteen-nineties that Ernest Hogan, pioneer comedian of the better type, changed the

tradition of the merely funny, rather silly "end-man" into a character with a definite plot in a rather loosely constructed but none the less well-outlined story. The method was still humorous, but less broadly, less exclusively. A little of the hard luck of the Negro began to creep in. If he was a buffoon, he was a buffoon wearing his rue. A slight, very slight quality of the Harlequin began to attach to him. He was the clown making light of his troubles, but he was a wounded, a sore-beset clown.

This figure became the prototype of the plays later presented by those two great characters, Williams and Walker. The ingredients of the comedies in which these two starred usually consisted of one dishonest, overbearing, flashily dressed character (Walker) and one kindly, rather simple, hard-luck personage (Williams). The interest of the piece hinged on the juxtaposition of these two men. Of course these plays, too, were served with a sauce of humor because the public, true to its carefully taught and rigidly held tradition, could not dream of a situation in which colored people were anything but merely funny. But the hardships and woes suffered by Williams, ridiculous as they were, introduced with the element of folk comedy some element of reality.

Side by side with Williams and Walker, who might be called the apostles of the "legitimate" on the stage for Negroes, came the merriment and laughter and high spirits of that incomparable pair, Cole and Johnson. But they were essentially the geniuses of musical comedy. At that time their singers and dancers outsang and outdanced the neophytes of contemporary white musical comedies even as their followers to this day outsing and outdance in their occasional appearances on Broadway their modern neighbors. Just what might have been the ultimate trend of the ambition of this partnership, the untimely death of Mr. Cole rendered uncertain; but

speaking offhand I should say that the relation of their musical comedy idea to the fixed plot and defined dramatic concept of the Williams and Walker plays molded the form of the Negro musical show which still persists and thrives on the contemporary stage. It was they who capitalized the infectious charm of so much rich dark beauty, the verve and abandon of Negro dancers, the glorious fullness of Negro voices. And they produced those effects in the *Red Shawl* in a manner still unexcelled, except in the matter of setting, by any latter-day companies.

But Williams and Walker, no matter how dimly, were seeking a method whereby the colored man might enter the "legitimate." They were to do nothing but pave the way. Even this task was difficult but they performed it well.

*   *   *   *   *   *

Those who knew Bert Williams say that his earliest leanings were toward the stage, but that he recognized at an equally early age that his color would probably keep him from ever making the "legitimate." Consequently, deliberately, as one who desiring to become a great painter but lacking the means for travel and study might take up commercial art, he turned his attention to minstrelsy. Natively he possessed the art of mimicry; intuitively he realized that his first path to the stage must lie along the old recognized lines of "funny man." He was, as few of us recall, a Jamaican by birth; the ways of the American Negro were utterly alien to him and did not come spontaneously; he set himself therefore to obtaining a knowledge of them. For choice he selected, perhaps by way of contrast, the melancholy out-of-luck Negro, shiftless, doleful, "easy"; the kind that tempts the world to lay its hand none too lightly upon him. The pursuit took him years, but at length he was able to portray for us not only that "typical Negro" which the white world thinks is universal but also the special types

of given districts and localities with their own peculiar foibles of walk and speech and jargon. He went to London and studied under Pietro, greatest pantomimist of his day, until finally he, too, became a recognized master in the field of comic art.

But does anyone who realizes that the foibles of the American Negro were painstakingly acquired by this artist, doubt that Williams might just as well have portrayed the Irishman, the Jew, the Englishman abroad, the Scotchman or any other of the vividly etched types which for one reason or another lend themselves so readily to caricature? Can anyone presume to say that a man who travelled *north, east, south* and *west* and even abroad in order to acquire accent and jargon, aspect and characteristic of a people to which he was bound by ties of blood but from whom he was natively separated by training and tradition, would not have been able to portray with equal effectiveness what, for lack of a better term, we must call universal roles?

There is an unwritten law in America that though white may imitate black, black, even when superlatively capable, must never imitate white. In other words, grease paint may be used to darken but never to lighten.

Williams' color imposed its limitations upon him even in his chosen field. His expansion was always upward but never outward. He might portray black people along the gamut from roustabout to unctuous bishop. But he must never stray beyond those limits. How keenly he felt this few of us knew until after his death. But it was well known to his intimates and professional associates. W. C. Fields, himself an expert in the art of amusing, called him "the funniest man I ever saw and the saddest man I ever knew."

He was sad with the sadness of hopeless frustration. The gift of laughter in his case had its source in a wounded heart and in bleeding sensibilities.

* * * * * *

That laughter for which we are so justly famed has had in late years its over-tones of pain. Now for some time past it has been used by colored men who have gained a precarious footing on the stage to conceal the very real dolor raging in their breasts. To be by force of circumstances the most dramatic figure in a country; to be possessed of the wells of feeling, of the most spontaneous instinct for effective action and to be shunted no less always into the role of the ridiculous and funny—that is enough to create the quality of bitterness for which we are ever so often rebuked. Yet that same laughter influenced by these same untoward obstacles has within the last four years known a deflection into another channel, still productive of mirth, but even more than that of a sort of cosmic gladness, the joy which arises spontaneously in the spectator as a result of the sight of its no less spontaneous bubbling in others. What hurt most in the spectacle of the Bert Williams' funny man and his forerunners was the fact that the laughter which he created must be objective. But the new "funny man" among black comedians is essentially funny himself. He is joy and mischief and rich, homely native humor personified. He radiates good feeling and happiness; it is with him now a state of being purely subjective. The spectator is infected with his high spirits and his excessive good will; a stream of well-being is projected across the footlights into the consciousness of the beholder.

This phenomenon has been especially visible in the rendition of the colored musical "shows," *Shuffle Along, Runnin' Wild, Liza,* which livened up Broadway recently for a too brief season. Those of us who were lucky enough to compare with the usual banality of musical comedy, the verve and pep, the liveliness and gayety of those productions will not soon forget them. The medley of shades, the rich colorings, the abundance of fun and

spirits on the part of the players all combined to produce an atmosphere which was actually palpable, so full was it of the ecstasy and joy of living. The singing was inimitable; the work of the chorus apparently spontaneous and unstudied. Emotionally they garnished their threadbare plots and comedy tricks with the genius of a new comic art.

The performers in all three of these productions gave out an impression of sheer happiness in living such as I have never before seen on any stage except in a riotous farce which I once saw in Vienna and where the same effect of superabundant vitality was induced. It is this quality of vivid and untheatrical portrayal of sheer emotion which seems likely to be the Negro's chief contribution to the stage. A comedy made up of such ingredients as the music of Sissle and Blake, the quaint, irresistible humor of Miller and Lyles, the quintessence of jazzdom in the Charleston, the superlativeness of Miss Mills' happy abandon could know no equal. It would be the line by which all other comedy would have to be measured. Behind the banalities and clap-trap and crudities of these shows, this supervitality and joyousness glow from time to time in a given step or gesture or in the teasing assurance of such a line as: "If you've never been vamped by a brown-skin, you've never been vamped at all."

And as Carl Van Vechten recently in his brilliant article, *Prescription for the Negro Theater,* so pointedly advises and prophesies, once this spirit breaks through the silly "childish adjuncts of the minstrel tradition" and drops the unworthy formula of unoriginal imitation of the stock revues, there will be released on the American stage a spirit of comedy such as has been rarely known.

*   *   *   *   *   *

The remarkable thing about this gift of ours is that it had its rise, I am convinced, in the very woes which beset us. Just as a person driven by great sorrow may finally go into an orgy of laughter, just so an oppressed and too hard driven people breaks over into compensating laughter and merriment. It is our emotional salvation. There would be no point in mentioning this rather obvious fact were it not that it argues also the possession on our part of a histrionic endowment for the portrayal of tragedy. Not without reason has tradition made comedy and tragedy sisters and twins; the capacity for one argues the capacity for the other. It is not surprising then that the period that sees the Negro actor on the verge of great comedy has seen him breaking through to the portrayal of serious and legitimate drama. No one who has seen Gilpin and Robeson in the portrayal of *The Emperor Jones* and of *All God's Chillun* can fail to realize that tragedy, too, is a vastly fitting role for the Negro actor. And so with the culminating of his dramatic genius, the Negro actor must come finally through the very versatility of his art to the universal role and the main tradition of drama, as an artist first and only secondarily as a Negro.

*   *   *   *   *   *

Nor when within the next few years, this question comes up—as I suspect it must come up with increasing insistence, will the more obvious barriers seem as obvious as they now appear. For in this American group of the descendants of Mother Africa, the question of color raises no insuperable barrier, seeing that with chameleon adaptability we are able to offer white colored men and women for *Hamlet, The Doll's House* and *Second Mrs. Tanqueray;* brown men for *Othello;* yellow girls for *Madame Butterfly;* black men for *The Emperor Jones.* And underneath and permeating all this bewildering array of shades and tints is the unshakable precision of an instinctive and spontaneous emotional art.

All this beyond any doubt will be the reward of the "gift of laughter" which many black actors on the American stage have prof-

fered. Through laughter we have conquered even the lot of the jester and the clown. The parable of the one talent still holds good, and because we have used the little which in those early painful days was our only approach, we find ourselves slowly but surely moving toward that most glittering of all goals, the freedom of the American stage. I hope that Hogan realizes this and Cole and Walker, too, and that lastly Bert Williams the inimitable, will clap us on with those tragic black-gloved hands of his now that the gift of his laughter is no longer tainted with the salt of chagrin and tears.

—1925

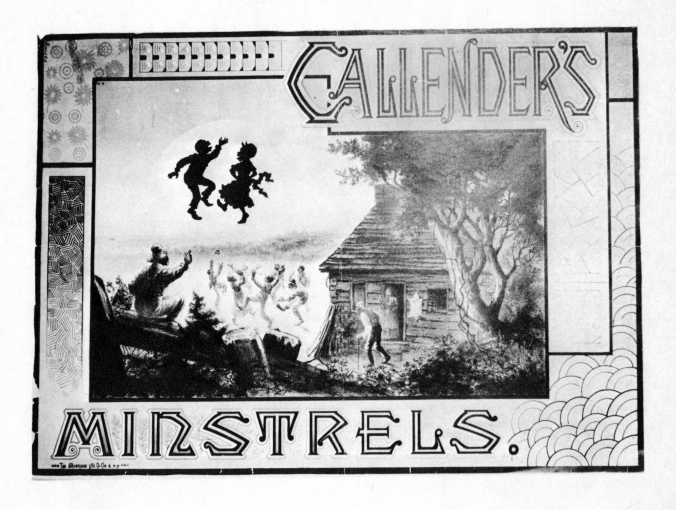

To-night, Saturday, Feb. 7th,   DAVIS' Jubilee Singer.
At Church of Messiah, S. E. Cor. 23d St. & Michigan Ave.
Come and hear the Finest Singers in the World.

ADMISSION,   -   -   15 and 25 Cents.

Bob Cole

J. Rosamond Johnson

Musical Comedy

by Maud Cuney-Hare

FROM a judicious use of syncopation, Ragtime, quickly followed by Jazz and the Blues, gave unrestrained zest to the stage-dances. Negroes had been engaged in the theatre, in the comedy type of entertainment, as early as 1820, when the African Players performed in New York. In 1873, Lyles and Lyles, a musical comedy team played *Free and Easy,* a variety show. Twenty years later there were many companies on the road. On August 4, 1890, Sam T. Jack's *Creoles* opened at Haverhill, Massachusetts, with the novelty of Negro women on the professional stage. John V. W. Isham followed in 1895 by presenting the Octoroons abroad, in a comedy called *Oriental America.* About 1896, S. H. Dudley's *Smart Set,* including Walter Smart, who wrote his own songs as well as the lyrics for his wife, Marion, one of the beauties of the play, became known far and wide for the chorus of extremely pretty colored girls.[1]

Ernest Hogan was one of the best known comedians who sang and acted. His real name was William Fields. He assumed the stage name of Ernest Hogan in taking that of his patent medicine vending employer who gave the young man his first histrionic opportunity in having him do "stunts" of singing

and dancing from his wagon to attract buyers. He wrote many songs, one of which was "All Coons Look Alike to Me." This song, he explained to a friend, was suggested by his being in a place which was raided because of the misdemeanor committed by one of the party. In explaining to the police that he was not the offender, the undiscriminating guardian of the peace replied, "All Coons Look Alike to Me." In all but similar fashion was suggested to Kip Taylor "Please, Mr. Johnson, Turn Me Loose; I Got No Money But a Good Excuse." The composer, living in an Indiana town, frequently got into mischief with fellows playing on the sand lots. Often when arrested they appealed to the policeman in the language of this song.

In 1895, Hogan wrote the dance-song, "Pas Ma La," popularized in *By the Sad Sea Waves,* a white comedy. Hogan became very prominent about 1899 and traveled extensively. In 1902 he was with Gus Hill, widely known as a producer until his death. From 1905 to 1907, Hogan starred in *Rufus Rastus,* for which he and Joe Jordan wrote the music to his own book. The lyrics were by Lester A. Walton and Frank Williams. Walton and Creamer wrote the lyrics for the *Oyster Man,* in which Hogan starred in 1907-08. The music was by Will H. Vodery to the book by Miller and Lyles.

These productions tended to develop toward higher ground. In 1898, the first Negro

---

[1] *Before 1860 a concert troupe known as "The Extraordinary 7 Slaves," from Alabama, were billed in Massachusetts, "under guidance of Northern friends and guarantees, to purchase their freedom."*

musical comedy worked out by a Negro for Negro talent, was written and produced by Robert Cole[2] and William Johnson. This was called *A Trip to Coontown.* Cole also wrote *A Shoo Fly Regiment.* Among his popular songs we find "Louisiana Lize," "I Must Have Been A-Dreaming," "No One Can Fill Her Place," "Katydid," "The Maiden with Dreamy Eyes," and "The Cricket and the Frog." For a long time Cole amused a wide public with his "Tramp" act. All of these companies featured dance novelties.

In 1899 a new stage was reached when *Sons of Ham* was produced at the Grand Opera House, New York City, by Williams and Walker. The partnership between Bert (Egbert Austin) Williams and George Walker lasted until 1909, the time of the latter's death. The two comedians starred in *Abyssinia,* from 1906 to 1907, and in *Bandana Land* from 1907 to 1909—two widely heralded productions, the lyrics of which were written by Alex C. Rogers, the collaborator with Jesse A. Shipp in the writing of the book. The music was by Will Marion Cook, who also composed the music for *In Dahomey,* in which Williams and Walker appeared from 1902 to 1905. The lyrics were by Paul Laurence Dunbar. On September 12, 1902, the piece was produced at the Globe Theatre, Boston, after which Cook took the aggregation of performers abroad. They gave one hundred and fifty performances at the Shaftesbury Theatre in 1903, with Williams as Shylock Homestead, and Walker as Rareback Pinkerton. The Boston *Herald* mentioned Bert Williams as having never appeared to better advantage . . . and that "His song 'I May Be Crazy But I Ain't No Fool' was the humorous piece de resistance."

The best liked songs in this comedy were "On Emancipation Day" and "Happy Jim," sung by J. Leubrie Hill, together with "That's

How the Cake-walk's Done." The play was seen again in Boston in March, 1905. The Boston *Evening Transcript* said, in comment thereupon, "Musical comedies with real music are rarities, but this is one"; and in reference to Cook the reviewer added, "The composer has succeeded in lifting Negro music above the plane of the so-called 'Coon Song' without destroying the characteristics of the melodies, and he has provided a score which is likewise unusually diversified. James Vaughn, who has written some of the added music, conducted the orchestra, and his piano accompaniments were one of the features of the performance."

Before this time, Williams and Walker had been the stars in *Two Real Coons, The Gold Bug* and *Senegambia Carnival.* After Walker's death Williams, who had performed for some time alone, made a contract in 1911 to appear in the *Ziegfeld Follies* for ten years. Williams, who was born in Nassau, British West Indies, November 12, 1874, died in New York in 1922. He was a handsome man whose visage was masked by Negro makeup needed in his character roles. He was last seen in *Under the Bamboo Tree,* a rewritten play of 1918-19. The New York *Evening Post* said of him, "His admirable art was not for the orgiastic jazz, but for that plaintive humor of the 'blues' that is now coming to the front." Williams compellingly followed the path of Negro dance and comic song, but as an artist he was above his medium.

During these years, too, other artists were active. *Put and Take,* the lyrics and music by Spencer Williams, Perry Bradford and Tim Brymn, book by Irvin C. Miller, appeared on the boards in 1921-22, a year before *This and That,* with lyrics and book by Alex C. Rogers, the music by C. Luckeyth Roberts. In 1912 Rogers collaborated with Henry S. Creamer in writing the lyrics and book of *The Traitor,* music by Will Marion Cook, in which he and Creamer appeared as stars.

---

[2] *Cole was born in Athens, Georgia, July 1, 1868, and died in New York City on August 2, 1911. He was a graduate of Atlanta University.*

The latter, with J. Turner Layton, wrote the lyrics and music of *Strut Miss Lizzie,* book by Creamer, in 1922. Mr. Layton was born in Washington, D.C., the son of John T. Layton who was director of music in the Washington Public Schools and the first conductor of the Samuel Coleridge-Taylor Society. The father was a bass singer, a pupil of Esputa. He died in 1915. The son received his academic education at Howard University and his musical training from his father who followed the classic school. The son wrote songs of more than ephemeral quality, "The Little Gray Road of Love," "Thank God the Drums Are Silent," and other ballads. Layton's co-worker, Henry S. Creamer, a product of New York schools, was born in Richmond, Virginia, June 21, 1879, the son of the Rev. H. Creamer. Young Creamer was one of the founders of the Clef Club, one of the first organizations to win notice in syncopated orchestral music. As song writers they have composed music for Nora Bayes, Al Jolson, Eddie Cantor, Eva Tanguay, Bert Williams and Mr. and Mrs. Coburn, who played at the Harris Theatre, in New York.

Miller and Lyles starred in *Darkeydom* in 1914-15; the lyrics were by Lester A. Walton and the book by Henry Troy, with music by Will Marion Cook. In 1927-28 they appeared in *Rang Tang,* the music of which was written by Ford Dabney to lyrics by Joe Trent. The book was by Kaj Gynt. *Keep Shufflin',* a Miller and Lyles production of 1929, succeeded in reaching Broadway. In the meantime, 1924-25, they starred in their own vehicle, *Runnin' Wild,* for which Jimmie Johnson wrote the music, and R. C. McPherson the lyrics.[2a]

James J. Vaughn, son of Wiley Vaughn, also deserves notice here. He was born in Boston and educated at the Ridge Technical School in Cambridge, where he became a noted football star. Bert Williams and George Walker, visiting Boston, heard the young man play the piano at a club which catered to a theatrical patronage, and noted his unusual gifts as a pianist. His first engagement was with Graham's Specialty Company, that featured the cakewalk in performances of Goodman's Alabama Troubadours. While in need of funds, he met Alex Rogers in Philadelphia, and together the two men wrote the *Sultan of Zulu,* which was bought by George Walker. Vaughn then became the musical director for Williams and Walker with whom he remained for eight years. He made a reputation as a jazz pianist and wrote many songs for their productions. "Men and the Minstrel Bard," "It's Hard to Find a King Like Me," "When the Moon Shines," and "When Susie Comes," became general favorites. In 1902, the musician went to Europe with the *In Dahomey* company.

For three seasons Vaughn was musical director of shows produced by J. Leubrie Hill, and opened Dudley's first picture house in Washington. He toured with Black Patti and her company, and collaborated with Tutt of the Tutt Whitney team. After a period of organizing orchestras in Albany, New York, in 1929 he joined the *Darktown Frolics* as director. Tutt Whitney and J. A. Shipp were of *The Green Pastures* cast.[3] Leubrie Hill starred in *My Friend from Dixie,* for which he wrote lyrics and book, and in *Here and There,* by Alex C. Rogers, from 1913 to 1916.

The Policy Players, book by Jesse A. Shipp with music by Will Marion Cook, was a comedy in which Williams and Walker appeared in 1900. Williams starred in *Mr. Lode of Koal,* lyrics by Alex C. Rogers, with music written by Rosamond Johnson in 1909-10. *Dr. Beans from Boston,* lyrics by Henry

---

[2a] *The popular hit, "Good Morning, Carrie," was one of the many by R. C. McPherson and Tim Brymn.*

[3] *Jesse A. Shipp, born 1859, died June, 1934. He took the part of Abraham in* The Green Pastures. *Tutt Whitney died Feb. 10, 1934.*

S. Creamer, book by S. H. Dudley and Henry Troy, with music by Will H. Vodery,[4] appeared in 1911-1912 with S. H. Dudley as the star. *Dixie to Broadway,* the music by Mr. Vodery (practically the same play as *Dover to Dixie*), presented at the Broadhurst Theatre, New York City, on October 19, 1924, was the first real revue by Negroes. Florence Mills was the star during 1924-25. For 23 years Vodery arranged music for the Ziegfeld productions and also for those of the English producer, Charles Cochran.

Florence Mills, a singing comedienne and dancer, was an exponent of Negro dances and became the "rage" for her cakewalking and buck-dancing. She was born in Washington, D.C., January 25, 1895, and died November 1, 1927, in New York City. From vaudeville appearances with her two sisters, the slender, talented dancer soon earned a wide reputation in *Shuffle Along,* a musical comedy with F. E. Miller and Aubrey Lyles as the stars, the lyrics and music by Noble Sissle and Eubie Blake. This musical melange had a long run, following the opening on May 23, 1921, in 63rd Street Music Hall, New York.[5] *Shuffle Along,* a phenomenal success, was followed by *Liza,* lyrics and music by Maceo Pinkard, the book by Irvin C. Miller, in 1922-23; but tunes from the former play such as "I'm Just Wild About Harry," "Love Will Find A Way," "Shuffle Along," and "In Honeysuckle Time," continued to be whistled and sung. For three seasons, 1921 to 1923, Sissle and Blake were the foremost stars in Negro comedy. Blake pleased a wide public as a skillful Jazz pianist, and his keyboard manipulations were always a part of the show. Eubie Blake and Noble Sissle wrote their own book and music for their musical com-

edy *Chocolate Dandies,* in which they appeared in 1924-25.

It was in 1925 that musical plays with white casts featured Negro attractions. Miller and Lyles were in *George White's Scandals,* and next appeared (in 1929) with Cora Green, a singer of "blues," in Vincent Youmans' *Great Day.* In 1927, ten Negroes appeared in *Sidewalks of New York* while twenty were in the play *Americana.* When Oscar Hammerstein opened his memorial theatre on Broadway, he presented fifty colored singing actors in the cast.

Sissle later traveled with his own orchestra, and Blake, also temporarily out of musical comedy, had an independent orchestra. His band in *Harlem Is Heaven,* produced by the Lincoln Pictures Corporation, New York, together with the dancing of "Bojangles" Robinson (1932) were the leading features of a hodge-podge attraction.

It was through the Sissle and Blake shows that the comedienne Josephine Baker best exhibited her talent as a dancer. She was seen in *Chocolate Dandies* before becoming a sensation in the music halls of Paris. Negro revues served to introduce singers of the "blues." Ethel Waters became a Broadway star and after singing in *Africana,* a revue conceived by Earl Dancer, lyrics and music by Donald Hayward, became a popular radio singer of Negro song.

Negro actors of this period owe much to S. H. Dudley, a man of long stage experience, who rose from a small part as assistant to a patent-medicine street hawker in Texas to the status of one of the greatest comedians of all time. He entertained in music halls, organized groups of musicians, wrote songs and "hits" for many vaudeville performers, and managed his own companies. As already stated above, he appeared in 1904, in the new *Smart Set,* and became popular in vaudeville billed as "Dudley and His Mule." Some of his biggest hits were the familiar invitation,

[4] *In 1929, Will Vodery, for a number of years arranger of music for Ziegfeld's Follies, was given a three year contract with the Fox Film Company, Hollywood.*

[5] *Lyles, who was born in Jackson, Mississippi, lived in Indianapolis, Indiana, and followed a musical profession in Chicago, died in New York City on August 4, 1932, at the age of 49.*

Richard B. Harrison (left) played "De Lawd" in the original stage production of Marc Connelly's *The Green Pastures*. William Warfield (right) played the role in the 1957 television production.

The Hall Johnson Choir in rehearsal for the movie version of *The Green Pastures,* in 1936.

"Come After Breakfast, Bring Your Lunch, and Leave Before Dinner Time," " 'Deed I Ain't See'd No Messenger Boy," and "Good Morning, Carrie." Dudley retired from the stage to enter business. He organized the Colored Actors' Union, and devoted his time to the management of a circuit of theatres with headquarters in Washington, D.C.

Foremost among the colored composers of musical comedy was Will Marion Cook, an erratic genius, a man of more than ordinary talent. He was born of educated parents in Detroit, Michigan. While a boy soprano, he began the study of the violin. For three years he attended Oberlin College, after which he went to Berlin where he became the pupil of Joachim, the violinist. Ill health forced him to return home, about the time "Ragtime" was spreading northward. According to Cook, this was about 1898. A number of Negro companies had been organized about this time, and at the suggestion of George Walker, Cook wrote some of the choruses. Lyrics by Paul Laurence Dunbar were set to melodies founded upon plantation hymns, and finally Cook's operetta, *Clorindy, the Origin of the Cakewalk* was produced at the Casino Roof Garden in New York, and created a sensation. The song "On Emancipation Day" became a pattern for later white composers, while the swaying rhythms of "That's How the Cake-walk's Done," greatly influenced the stage dances that followed. In 1919-20 Cook toured America and Europe with his "American Syncopated Orchestra" which was the finest aggregation of musicians ever before heard in what is termed distinctly Negro music.

Cook later conducted the Clef Orchestra, a like organization of skilled Negro performers. He held to his avowed intention to work only in the Negro idiom, but while doing so, he produced music of undoubted worth. Cook, who was a pupil of Anton Dvorak, received universal praise for his orchestrations. A London paper of May 16, 1903, stated, "The work of Mr. Cook, the composer, stands out prominently . . . in several of the numbers one could not listen to more excellent orchestration. He conducted with remarkable vigor and enthusiasm, and . . . his music displays true dramatic perception."

As an orchestral leader, Mr. Cook was musically well-equipped, and able to discern the excellent points in music of a syncopated type. He developed the primitive Jazz and selected trained musicians for interpreters. Of four characteristic songs written by the composer, "Exhortation," a Negro Sermon, the "Rain Song," "Swing Along," and "Wid de Moon, Moon, Moon," Kurt Schindler said:

"Mr. Cook's work at its best means no less than finding the proper musical correlative to the Negro idiom, and thus adding a new territory to musical geography.

"Besides his larger works, Mr. Cook has been writing a great many songs in a more popular vein, but it is the development of his serious work along the lines of the 'Rain Song' and the 'Exhortation' which especially interests us, since here he will not only perform a lasting service to his race, but intrinsically enrich the entire musical world."

Mr. Cook has just completed a Negro music-drama *St. Louis 'ooman,* which is based on life on the Mississippi River in the gay 90's. The lyrics have been written by his son who wrote "Stop the Sun, Stop the Moon."

By 1901, the group of Negro companies which were featuring the sentimental and comical ballad of the day, had reached their ascendancy. The press commented upon the passing of the "buck and wing" dancing that was to be outlived by the cakewalk, and a number of trained musicians came forward in the dual capacity of orchestral leader and musical-comedy promoter. They were largely responsible for the growth of Ragtime in the large cities, and their names became known wherever Ragtime succeeded in securing a

foothold. Under Cook's baton, the cakewalk reached its highest artistic expression.

J. Rosamond Johnson, who was born in Jacksonville, Florida, 1873, the son of a Baptist minister, worked simultaneously with Mr. Cook. Both he and his brother, James Weldon Johnson, received the advantage of an academic training. But while James Weldon pursued his studies through a collegiate course and developed as a man of public affairs and an author of recognized ability, Rosamond came to Boston where he entered the New England Conservatory of Music and received a thorough musical education.

Rosamond Johnson's career is an unusual one. From an exponent of distinct Negro music, as typified in Ragtime, both as a vaudeville performer and as a composer-producer, he rapidly rose from partnership with "Bob" Cole, comedian (a graduate of Atlanta University), to a successful directorship of musical comedies, thence to a professorship, but to return again to the vaudeville stage.

An early work, *The Red Moon,* written and staged by Cole and Johnson, and performed by an aggregation of young Negro men and women, was one of the cleanest and brightest musical comedies of the day and from a musical standpoint, marked a decided advance in this sphere. "Wrap Me in Your Little Red Shawl," one of the "hits" of the operetta, was long remembered after the ill-starred *Red Moon* had passed from the stage. The presentation was a financial failure, but its influence lived.

At this time Johnson was collaborating with his brother, James Weldon, whose later poetry reached a high standard. At the same time, Cole and Johnson were writing "extravaganzas" for Klaw and Erlanger, white New York producers, and popular airs for Marie Cahill and other white musical comedy stars. "Under the Bamboo Tree," "The Congo Love Song," "Nobody's Looking but the Owl and the Moon," and "My Castle on the Nile" won national popularity.

After Cole's death, Johnson was engaged (in 1912) in vaudeville work with Charles Hart. "Lovely Daughter of Allah," a setting of one of his brother's lyrics, was equally popular with "Excuse Me, Mister Moon," a song written for Alice Lloyd in the musical play *Little Miss Fix-It.* In 1913, Johnson went abroad and, while in London, directed musical comedy at Hammerstein's Opera House, where he gained new honors. He appeared in a new musical comedy act at the London Pavilion, then returned to this country in the spring of 1914. His first appearance after his return was made at the New Standard Theatre in Philadelphia.

Shortly after this Johnson accepted a position as director of music at the newly established Music School Settlement in New York. The musician remained at this institution for a few years, giving lessons and composing for voice, chorus and orchestra. It was at this period that his best pieces were written. About 1917, when the author visited the New York Music School Settlement for colored pupils, Johnson whimsically said, "When I was single, I was in vaudeville, earning a lucrative salary; now that I am married, I am giving music lessons in a Music School Settlement!" It may be that the economic pressure and the untoward conditions resultant from the war persuaded him to return to the vaudeville stage. This he soon did and for two years he was engaged on the Orpheum and Keith Circuits with the "Rosamond Johnson Quintet."

Johnson rendered another service in 1925 when the Viking Press published his brother's excellent collection called *The Book of American Negro Spirituals,* for which he made the musical arrangements. Additional numbers were by Lawrence Brown. The introduction by James Weldon Johnson is a valuable contribution to the history of the Negro in music.

Juanita Hall in Hall Johnson's
Run, Little Chillun.

After this, the musician proved most successful in a new field; and for two or three years thereafter, the Taylor and Johnson programs of Negro Spirituals, presented by white concert management, met with much favor. The songs were sung in duet form in which Gordon Taylor joined his tenor voice with that of the basso cantante of Johnson's.

This prolific writer has composed pieces for solo voice, chorus, and orchestra. "Lift Every Voice and Sing," a national patriotic hymn sung by Negroes, is not only a melodically beautiful production but tremendous in its racial and national appeal. It is widely used by Negro organizations everywhere. Apart from this composer's lighter music in the Negro vein, are found serious songs, the words of which are by his brother.[6]

A list of his compositions include: "Walk Together, Children," which is a plantation melody transcribed as a majestic marching song for full chorus and orchestra. It was written for the Negro Pageant held in Washington, D.C., in 1915. Of this setting of a Negro camp-meeting hymn, the Boston *Evening Transcript* of Feb. 17, 1917, said:

> The few touches which he has added in the development are those of the trained musician, with an accurate instinct for musical organization. Like all great music, whether of individual or folk-origin, it has the property of suppressing the conscious judgment and liberating the sensuous reactions into full play. Many observers have noted that the most promising signs in American drama are to be found in the popular "topical" plays of George Cohan and a few of his fellows. The same hypothesis seems reasonable as applied to music. . . . Negro Ragtime appears to have the greatest vitality of any American musical strain and seems most likely to supply the materials for American orchestral works of incontestable originality.

6 *The libretto of Enrique Granados' opera,* Goyescas, *which was written by Fernando Periquet, was translated from the Spanish by James Weldon Johnson in order that it might be presented in English at the Metropolitan Opera House in New York. The opera was given in 1916, under the direction of Gatti-Casazza.*

For the past ten years, musical comedies with all Negro casts have reached Broadway, which is the height of ambition of all theatrical folk. After Lew Leslie's *Blackbirds* had the run of one year in New York—an unsurpassed record for this particular type of show—the manager organized a second company with Harriet Calloway as the star. Florence Mills appeared in the 1926-27 production for which the words and music were written by George W. Meyer. Aida Ward was the star of the *Blackbirds of 1928,* in which the tap-dancing of Bill Robinson won applause.

Of Robinson's foot-tapping, Mary Austin wrote in *The Nation,* "The postures of his little dark body and the motions of his slender cane so puncture this rhythmic patter as to restore, for his audience, the primal freshness of their own lost rhythmic power." When a boy, Robinson (known as "Bojangles" Robinson) danced in the streets of Washington for any amount the amused passerby cared to throw at his feet. He is now the highest paid tap-dancer in the world. When seen in *Blackbirds* in 1926, he divided the applause with the song hit of the show—"I Can't Give You Anything But Love."

Recent plays of a serious nature, dramas of Negro folk life, owe much of their success to the incidental music employed. Naturally they are in an entirely different genre from the revue, and appeal to thoughtful audiences. *Porgy* (dramatized by DuBose Heyward, a white writer), a Theatre Guild production of 1927, played to crowded houses. South Carolina musical street-cries and Negro Spirituals served to create atmosphere and to deepen the emotional appeal. Frank Wilson, actor and playwright, who had the leading role, is a singer of Negro songs of which he makes effective use in his own plays. He is an earnest and serious actor of artistic ideals. His play, *Meek Mose,* was given at the Princess Theatre, New York, with a Negro repertory com-

pany and marks the first time a Negro has appeared as producer of a dramatic work on Broadway. Lester A. Walton was the manager.

Heralded in 1930, by Richard Watts, Jr., dramatic critic of the New York *Herald Tribune* as "one of the loftiest achievements of the American Theatre," *The Green Pastures,* a Negro miracle play, proved to be a masterpiece. With a cast of ninety-five Negroes, it became a great attraction in the theatrical world. Richard B. Harrison, who played the role of "De Lawd" 1,658 times, passed away on March 14, 1935. This was a drama, a prize winning play from the book *Ol' Man Adam and His Chillun,* by Roark Bradford, the work of Marc Connelly. It is a religious play dramatizing Biblical scenes as the two white authors conceive the illiterate Negroes' visualization of the mysteries of the Book of Genesis—of a God of wrath who is a personal deity. The Celestial Choir of the play, that sings off stage or in the orchestral pit, are heard in Negro Spirituals "a capella." The choir was first organized and conducted by Hall Johnson, whose chorus had been reaping fame at the concerts at the International House and at the Lewisohn Stadium of New York City College. Ulysses Chambers,[7] tenor, followed Hall Johnson as director of the choir of *The Green Pastures* when the play went on tour. Chambers made the choral arrangements and trained the chorus for the second season of Lew Leslie's *Blackbirds.*

Daniel Haynes was one of the leading singing-actors in *The Green Pastures* in which he played the dual role of Adam and Hezdrel. This versatile artist, successful on the stage and screen, was also an amateur painter and belonged to the Art Students League of New York. Haynes studied for the ministry in Atlanta, Georgia, his native city and came to New York with the idea of receiving advanced theological training. Instead he was drawn into accepting a place as understudy to the actor Charles Gilpin in *The Bottom of the Cup.* Owing to Gilpin's illness, he opened the play at a moment's notice and was triumphant in the star role. Haynes next appeared in *Earth;* in *Rang Tang,* a review; and in *Show Boat* as the understudy to Jules Bledsoe. Haynes' work in the two motion pictures, *Hallelujah* and *The Last Mile,* added to his reputation as an actor and singer. The producer Reinhardt has declared that in *Hallelujah* Haynes gave the most artistic performance he has seen in an American photoplay.

Ziegfeld's *Show Boat,* drawn from Edna Ferber's story of romantic days on the Mississippi, gave an opportunity for Negro talent. The singing and dancing in this musical play which is far above the standard of the comedy and revue of the Jazz school, is excellently done, while Jules Bledsoe brought an individual interpretation to the outstanding song, "Ol' Man River," which has placed it by the side of the best liked art songs of the present day.

---

[7] *Chambers, who was born in Baltimore, is a teacher of piano and organ. He was educated at Morgan College in that city, and also studied privately with white professors of Peabody Institute. However, he received his first lessons in this field from his parents, both of whom were musicians. Advanced musical studies were followed at the Musical Institute of Art, where he was graduated in 1916 and completed a post-graduate course in 1917. He studied further at the Teachers' College of Columbia University, where he finished a course in 1921 and was awarded the degree of Bachelor of Music and of Science. He has held many important positions as teacher and executant.*

From the supervisorship of music of the Baltimore colored public schools in 1921, he held, successively, similar positions at the Dunbar High School, Washington, D.C., and at the combined public schools of St. Louis. As organist, he has held positions at the "Lafayette," a white theatre of Newark, New Jersey, and at the Royal Theatre, Chicago. As tenor soloist and organist, Chambers has been connected with various white churches, including St. Luke's Cathedral, Trinity Parish and the Chapel of the Incarnation in New York City, and the First Presbyterian Church of South Hampton, Long Island. As solo organist he has been heard in the Wanamaker Auditorium in New York as well as in the largest cities in the United States.

A number of recent concoctions in the form of Negro revues have been short-lived owing to the fact that they are unfinished, trivial even for that particular medium, and lacking in distinction. Among the plays that received mention we find *Blackberries of 1932,* a revue in two acts and twenty-six scenes by Eddie Green, lyrics and music by Donald Heywood and Tom Pelusco and dances arranged by Sidney Sprague and Lew Crawford. The play was staged by Ben Bernard and produced at the Liberty Theatre, New York.

Of the character of the Negro musical comedy today, S. H. Dudley, the veteran actor-producer, says, "It seems to me that there is room in New York for a Negro show different from the present one. I may be wrong. *Blackbirds* and other shows like it have been a success, but I would like to see something nearer the Negro's genius."

There are two factors which may account for the present dearth of first-class Negro musical comedies. First, the present economic conditions of stress in the United States and in the world at large prohibit at the moment any new venture that entails the risking of the necessary sum to further début artist recitals or the financing of the elaborate and costly revue entertainment demanded by modern theatre-goers. A large growing body of educated Negroes, moreover, are turning their attention to the dramatic stage, and are questioning the successful, serious Negro drama of the times, written by white playwrights. They realize that in order to produce a good musical comedy or an opera, one must have a knowledge of what constitutes "good theater." Nevertheless it has become more than a suspicion that distinctive plays can be written, in which the drama of the lowly can be treated as but one phase of the realities of Negro life. Young Negro writers, on the wave of the new art awakening in America, therefore, have accepted the advice of Alain Locke who, in

writing of race-drama, has said, "The vehicle of all sound art must be native to the group." Americans of all racial affiliations are writing better stage music—it is not too much to expect that the Negro too will make progress in both the Negro folk-drama and his racial theatrical music. The distinct form of musical comedy and revues, frankly that of entertainment and no more, will be benefited by an improved taste.

For some time—since 1921—groups of Negro men and women have been experimenting in a new artistic medium. They are found in colleges and in amateur dramatic organizations. The Howard University Dramatic Department organized from the school club by Montgomery Gregory, and guided by Alain Locke; the Morgan College Dramatic Club in Baltimore; and the Dramatic Club of Hampton Institute where students paint the sets, perform the roles and compose the chorus— these are at the head of a long list of Negro college dramatic groups which are seriously studying the drama and giving commendable performances.

In 1921, the Colored Players Guild of New York, under Dora Cole Norman, talented dancer, a sister of Bob Cole, the comedian, was formed to produce original plays. A few years later, the Krigwa Players, Little Negro Theater, a nation-wide movement sponsored primarily by W. E. B. Du Bois, and directed by Charles Burroughs in New York, won prizes and praise from Belasco and other authorities. These activities were actuated within the race, thus differing from the presentation of the "Negro Players" in three Negro dramas written by Ridgely Torrence in 1917.

Other such efforts should be noted. The Little Theater group in Washington, D.C., has been working under the direction of Willis Richardson, a Negro playwright, and Georgia Douglas Johnson, the Negro woman poet who is now writing Negro one-act plays. The Dixwell Community Players of New Haven are

acting alertly under the shadow of the Theatre of Yale University. The Aldridge Players of St. Louis, who have just celebrated their eighth anniversary (1927-35), are producing Plays of Negro Life. The Gilpin Players of Cleveland, Ohio, for fourteen years have been widening their reputation in the longer, serious Negro plays written by white playwrights, but ever seeking new material. The San Antonio Little Theater Players are presenting Negro shows throughout the State of Texas. The Allied Arts Players of Boston have been presenting for five years romantic and historical plays in the search for the jewel that hangs from Ethiopian ears.[8] These and other groups West and South have started an influence that may prove tremendous in its appeal.

Not only are the Negro amateur theatres serving to create colored audiences capable of recognizing and appreciating productions of excellence, they are proving a means of giving the would-be-playwright a knowledge of the technique of the drama. The talented colored musician with something to say through the alliance of the arts and the theater, must perfect himself in dramatic technique if he is to write his own race-drama, the interpretation of which is now largely in the hands of white writers of the theatrical world.

Even as the author writes, a decided trend toward a certain form of music-drama is being evinced. For over three months, beginning in March, 1933, Hall Johnson's *Run, Little Chillun,* the title taken from that of a Negro Spiritual, was witnessed at the old Lyric Theater at New York. The scene is laid on the outskirts of a small southern town on an August evening. The second scene, that of the Hope Meeting House, gives opportunity for prayer-meeting scenes, shouting and

preaching, praying and singing of Negro Spirituals. The folk material used in the first scene—in the orgiastic rites of the New-Day Pilgrims led by the prophet and the voluptuous Sulamai, was taken from the Bahamas. There Negro superstitions hold sway to a far greater extent than in the southern United States. The weakest part of this folk play, which was written and prepared by Mr. Johnson, leader of the Negro choir which was so favorably received in *The Green Pastures* (and independently as well), is said to be the portrayal of character, perhaps due to inexperience in play-writing.

This music-play has commanded the notice of the press. H. T. Parker, late music editor and critic of the Boston *Evening Transcript,* stated that, "Outside the two spectacular scenes and his use in them of ritual and music and amassed song, he remains an inarticulate playwright in a flood of talk. . . . The root of the matter is in him, but for the present lack of adaptability and resource, he cannot bring it to stage-flower." Writing further, Parker concludes that "the power that is implicit in *Run, Little Chillun,* proceeds from the two scenes of spectacle and music. . . . Give Mr. Johnson primitive music and he is dramatist indeed. In these two contrasted scenes he has wrought something very like American music-drama."

The film of Eugene O'Neill's play, *The Emperor Jones,* completed in July, 1933, was presented during the first week in October, 1933, at the Rivoli Theatre, New York City. The cinema was produced in Boston, beginning the week of September 23, with Fredi Washington and Paul Robeson in the leading roles. The title role is superbly acted by Robeson. The music was arranged by Rosamond Johnson. The movie version differs greatly from the original play, and it has no relation to Gruenberg's opera of like name. DuBose Heyward has written a long American sequence which includes scenes of the lowest

---

[8] *Following the closing of the Allied Arts Centre, training school and sponsor of the Allied Arts Players, individuals have been employed in government dramatic groups and in leading professional productions in New York and in Boston.*

class and types of Negro life. The scenes of folk life include an African ceremony with dancing and beat of the tom-tom, and the interior of a church in the United States, south, with . . . shout and hysterical singing of the Spirituals, as inevitable as the pictures of Harlem night life, also portrayed. The statement by the press that the play-cinema "represents three stages in the spiritual growth of the race" is misleading, for the much-heralded use of folk music and musical sound proved to be abortive and devoid of any true "spiritual" portrayal. It is calculated to please the masses and to fill the coffers of those most interested. Offensive racial terms and scenes have been deleted.

—1936

Florence Mills, a singing comedienne and dancer, became famous for her cakewalking and buck dancing. She is seen here with the other members of the Florence Mills Trio, U. S. Thompson, her husband (right) and Fredi Johnson (left).

Will Marion Cook

Clorindy, the Origin of the Cakewalk

by Will Marion Cook

WHEN BERT Williams and George Walker met in California, the Negro god of comedy and drama must have opened his thick lips and wide mouth and laughed loud, long, raucously! After failures around the country in medicine shows and cheap vaudeville houses, the team found themselves at French Lick Springs where Canary, George W. Lederer's partner, happened to catch their act. Immediately he put them on a train for New York and Lederer's Casino Theatre, where the famous producer introduced them between the acts of *The Gold Bug*. They swamped New York and then went on to one of the longest runs that had ever been made at Koster and Bial's. That was where I came into the picture.

Since I had come to New York to learn to write good music, I met Williams and Walker and gave them my ideas on creating a story of how the cakewalk came about in Louisiana in the early Eighteen Eighties. *Clorindy, the Origin of the Cakewalk* was the result and though, when the time came, Williams and Walker were unable to play in it, it was for them that I wrote the show.

But all that came later. At our first meeting Williams and Walker made a few suggestions to me and then introduced me to their manager, Will McConnell, who lent me ten dollars to go back home to Washington. I was barred anyhow from the classes at the National Conservatory of Music because I wouldn't play my fiddle in the orchestra under Dvorak. I couldn't play; my fingers had grown too stiff. Dvorak didn't like me anyway; Harry T. Burleigh was his pet. Only John White, the harmony and counterpoint teacher, thought I had talent, and insisted that I attend his classes.

With McConnell's ten dollars I returned home with my tremendous idea. After a long siege of persuasion, I finally got Paul Laurence Dunbar to consent to write the *Clorindy* libretto (which was never used) and a few of the lyrics. We got together in the basement of my brother John's rented house on Sixth Street, just below Howard University, one night about eight o'clock. We had two dozen bottles of beer, a quart of whiskey, and we took my brother's porterhouse steak, cut it up with onions and red peppers and ate it raw. Without a piano or anything but the kitchen table, we finished all the songs, all the libretto and all but a few bars of the ensembles by four o'clock the next morning. By that time Paul and I were happy, so happy that we were ready to cry "Eureka!" only we couldn't make any noise at that hour so both of us sneaked off to bed, Paul to his house three blocks away and I to my room.

The following morning or rather later that morning, I was at John's piano trying to learn to play my most Negroid song, "Who Dat Say Chicken in Dis Crowd?" My mother, who was cooking my breakfast, came into the

parlor, tears streaming from her eyes, and said:

"Oh, Will! Will! I've sent you all over the world to study and become a great musician, and you return such a nigger!" My mother was a graduate of Oberlin in the class of 1865 and thought that a Negro composer should write just like a white man. They all loved the Dunbar lyrics but weren't ready for Negro songs.

After the writing of *Clorindy,* many days are to elapse before I get any kind of action. Williams and Walker come through Washington with the Hyde and Behman show, on their way to the coast. They listen to my music and, after praising it highly, again get McConnell to lend me ten dollars, so that I may go to New York and play it for Isidore Witmark, the head of Witmark and Sons, then located in Thirty-seventh Street just beyond Broadway.

That weekend I go to New York. McConnell makes an appointment by telephone for me for Saturday afternoon at one o'clock which was the Saturday closing hour. After keeping me waiting for two hours, the cooling-off process, Isidore Witmark comes into the large front professional office and curtly says, "Go ahead! What's you got?" I am not now and never have been a great pianist, and I could sing only a little bit, but for forty minutes I struggled to give this man some idea of the songs and ensembles. At last, starting for the door of his private office, he interrupted me long enough to say that he thought I must be crazy to believe that any Broadway audience would listen to Negroes singing Negro opera.

There I was, on a Saturday afternoon in New York, with only a few pennies in my pocket, and no place to eat or sleep. I started to walk to the Twenty-third Street ferry, hoping for some good luck and found it. An old pal of mine, Sol Johnson, was on the same boat, on his way to the Penn Depot in Jersey City, where he was a porter on the Washington train. As his train did not leave until night, I loafed about for a while. Later he locked me in a closed dining car, telling me to be quiet until we reached Washington.

And so I got back, hungry, mad with the world and heartbroken at such a failure. It took me some months to recover my spirit, and by this time my brother John, who worked at the pension office and was always good for a touch, became disgusted with the whole idea and wanted me to go to work at something that would at least take care of me. What was more tragic, he even refused to lend me any more money! Bill Higgins, secretary to Congressman White, one of the last colored congressmen from North Carolina, lent me ten dollars. Higgins had been a classmate of my brother at Howard University.

This time it's do or die. So I hunt up Sol Johnson again, and again he hides me on his train, but he charges me two dollars for the favor, since I seem to have become a regular passenger. A long, long struggle and much suffering is to ensue until George Archer, head usher at the Casino Roof Garden, says, "Why don't you go to see Ed Rice? His office is in the Standard Theatre Building at Sixth Avenue and Thirty-second Street. He runs the show up on George Lederer's Roof and needs an outstanding attraction."

For weeks, whenever I could get three or four of my prospective cast together or find a place to rehearse, I had been teaching them the *Clorindy* music. I taught them with or without a piano; sometimes just singing or trying to sing the different parts. But this was a genius aggregation, Negro talent that had made much of little. And besides, they believed in me.

As directed by George Archer, I went to see Ed Rice, and I saw him every day for a month. Regularly, after interviewing a room full of people, he would say to me (I was always the last): "Who are you, and what do

you want?" On the thirty-first day—and by now I am so discouraged that this is my last try—I heard him tell a knockabout act: "Come up next Monday to rehearsal, do a show and, if you make good, I'll keep you on all the week."

I was desperate. My feet, with soles worn through, were burnt black by walking on the hot cobblestones of New York streets. I was hungry almost all the time, except when I could meet Harry Burleigh, who had recently become soloist in St. George's Church. He only made a small salary but always had enough to treat me to coffee and crullers at a little dairy called Cushman's, on the corner of Fifteenth Street and Third Avenue, or to a twenty-five-cent dinner at a German restaurant near Union Square.

On leaving Rice's office, I went at once to the Greasy Front, a Negro club run by Charlie Moore, with a restaurant in the basement managed by Mrs. Moore. There I was sure to find a few members of my ensemble. I told them a most wonderful and welcome story; we were booked at the Casino Roof! And I sent them to contact all the others. Everybody was notified to be at the Casino Roof Garden on Monday at eleven a.m. Only Ernest Hogan, my comedian, could not be reached because, unless he was working (and sometimes even then), he stayed up all night carousing. Consequently he slept all day. Just to play safe, I sent him a note in care of his landlady. "We were booked!" I exclaimed. That was probably the most beautiful lie I ever told.

Hogan, whose real name was Rube Crowders [sic], had become my comedian because Williams and Walker, for whom Clorindy had been written, had been delayed on the Coast by the terrific success of the Hyde and Behman show. I had come in contact with Hogan one day in the back room of the Greasy Front where I was playing "Who Dat Say Chicken?" for a couple of unimpressed come-

dians. Suddenly I heard a full-bellied laugh and a loud but musical voice: "That's great, son! Who are you? Come on and have a glass of beer."

As I went into the front room to join the man who had called me, Charlie Moore whispered: "That's Ernest Hogan, leading comic with Black Patti's Troubadours, and the man who wrote 'All Coons Look Alike to Me.' He's a great comedian and can do lots for you." That same night Hogan learned "Who Dat Say Chicken?" and my "Hottes' Coon in Dixie."

Back to Clorindy. On Monday morning, in answer to my call, every man and woman, boy and girl that I had taught to sing my music was at the Casino Roof. Strange to say, Hogan was the first one to show up.

Luckily for us, John Braham, the English conductor of the Casino orchestra, was a brick. And, still more luckily for us, Ed Rice did not appear at rehearsal that morning until very late. When Braham had finished with the smaller acts, he turned to me questioningly. There I sat, orchestra books in hand. In two minutes I told him how I had studied violin under Joachim, a bit of composition under Dvorak, harmony and mighty little counterpoint under John White. I explained that I had some new music, a Negro operetta. Right then he stopped me, turned to his orchestra men and said: "Gentlemen, a new composer!" He held out his hand for my orchestra parts. Again I got his ear and told him that my singers understood my direction, they understood my gestures and that I was afraid. . . . He again turned and announced: "Gentlemen, a new composer and a new conductor."

By this time my singers were grouped on the stage and I started the opening chorus, an orchestral and choral development of "Darktown Is Out Tonight." Remember, reader, I had twenty-six of the finest Negro voices in America, twenty-six happy, gifted

Negroes, who saw maybe weeks of work and money before them. Remember, too, that they were singing a new style of music. Like a mighty anthem in rhythm, these voices rang out.

Rice must have heard the voices and the pulsing Darktown rhythm as he came up Broadway, but his only comment when he came was shouted to Braham: "No nigger can conduct my orchestra on Broadway!" And Braham—God bless him! and He must still be blessing him if there is a place for the great-hearted—simply said: "Ed, go back to your little cubby-hole"—Rice had a little pagoda at one end of the roof, where he "entertained" some of his pretty girls after the show at night—"Go back to your little cubby-hole and keep quiet! That boy's a genius and has something great!"

Well, we didn't get on that Monday night after all. It rained pitchforks until about nine o'clock and the Roof, which was uncovered, was in no condition to receive the high-class habitués. We were sent home about nine-thirty. A more disappointed bunch of people you've never seen. I was heartbroken. Another failure! Was I never to get going? Only Hogan was in good spirits. He had taken charge of things by now, and had spent the day staging the different numbers. Naturally, he had eliminated Dunbar's dialogue, for a lot of dialogue on an uncovered roof garden after eleven p.m. would have been impossible. Hogan also hurriedly gathered three or four sensational dancers. He seemed to know everybody. In short, it was just as well that we didn't go on that night, for Hogan really needed the extra time to whip the dancers into shape, especially the cakewalk. After all, our subtitle was "The Origin of the Cakewalk" and we mustn't fall down on that part of the performance.

Our opening for Rice was postponed until the following Monday and by then all was ready. About 11:45 Mr. Price, Rice's mana-ger, made the simple announcement that the Negro operetta, *Clorindy, the Origin of the Cakewalk,* would now be produced for the first time on any stage. Immediately I struck up the introduction and opening chorus. When I entered the orchestra pit, there were only about fifty people on the Roof. When we finished the opening chorus, the house was packed to suffocation. What had happened was that the show downstairs in the Casino Theatre was just letting out. The big audience heard those heavenly Negro voices and took to the elevators. At the finish of the opening chorus, the applause and cheering were so tumultuous that I simply stood there transfixed, my hand in the air, unable to move until Hogan rushed down to the footlights and shouted: "What's the matter, son? Let's go!"

So I started his strut song, which began and ended with an ensemble, "Hottes' Coon." This was hardly Dunbar's finest lyric, but the chorus, the dancers and the inimitable Ernest Hogan made that Broadway audience think it was. The rest of the performance kept them at the same pitch, especially "Who Dat Say Chicken in Dis Crowd?" This number (which Rice had thought too slow) had to be repeated ten times before Hogan could leave the stage, and there were encores galore when Belle Davis sang "Jump Back, Honey, Jump Back!"

The Darktown finale was of complicated rhythm and bold harmonies, and very taxing on the voice. My chorus sang like Russians, dancing meanwhile like Negroes, and cake-walking like angels, black angels! When the last note was sounded, the audience stood and cheered for at least ten minutes. This was the finale which Witmark had said no one would listen to. It was pandemonium, but never was pandemonium dearer to my heart as I stood there sweating in Charles W. Anderson's old full dress coat (Charlie weighed 200 pounds; I, 126), Harry T. Burleigh's vest (Harry was very short; I, quite tall) and my own out-at-

the-seat and frayed-at-the-cuffs light street pants, and the same feet-mostly-on-the-ground shoes. These, with a clean shirt and tie (thank heaven), completed my evening clothes.

But did that audience take offense at my rags and lack of conducting polish? Not so you could notice it! We went on at 11:45 and finished at 12:45. Boy, oh boy! Maybe, when the pearly gates open wide and a multitude of hosts march in, shouting, laughing, singing, emoting, there will be a happiness which slightly resembles that of *Clorindy's* twenty-six participants. I was so delirious that I drank a glass of water, thought it wine and got gloriously drunk. Negroes were at last on Broadway, and there to stay. Gone was the uff-dah of the minstrel! Gone the Massa Linkum stuff! We were artists and we were going a long, long way. We had the world on a string tied to a runnin' red-geared wagon on a down-hill pull. Nothing could stop us, and nothing did for a decade.

—1944

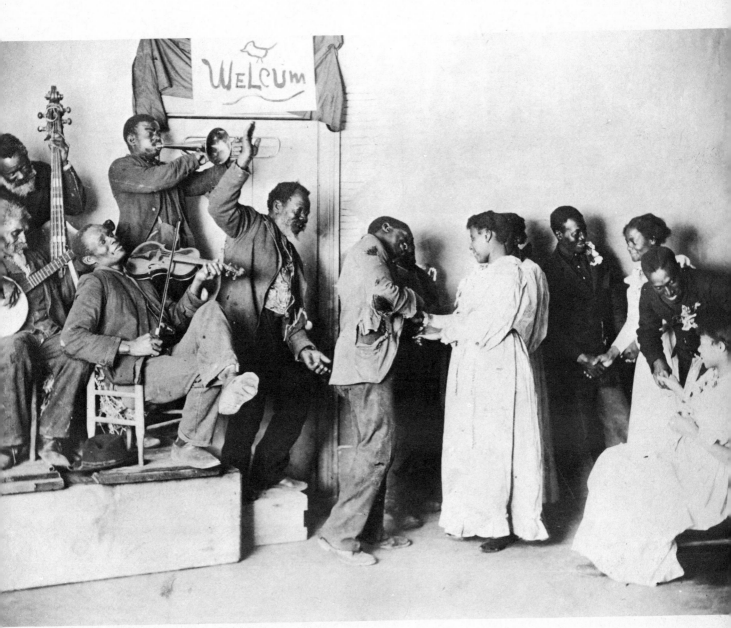

The cakewalk

MANSFIELD THEATRE

THE · PLAYBILL · A · WEEKLY · PUBLICATION · OF · PLAYBILL · INCORPORATED

Beginning Wednesday, August 30, 1944   Matinees Wednesday and Saturday

JOHN WILDBERG
presents

HARRY WAGSTAFF GRIBBLE'S
production

ANNA LUCASTA

by
PHILIP YORDAN

Settings by
FREDERICK FOX

Costumes by
PAUL DUPONT

Assistant to Mr. Gribble,
Walter Thompson Ash

CAST
(In order of their appearance)

KATIE .... THEODORA SMITH
STELLA .... ROSETTA LeNOIRE
THERESA .... GEORGIA BURKE
STANLEY .... JOHN PROCTOR
FRANK .... FREDERICK O'NEAL

FORTY-EIGHTH STREET
THEATRE
BERNARD KLAWANS, MANAGER

PROGRAM · PUBLISHED · BY · THE · NEW · YORK · THEATRE · PROGRAM · CORPORATION

BEGINNING
MONDAY EVENING,
FEBRUARY 27, 1933

MATINEES
WEDNESDAY AND
SATURDAY

GEORGE L. MILLER

FOR

THE NEGRO THEATRE GUILD

OFFERS

"LOUISIANA"

A PLAY OF THE SOUTH

BY

J. AUGUSTUS SMITH

STAGED BY SAMUEL J. PARK

CAST
(As you meet them)

THE PROLOGUE

AUNT HAGAR, The Voodoo Priestess . . *Played by* LAURA BOWMAN
EBENEZER, Her Nephew . . . . "   " LIONEL MONAGAS

(Program Continued on Fourth Page Following)

The Negro as Playwright

THE NEGRO PLAYWRIGHT ON BROADWAY
by Raoul Abdul

THE NEGRO DRAMATIST'S IMAGE OF THE UNIVERSE, 1920-1960
by Darwin T. Turner

A WOMAN PLAYWRIGHT SPEAKS HER MIND
by Alice Childress

AMERICAN THEATER: FOR WHITES ONLY?
by Douglas Turner Ward

HOW I BECAME A PLAYWRIGHT
by Garland Anderson

Rose McClendon in Langston Hughes' *Mulatto*.

Hilda Simms and Lou Gossett as lovers in Langston Hughes'
Tambourines to Glory.

Vinnette Carroll in Errol John's
Moon on a Rainbow Shawl.

The Negro Playwright on Broadway

by Raoul Abdul

THE FIRST known play by a Negro playwright was *Escape, or a Leap to Freedom,* by William Wells Brown, dated 1858. It was an abolitionist drama involving a beautiful slave heroine, a dastardly master, an heroic slave and an abolitionist who helps the lovers escape. Although it was never staged, records show that it was frequently read publicly by its author. A contemporary account of Brown's readings can be found in the *Poughkeepsie Eagle* which reported: "His drama interested and amused his audience, bringing the subject before them more vividly than any argument could have done." The first published play by a Negro was *Caleb, the Degenerate* by Joseph Cotter, Sr., in 1903.

The pioneering efforts of these two men did not lead to an outpouring of Negro talent in the area of playwriting. This was to come much later after Negro *performers* were accepted in the legitimate theatre and serious *plays* about Negro life were written by experienced white dramatists.

The true beginning of serious Negro theatre can be precisely dated April 5, 1917, when three one-act plays by Ridgely Torrence—*The Rider of Dreams, Simon the Cyrenian* and *Granny Maumee*—were presented by Mrs. Emilie Hapgood with an all-Negro cast. These plays by a white poet opened two great doors: the door to the use of Negro life as material for serious theatre and the door

to acceptance of Negro actors as performers in non-musical theatre.

Shortly afterwards Eugene O'Neill began writing plays of Negro life including *Dreamy Kid,* the classic *Emperor Jones,* and *All God's Chillun Got Wings.* Paul Green turned out many wonderful plays including *In Abraham's Bosom,* which won the 1926 Pulitzer Prize. Dorothy and DuBose Heyward's *Porgy* appeared. Last in this group is Marc Connelly's *The Green Pastures,* which was originally produced in 1930.

The prerequisites had been met. Serious plays about Negro life had been accepted in the theatre and the Negro actor had not only been accepted, but acclaimed. The first nonmusical play by a Negro playwright to reach Broadway was a one-act play by Willis Richardson entitled *The Chip Woman's Fortune.* Opening May 15, 1923, at the Frazee Theatre, it was presented by the Ethiopian Art Players and ran eight performances. The critics received Richardson's play most favorably. Although he never returned to Broadway, Richardson won a contest sponsored by *Crisis* in 1925 for his play *Broken Banjo* and published *Plays and Pageants of Negro Life* and *Negro History in 13 Plays.*

Garland Anderson's *Appearances,* opening at the Frolic Theatre on October 13, 1925, was the first full-length play by a Negro to be produced on Broadway. Although it is a message play, it does not primarily concern

itself with the race problem. It shows how an inspired person, through the mobilization of his subconscious forces, can achieve what seems impossible. The original run of *Appearances* was 23 performances, with two subsequent revivals on Broadway, and a London production.

While Frank Wilson was making theatrical history in the title role of *Porgy* a few blocks away, his play *Meek Mose* opened on January 23, 1928, at the Princess Theatre, where it ran 32 performances. It was later revived by the Federal Theatre under the title *Brother Mose*.

Capitalizing on the Harlem mania of the late twenties, Wallace Thurman's *Harlem* stormed into the Apollo Theatre on 42nd Street on February 20, 1929, and became the first *successful* play by a Negro playwright on the great white way. Brooks Atkinson wrote in the *New York Times*: "Even if the drama were omitted, you can rest assured the entertainment would go on—or will if the police censors who were in the audience last evening do not clang down 42nd Street with their patrol wagons." They didn't and *Harlem* ran 93 performances.

A play about weird voodoo rites in Southern swamplands entitled *Louisiana* by J. Augustus Smith opened at the 48th Street Theatre on February 27, 1933. It ran 8 performances. At that time, John Mason Brown remarked: "This is the stuff out of which real folk plays can be made."

The line of the Negro folk play which began with Ridgely Torrence's three one-act plays in 1917 and continued with *In Abraham's Bosom, Porgy* and *Green Pastures,* culminated in *Run, Little Chillun,* by Hall Johnson, which opened on March 1, 1933, for a run of 126 performances. Mrs. Edith Isaacs, in her book *The Negro in the American Theatre,* says: ". . . the play stands as an important milestone in the history of the Negro theatre."

Run, Little Chillun marked the end of an era as far as Broadway was concerned. The folk play gave way to the protest play. The first of this new cycle by a Negro was *Legal Murder* by Dennis Donoghue, which opened at the President Theatre on February 15, 1934, and ran only seven performances. Based on the case of the Scottsboro boys, the play was accurate reporting, but not dramatically effective.

Climaxing the cycle of protest plays was Langston Hughes' *Mulatto,* which opened on October 24, 1935, at the Vanderbilt Theatre and ran for 373 performances—the second longest run by a Negro playwright. Brooks Atkinson said in the *New York Times*: "*Mulatto* is flaming with sincerity . . . after a season devoted chiefly to trash, it is a sobering sensation to sit in the presence of a playwright who is trying his best to tell what is on his mind."

It was not until 1941 that another play by a Negro reached Broadway. But, these six years were full of playwriting activity, most of it as part of the Federal Theatre which was organized in 1935. The honor of having the first Federal Theatre production in New York went to Frank Wilson's *Walk Together, Chillun.* It ran for 29 performances, opening at the Lafayette in Harlem on February 2, 1936. It was an appeal for Negro solidarity in the face of white hostility. How timely even today!

The best play by a Negro written during the Federal Theatre days was *Big White Fog* by Theodore Ward. Originally produced by the Chicago unit, Ward's play was scheduled for New York when the Federal Theatre was abolished by Congress. So, Ward simply organized the Negro Playwrights Company which brought his play to the Lincoln Theatre in Harlem on October 22, 1940. Brooks Atkinson found it to be "the best serious play of Negro authorship about race problems . . .

no concessions to the white man's taste." And it ran 64 performances!

Finally, the Negro playwright returned to Broadway. In collaboration with Paul Green, Richard Wright brought his *Native Son* to the St. James Theatre on March 24, 1941. Although it lasted only 97 performances, it was selected by Burns Mantle as one of the ten best plays of the season. Brooks Atkinson found it "an overwhelming play" and the *World Telegram* said it was "stamped with genius." Maybe so, but Mr. Wright never returned to Broadway with a play.

Although we are concerned here with the commercial theatre, the story of the Negro as playwright can hardly be complete without some mention of the work going on in the Negro colleges and universities and in tributary theatres. Pioneering in this field were Alain Locke and Montgomery Gregory who established the Howard University Players. Their efforts were expanded and coordinated through the Negro Intercollegiate Drama Association in 1930 under the direction of a fine playwright, Randolph Edmonds. Owen Dodson, now head of Howard's drama department, turned out several outstanding plays including *Divine Comedy,* which received its premiere at Yale University. Today, every Negro college has some kind of dramatic activity.

In Harlem in the late thirties, Langston Hughes founded The Suitcase Theatre which produced his own *Don't You Want to Be Free?* It established the longest run of any play in that community. The Rose McClendon Players under the direction of Dick Campbell produced plays by George Norford and Wilson Williams. In the 40's the American Negro Theatre produced Abram Hill's *On Striver's Row*; but when it took its production of white playwright Philip Yordan's *Anna Lucasta* to Broadway, Harlem lost what might have been its permanent repertory theatre. Today, Harlem remains in a cultural void, without a theatre, and without those who care enough to do something about it.

Unquestionably, the leading Negro theatre group in the United States is Cleveland's Karamu Theatre. Founded by two white people of great vision, Russell and Rowena Jelliffe, it is over fifty years old. Karamu gave almost all the premieres of Langston Hughes' plays during his residence in Cleveland and has in recent times given exciting productions of Hughes' *Simply Heavenly,* William Branch's *In Splendid Error,* Lorraine Hansberry's *Raisin in the Sun* and the world premiere of Branch's *A Wreath for Udomo.*

Returning to the Broadway scene, the next play by a Negro playwright was Theodore Ward's *Our Lan'.* After having great success at the Grand Street Playhouse (off-Broadway), it moved to the Royale Theatre on September 27, 1947. It had only a short run of 41 performances because the very same critics who had praised it downtown, reversed their opinions. "It has lost its soul," wrote Robert Garland.

A giant step seemed to be taken on September 24, 1953, when Louis Peterson's *Take a Giant Step* opened at the Lyceum Theatre. "It is very much Mr. Peterson's point that a Negro adolescence is not very different from any other kind of adolescence," wrote Walter Kerr in the New York *Herald Tribune.* Perhaps that made the play less picturesque, but it made it more true. The emphasis here was on the universal, not the special. And that was something *new* in Negro playwriting. Broadway audiences were not ready for *Take a Giant Step,* and it ran only 76 performances.

A charming little quasi-fantasy on Negro adolescence in the South, *Mrs. Patterson* by Charles Sebree (with Greer Johnson), opened December 1, 1954, at the National Theatre where it ran 101 performances. And, after a highly successful off-Broadway production, Langston Hughes' *Simply Heav-*

enly moved to Broadway on August 20, 1957, where it ran 62 performances at the Playhouse.

The myth that Negro plays are "box-office poison" was shattered when Lorraine Hansberry's *A Raisin in the Sun* became a hit. It is without question the most successful play by a Negro to reach Broadway. Opening at the Ethel Barrymore Theatre on March 11, 1959, it ran 530 performances, was chosen "Best Play of the Season" by the New York Drama Critics Circle, and was made into a moving picture.

With a good-humored satire on Negro-white relationships in the South, *Purlie Victorious,* Ossie Davis managed to captivate audiences for 261 performances at the Cort Theatre where he and his charming wife Ruby Dee set up housekeeping on September 28, 1961.

A case of bad timing contributed to the failure of Langston Hughes' *Tambourines to Glory,* which opened at the Little Theatre on November 2, 1963, and ran 24 performances. The public expected a play dealing with the more urgent civil rights problems at that time and seemed disappointed with this melodrama about storefront churches in Harlem.

Timely indeed was James Baldwin's first venture on the Broadway scene, *Blues for Mister Charlie,* which opened April 23, 1964, at the ANTA Theatre. It dealt with the racial situation in the South. Even a fine acting ensemble could not disguise the fact that Baldwin was not yet a good technician in the field of playwriting. It closed after 44 performances.

Although not a success, Lorraine Hansberry's *The Sign in Sidney Brustein's Window* (opening October 15, 1964, at the Longacre) had the distinction of being the first play by a Negro in which Negro characters and themes were only incidental. Much of the writing was fine, but the playwright

tried to say too many things in one play. Miss Hansberry died on the day her play reached its 100th performance, and a bright light was extinguished from the American theatre.

With a company from the West Coast, James Baldwin's *The Amen Corner* reached New York's Ethel Barrymore Theatre on April 15, 1965. This sensitively written character study of a lady preacher in a Harlem storefront church proved too exotic for the theatre-going public.

The "Off-Broadway" theatre movement has developed several Negro playwrights of great promise. LeRoi Jones' *Dutchman* (1964) at the Cherry Lane Theatre created a sensation, as did *The Toilet* and *The Slave* later the same season at the St. Mark's Playhouse. His plays reflect the young Negro's disenchantment with white society and Jones uses a language which is brutal, vulgar, but exciting. *Dutchman* won an Obie award from the *Village Voice* and was filmed in England. Another award-winning playwright is Douglas Turner Ward (Vernon Rice Award), who spoofed the race problem in a style similar to *Purlie Victorious* in his two one-act plays *Happy Ending* and *Day of Absence* at the St. Mark's Playhouse (1965).

Other fine plays by Negroes produced off-Broadway include *In Splendid Error* by William Branch (1954), *Trouble in Mind* by Alice Childress (1955), *Moon on a Rainbow Shawl* by Errol John (1962), *Walk in Darkness* by William Hairston (1963), *Funnyhouse of a Negro* by Adrienne Kennedy (1964), and *Who's Got His Own?* by Ronald Milner (1966).

* * * * * *

The Negro playwright, with few exceptions, has written about his own world. He has been preoccupied with the problems of being black in white America. Thus, he has usually emphasized the ways in which Negroes are different. But the Broadway theatre caters to

the common culture of all. The Negro playwright who hopes for a commercial production must recognize that there is only a limited audience for folk and protest plays. He can write about Negro life—but primarily about life and only secondarily about Negroes.

Some of the young Negro playwrights of today, acutely conscious of being Negro, may choose to by-pass Broadway. For them, off-Broadway offers opportunities, but a more challenging alternative would be the establishment of a professional working theatre in the Negro community.

—1966

Billie Allen in Adrienne Kennedy's *Funnyhouse of a Negro*

Al Freeman, Jr., and Diana Sands in James Baldwin's *Blues for Mister Charlie.*

Robert Dean Hooks and Jennifer West in LeRoi Jones' *Dutchman*, which received unanimous acclaim from New York theatre critics.

A Raisin in the Sun

Claudia McNeil is Mrs. Younger, Diana Sands is the daughter, and Ruby Dee, the wife of Walter Lee Younger in the screen version of Lorraine Hansberry's award-winning drama of a Southside Chicago slum family.

Diana Sands does an African dance.

Walter Lee (Sidney Poitier), asserting his newly discovered manhood, encourages his family to make the move to an all-white neighborhood.

Claudia McNeil does the marketing for the family.

The Negro Dramatist's Image of the Universe, 1920—1960

by Darwin T. Turner

IN DRAMA, as in his other media of self-expression, the Negro artist has retouched his image of the universe as the Negro's shifting position in American society has afforded new perspectives. For the Negro, the stage represented, first, a pulpit from which to denounce the injustices meted out to him in America or a platform on which to parade idealized heroes to supplant the grinning dancing Jim Crows of the white playwrights. His universe was a checkerboard of black and white: the white purity lauding both the Negro and the benevolent people who struggled to elevate the Negro; the black of corruption castigating both the treacherous Uncle Toms and the people who chained the race in ignorance and deprivation. As the Negro has been guaranteed additional rights, however, the playwrights have perceived a universe of shades of grey, a universe of non-noble, non-villainous human beings who wrestle with life.

Beginning as a crusader, a preacher, an instructor, the Negro dramatist has become a delineator, a psychologist cognizant of his artistic responsibility to represent life faithfully. The maturing of the Negro dramatist to a standard-conscious, accurate painter of his universe can be observed by comparing characteristic images in Negro dramas of the Twenties and Thirties with similar images in dramas of the Fifties. In order to restrict the topic, the examination will be limited to the dramatist's delineating of the hero; his treatment of education, religion, and superstition; his attitude towards life in the North; and his discernment of the relationship between Negroes and the larger American society.

THE IMAGE OF THE HERO

Since most individuals view the universe as a macrocosm and themselves as the microcosm, the first aspect of the Negro's image of the universe which warrants study is his image of himself. To efface the Negro stereotype paraded in plantation novels of the "Old South" tradition and exhibited in minstrel shows, the Negro protest dramatists of the Twenties and Thirties created a counter-stereotype: a dark-skinned physically impressive adult—noble, courageous, rebellious, and proud.

Carving his characters to the "noble savage" Indian prototype of Aphra Behn and James Fenimore Cooper, Willis Richardson emphasized the physical strength, the nobility, and the courage of his heroes. In *The Flight of the Natives* (1927), Mose refuses to permit any man to flog him. When his master, cowed from the attempt, threatens to sell him "down the river," Mose reluctantly decides to escape without his wife, who is physically incapable of withstanding the rigors of flight. As he leaves, however, he swears to rescue her eventually. The heroes of *The Black Horseman* (1929) are tall, ath-

letic Africans eulogized for their bravery. Massinissa, a tall, dark-skinned hero, contrasts with Syphax, his smaller, fairer antagonist. Massinissa unmasks a Roman spy by torturing him. An African, he argues, would never reveal secrets, no matter how severely he might be tortured. In both works, Richardson glorified qualities which he considered intrinsic virtues of the Negro: dignity, nobility, and courage.

Although John Matheus, in *Ti Yette* (1929), centered his story about a Creole quadroon, Matheus invested him with qualities typical of Richardson's heroes. Racine, the quadroon, idolizes Negroes who have died rather than submit to indignity. Determined to marry his sister to an African prince, Racine kills her when he learns that she plans to reject her African ancestor in order to marry a white man.

One of the most productive Negro dramatists of the Thirties, S. Randolph Edmonds, continued the pattern in such dramas as *Bad Man* and *Nat Turner,* both published in 1934. Thea Dugger, the Bad Man, leaps from the mold of Bret Harte's heroes. Although his animal savagery has wrenched fearful respect from Negro workers in a saw-mill camp, a girl's faith ennobles him. When the sister of one of the workers visits her lover in the camp, Thea, flattered by her admiration, protects her from the other workers. When a lynch mob attacks the camp to capture the murderer of a white man, Thea prefers to sacrifice himself rather than to risk endangering the girl's life in a fight.

Proud and courageous, he detests cowards. When the lynchers approach, he refuses to join the Negroes who seek escape. He will fight, or he will die; he will not run.

Edmonds' Nat Turner possesses Thea's courage although he lacks Thea's physical strength. Respected by some of his enslaved followers, feared as a witch-doctor by others, judged untrustworthy or even insane by still

others, Nat desires to inspire the Virginia slaves with his pride and his fearlessness. "No real man," he tells them, "ain' willing tuh be wurked lak a mule in de field, whupped lak a dog, and tied tuh one farm and one master. . . . We mus' let dem know dat jes' because our skins is black we is not afraid tuh die."[1]

Thea and Nat project a twin image dominant in the protest dramas of the Twenties and the Thirties. Thea typifies the hero whose pride and physical strength provoke his defying tyranny. He sometimes wins followers when others seek the protection of his strength; he sometimes becomes a martyr when he refuses to bend even though he stands alone. In contrast, Nat Turner typifies the leader who, less strong physically, uses religion and inspiration to teach other Negroes the necessity of rebelling.

The submissive Negro, trusting God and the white man to resolve his problems, rarely is the protagonist of the protest dramas. Such a character can be observed in Frank Wilson's *Meek Mose* (1928). Scorned by his neighbors, who call him a white man's tool, Mose suffers eviction and an attempt upon his life. Continuing to advise faith in God, he triumphs when oil is discovered.

More often, however, the submissive Negro is the villain. In both *Nat Turner* and *Bad Man,* the despicable characters are the cowards who advise surrender.

Significantly, although they drew stereotypes, Negro dramatists revealed weaknesses in their heroes by the mid-Thirties. Thea bullies weaker Negroes. Nat is fanatic. Their virtues are magnified, but their vices distinguish them from the noble savages of Richardson's dramas.

The hero image in the more recent dramas has been that of an ordinary human being rather than an idealized stereotype. Three significant developments merit attention.

First, although the hero or protagonist

---

[1] Randolph Edmonds, *Six Plays for a Negro Theatre* (Boston, 1934), pp. 71–72.

elicits sympathy, he does not necessarily arouse admiration. Richard Wright's Bigger Thomas, in *Native Son* (1941),[2] embodies Thea Dugger's weaknesses with none of Thea's redeeming qualities. Uncouth and cowardly, he lies, rapes, and murders; yet he is the sympathetic protagonist of a protest drama.

Recognizing the unreality of both the "noble-savage" drawn by Negro polemicists and the "savage-beast" drawn by Dixon and other Negrophobes, Wright blended in Bigger the weaknesses for which the race has been criticized. Then he charged non-Negro America with the responsibility of breeding such individuals. Although he offered a stereotype as obvious as Massinissa had been, Wright evidenced the new confidence of the Negro writer in revealing the vices of race, not in comedy, but in work intended to evoke sympathy.

In the Forties and the Fifties, Negro dramatists have delineated credible protagonists both in dramas intended to be produced before Negroes and in those intended to be produced before predominantly non-Negro audiences. In A. Clifton Lamb's *Roughshod up the Mountain* (1956), the central figure, an uneducated minister desiring to retain his post, ignores his inability to guide his sophisticated, educated congregation.

The hero of Langston Hughes' *Simply Heavenly* (1957) is Jesse B. Semple. Ordinary—even weak in character, Semple carouses, squanders his money, and philanders. A comic and a pathetic figure, he typifies the dramatist's realistic appraisal of some Negroes who comprise the group which Hughes has described as the lower class of Negro society. But *Simply Heavenly* does not dramatize the problems of all Negroes of that group: it tells the story of Jesse B. Semple. Hughes displayed Semple before the Broadway audience confident that the Negro had

attained sufficient dignity in American life that the audience would not confuse Semple with all Negroes.

To point to Biggers and Semples is not to imply that the stereotyped noble Negro has disappeared from the stage. He lives in idealizations of school teachers who sacrifice life and love for their children and in idealizations of such leaders as Frederick Douglass. Nevertheless, the contemporary Negro dramatist exercises greater freedom in delineating the weaknesses of a character whom he wishes to have accepted as an individual rather than as a representative of a race.

A second development in the characterization of Negro protagonists has been that the educated Negro is no longer regarded as an individual significantly different from other Negroes. The development undoubtedly reflects the change in the Negro's position. Whereas in the Twenties and the Thirties, a college education was still considered an opportunity for only the "Talented Tenth" or those whose families possessed wealth, today a college education lies within the reach of many Negroes in urban communities.

Evidence of the earlier attitude toward the educated Negro appears in May Miller's *Riding the Goat* (1929). Jones, the antagonist of the play, dislikes Dr. Carter because he believes that Carter's education has enabled him to win the love of Ruth Chapman. Even Ann Hetty, Ruth's grandmother, suspects Carter's education. She says, "Course I thinks Doctor's all right in some ways, but them educated chaps always manages to think a little diff'rent."[3]

In contrast, in *Simply Heavenly* (1957), Boyd, a young, educated Negro, gains respect as a person who will succeed in life. Significantly, however, the protagonist is not Boyd but Jesse Semple, who survives by means of

---

[2] Dramatized by Richard Wright and Paul Green.

[3] May Miller, *Riding the Goat, Plays and Pageants of Negro Life,* Willis Richardson, ed. (Washington, 1930), p. 156.

common sense rather than formal education. Hughes has not ridiculed the educated Negro, at the same time, however, he has not pedestaled Boyd as the individual carrying the hopes of the race.

Third, recent dramatists have studied the intelligent or even intellectual hero as an individual rather than as a representative of the race. In *Bad Man,* Ted James had cried, "We ain't s'posed tuh pay no 'tention tuh a burnin' man . . . but ef de people wid larnin' can't do nothin' 'bout hit, 'tain nothing we can do."[4] Implicit in the cry is a prayer for an educated Negro to solve the race's problems.

In *Simply Heavenly,* Boyd attracts not as a leader but as a respected individual.

In Louis Peterson's *Take a Giant Step* (1953), the hero is a sensitive, intelligent young Negro who acquires education routinely. Although he discerns a difference between himself and the people whom he encounters when he seeks companionship in a tavern, he does not envision himself as a person with a mission. He desires merely to adjust to a society which accepts him intellectually but not socially.

EDUCATION, SUPERSTITION, AND RELIGION

The new attitude toward the education of the hero reflects a changed attitude towards a second area of his universe: education, superstition, and religion.

As has been suggested, most dramatists of the Twenties and Thirties, writing during a time in which the average Negro could not secure a college education, viewed education as the curse of individuals or as the hope of the race, an attitude still evidenced occasionally in such a work as William Robinson's *The Passing Grade* (1958), which castigates the unjust administration of the rural Negro schools in the South. Those who hailed education as the need of the race assumed ignorance to be a major cause of the Negro's inferior position and echoed Dr. W. E. B. Du Bois' pleas for educated men and women to serve as spokesmen and as leaders. Those distrusting education demonstrated an anti-intellectualism characteristic of American society as a whole rather than the Negro race alone. From the first American comedy, Royall Tyler's *The Contrast* (1787), through the era of Will Rogers, to the present disparagement of "eggheads," American society has mocked the college-bred, cultured individual and has praised the shrewd, ingenious wit educated in the school of hard knocks. Consequently, the reflection of that attitude in dramas by Negroes should surprise no one.

Negro playwrights of the Twenties and Thirties who pictured superstition as a characteristic of the race used it for three purposes: local color, criticism, and comedy. Significantly, however, by associating superstition with the older characters in the plays, they identified it with the past rather than with the future of the race.

In John Matheus' *'Cruiter,* for example, the grandmother superstitiously anticipates bad fortune for business begun on Friday. Matheus has characterized her, however, as one of the older Negroes bound to tradition. Although she sends her son and her daughter North to find a freedom impossible in the South, she refuses to accompany them.

Similarly, in Edmonds' *The New Window* (1934), Lizzie, the middle-aged wife, superstitiously awaits fortuitous omens while Hester, her daughter, assists destiny. Offered an opportunity to free herself from sixteen years of marriage to a bully, Lizzie is impotent; but, knowing his intentions to fight a duel, Hester dulls the firing pin of his gun so that he will be killed.

The danger of depending upon superstitions provided a theme for Georgia D. Johnson's *Plumes.* Distrusting modern medical practice, Charity Brown, a middle-aged

[4] Randolph Edmonds, *op. cit.,* p. 35.

woman, debates the advisability of submitting her child to an operation. Before she decides whether to risk the operation, the child dies.

Often, a satirical treatment of superstition has distinguished the older generation from the younger generation. In James W. Butcher's *The Seer,* Bucephalus Wilson, a charlatan, has preyed upon the superstitions of older Negroes in order to further his selfish plans. When Wilson schemes to use Ivory Toles' fear of ghosts as an instrument to force Toles to consent to Wilson's marrying Toles' daughter, the girl's young suitor unmasks Wilson by posing as a ghost. All three of the comedy's older characters—Toles, Wilson, and Wilson's henchman—behave superstitiously. Even Wilson, who recognizes most of the ignorance of superstition, fears ghosts. In contrast, the intelligent ingenious young hero and heroine fear nothing.

In *The Conjure Man Dies* (1936) Rudolph Fisher used voodoo and sorcery as a background for melodrama and horror. Although they have employed superstition for their dramatic purposes, most Negro dramatists have avoided picturing voodoo as a unique, important, or necessary part of the Negro's faith.

Perhaps because it has been considered characteristic of Negro thought, religion has been a popular element for dramatists, who have used it both as a theme and as background for the plot. Some dramatists have suggested the hope which Negroes have sought in religion. Mammy, in Edmonds' *Breeders* (1934), verbalizes the attitude: "Lawd, Ah don't want tuh question Yo' justice an' murcy, but Ah kain't help but axe how long Yuh will let Yo' chilluns be sold down de river lak horses an' cows, an' beat wussen de mules dey water down at de waterin' branch. . . . Stop it soon, Lawd! Stop it soon an' let Yo' chilluns drink of de water of freedom, an' put on de garments of righteousness."[5]

Other dramatists, however, have criticized the delusion of accepting religion as a panacea. In *Meek Mose* (1928), Wilson suggested that religion is offered to Negroes to make them forget the discriminatory practices of American society. In *Bleeding Hearts* (1934), Edmonds revealed the despair of a Negro who could not find solace in religion. In *Divine Comedy* (1938), Owen Dodson castigated the religious fanatics who delude Negroes just as charlatans have deceived them with superstition.

Other dramatists have not suggested attitudes toward religion but have used it merely as background for purposes of humor, history, local color, or social criticism. In *Jedgement Day,* Pawley contrasted Zeke's superstition with the sincere religious conviction of his wife and of the minister. George Norwood dramatized the Father Divine movement in *Joy Exceeding Glory.* A. Clifton Lamb, in *Roughshod up the Mountain* (1956), used religion as a vehicle for dramatizing the conflict in Negro society resulting from the transition of the race. Having ascended to the pulpit when "the call" has inspired him to leave his trade as a bricklayer, a Negro minister attempts unsuccessfully to prevent his congregation from replacing him with a young minister trained in the Harvard School of Divinity. To the author, however, the theme is not religious but social: it states the demand of the Negro populace for educated and rational, rather than emotional, leadership.

Two interesting aspects of the Negro dramatist's treatment of education and religion appear in the plays. First, dramatists have ignored the Negro's interest in culture and in the fine arts. Perhaps part of the reason for the neglect of this phase of Negro life lies in the dramatists' tendency to focus upon Negroes of lower economic positions.

Second, as protest drama has diminished, dramatists have become less constrained in

---

[5] Randolph Edmonds, *op. cit.,* p. 101.

Langston Hughes' *Simply Heavenly*.

Canada Lee as Bigger Thomas in Richard Wright's
Native Son.

Melvin Stewart and Ethel Ayler in *Simply Heavenly*.

their treatment of immorality. Many protest dramatists created images to refute the allegation that sexual immorality characterizes Negro behavior. In *The Flight of the Natives,* the Negroes remain faithful to their mates even though they have not been married legally. In *Breeders* the heroine kills herself rather than submit to a relationship with the plantation stud.

Recent playwrights, however, have depicted immoral sexual relationships more objectively; sometimes they have even sanctioned such relationships. The young hero of *Take a Giant Step* attempts to prove his masculinity and to weld himself to Negro society by consummating a physical relationship with a prostitute after his desire for a more spiritual relationship has been rebuffed by a seemingly virtuous young woman who, weary of poverty, wishes to offer her body to any man who has enough money to escort her on a tour of nightclubs. In *Roughshod up the Mountain,* the young minister who represents the intelligence of the new Negro is romantically associated with a reformed prostitute, a twentieth century Mary Magdalene. Although the heroine of *Simply Heavenly* refuses to risk remaining alone with Semple before their marriage, the hero sometimes relapses into the arms of another woman, who wears morality more loosely.

ATTITUDES TOWARD THE NORTH

A third important facet of the Negro's image of his universe is his attitude towards life in the North, particularly Harlem. In much of the drama of the Twenties and the Thirties, the North represented a vaguely defined section of America in which the Negro might find freedom. Harlem, however, often symbolized a modern Babylon in which damnation awaited the unsuspecting Southern Negro.

The conflicting attitudes towards the North appear in Frank Wilson's *Sugar Cane* (1920). Paul Cain distrusts all Northern Negroes, whereas his son envisions the North as a place where Negroes can acquire education. In Jean Toomer's *Balo* (1927), Balo's father desires to remain in Georgia to farm and preach. The mother, however, dreams of the happiness which she can find in the North. Although Granny, in *'Cruiter,* sends her grandson North to find economic security in a munitions factory, she prefers to remain in the section which has been her home.

Historical, anti-slavery dramas, of course, pictured the North as a world of freedom for Negroes, to whom any place would have offered more happiness than the South offered. The same attitude persisted in early protest dramas. For instance, in *Bleeding Hearts,* embittered because his employer has refused to permit him to stop work to comfort his dying wife, Joggison Taylor leaves the South. He feels that he will kill his employer if he remains.

The contrasting attitude—suspicion of the North—is evident in *Harlem* (1922), by Wallace Thurman, a Negro, in collaboration with William J. Rapp. After their migration to Harlem from South Carolina, the Williams family experiences only misery. Cordelia, the daughter, prostitutes herself. Financial failure forces the family to give rent parties. Cordelia becomes involved in murder when her West Indian lover is accused of having murdered a gambler who had been a former suitor. Eulalie Spence, in *The Starter* (1927), satirized Negro life which spawns such individuals as T. J., indolent, conceited, dependent upon the support of Georgia, his industrious sweetheart. The most violent condemnation of the North in drama of the Twenties and Thirties, however, is Edmonds' *Old Man Pete.* Having come North at their children's invitation, Pete Collier and his wife offend their sophisticated children by shouting in

church and by dressing and conducting themselves in rural, Southern ways which the children wish to forget. When the parents realize the children's feelings, they decide to return to the South. Trying to walk from Harlem to Grand Central Station on the coldest night in the history of New York, they freeze to death while resting in Central Park.

Recent dramatists, such as Hughes and Peterson, however, have depicted life in the North more objectively, revealing the vices of life among the lower classes but viewing the North neither as a heaven nor a hell.

NEGRO SOCIETY

The final aspect of Negro life to be examined is the Negro's picture of his society and of the relationship between that society and America.

Perhaps because they dramatized protest themes, many Negro playwrights of the Twenties and the Thirties saw Negro society only as it was affected by white society. In such works as *Sugar Cane* (1920), *'Cruiter, Ti Yette* (1929), *Bad Man* (1934), and *Bleeding Hearts* (1934)—as well as those works which condemn slavery, the basic conflict results from the inability of Negroes to protect themselves from unjust impingements by other Americans. In *Sugar Cane* and *Ti Yette,* white men exploit Negro women sexually. In *Bad Man,* friction between the races costs Negro life, and in *Bleeding Hearts,* the inhumanity of the white employer precipitates the conflict. The attitude of these dramatists is effectively expressed in *'Cruiter* when Sonny says, "Whatevah whi' folks wants o' we-all, we-all jes' nacherly got tuh do, Ah spose."[6]

Interference with the lives of Negroes is dramatized effectively in Ransom Rideout's *Going Home* (1928). Having settled abroad after World War I, Israel Du Bois marries a European girl who believes him to be a wealthy American. When American troops pass through the town where Du Bois lives, Major Powell, the son of the family which reared Du Bois as a servant, foments a race war but finally persuades Du Bois to leave his wife and to return to America.

In some of the drama of the Twenties and the Thirties, however, and in more recent plays, the Negro playwright has considered conflicts caused by internal rather than external forces. Richardson's *The Broken Banjo* (1925) describes the problems of a Negro betrayed by his wife's parasitic relatives. Langston Hughes's *Soul Gone Home* (1938) introduces the ghost of a son who charges his mother with misconduct because she was not able to provide him with the food, the clothing, and the example of moral purity which a child should have.

Other dramatists have drawn their characters so racelessly that one cannot identify them as Negroes. In *The House of Sham* (1929), Richardson dramatized the problem of a real estate broker who, by fraudulent practices, enables his wife and his daughter to live extravagantly. Thelma Duncan, in *Sacrifice* (1930), told the story of a youth who protects a friend by assuming the blame for stealing an examination. In *The Anger of One Young Man* (1959), William Robinson has described the frustration of a writer whose idealism is blighted by the mercenary materialism of the publishing trade.

Still other dramatists have emphasized the uniquely Negroid existence of their characters. In *Big White Fog* (1938), Theodore Ward dramatized problems of a Negro family affected by the depression, Communism, domestic quarrels, and anti-Semitism. As Americans they respond to issues which touch all Americans. As Negroes they react to such other matters as Garveyism and the attempt of a white man to buy the affection of one of the daughters.

---

[6] John Matheus, *'Cruiter, The Negro Caravan,* Sterling Brown and others, eds. (New York, 1941), p. 192.

The Harlemites of *Simply Heavenly* dwell in an isolated world. The central problem is Semple's effort to amass enough money to persuade Joyce to marry him. Conflicts within that society and the economic status of the characters remind the audience that the figures are lower class Negroes. Rather than being embarrassed about their lives, however, they defend their ways. When a Negro stranger condemns as stereotypes the other Negroes in a neighborhood tavern, Mamie justifies her enjoyment of watermelons, chitterlings, red dresses, gin, and black-eyed peas and rice. "I didn't come here to Harlem to get away from my people," she says. "I come here because ther's more of 'em. I loves my race. I loves my people."[7]

In *Take a Giant Step,* Louis Peterson has dramatized the manner in which an educated Negro may become isolated from both Negro and white society. When he reaches the age at which he and his friends begin to seek the companionship of females, Spencer Scott, whose family is the only Negro one in the neighborhood, is rebuffed by his former playmates. Seeking association within his race, he perceives equally his inability to adjust to the Negroes who visit taverns.

A. Clifton Lamb, in *Roughshod up the Mountain,* has pictured the chasm dividing the traditional Negro society from the new Negro society. On one side are the uneducated Negro laborers; on the other side are Negroes who, by means of education, have attained professional positions.

Perhaps the most dominant and the most important idea in recent drama by Negroes is the impossibility of typifying the Negro race. Lorraine Hansberry's *A Raisin in the Sun* (1959) effectively dramatizes this idea.

Lorraine Hansberry has not idealized the Younger family. Descended from five gen-erations of slaves and sharecroppers, the Youngers, domestic laborers, have little which other people would covet. Desiring to free his wife and his mother from the burden of helping to support the family and desiring to provide his son with an inheritance of which he can be proud, Walter Lee Younger experiences bitter frustration because no one else in his family agrees to his scheme to invest his mother's insurance money in a liquor store. Far from epitomizing nobility, he searches for pride and for maturity. As he says, "I'm thirty-five years old; I been married eleven years and I got a boy who sleeps in the living room—and all I got to give him is stories about how rich white people live."[8] He believes that the Negro who wishes to succeed must imitate white people.

In contrast, his sister, Beneatha (Bennie), inspired partly by racial pride and partly by the lectures of her African suitor, argues against the assimilation of the Negro race into the American culture. Whereas Walter materialistically concentrates upon acquiring money, Bennie wants to become a doctor because her desire since childhood has been to help other people.

Concerned neither with money nor with crusades, their mother desires merely to provide cleanliness and decency for her family. When she receives the insurance money left by her husband, she restrains herself from donating the ten thousand dollars to the church only because she wishes to help her children realize their dreams. She wants her children to respect themselves and to respect others. She refuses to consent to her son's purchasing a liquor store because she believes that it is morally wrong to sell liquor. She wants to maintain a household characterized by the simplicity of Christian ethics. She sees herself symbolized in a ragged plant which she has nursed and has treasured because, in

[7] Langston Hughes, *Simply Heavenly, The Langston Hughes Reader* (New York, 1958), p. 258.

[8] Lorraine Hansberry, *A Raisin in the Sun* (New York, 1959), p. 17.

the North, she has never had sufficient space for the garden which she desires.

Separated by personality and belief, the members of the family conflict incessantly in their attitudes towards education and religion. Although Walter does not oppose education, he resents the fact that Bennie's desire to become a doctor rather than a nurse will necessitate expenses which he wishes to avoid. Bennie, an atheist, seeks education, not to help her race collectively, but to help individuals. Lena Younger, their mother, comforts herself with the belief that God helps the good.

The Youngers are basically moral. Walter would not commit adultery; in fact, he argues that wives are excessively suspicious in believing that their husbands are running to other women when the husbands merely want to be alone. Bennie refuses to become involved in a casual affair with a man to whom she is attracted. To save money, however, Walter's wife Ruth deliberates abortion, and Walter fails to oppose her.

The North has not brought prosperity to the Youngers, emigrants from the South. On the other hand, it has not harmed them. Life in the crowded slums of Southside Chicago has not been pleasant. They have shared a bathroom with other tenants, and they have lacked sufficient space for separate bedrooms or for a garden. Miss Hansberry has reported the situation, however, rather than used it as a basis for protest. The only major conflict with American society stems from the Youngers' decision to move into an all-white neighborhood because they cannot afford to purchase a home at the inflationary prices charged in suburban developments for Negroes.

The Youngers disagree even in their attitudes toward their race. Although Walter blames the backwardness of the race for the inferior economic status of the Negro, he responds to the rhythms of recordings of African music. Bennie recognizes the barrier which separates her from the snobbish Negroes who possess wealth; yet she considers herself a crusader for and a defender of her race. Individual in their characters and their attitudes towards life, the Youngers find unity only in their common belief in the importance of self-respect, a philosophy not unique to the Negro race.

THE FUTURE IMAGES OF NEGRO DRAMA

The changes in the Negro dramatist's image of his hero, his attitude toward education, his attitude toward the North, and his image of his society and its problems parallel those which can be observed in other media utilized by Negro literary artists: from idealization of Negroes to efface the caricatures created by white authors, to strident, self-conscious defense of the vices of Negroes, to objective appraisal. Unlike the Negro novelist, the dramatist cannot escape easily into a world of racelessness. If he employs Negroes to enact his stories, he identifies the characters with Negroes. For that reason, perhaps, the Negro dramatists, more than the novelists, have continued to emphasize problems unique to the Negro race. As reasons for protest have faded, however, they have become more concerned with dilemmas of individuals rather than of the entire race. They have created individuals in the confidence that America has become educated to a stage at which audiences will not assume these characters to typify the Negro race. The Negro dramatists of the present and of the future are no longer compelled to regard themselves as spokesmen for a race which needs educated and talented writers to plead its cause. Now they can regard themselves as artists, writing about the Negro race only because that is the group with which they are the most familiar.

—1960

A Woman Playwright Speaks Her Mind

by Alice Childress

I AGREE that the Negro woman has almost been omitted as important subject matter in the general popular American drama, television, motion pictures and radio; except for the constant, but empty and decharacterized faithful servant. And her finest virtues have been drawn in terms of long suffering, with humility and patience.

Today, the Negro woman's faults are sometimes pointed out, that she is too militant, so domineering and aggressive with son, husband and brother, that it is one of the chief reasons for any unexpressed manhood on the part of the black man in America.

There must be some truth in this charge. The mother in James Baldwin's *Amen Corner* attempts to restrict her son and husband to her passive and withdrawn way of life, but fails. The husband abandons her and seeks to find himself in music. He returns home to die, then advises the son she has raised to break free of her gentle domination. The son leaves home.

In Lorraine Hansberry's *A Raisin in the Sun,* the strong, loving mother so dominates the home that she restricts her children and infringes upon the rights of her son as a man.

In Louis Peterson's *Take a Giant Step,* a Negro mother tries to separate her son from his black heritage in order to shield him from the realities of life.

All Negro writers have written, first, about that strong, matriarchal figure. I did in a one-act play, *Florence,* and in *Trouble in Mind.*

But now we frequently hear that strength has taken femininity away from her with the end result that she is the main culprit in any lack of expressed black manhood, and that she has been masculinized in the process.

Certainly this is too easy and too misleading a conclusion. We know that most alien visitors are guaranteed rights and courtesies not extended to at least one-fifth of America's citizens. They are entitled to travel without restriction, reside in hotels, eat at restaurants and enter public and private places closed to Americans who have built up the country under bondage and defended it under a limited and restricted liberty.

But the American Negro woman has been *particularly* and deliberately oppressed, in slavery and up to and including the present moment, above and beyond the general knowledge of the average American citizen.

After the Emancipation, the white South was faced with a dilemma. How could it protect itself against the legal claims of slave-owners' half-black children? Some of them were the only offspring of a white master. Many black women had been purchased to fulfill the role of wives, but most were used as sexual outlets under degrading circumstances

and none had the privileges of consent or refusal concerning the use of her body. She was forced to bear children and her offspring belonged legally not to her but to her owner-master.

There were many black men who were resentful of being named father to the white slaveowners' children and eager to escape the additional bondage of an enforced family set-up.

There were also some cases of whites who wished to acknowledge their colored children and leave property to them. Laws were passed, declaring what percentage of "black blood" made human beings all-black and thus no responsibility to their white parents.

To spare white men the responsibility of support claims, and to avoid black men challenging in court the paternity of some fair-complexioned child, the white South took action against the Negro woman.

State after state passed legislation declaring that all children born to black women during slavery shall be known as the legitimate children of *their mothers only*.

In the first generation of "freedom," the black woman was abandoned, not only by the white father-owner, but by any black man faced with acknowledging children bred by the slave-master, or by other black men, since women were mated by the owners with various men to bring forth various kinds of offspring—mated for strength, endurance, size, color, and even docility.

With one stroke of the pen, she was told that no man, black or white, owed her anything, and her children were disinherited of all property rights. Her brothers, her father, male cousins, all family ties had been sold, resold, scattered, and so lost that she was, in the majority of cases, without family of any kind.

In so-called freedom, she could now seek a Negro husband. A man who, like herself, was jobless, without education, and doomed to petition for basic human rights and needs for the next century, and God knows how many more years past that century mark of 1963.

The white South, and much of the North, destroyed reconstruction efforts and passed laws designed to subjugate and keep the ex-slave in a state of ignorance. He was not allowed to attend schools, churches, parks, libraries, and most certainly, not the concert halls or theaters.

Two hundred years of outlawing the use of African languages has divorced Africans from their folk stories, songs, ritual ceremonies, even the ability to pass on crafts and handiworks.

The Negro was ridiculed, he was emancipated in rags and tatters. Cartoonists lampooned his appearance, vaudeville performers blackened their faces and made mocking, comic characters of "Mandy" and "Sambo."

The mainstay of television and movies has been the big fist fight scene: the hero fights the villain for mistreating or manhandling a defenseless woman. How many times have you seen these men fighting for the honor of a Negro woman? How many guns have been fired for *her* protection? How many detectives have rescued *her* in the nick of time?

She came out of bondage with the burden of the white and the black man's child. Her former master passed laws absolving him of all moral and financial obligation to his children, and she has to feed, raise and educate them by her own effort.

And today, the slaveowners' acknowledged children fight to keep their own, as well as ours, out of the school and out of the voting booth.

Writers, be wary of those who tell you to leave the past alone and confine yourselves to the present moment. Our story has not been told in any moment.

Have you seen us in any portrayal of the Civil War? *Gone With the Wind* is not our story. And our history is not gone with the wind, it is still with us.

For a time, Hollywood seemed to concern itself with the question of "passing"—*Imitation of Life,* a black woman and her almost-white child; *Pinky,* an almost-white girl, played by a white girl.

"Pinky" toyed with the idea of marrying a white man and passing for white. Her grandmother made her kneel and pray for being so sinful.

Lost Boundaries—there is a title, losing your boundaries—all of the light colored people were played by white actors.

Do you think any part of the Negro woman's story has been told in these films? Not yet.

Most colored people who are light enough to pass and wish to pass, do so and get away with it without any complications. They are scattered through the land, thousands upon thousands—thousands upon thousands since that emancipation time, year after year after year, marrying with the so-called white population, and the black community does not turn them in.

It is *the law* that has made these "passers" deny themselves and undo that security which the lawmakers thought they were establishing.

Oh, there are black people who pass, also. They say they were born in other places, or of half this or that other origin, hiding, trying to free themselves from that yoke of bondage which weighs heavy on all, but heaviest on the shoulders of the Negro woman.

Let the psychiatrists tell us how to raise our children to be good citizens, and to be healthy and strong in mind and body . . . in the face of racist laws working against their human rights.

Let there be plays and movies and books about these things.

There are thousands of state laws on the books which shape our lives and the opinions formed about us. Attorney Pauli Murray, a Negro woman, reports in her book, *State Laws and Race and Color,* of many such laws. Let me tell you a few gathered from several states.

"The State Training School for Feeble-minded shall admit white only."

"It is unlawful for any place of business to permit laborers of different races to work within the same room." "This action shall not apply to floor scrubbers, lavatory cleaners, firemen in boiler rooms."

Now, another one: "Mestizos shall be defined as mixed blood, such as Mexican and 'United States'—United States blood. Mixtures of Chinese, Spanish, Indian and Filipino bloods."

"A bus driver has the power to make arrests. He shall be the judge of the race of each passenger, whenever such passenger refuses to disclose his or her race." "Anyone ejected from the bus by the driver shall not be entitled to the return of his fare."

"False statement on marriage license concerning race is a felony, punishable by two to five years in prison."

"Passing for white, or colored—punishable by one to two years in prison." Oh, many people have passed for colored, who wish to marry a colored person in the South. Where is the security in racist law?

"When any birth certificate shows the birth of a legitimate child to parents, one of whom is white, the other colored, and is forwarded to the Bureau of Vital Statistics, it shall be the duty of the State Board of Health to report the same to the attorney general of the State. It shall be the duty of the attorney general to institute criminal proceedings against the parents of such child."

"Any charge or intimation against a white female of having sexual intercourse with a

person of color is slanderous without proof of special damage."

There is no provision for slandering a Negro woman.

Alabama College is listed for "any white girl or woman residing in Alabama of good moral character." It was not intended for Autherine Lucy.

But the school for the deaf and blind in Alabama is open to all races. Perhaps the lawmakers think that those whites who can't see or hear do not need the "protection" of the law.

"White women are not to nurse where Negro men are patients, either private or public."

Any woman who shall have been delivered of a mulatto child, the child shall be evidence of guilt, without further proof, and shall justify the conviction of the woman, but no person shall be convicted of concubinage upon the testimony of the female, unless the same is corroborated by other evidence."

"This act can only be applied to persons of opposite races."

In Florida, ". . . intermarriage shall be null and void, and the issue of any such surreptitious marriage shall be regarded as bastard, and incapable of having or receiving any estate, real, personal or mixed, by inheritance."

There are anti-woman laws in Idaho, Colorado, Indiana, Maryland, Kentucky—over and over, marriage void, issue of marriage illegitimate. It is "fornication" for any white woman to "suffer herself to be got with child by a Negro or mulatto." There are laws against suggesting racial equality, laws against *pernicious* political activity, laws against concubinage, cohabitation, fornication and laws against marriage. Many citizens claim one cannot legislate *for* civil rights and better race relations but it is obvious that legislation against rights has worked to the detriment of the country.

Facing the world alone makes a woman strong. The emancipated Negro woman of America did the only thing she could do. She earned a pittance by washing, ironing, cooking, cleaning, and picking cotton. She helped her man, and if she often stood in the front line, it was to shield him from a mob of men organized and dedicated to bring about his total destruction.

The Negro mother has had the bitter job of teaching her children the difference between the White and Colored signs before they are old enough to attend school. She had to train her sons and daughters to say "sir" and "ma'am" to those who were their sworn enemies.

She couldn't tell her husband "a white man whistled at me, or insulted me, or touched me," not unless she wanted him to lay down his life before organized killers who strike only in anonymous numbers. Or worse, perhaps to see him helpless and ashamed before her.

Because he could offer no protection or security, the Negro woman has worked with and for her family. She built churches, schools, homes, temples and college educations out of soapsuds and muscle.

It seems a contradiction for a woman to be degraded by law, and by popular opinion which was shaped and formed by that law, and yet also take her rightful place as the most heroic figure to emerge on the American scene, with more stamina than that shown by any pioneer.

Finally, I would like to say, today we hear so much about the *new Negro.* As though we never breathed a protest until a few years ago.

But the story of the old Negro has not been told.

Denmark Vesey, Francis Watkins Harper, Monroe Trotter—if their true stories were told, there would not be so many school drop-outs.

Who wants to sit in a classroom and be taught that he is nobody?

The Negro woman will attain her rightful place in American literature when those of us who care about truth, justice and a better life tell her story, with the full knowledge and appreciation of her constant, unrelenting struggle against racism and for human rights.

—1966

GREENWICH MEWS THEATRE

141 West 13th Street

FIRE NOTICE: The exit indicated by a red light and sign nearest to the seat you occupy is the shortest route to the street. In the event of fire please do not run — WALK TO THAT EXIT.

EDWARD CAVANAGH, FIRE COMMISSIONER.

THE GREENWICH MEWS THEATRE

presents

TROUBLE IN MIND

by ALICE CHILDRESS

Directed by CLARICE TAYLOR and ALICE CHILDRESS

Setting and Lighting   by Vincent Sorrentino

A community project sponsored by the Village Presbyterian Church and Brotherhood Synagogue

THE CAST

(In order of appearance)

Hoodan	JOHNNY BARRACUDA
Pop	LIAM LENIHAN
Wiletta Mayer	CLARICE TAYLOR
John Neville	CHARLES BETTIS
Millie Davis	HILDA HAYNES
Sheldon Forrester	HOWARD AUGUSTA
Judith Sears	STEPHANIE ELLIOT
Al Manners	JAMES McMAHON
Eddie Fenton	HAL ENGLAND

ACT ONE: The Brick Box Theatre in New York City. 10 a.m. Monday morning.

ACT TWO: Ten Minutes later.

There will be a ten minute intermission between the acts.

PRODUCTION STAFF

Artistic Director	LILY TURNER
Administrative Coordinator	STELLA HOLT
Stage Manager	HOWARD AUGUSTA
Production Assistants	DOROTHY BARRY, MAURICE BUGEAUD, ANITA HONIS, BILL KELLOGG, LINDA STEINBERG

Beah Richards (top) was the mother in the 1965 production of James Baldwin's *Amen Corner;* and Ethel Waters (bottom) played the grandmother in the Hollywood production of *Pinky.*

Douglas Turner Ward with Allen Miller in the Off-Broadway drama
The Blood Knot.

American Theater: For Whites Only?

by Douglas Turner Ward

DURING the last decade—coinciding with the explosion of Negro civil rights movements into public consciousness—a number of Negro playwrights have gained considerable notice. Louis Peterson, Lorraine Hansberry, Ossie Davis, James Baldwin, LeRoi Jones, and others . . . collectors of awards and honors . . . a few catapulted into international fame and dramatic prominence . . . critical barometers and geiger counters whipped out to gauge possible winds, trends and resulting fallout.

However, this flurry of attention has tended to misrepresent the *real* status of Negro playwrights. Despite an eminent handful, Negro dramatists remain sparse in number, productions sporadic at most, and scripts too few to indicate discernible trends. (Last year, during a forum on "What Negro Playwrights Are Saying," not even panel members could cite enough plays to make the plural subject matter viable.) Moreover, even when deemed successful—the critical and financial rewards reaped by *A Raisin in the Sun* excepted, and on a smaller scale, LeRoi Jones's *Dutchman*—few productions have managed to recoup capitalization. No, the millennium has not been reached.

Many factors contribute to this situation but, surveying the total landscape of American theater, results could hardly be otherwise.

The legitimate theater, that fabulous in-valid which, compared to its electronic bed-partner, is still dreamed of as the repository of high culture and artistic achievement in America, hardly qualifies when examined from a Negro viewpoint.

Tirelessly, predictably, almost repetitiously on cue, theater critics and other Jeremiahs deplore rampant commercialism, the monopoly of escapist musicals, the dominance of brittle, frothy comedies, and the inadequacy of experimental ventures. They also leave the impression that a little minor surgery would work wonders, that palliatives could restore health. But the patient is sicker than even the most pessimistic diagnosis suggests. No matter how severe their prognosis, pundits seldom question the basic structures or assumptions of their theater.

With rare exceptions—an occasional native play of quality, or intermittent foreign infusions—American legit theater, even at its most ambitious seriousness, is essentially a theater of the Bourgeois, by the Bourgeois, about the Bourgeois, and for the Bourgeois. A pretentious theater elevating the narrow preoccupations of restricted class interests to inflated universal significance, tacitly assuming that its middle-class, affluent-oriented absorptions are central to the dominant human condition. A theater rarely embracing broader frames of reference or more inclusive concerns. A theater—even if it tried—incapable

of engaging the attention of anyone not so fortunate as to possess a college diploma or five-figure salary.

More specifically, a theater in its lofty-modern niche—Broadway, off-Broadway, off-off-Broadway, Happeningsland, wherever—overwhelmingly riddled with works of ingroup concerns, belles-lettres pomposity, instant despair, stultifying boredom, humorless humor, hasty-pudding hi-jinks, pseudo-absurdity and closet-avant daring.

A Theater of Diversion—a diversionary theater, whose main problem is not that it's too safe, but that it is surpassingly irrelevant.

Occasional productions of stature and significance must usually display a cachet of foreign authorship and reputation to justify presentation.

Maybe this is all as it should be: Computer consensus—as yet—doesn't spawn meaningful plays; the most powerful country in the Western world doesn't necessarily usher in a golden age of drama.

DISTURBING PRESENCE

It is not surprising that the Negro playwright and the power of his potential fits only peripherally into this spectrum. By his mere historical placement in American society, the Negro exists as a disturbing presence, an embarrassment to majority comfort, an actuality deflating pretenses, an implicit witness and cogent critic too immediate for attention.

Also, just as in real life, a black playwright—sight unseen, play unheard—is soothsayed as too bothersome a prod to the sleeping conscience of numerical superiors. The stage establishment, like Hollywood, consigns even the most innocuous Negro subject matter to an ogre-category of problem drama. Even sympathetic advisers constantly bug the dark craftsman to shun racial themes and aspire to that pantheon of Olympian universality which all white playwrights, ironically enough, can enter by merely getting themselves born. As

one naive, well-meaning, but frighteningly boorish scribe put it—"No longer Negro playwright, just playwright. . . ." Whoever heard of batting an eyelash of lower-caste condescension when Sean O'Casey is mentioned as an Irish playwright?

NOT ABC'S, BUT ALGEBRA

That the Negro playwright is more or less excluded from legit boulevards is not a revelation for concern. More important is the fact that, even when produced within this environment, the very essence of his creative function is jeopardized. His plays stand to be witnessed and assessed by a majority least equipped to understand his intentions, woefully apathetic or anesthetized to his experience, often prone to distort his purpose. Spectators who, though afflicted with self-imposed ignorance, demand to be taught ABC's at the very moment when the writer is impatient to explore the algebra of his thematic equations. Observers, even when most sympathetic, whose attitudes have been repeatedly shaped by preconceptions and misconceptions, warped by superficial clichés and platitudes—liberal, conservative or radical though they may be. Catering to such insistences presages barren results. With imagination short-circuited, valuable time is wasted clueing in, exposition is demanded when action should be unfolding, the obvious must be overillustrated, and fantasy literalized.

Finally, when the curtain descends, whether the writer has pampered illusions, lectured ignorance, comforted fears, shouted for attention or flagellated consciences, probability dictates his defeat and the victory of customers—triumphantly intact in their limitations. With tears dried, the shouting quieted, or the aches of the cat-o'-nine-tails subsided, the writer has been neatly appropriated, usurped, his creativity subverted.

For those Negro playwrights eager to volunteer for this function, there's no advice to offer. They know the rules, they play the game and take their chances.

But for a Negro playwright committed to examining the contours, contexts and depths of his experiences from an unfettered, imaginative Negro angle of vision, the screaming need is for a sufficient audience of *other Negroes,* better informed through commonly shared experience to readily understand, debate, confirm, or reject the truth or falsity of his creative explorations. Not necessarily an all-black audience to the exclusion of whites but, for the playwright, certainly his primary audience, the first persons of his address, potentially the most advanced, the most responsive or most critical. Only through their initial and continuous participation can his intent and purpose be best perceived by others.

UNAPOLOGETICALLY NEGRO

The validity of this premise has been borne out previously in other productions and, most recently, during the current run of my own plays, *Happy Ending* and *Day of Absence,* two works of satirical content written from an unapologetic Negro viewpoint. Throughout the run, Negro attendance has averaged close to 50 per cent—hundreds witnessing a professional play for the first time. Besides contributing immeasurably to the longevity of the run, the freshness of their response, immediacy of involvement, and spontaneity of participation have significantly underscored the essence of the works themselves and provided crucial illuminations for others. With Negroes responding all around, white spectators, congenitally uneasy in the presence of Negro satire, at least can't fail to get the message.

Any future hope for the Negro playwright depends upon whether or not this minuscule, singular, all-too-infrequent experience can be extended, multiplied, and made permanent.

As long as the Negro playwright remains totally dependent on existing outlets, he stands to continue as a pauper begging sustenance, never knowing from day to day, year to year, whether a few scraps will be tossed his way. Even burgeoning, tax-supported, privately endowed repertory companies are beyond the reach of his ambition (imagine rushing to present *Day of Absence* or any other work which would require jobbing-in 15 Negro actors when your roster only allows for two or three at most—often tokens at that).

Eventually, an all-embracing, all-encompassing theater of Negro identity, organized as an adjunct of some Negro community, might ideally solve the Negro dramatists' dilemma, but such a development—to me—must arise as part of a massive effort to reconstruct the urban ghetto. Small-scale cultural islands in the midst of the ghettoes, separate and apart from a committed program of social and economic revitalization of slums, are doomed to exotic isolation.

Meanwhile, potential talent ready for exercise cannot wait. Without engagement, it lies dormant, still-born. Time passes, aging proceeds. The talent withers and eventually dies of nonuse.

If any hope, outside of chance individual fortune, exists for Negro playwrights as a group—or, for that matter, Negro actors and other theater craftsmen—the most immediate, pressing, practical, absolutely minimally essential active first step is the development of a permanent Negro repertory company of at least off-Broadway size and dimension. Not in the future, but now.

A theater evolving not out of negative need, but positive potential; better equipped to employ existing talents and spur the development of future ones. A theater whose justification is not the gap it fills, but the achievement it aspires toward—no less high than any other comparable theater company of present or past world fame.

A theater concentrating primarily on themes of Negro life, but also resilient enough to incorporate and interpret the best of world drama—whatever the source. A theater of permanence, continuity and consistency, providing the necessary home base for the Negro artist to launch a campaign to win his ignored brothers and sisters as constant witnesses to his endeavors.

This is not a plea for either a segregated theater, or a separatist one. Negroes constitute a numerical minority, but Negro experience, from slavery to civil rights, has always been of crucial importance to America's existence. There's no reason why whites could not participate in a theater dedicated to exploring and illuminating that experience if they found inspiration in the purpose.

Also, just as the intrusion of lower middle-class and working-class voices reinvigorated polite, effete English drama, so might the Negro, a most potential agent of vitality, infuse life into the moribund corpus of American theater.

—1966

Robert Dean Hooks and Barbara Ann Teer in Douglas Turner Ward's *Day of Absence*.

Appearances, by Garland Anderson, was the first full-length drama by a Negro to be presented on Broadway. It opened at the Frolic Theatre in New York on October 13, 1925, and received good notices; but it lasted only 23 performances. However, the play later had two more productions in New York, and it also played in London.

How I Became a Playwright

by Garland Anderson

I AM OFTEN asked how I happened to write this play. At the time it occurred to me to do so the thought of service was in my mind. Service to me is the rent I pay for the space I occupy on earth. I felt that unless I could be of some service to my fellow men, there was no excuse for my occupying space here.

It was after seeing Channing Pollock's play, *The Fool,* that I definitely decided on writing a play. At first the idea seemed absurd because I had only four years' schooling, as my mother died when I was eleven years old,

and I ran away from home. No one realized more than myself that, though I wanted to write this play, I had no training in the technique of dramatic construction; but I also realized that to shirk what I wanted to do could be likened to the outer shell of the acorn after it was planted in the ground saying to that inner stir of life for expression, "What are you stirring for? Surely you don't expect to become a great oak tree? Why, you are only the inside of a mere acorn."

With this firm conviction I determined to

write a play. The fact that I did not know how seemed to me the very reason why I must. I realized that if I succeeded, in spite of apparently unsurmountable obstacles, in writing a play sufficiently interesting to hold an audience, the production of that play would prove to my audience, with every advantage in life over me, that they would be able to do the thing they wanted to do.

The next question was how to concentrate. At first it seemed impossible, as I was working in a busy hotel in San Francisco, sitting at the switchboard with constant interruptions at the telephone and bell. But I determined that nothing should interfere with me, except that which I myself permitted. And so I decided that, rather than resist my surroundings, I would put love into my work. In other words, I would love what I had to do rather than hate it. So, after that, whenever the switchboard rang while I was writing, I would say to myself, "This is just a loving call coming at exactly the right moment to refresh my thoughts so that I can write better." And if someone came up and spoke to me I would say, "This is a loving interruption coming just at the right time to prevent me from writing the wrong thing." In this way all things worked together for good, and at the end of three weeks the play was completed.

Al Jolson was a real pal to me. He paid all my expenses from San Francisco to New York, where for seven months I went from producer to producer endeavoring to interest them in my play—but without success. I felt, however, that the only failure a man ought to fear is failure in cleaving to his purpose. Although failure in any cause produces misery in the soul, yet it is in a sense the highway to success, inasmuch as every discovery of what is false leads us to seek what is true, and every fresh experience enables us to rectify and avoid our previous mistakes. Thus do stumbling blocks become stepping stones!

Without earnestness there is nothing to be done in life, and I was so full of confidence in my play that I wrote to President Coolidge, offering to present him with a copy of my play. A polite letter from the Secretary shattered my hopes, but, undaunted, I went to Washington, and one fine morning presented myself at the White House. I was lucky in obtaining, after talks with many minor officials, an interview with the President's Secretary, Mr. Saunders. He gravely pointed out that no one, however important, could be admitted to the President's presence without an appointment, and that the President's time was fully occupied by important matters of State. Full of fear and hope, I appealed to him to help me, so he said, "Give me your book and I will give it to President Coolidge, and come back at 12:30, when you can go in with Senator Wheeler's party and shake hands with the President."

You can't imagine how grateful I felt to him for this great service, and when later I joined Senator Wheeler's friends I was the last to enter the President's study. The great opportunity of my life had come. Firmly grasping President Coolidge's hand, I realized that we were alone, and I told him all about my work and my ambition. It was due in no small measure to his interest in my work that my play was produced in New York, where it ran for over three years.

The one thought I want to leave in the minds of the readers of *Everyman* is this: I was not seeking to write a wonderful play, a technically perfect play, but merely a play that would be sufficiently interesting and entertaining to provide the public with a pleasant evening—plus, possibly, an inspiration to many. If I have succeeded, then they can say, "If with his very limited opportunities he has succeeded in writing a play that has held my interest, then what can prevent me from doing the thing I want to do?"

—1928

First on Broadway

THE CHIP WOMAN'S FORTUNE
by Willis Richardson

Frazee Theatre

42d Street, West of Broadway
Telephone Bryant 0031
Direction of H. H. Frazee

Manager..................................Richard E. H. French
Treasurer ....Walter Heyer
Treasurer's Assistant..........................Lester Worden

NOTICE: This Theatre, with every seat occupied, can be emptied in less than three minutes. Choose NOW the Exit nearest to your seat, and in case of fire walk (do not run) to that Exit.
THOMAS J. DRENNAN, Fire Commissioner.

BEGINNING TUESDAY EVENING, MAY 15, 1923
Matinees Wednesday and Saturday

ETHIOPIAN ART THEATRE
Raymond O'Neil, Director

Announces

A REPERTORY SEASON

"THE CHIP WOMAN'S FORTUNE"
By Willis Richardson

Characters

LIZA ....EVELYN PREER
SILAS ....SYDNEY KIRKPATRICK
EMMA ....MARION TAYLOR
AUNT NANCY............................LAURA BOWMAN
JIM ....SOLOMON BRUCE
A MAN.....................................ARTHUR RAY

Scene—The Home of Silas.

PROGRAM CONTINUED ON SECOND PAGE FOLLOWING

THE CHIP WOMAN'S FORTUNE

BY WILLIS RICHARDSON

THE CHIP WOMAN'S FORTUNE, a one act play by Willis Richardson, was the first drama by a Negro to appear on Broadway (May 15, 1923). It was part of a triple bill (Oscar Wilde's SALOME and Shakespeare's A COMEDY OF ERRORS, *an original interpretation,* were the other two) presented by The Ethiopian Art Players organized by Raymond O'Neill and Mrs. Sherwood Anderson. (EDITOR'S NOTE: Most available source materials place the opening date of THE CHIP WOMAN'S FORTUNE as May 7, 1923. The date is inaccurate. On the 7th of May, THE CHIP WOMAN'S FORTUNE was presented at the Lafayette Theatre in Harlem and then subsequently had its Broadway opening at the Frazee Theatre on May 15, 1923.)

CHARACTERS

SILAS GREEN, a store porter

LIZA, his wife

EMMA, their daughter

AUNT NANCY, the chip woman

JIM, her son

TWO OTHER MEN

The scene is the very plain dining room of a poor colored family. The floor is without covering and the walls are without pictures. At the center of the floor is a rectangular table with a couple of chairs near it. In the rear wall is a fireplace in which a low fire is burning, and at the left of this sits LIZA *in a rocker. She is wrapped from shoulder to ankles in blankets, for she is just up from a spell of sickness. At the right of the fireplace is a window. A door at the right leads through to other rooms and to the back yard. Another door at the left leads to the front of the house. Against the left side near the door stands a Victrola. There is a deep silence as* LIZA *sits gazing into the fire. She looks up at the clock on the mantle, then looks towards the right and calls.*

LIZA (*calling*). Emma! Emma!

Presently AUNT NANCY *appears at the right. Everyone of us has seen her kind—those old women who go about the streets picking up chips of wood and lumps of coal, or searching in trash cans for whatever they can find. Such is* AUNT NANCY. *She is old and her back is bent on account of constant stooping. She is wearing a bonnet which partly hides her black, wrinkled face, and is wearing a shawl over her shoulders.*

AUNT NANCY. You callin' Emma, Miss Liza?

LIZA. Yes'm, Aunt Nancy. You seen her?

AUNT NANCY. No'm I ain't seen her.

LIZA. Wonder where she is? Ah want her to go to the store for me.

AUNT NANCY. Ah don't know where she is. Ah ain't seen her for the last two hours, but I reckon she'll drop in in a minute or two. How you feelin' now?

LIZA. Ah'm feelin' pretty good. The medicine you give me last night must be doin' me good.

AUNT NANCY. Ah don't reckon you need no more medicine today.

LIZA. Ah reckon not. How you feelin'? Seems

like *ah* ought to be askin' you that instead of you askin' me.

AUNT NANCY. Ah'm feelin' right sharp for a old woman. To tell you the truth, *ah* ain't felt better since the day *ah* got married. Ah'm 'spectin' somethin'?

LIZA. You 'spectin' somethin'?

AUNT NANCY. Yes'm.

LIZA. What you 'spectin'?

AUNT NANCY. Ah can't tell you that, Miss Liza; but maybe you'll find out before the day's gone.

LIZA. Is it anything good?

AUNT NANCY. Didn't *ah* tell you *ah* ain't felt better since the day I got married?

LIZA. Ah'm glad somethin' good's happenin' to somebody. Ain't nothin' good happenin' to me.

AUNT NANCY. You gettin' better, ain't you?

LIZA. Yes'm *ah'm* gettin' better.

AUNT NANCY. That sure is good; and besides, you're young yet; lot o' good things can happen to you before you die.

LIZA. Ah hope so.

AUNT NANCY (*going close to her*). Lemme look in your eye.

After looking into her eyes.

Your eyes startin' to shine. You'll be gettin' all right pretty soon.

She whispers something into LIZA'S *ear.*

LIZA. (*blushing*). Oh, no'm Aunt Nancy!

AUNT NANCY (*laughing*). That's all right, you wait. Ah likes to see a woman's eyes shinin'. It shows she's got some life in her. Ah don't like to see no woman with dead eyes, 'specially a young woman. Ah likes to see 'em pert.

LIZA. You ain't by yourself. Everybody likes to see a young woman pert.

AUNT NANCY. Ah was goin' in the woods to dig up some roots, but *ah* reckon *ah'll* wait 'til tomorrow.

LIZA. Tomorrow'll be all right. You don't have to go today.

AUNT NANCY. Ah'll go now and set out on the back steps and think. Ah like to set in the sun and think.

LIZA. Think about what?

AUNT NANCY. Ah got somethin' to think about.

LIZA. What?

AUNT NANCY. Ah can't tell you everything. It ain't good to tell everything you think about, you know. 'Spose everybody told all their thoughts?

LIZA. That wouldn't never do.

AUNT NANCY. 'Deed it wouldn't never do. Everything *ud* be upside down with other people knowin' what you was thinkin' about.

She starts out right.

LIZA. If you see Emma out there send her in to me.

AUNT NANCY. All right, *ah* will.

She looks through the right door.

Here comes Emma now.

EMMA *enters. She is a pretty brown girl of eighteen.*

EMMA. You want me, Ma?

LIZA. Yes, *ah* want you, where you been?

EMMA. Upstairs.

LIZA. Upstairs doin' what?

EMMA. Combin' ma hair.

LIZA. Combin' your hair this time o' day? You combed your hair once this mornin'. What you comb it again for?

EMMA. Ah wanted it combed.

LIZA. You wasn't always so fond o' combin' your hair. What's comin' off?

EMMA. Nothin'.

LIZA (*Looking at her more closely*). Come here, gal.

EMMA *moves nearer to her.*

Ah believe before God you been puttin' powder on your face. Is you been puttin' powder on your face?

EMMA *looks away without answering.*

Where'd you get that powder from?

EMMA. Ah bought it.

LIZA. Bought it with what?

EMMA *is silent.*

Don't you hear me talkin' to you? Bought it with what?

EMMA. Bought it with some change Pa gave me.

LIZA. Well wipe it off! Wipe it right off and don't put no more on! Leave it up there and *ah'll* use it when ah get on ma feet. You too young to be powderin'.

AUNT NANCY (*who still stands near*). Let the gal alone, Liza. You was young like that once and she ain't goin' to be that young but once.

LIZA. She don't have to paint herself up like a billboard just because she's young.

> *To* EMMA.

Get the basket, *ah* want you to go to the store for me.

> EMMA *goes out right.*

AUNT NANCY. Ah'll be out on the back steps if you want me.

LIZA. All right'm. Ah hope *ah* won't need you.

> AUNT NANCY *goes out right and* LIZA *sits rocking until* EMMA *returns. She speaks just as* EMMA *comes in.*

There's somethin' mighty funny goin' on round here. You primpin' and Aunt Nancy thinkin'. Ah reckon we goin' to have a thunder storm.

EMMA. Ain't nothin' funny goin' on.

LIZA. What you doin' plasterin' your face up and combin' your hair if somethin' funny ain't goin' on? You know you ain't never combed your hair twice the same day in your life if it wasn't Sunday.

EMMA (*anxious to change the subject*). What did you say to get from the store?

LIZA. Get some potatoes and chops and some cakes. Some o' the little ones your Pa likes so much.

EMMA. Is that all?

LIZA. Yes, that's all. Look a here tell me this. Did Aunt Nancy take you in the woods and show you how to dig them roots yesterday?

EMMA. Yes'm, she showed me, but *ah* don't remember much.

LIZA. Why don't you? You ain't got your mind on no boy, is you?

EMMA. No'm. She says she's goin' to show me all over again so *ah'll* know how to find 'em for you when she's gone.

LIZA. Aunt Nancy ain't goin' nowhere.

EMMA. Ah hope she won't, but if she does *ah'll* be sorry. She's so good to me *ah* love her a lot.

LIZA. 'Deed she is good. Everybody loves her and they can't help it. Ain't no way in the world to help lovin' somebody that's good to you.

EMMA. And Aunt Nancy sure has been good to us.

LIZA. Nobody knows that like *ah* do.

EMMA (*starting out*). Ah'm goin' now.

LIZA. Wait a minute. Start the Victrola off before you go, and go out the back way, it's nearer.

EMMA (*adjusting the needle*). When we goin' to get some new records, Ma?

LIZA. New records? You better wait 'til the Victrola gets paid for. You got plenty o' records.

EMMA. But they're all old.

LIZA. That's all right, you can keep on usin' 'em. You ought to be glad to get bread to eat and let new records alone.

> LIZA *is listening to the Victrola when* SILAS, *her husband, enters from the left. He is a man about forty and is wearing the uniform of a store porter. As he enters* LIZA *looks up at him in surprise.*

LIZA. Why, Silas, what you doin' home?

SILAS (*throwing his cap down and moving to the table*). They sent me home.

LIZA. Not discharged?

SILAS (*not in the best of spirits*). No, *ah* ain't discharged, but it's almost as bad; *ah'm* furloughed a couple o' days without pay.

LIZA. Furloughed for what?

SILAS (*motioning towards the Victrola*). On account o' that old Victrola. Seems like it's bringin' us more trouble than it's worth.

LIZA. What's the Victrola got to do with your job?

SILAS. It's just like everything else. When a man's got trouble o' one kind seems like everything goes wrong.

LIZA. That ain't tellin' me nothin'.

SILAS. Well, you know we ain't paid nothin' on that Victrola since the first payment, don't you?

LIZA. Yes, *ah* know that. But you been promisin'.

SILAS. That's the trouble. Ah been doin' a lot o' promisin' and no payin'.

LIZA (*impatiently*). Well, what else. You just as well tell me all of it at once. Ah don't feel like askin' a million questions.

SILAS. The man said he was goin' to send here and get the thing if we didn't pay this month, didn't he?

LIZA. Yes.

SILAS. Well, you know we ain't been able to pay, so he's goin' to send after it.

LIZA. Goin' to take it away?

SILAS. Yes.

LIZA. So, that's why you got furloughed, is it? 'Cause they goin' to take the Victrola away.

SILAS. No, that ain't it exactly.

LIZA. Ah see you ain't told me. What is it exactly?

SILAS. The manager o' that music place is a friend o' ma boss; and this mornin' while *ah* was sweepin' off the pavement he passed by me goin' in the store. When he seen me he stopped and looked at me hard, then he went in. Ah thought trouble was comin' when *ah* seen him look at me so hard. After he came out the boss called me in and told me they was goin' to send after that Victrola; and then he says, 'Go home and stay a few days and maybe you'll learn how to pay your debts.' So here *ah* am.

LIZA. Ah'll be mighty sorry to lose that Victrola; but if it can't be helped, it can't be helped.

SILAS. No, it can't be helped, but that ain't the worst of it. If *ah* don't pay and they take it back, when *ah* go back, the boss'll always have his eyes on me, and *ah* bet it won't be long before *ah'll* be losin' ma job.

LIZA. What you goin' to do?

SILAS. Ah'll do anything to save ma job.

LIZA. Ah know you'd like to pay and keep the Victrola; but *ah* don't see where you goin' to get the fifty dollars from.

SILAS. Ah know one thing.

LIZA. What?

SILAS. Aunt Nancy's got to start to payin' for her room and board.

LIZA (*surprised*). Aunt Nancy!

SILAS. Yes. We can't keep her around here as high as everything is.

LIZA (*earnestly*). But look what she done for me. She brought me from flat o' ma back. Ah had one foot in the grave before she come here. And look at me now. Ah'm almost on ma feet.

SILAS. Ah can't help it. Ah know she done a whole lot for us, but *ah* can't keep things goin' if she don't pay.

LIZA. She helps along. She picks up chips and pieces o' coal on the street. That keeps you from havin' to buy 'em.

SILAS. Everything you sayin' is true, but she's either got to give us some money for stayin' here, or she's got to go.

LIZA (*greatly concerned*). If she goes who's goin' to nurse me? Who's goin' in the woods to get the roots to make ma medicine?

SILAS. If that old woman didn't have money *ah* wouldn't say nothin'.

LIZA (*not understanding*). If she didn't have what?

SILAS. If she didn't have money; but *ah* know she's got money.

LIZA (*angrily*). Where in the devil would Aunt Nancy get any money from?

SILAS. Ain't no use to get mad about it. Ah know what *ah'm* sayin'.

LIZA. How do you know she's got money?

SILAS. Ah know because *ah* been watchin' her the last week or so.

LIZA. You been watchin' her, is you? Well, what did you find out?

SILAS. Ah found out that people passin' in the street give her money every day.

LIZA. You ain't talkin' about a cent or two anybody might give a poor old woman, is you?

SILAS. No, every day *ah* see people givin' her dimes and nickels and quarters. And it ain't no longer than yesterday that *ah* seen two rich lookin' men givin' her greenbacks.

LIZA. Ah ain't never seen her with no money.

SILAS. Ah know you ain't. She hides it.

LIZA. Hides it where?

SILAS. In the back yard. I know the very place.

LIZA. Did you see her hide it there?

SILAS. No, *ah* didn't see her hide it there, but every time I go out there by that spot she comes right behind me.

LIZA. Ah hope you ain't mean enough to try to take her money. Ah mean if she's got any.

SILAS. No, *ah* ain't been tryin' to take it. Ah just wanted to see what she had there. Ah tried it time and time again, and every time I went close to that spot she come right up.

LIZA. Why.didn't you wait 'till she went away?

SILAS. I done that twice; but every time *ah* went out there she come right back just like somethin' drawed her back. Once *ah* went out there with a spade and up she comes and stands right on the spot. Ah told her *ah* wanted to dig a hole for a post and she said, "Please don't dig it right here, Mr. Silas; *ah* got somethin' planted here." You know if somebody has anything planted they wouldn't go and stand right on the spot.

LIZA (*after a moment's thought*). Well, whether she's got money or not, *ah* don't think you ought to put her out after what she's done for us.

SILAS. That's the only way I know we can get by.

LIZA. That won't make it the right thing to do. A lot o' people get by doin' the wrong thing. Ah know Emma won't like it.

SILAS. It's got to happen just the same if she don't hand out some money. Where's Emma?

LIZA. She went after somethin' for dinner.

SILAS. When she comes in tell her what *ah* said. 'Course the old woman might get open hearted and let us have fifty dollars or so; then we won't have no trouble at all and *ah* can go back to work tomorrow.

LIZA. Maybe she'll let us have that much if she's got it, but *ah* don't believe she's got that much.

SILAS (*determined*). Somethin's got to be done.

He starts out.

Ah reckon *ah* better change these clothes so they'll be clean when *ah* do go back.

He goes out leaving LIZA *gazing into the fire. Presently* EMMA *returns with the basket on her arm.*

LIZA. Ah got a lot o' sad news for you, Emma.

EMMA (*a little frightened at her mother's tone rests the basket on the table and gazes at her*). What's the matter? Anything bad happened?

LIZA. They goin' to take the Victrola away.

EMMA. The Victrola! Who's goin' to take it away?

LIZA. The men from the store's comin' 'cause we ain't been makin' no payments.

EMMA. Does Pa know about it?

LIZA. Yes, he's the one told me.

EMMA. He been here?

LIZA. He's here now. They sent him home from work because we ain't been makin' no payments.

EMMA (*fearfully*). He ain't been discharged, is he?

LIZA. He ain't been discharged, but he's furloughed and that's just as bad.

EMMA. You mean they goin' to let him go back?

LIZA. Yes, they'd let him go back today if he could make a good payment on that Victrola; but he reckons he'll have to stay out two or three days as it is.

EMMA. Ah'm mighty sorry they put him off, and *ah'm* mighty sorry we can't keep that Victrola. Hearin' that thing was about the only pleasure ah had.

LIZA. That ain't the worst yet.

EMMA. What, somethin' more? What else is it?

LIZA. Your Pa says if Aunt Nancy don't pay any money for stayin' here she's got to go.

EMMA. Where's Aunt Nancy goin' to get any money from?

LIZA. He says he's been seein' people give her money almost every day, and she's got it buried in the back yard.

EMMA. If she's got any money at all it's just a few cents; but *ah* don't believe she's got none.

SILAS (*entering just in time to hear what* EMMA *says. He is now wearing overalls*). Yes, she is got money, too; and she'll either have to pay some or get out.

EMMA (*turning to him*). Ah don't see nothin' fair in that. She picks up chips, she brings home wood and coal, and she nurses Ma. What more do you want?

SILAS (*sitting at the right of the table*). If she'll give me a few dollars or let me borrow a few dollars maybe *ah* can go back to ma job tomorrow.

EMMA. If you put her out *ah* believe Ma'll go right back to bed, 'cause there won't be nobody that'll know what to do for her. So *ah* don't see nothin' you'll gain by puttin' her out.

SILAS. If she'll let us have the money—

EMMA. If she's got any money it's just a little she's savin' for her son.

SILAS (*surprised*). Her son! Ah didn't know she had no son.

EMMA. Yes, seh, she's got a son.

SILAS. Where's he? Ah ain't heard nothin' about him.

EMMA. He's been in the pen a long time, but *ah* reckon he's out now.

SILAS. In the pen?

EMMA. Yes, seh.

SILAS (*still puzzled*). And she's savin' money for him?

EMMA. Ah reckon that's what she's savin' it for if she's got any.

SILAS (*in disgust*). Well, for God's sake! Savin' money for a jail bird!

EMMA. She says she wants him to have a few cents to keep him 'til he can get a job.

SILAS. Did she tell you all this?

EMMA. Yes, seh. Ah wrote a letter for her the other day.

SILAS (*turning to* LIZA). Did you know anything about this, Liza?

LIZA. No, this is the first time *ah've* heard a word about it.

SILAS. Why didn't you say somethin' about it?

EMMA. You always told me to tend to ma own business. Ah didn't want to be tellin' her business around.

SILAS. It's all right to tend to your own business, but it ain't all right to keep secrets from your parents when it concerns 'em. You say her son's out now.

EMMA. He was to be out yesterday. She's lookin' for him to come here today.

SILAS. What was he sent up for?

EMMA. Ah don't know, seh; somethin' about a woman, *ah* believe.

SILAS. And he means to come here, does he?

EMMA. Yes, seh.

SILAS. You hear that, Liza?

LIZA. Yes, and *ah* ain't particular about havin' no jail bird comin' here neither.

SILAS. Ah reckon *ah* just as well talk to her now as any other time. Was she out there when you come in, Emma?

EMMA. Yes, seh, she was sittin' out on the back steps; but she got up when *ah* came in and started off.

SILAS. Well, go tell her to come in here a minute.

EMMA (*as she goes out*). Ah'll have to catch her 'cause *ah* reckon she's gone.

SILAS. Just go out there and stand by that middle clothes prop and she'll come right in sight. Ah've already tried it a lot o' times myself.

EMMA *goes out.*

Liza, *ah* want you to understand *ah'm* not actin' this way 'cause *ah* mean to be hardhearted. Ah've just got to get out o' this trouble.

LIZA (*discouraged*). Ah'm sorry everything turned out like this, 'cause I reckon *ah'll* have to go back to bed if she goes.

SILAS (*concerned*). Don't say that. The Lord couldn't be that hard on us.

LIZA. Ah hope you're right; goodness know *ah* do.

SILAS. If *ah* can get her to do us this favor before the men come after that Victrola, everything'll be all right.

There is a pause while they ponder over their situation.

And even if she will agree to help us, *ah'm* tired o' this kind o' life. Ah'm sick o' livin' from hand to mouth.

LIZA. Ah reckon we ought to be thankful to be livin' any kind o' way with the trouble we had. Some people get along better'n we do, but a whole lot o' others don't get along as good. Ah only got one consolation besides believin' in the Lord.

SILAS. What's that?

LIZA. That things ain't always been like this, and they might not always be like this.

SILAS. Ah hope not.

He listens.

Here they come.

LIZA. Now don't be hard on her, Silas. You know she's been mighty good to us.

SILAS. I ain't goin' to be hard on her. Ah'm goin' to be as fair as ah can.

EMMA *enters followed by* AUNT NANCY.

AUNT NANCY (*moving to the table and speaking to* SILAS). You want to see me, seh?

SILAS (*kindly*). Yes'm, Aunt Nancy, *ah* want to talk to you. Get a chair so she can sit down, Emma.

AUNT NANCY *looks around for a chair.* EMMA *brings her one and she sits above the table.*

SILAS. The first thing *ah* want to do, Aunt Nancy, is to thank you for all the good things you done for us. And then *ah* want to tell you that we're in trouble.

AUNT NANCY. You all in trouble, Mister Silas?

SILAS. Yes'm. The men'll be here today after the Victrola, and *ah'm* put off from work a few days 'cause *ah* didn't pay for it.

AUNT NANCY. Ah'm mighty sorry for that.

SILAS. And you know you been stayin' here with us for six months or more and we ain't been chargin' you a thing.

AUNT NANCY. No, and *ah* wouldn't a been able to pay you nothin' no how.

SILAS. Now *ah'm* askin' if you'll pay us for stayin' or let us borrow a few dollars from you?

AUNT NANCY (*with a long face*). 'Deed the Lord knows *ah* can't pay you nothin', Mister Silas. Ah ain't got nothin' for maself.

SILAS. But we know you got money hid out there in the back yard.

AUNT NANCY. Ah got a little money out there, but that ain't for me, that's for ma child.

SILAS (*feigning surprise*). You didn't tell us you had no child.

AUNT NANCY. Ah reckon you'd call him a man, but *ah* call him ma child. He's grown.

SILAS. Where is he?

AUNT NANCY. Ah reckon he's on his way here now.

SILAS (*still pretending ignorance*). Ah don't see what a old woman like you wants to be savin' money for a grown man for. He ought to be workin' and takin' care o' you. Ain't he workin'?

AUNT NANCY. He's been locked up.

SILAS. In jail?

AUNT NANCY. In the pen.

SILAS. That's so much the worse. You ought'n to be savin' money to give to a jail bird.

AUNT NANCY (*offended*). He ain't no jail bird, Mister Silas; don't call him that. He's ma son.

SILAS. He ought to be ashamed of hisself for not workin' and takin' care o' you.

AUNT NANCY. That used to be the way when *ah* was comin' up. When children used to get grown they used to take care o' the old folks, but now it's different. The old folks has to take care o' the children.

SILAS. And 'specially if he went to the pen.

AUNT NANCY. Goin' to the pen ain't nothin'. Some o' the best men in the world's been to the pen. It ain't the goin' to the pen that counts, it's what you go there for. Once it used to be a big disgrace to be locked up. No, seh, it ain't the bein' locked up, it's what you locked up for. If the Lord had a got locked up for stealin' somethin' or killin' somebody do you think people would be praisin' him like they do?

SILAS. I know they wouldn't; but what did your son get locked up for?

AUNT NANCY. He got locked up about a woman, but he done what any other man might a done. He was goin' with a woman what he thought was clean, but she was crooked. He run up on her one night when another man was handlin' her kind o' rough and beat the man up—he beat the man up bad. Then he found out the woman was crooked and he lost his head and beat her up too. That's the worse part of it.

SILAS (*doubtfully*). And they sent him to the pen for that? Just for that?

AUNT NANCY. Yes, seh. The man he beat up was one o' these big fellows what went to church every Sunday, and looked so clean and nice in his biled shirts and white collars and fine clothes all through the weekdays, but in the night he trailed in the gutter. He used his pull and put up a job on Jim that sent him to the pen.

SILAS. Ah don't mean to hurt your feelin's, Aunt Nancy, but your boy can't be much if he beat a woman up.

LIZA. 'Deed he can't. That's the worse part of it. Ah didn't mind him beatin' the man, but *ah* never did care much for a man that *ud* hit a woman—no man but ma own son.

Looking him in the eyes.

And you know a mother can't help that.

SILAS. Ah always did think some mothers was too kindhearted.

AUNT NANCY. No, they ain't. Mothers ain't half as kindhearted as God is. If God was hard as some people is, everybody in this world would be farin' mighty bad. You know there ain't no man perfect, and no woman either.

SILAS. I reckon you might be right about that, but the main reason I sent for you was to ask you if you wouldn't let us have a little money. If you can't do it we'll be in a hole sure enough.

AUNT NANCY. Ah wish *ah* could. Ah'd be willin' to do anything in the world for you, but he comes first, you know.

SILAS. Do you reckon he'll let us have it?

AUNT NANCY. Ah don't know; he's mighty kindhearted. He's takin' a mighty long time to come here too.

At this time there is a loud knocking on the outside door.

AUNT NANCY (*starting to rise*). Ah reckon that's him now.

LIZA. Don't get up, Aunt Nancy; Emma'll let him in.

EMMA *goes out.*

SILAS (*to* AUNT NANCY). Why don't you take your bonnet off? You don't want to look like you ain't home.

AUNT NANCY. Never mind *ah'll* keep it on. We won't be here long, *ah* reckon.

EMMA (*returning*). It's the men after the Victrola.

SILAS *hastens out left.*

AUNT NANCY (*sighing*). Oh, Lord, *ah* thought that was Jim. Ah wonder why he don't come?

LIZA. Don't worry, Aunt Nancy, it ain't late.

EMMA. Ah reckon he might be lookin' for the place.

AUNT NANCY. But you put this number in the letter, didn' you?

EMMA. Yes'm, *ah* put it in.

SILAS (*returning*). Ah don't know why *ah* done it, but *ah* told 'em to wait a few minutes.

He sits again.

AUNT NANCY. Ah don't know, Jim might come in a few minutes.

There is another knock on the door.

SILAS (*rising*). Ah wonder what they want now?

He goes out again.

AUNT NANCY. That might be Jim.

LIZA. Ah hope it is.

SILAS *returns followed by Jim. When* AUNT NANCY *sees him she flies towards him.* JIM *opens his arms and draws her to him.*

AUNT NANCY (*holding him off and looking at him*). Is it you, sure enough? Jim is it you?

JIM (*smiling*). Yes'm, it's me.

AUNT NANCY. Come over here.

She draws him over to the table and we have an opportunity to get a good view of him. He is about six feet in height and large in proportion. He is wearing a blue shirt with collar attached and a blue suit.

These is the people *ah* been stayin' with all the winter, Jim.

She names each one in her way of introduction.

This is Mr. Silas.

JIM (*smiling as they shake hands*). Glad to meet you, Mr. Silas.

AUNT NANCY. This is Miss Liza.

JIM (*bowing to* LIZA). Glad to meet you, Miss Liza.

AUNT NANCY. And this is Emma.

JIM *and* EMMA *bow and smile at each other.*

These people been mighty good to me, Jim.

JIM (*speaking to all of them*). Ah'm glad to hear that and *ah* thank you all for it.

LIZA. We ain't been half as good to her as she's been to us.

EMMA. Indeed we ain't.

AUNT NANCY (*to* JIM). What made you take so long to get here?

JIM. Well, *ah* hung around a little while—.

AUNT NANCY. Now, Jim, you ain't got no business hangin' 'round when *ah'm* waitin' for you.

JIM. And even when *ah* got here *ah* wasn't sure this was the right place 'cause *ah* seen two men hangin' 'round on the outside and they looked kinder like bootleggers.

SILAS. Them's the men that come to take the Victrola away.

JIM (*turning to* AUNT NANCY). You say these people been good to you, Ma?

AUNT NANCY. Yes, they been mighty good to me.

JIM (*reaching into his pocket*). Ah got fifteen dollars. You can have that if it'll do you any good.

He gives it to SILAS.

SILAS (*taking the money*). Thanks for that. Maybe some o' these days—.

The two men who have been waiting outside enter.

FIRST MAN. Ah'm sorry, but we can't wait all day; we got to get back to the store.

JIM (*to* SILAS). How much do you owe on it?

SILAS. Fifty dollars.

JIM. Fifteen dollars won't do much good then, will it?

SILAS. Well, it'll help. Ah been tryin' to borrow it from your Ma.

SECOND MAN (*roughly*). Come on, Dan, let's take it; they ain't got nothin'.

SILAS (*as they take hold of the Victrola*). Wait a minute!

JIM (*turning to his mother*). You got any money, Ma?

AUNT NANCY. Ah got a little *ah* been savin' for you.

JIM. How much?

AUNT NANCY (*who is not very good at figures*). Ah don't know, but *ah* reckon it's enough. Ah'll get it.

She goes out right.

SECOND MAN (*impatiently*). Come on, Dan, this is all a bluff.

They move the Victrola towards the door.

JIM (*getting in the doorway*). There ain't nobody or nothin' goin' out o' here 'til she comes back!

JIM *is such a large man and so nearly fills the doorway that the two men stop and reconsider their plan. They decide to wait.*

Ah don't mean no harm to nobody and *ah* wouldn't hurt a hair in nobody's head; but when *ah* say wait, ah mean wait.

FIRST MAN. But you see, mister, we been waitin' a long, long time already.

JIM. Well, you won't have to wait much longer. She'll be back in a minute.

AUNT NANCY *returns with a rather dirty box which she puts on the table and opens. All gaze into it.*

AUNT NANCY (*pouring the contents of the box on the table*). This is yours, Jim, *ah* been savin' it for you ever since you went away.

JIM (*staring at the money*). All this for me?

AUNT NANCY. Yes, and you can do anything you want to do with it.

JIM (*pushing half of the money to* SILAS).

Here, take this; maybe it'll be enough.

Judging from the expression on AUNT NANCY'S *face* JIM *is giving away too much.*

SILAS (*drawing the money to him*). 'Deed it will be enough.

After counting the money he hands part of it to one of the men.

Here's your fifty dollars.

The FIRST MAN *takes the money and with the aid of the* SECOND MAN *pushes the Victrola back to its place. Having done this, they start out.*

JIM (*to* SILAS). You better get a receipt for that.

SILAS (*to the men*). Hey, wait a minute!

The MEN *stop.*

Gimme a receipt for that money.

The FIRST MAN *writes him a receipt and then they go out.*

That's better.

After indicating the money left on the table.

Ah reckon you better take the rest of it back, Jim.

JIM. No, you keep it. You all been good to Ma, and ain't nothin' *ah* got too good for you.

LIZA. She done a whole lot more for us than we could ever do for her.

AUNT NANCY. Ah'd a give you that money before, Mr. Silas, but *ah* was savin' it for Jim, and *ah* just didn't have the heart to give it away.

SILAS. That's all right, Auntie; *ah* 'preciate it just as much if you had give it to me when *ah* first ask you.

AUNT NANCY (*taking up her basket*). Well, Jim *ah* reckon we better be goin'.

LIZA (*quickly, in surprise*). Goin'? Where you goin'?

AUNT NANCY. Goin' to get a place to stay.

JIM. Then *ah'm* goin' to look for a job.

LIZA. But *ah* thought you was goin' to stay here with us.

AUNT NANCY. You ain't got no room for both of us, chile.

SILAS (*shifting the chairs around*). Yes'm, we is. We'll make room.

JIM. No, seh, *ah* don't want you to cramp yourself on ma account. It won't take us long to find another place.

LIZA. But how'll *ah* get along, Aunt Nancy, with you gone?

AUNT NANCY. Ah won't be far away. Ah'll come in and look after you every day.

LIZA. Ah'm mighty sorry you goin', and *ah* want to thank you for what you done for us.

AUNT NANCY (*as she and* JIM *stand near the door*). Maybe we'll ask you all to do us a favor sometime.

SILAS. And we'll be mighty glad to do it.

AUNT NANCY. Well, good day 'til tomorrow.

LIZA, SILAS, & EMMA. Good day.

AUNT NANCY *and* JIM *go out.*

EMMA. Ah'm sorry she's gone.

LIZA. You must be mighty sorry he's gone too by the way you looked at him.

SILAS. 'Deed she must be. She looked at him like her life depended on it.

LIZA. To tell the truth, *ah'm* mighty sorry she's gone too. She's sure goin' to be a loss to me.

SILAS. But she says she's goin' to come around every day to look after you.

LIZA. Yes, but that ain't like stayin' here.

SILAS. Well, there ain't nothin' *ah* can do.

EMMA. Ah reckon you're mighty glad you didn't put her out.

SILAS. Ah am, *ah'm* mighty glad.

LIZA. She got us out o' trouble, all right.

EMMA. Indeed she did.

SILAS. Ah got to go and get ma work clothes on and go and see about ma job.

LIZA. She saved your job, too, *ah'm* thinkin'.

SILAS. You bet your life she did.

CURTAIN

A Helping Hand

THE FEDERAL THEATRE
by Sterling A. Brown

The New York Federal Theatre project's production of *Macbeth*.

Turpentine, at the Lafayette Theatre in Harlem.

The Federal Theatre

by Sterling A. Brown

THE EMPLOYMENT of the Negro legitimate actor was always limited. The advanced, experimental and liberal groups such as the Provincetown Theatre and the Theatre Union gave Negro actors self-respecting roles but because of sharp competition with the commercial theatre could not give many of these. Broadway's saturation point for Negro plays seemed to be about one or two annually. There was no Negro theatre for legitimate drama. Even the houses for the popular song-and-dance vaudeville acts had a hard time staying open. The initials of the Negro booking agency for the South—T.O.B.A.—were supposed, in the words of barnstorming singers and dancers, to stand for Tough On Black Actors.

The depression that struck the American theatre was therefore exceptionally hard on Negro actors, who even in boom times had had a tough time.

In November 1935, the four arts projects of the Works Progress Administration were established to furnish employment for the large number of the unemployed in the fields of the theatre, writing, music, and the arts. The establishment of the Federal Theatre was doubly welcome to Negroes. It was not only a help in times of trouble, but was also the first opportunity for the Negro to participate fully in the theatre, as actor, technician, playwright, director and spectator.

Hallie Flannagan, the Federal director, and her co-workers were convinced that "freedom from racial prejudice . . . must exist at the core of any theatre for American people." Soon after the setting up of the Federal Theatre, there were nine Negro projects: two in New York City, and one each in Boston, Newark, Tampa, Chicago, Birmingham, Seattle and Los Angeles. There were also Negro units in smaller cities like Hartford and Raleigh that cooperated with acting groups from the community.

The opportunity to direct plays, denied to Negroes except in musical comedy or amateur drama, was one of the finest things afforded by the Federal Theatre. White directors were supposed to be working only temporarily until Negroes could be found to handle the work competently. John Houseman who, with Orson Welles, was an important figure in the Lafayette unit, said:

> Owing to the very limited opportunities hitherto open to Negroes in technical and directorial departments of the existing commercial theatre, such specialized workers are not easily available. It is therefore the function of Miss McClendon's [the late actress and one of the founders of the project] non-Negro technical associates to find and train Negroes who shall replace them in all departments at the earliest time possible.

Negroes participated in all of the complex activities of the theatre, from directing, reading and passing on plays, "doctoring" plays,

designing, staging, lighting, costuming, all the
way to ushering in white theatres. Here was
the best type of apprenticeship yet available
in the theatre. As the Federal Theatre pros-
pered, more and more Negro workers in the
theatrical arts were developing higher degrees
of skill in valuable collaboration.

The plays of the Negro units were of several types. As might be expected, the leaders
could not agree on a basic program. What
resulted from the trial-and-error method was
an eclecticism, showing at its best the versatility of Negro actors and Federal Theatre
producers, but really failing to make the social and artistic impact that sponsors of the
Federal Theatre had hoped. That no body
of plays comparable to the repertory of the
Abbey Theatre or the Yiddish Theatre was
produced is of course not the point, since the
Federal Theatre was extremely short-lived.
The workers involved were of many types: old
hoofers of the T.O.B.A., cabaret entertainers,
actors from the Lafayette Players, actors who
had played roles on Broadway, products of
the Little Theatre movement, ambitious young
students of contemporary dramaturgy. The
opinions on the Negro's place in American
life, on the functions of the theatre, on the
social questions of the time, were as varied as
the backgrounds of the actors and directors.

> There are those who would have a theatre
> produce a play having entertainment value
> only. Others would give plays of a functional
> nature, where people could come for clarifica-
> tion and enlightenment. Still others would like
> to continue reviving classics.

The same commentator goes on:

> It seems to us that a theatre that will be defi-
> nitely characteristic of the Negro will take
> a long time in coming. It will take years
> of hard work—years of constant testing of
> public responses before some members of the
> race will gather all the divergent trends and
> crystallize them into a dramatic form, genuine
> and vital enough to embody the needs,
> thoughts, and desires of the Negro people.

To imagine that a single play might do all of
this oversimplifies Negro life in America just

as the phrase "the Negro people" does. Nevertheless the point is well taken that before
the Negroes of Harlem and Southside Chicago could be brought into the theatre, public
responses had to be tested again and again.
One of the great difficulties was the introduction of the legitimate drama to people whose
only theatrical tradition was the song-and-
dance tradition. One Negro editor stated that
the average Negro theatregoer started laughing in the lobby as soon as he had put down
his money for a ticket. When he paid his hard
earned money he expected the theatre to make
him laugh, and he started early to get his
money's worth.

Feeling about for a type of play that would
be theatrically effective and would bring into
the theatre an audience most of whom had
never seen a legitimate drama, the directors
of the Negro units chose to present spectacles,
revivals of classics, social dramas, musical
revues and contemporary melodramas. The
biggest hit was the Haitian *Macbeth* produced
by the Harlem unit at the Lafayette Theatre.
This was the boldest of the contemporary
adaptations of Shakespeare. The scene was
shifted from Scotland to Haiti, the witches
scenes being changed to voodoo rites, the
costumes to those reminiscent of Haiti's struggle for freedom from France. The play received rave notices from the critics.

One of the Federal Theatre's spokesmen
was told that "Plays like *Macbeth* tend to
make the Negro theatre too spectacular. The
press stresses the Negro's love for riotous
color and glamorous productions so much
that I'm afraid ours will become a 'fad' theatre
and so lose in vitality and strength." She con-
fessed that this was an "interesting sidelight"
which she had not thought of before, a confession that illustrated the lack of understanding of Negro opinion on the part of some of
those in charge of the Federal Theatre.

There was much of the "fad," the seeking
for flamboyance on the part of the large white

audiences for *Macbeth*. *Fortune's* writeup reveals the tone of condescension and burlesque that many took to the novelty.

> When the U. S. Government produced William Shakespeare's *Macbeth* in Harlem, it stood them up, packed them in, and rolled them in the aisles. The opening was the blackest first night in New York history. The police roped off four city blocks and the sables from downtown and the high yallers from Harlem fought their way to their fifteen to fifty-five cent seats through the biggest crowd ever gathered on upper Seventh Avenue. . . . The play plus the price brought out white intellectuals as well as black enthusiasts.

Willson Whitman's history of the Federal Theatre stressed "racial" qualities, stating that the melodrama "came to life when played by a primitive people," Macbeth and his wife being "wrong headed children."

> The rich mouth-filling speeches . . . were well suited to be spoken by soft Negro voices; it was apparent that Negro actors can still soliloquize with naturalness and dignity in scenes where white actors are apt to sound like nervous idiots chattering to themselves.

But that Jack Carter and Edna Thomas, sophisticated cosmopolitan Negroes, should impress as primitive children, natural soliloquists, is overstressing "race." Many critics estimated them as actors not as Negroes, and gave them generous praise. Even *Fortune* stated that "Edna Thomas turned in one of the season's great performances as Lady Macbeth."

Macbeth played to a total audience of 117,244 . . . twelve weeks in New York, and in Bridgeport, Hartford, Dallas, Indianapolis, Chicago, Detroit, Cleveland and Brooklyn, for a total of 144 performances. This was the only Negro production for which white patrons stood in queues. The attendance of Negroes was not proportional, but many Negroes became acquainted for the first time with Shakespeare as a playwright. Up to that time, according to a Harlem wit, Shakespeare had been the name of a great halfback on Notre Dame's football team. A story that

went the rounds in Harlem was that one theatregoer, whose experience in the theatre had been confined to black-face comedy and prancing choruses, was asked how he liked *Macbeth*. "There was a lot of big words," he said, "and the folks talked too much, but the costumes was something, and there was some good knife-play in it."

> The gorgeous *Macbeth* in a Haitian setting was, as some serious-minded Negroes complained, no more typical of the Negro race than of Shakespeare; but it was no real disservice in either case. Harlem had lost its tourist trade, *Macbeth* its attraction for theatregoers, and the revival of both together was no mean accomplishment.

There were values in the play foreign to Shakespeare's. Many were probably more startled by the wild voodoo dance than by the tragedy; and many saw current pertinence in the fact that Macduff looked remarkably like Haile Selassie. *Macbeth* was sufficiently theatrical to be a smash hit, and it seemed an auspicious beginning for the Negro unit of the Federal Theatre. Unrelated in one sense to Negro life, it was related in its spectacular and melodramatic aspects to the Negro's theatrical tradition. All in all, it was a good opener.

The Federal Theatre, however, shared in the inclination of the commercial theatre to repeat smash hits. Because many of those connected with the Negro unit favored the novel and the odd in theatrical fare (Orson Welles being influential here), many other classics in costume were revived. It must be stated that plays of contemporary Negro life were difficult to find and were generally inexpertly written. Harlem was therefore shown revivals of Shaw's *Androcles and the Lion* and André Obey's *Noah,* a French play somewhat similar to *The Green Pastures*. But neither of these repeated the success of *Macbeth,* the reception bordering on the indifferent. William Du Bois' *Haiti* attempted to capitalize on the vogue of *Macbeth*. This was a historical romance celebrating the Haitian struggle for freedom. *Haiti* was frank melodrama with

intrigue, lost documents, sliding panels, eye-filling costumes and a romantic tropical set, blood and thunder, with the lines somewhat inclined to ranting. There was a rather trite situation in which the heroine, thought to be white, is revealed to be an octoroon. It furnished an exciting evening in the theatre, but its success as a historical drama of Negro life was tentative.

Closer to the American Negro were the two Federal Theatre plays on the legendary hero, John Henry. Frank Wells wrote a moving dramatization of the legend, with great sympathy for the Negro working-class. His use of John Henry as a proponent of working-class unity struck some observers as an anachronism and dramatically unconvincing. But the play had sustained flashes of poetry and understanding. It was surprising that a young white southerner could catch the idiom and character of these folk without any traces of condescension and quaintness. John Henry emerged a "man in full," a folk hero handled with becoming dignity. *John Henry* was produced on the West Coast, however, and never in New York.

The most ambitious effort of the Seattle Negro Repertory Company was *Natural Man,* a folk opera version of the John Henry legend. The script was done by a Negro project worker, Ted Brown. Vocal arrangements and original choral music were worked out by the chorus. *Natural Man* was a most interesting experiment in group composition of a play. This version inclined to symbolic and poetic fantasy more than to realism. Another fantasy, produced in Seattle, was a dramatization of the Uncle Remus stories of Joel Chandler Harris. In Boston, *Genesis,* a religious pageant of folk stuff that has never been written down but survives orally, was produced with the aid of the local Little Theatre and played to good crowds. This play, by Charles Flato and H. Jack Bates, continued the line of *The Green Pastures* fantasy.

The third type of play produced by Federal Theatre was the realistic play of Negro life. The first of these, *Walk Together, Chillun,* was by Frank Wilson, one of the best Negro actors. He had already written an unconvincing play called *Meek Mose* which had had a short run in Newark. A historian of Federal Theatre says that *Walk Together, Chillun* was concerned "with social justice or lack of it which customarily occupies dramatists who write for colored companies." As the work of an inexperienced playwright, it was not a distinguished play, but as the first Federal Theatre play, it was seen by large crowds. *Turpentine,* by Peter Morrell and Augustus Smith, a Negro who was important in the Lafayette Theatre unit, was of a leftist nature, dealing with Negro workers in the southern pine woods. *Turpentine* strongly denounced prejudice and exploitation but it

> went out of its way to be fair; its white men were not conscious oppressors, the real villain was colored, and it ended on a note of incredible optimism. But it contained such pearls of white speech as "Kill the black bastards!" and "You can't trust a nigger who looks a white man in the eye. . . ." Perhaps it was racial good nature, but it was noticeable that in the Lafayette Theatre during presentation of such plays as *Turpentine* there was less tension than in all-white audiences at Living Newspaper productions downtown. There was laughter, but no hissing, generous but not hysterical applause, indicating that the audience was content to rest the case as presented by the actors.

Called a "better and bitterer play," *Sweet Land,* by a white author, Conrad Seiler, dealt with "the tribulations of a World War veteran upon his return to the South." The Ku Klux Klan was attacked. Radical in purpose, *Sweet Land* showed understanding of Negro workers, presenting their well-founded hostility toward unity with white workers. Willson Whitman writes that "no plainer-spoken drama has been put on the stage than *Turpentine* and *Sweet Land."* *Stevedore* of course should be added. It is significant that the Fed-

eral Theatre included *Stevedore* in its repertory.

These plays were all concerned with the plight of the Negro in the South.

> To say that they were unqualified successes would not be exact; they were kindly received by the press and a certain section of the public, but they were not taken to Harlem's bosom. . . . The natural conclusion is that the Negro of the North is too much involved with his own problems to give much thought to the difficulties of his race in other parts.

Less of social realism and more of theatrical entertainment were in *The Case of Philip Lawrence,* by a Negro playwright, and *The Conjure Man Dies,* a thriller adapted from Rudolph Fisher's detective novel. The latter play, combining Harlem humor and "jive" with mystery—"a Harlem conjure man practised his evil art against a background of mystery, purple robes, secret panels and the burning of seductive incense—" was the most popular of all Federal Theatre productions to the Negroes of Harlem. Remaining dubious of the playwright's picture of working-class unity which they checked by a hard daily reality, rendered uncomfortable by the shameful indignities of southern life shown so powerfully in the social plays, they packed the house to see humor and suspense, to hear a language that they understood, to see something closer to the chief theatrical tradition they knew. In thirty-six performances, *The Conjure Man Dies* played to eighty-three thousand people, an audience largely Negro. In twenty-nine performances, *Walk Together, Chillun* played to ten thousand; in sixty-two performances, *Turpentine* played to twenty-three thousand. *The Conjure Man Dies* played to roughly two thousand per performance; the other two plays to less than four hundred per performance. The figures indicate that the Harlem audience wanted entertainment and not social criticism.

Judged by many as the best social play of Negro life produced by Federal Theatre was *Big White Fog* by Theodore Ward, a young Negro project worker. This play was produced in Chicago. Langston Hughes wrote of it enthusiastically:

> It is the greatest, most encompassing play on Negro life that has ever been written. If it isn't liked by people, it is because they are not ready for it, not because it isn't a great play.

Meyer Levin, Chicago novelist and dramatic critic, agreed with Hughes: "At last here is a play about Negro life as it is lived by Negroes, and not as it is interpreted by poetic white folks who get the esthetic shivers every time they hear spirituals being sung."

Unlike the social plays of the Lafayette unit, *Big White Fog* is about an urban, fairly well-educated, lower-middle-class family on Chicago's Southside. The father, angered by the Negro's lack of opportunity, has fallen heart and soul for Garvey's teachings. His visionary temperament is contrasted with his brother-in-law's Babbittry and his brother's hedonism. All, however, are caught in the "big white fog" of American prejudice. The family becomes more and more insecure. The father loses his hod-carrier's job yet continues to jeopardize his family by supporting Garveyism; the son has to give up college; the daughter has to sell herself for money for the home. The family's downward course is steady until they are finally threatened with eviction. In a scene reminiscent of *Stevedore,* a band of whites and Negroes join together protesting the eviction, and in the melee the father is killed.

Big White Fog is a play of the depression, and like others of that type loads hardships and indignities on the family. All of these are not convincing: the son loses a scholarship to a New England college when it is learned belatedly that he is a Negro; the daughter is arrested in a house of assignation at the very time when the woes of the family are heaviest. There are other traces of melodrama. The play

is a thesis play with differing philosophies of the Negro's way out represented by the characters. The father's Garveyism is done with sympathy and not caricature, and is developed more fully than the son's conversion to radicalism. The play has more discussion than action.

These, however, are the expected faults of a young playwright. Theodore Ward's virtues in *Big White Fog* are serious thoughtfulness and honesty. He has not been squeamish about certain subjects generally dodged in Negro playwrighting. He lampoons color-struck mulattoes, bourgeois climbers who are as ready as any to exploit their own people; he sees the restricted fields of choice open to ambitious young Negroes in the southside Ghetto.

> Its arguments on the familiar aspects of the Negro's sociological status in the United States never become tedious. Its picture of life in a self-respecting Negro home on the South Side is rich with realistic detail.

There was some difficulty about the production of *Big White Fog*. Some considered it "subversive." "Because of Mr. Ward's frankness in discussing the race problem, policemen and censors were on hand prepared to quell a riot. But contrary to the predictions of the "diehards" and Brahmins, both white and colored, the play won the hearts of all."

Naturally, many of the unemployed Negro actors were song-and-dance artists. To give their talents scope, Federal Theatre produced *Sing Out the News,* a well-received musical show in which one hit tune, "Franklin D. Roosevelt Jones," swept the nation, and *The Swing Mikado,* a jazzed up version of the Gilbert and Sullivan opera, making use of swift spirited dancing and startling musical effects. Many preferred the W.P.A. *Swing Mikado* to the *Hot Mikado,* starring Bill Robinson, which by an unusual quirk in producing procedure, came out immediately afterwards. *The Swing Mikado* was one of the last triumphs of the Federal Theatre. Shortly after, Congress got busy and doomed the Federal Theatre.

The Lafayette Theatre unit was considered more self-sufficient than any other within the project. It included a fully equipped costume department, a carpentry department, a lighting department with a crew of seven men, a crew of thirteen "grip men" to move scenery, six prop men, a scenic and costume designer; and the house staff of matrons, ushers, box office men, porters and firemen. There was a play-reading committee, consisting of J. Augustus Smith, Edna Thomas, Thomas Moseley and DeWitt Spencer, which kept in mind the Harlem audience and favored Negro playwrights; wherever possible, a casting director

LAFAYETTE THEATRE
2225 SEVENTH AVENUE
Phone: TIllinghast 5-1424   New York City

FIRE NOTICE: The exit, indicated by a red light and sign, nearest to the seat you occupy, is the shortest route to the street. In the event of fire or other emergency please do not run—WALK TO THAT EXIT. —JOHN J. McELLIGOTT, *Fire Chief and Commissioner.*

THE NEGRO THEATRE
FEDERAL THEATRE WORKS PROGRESS ADMINISTRATION
HALLIE FLANAGAN - - National Director — PHILIP W. BARBER - - Director for N. Y. C.
Presents
"MACBETH"
BY
WILLIAM SHAKESPEARE
Arranged and Staged by ORSON WELLES
Costumes and Settings by NAT KARSON
Lighting by Feder

The Federal Theatre Project is part of the W.P.A. program. However, the viewpoint expressed in this play is not necessarily that of the W.P.A. or any other agency of the Government

The Negro Theatre is also under the sponsorship of the New York Urban League
STAFF OF THE NEGRO THEATRE

Managing Producer ....John Houseman
Casting Director ....Edward G. Perry
Stage Manager ....Leroy Willis
Assistant Stage Managers............Edward Dudley, Jr. / Earl Shepherd / Jack Murray / Gordon Roberts
Press Representative ....James F. McDougald
Master Electrician ....Byron Webb
Master Carpenter ....James Kinard
Master of Properties ....Fred H. Marshall
Scenic Construction ....Charles White
Wardrobe Department ....Lena Tyers / Anne Gray
Display Department ....Tipp Beavers

CREDITS
Assistant Director ....Thomas Anderson
Musical Arrangements under the direction of Virgil Thomson.
Voodoo Chants and Dances under the direction of Asadata Dafora Horton.
Dances under the direction of Clarence Yates
Chorus under the direction of Leonard de Paur.
Costumes, Painting and Properties executed by the Federal Theatre Workshop.
Building by the Construction Staff of The Negro Theatre.
Masks executed by James Cochran.
The Negro Theatre Orchestra — Under the direction of Joe Jordan.

and a directorial staff. Where necessary, special music was composed by Leonard De-Paur, a musician on the staff. In charge of this production staff was J. Augustus Smith, Negro playwright, producer and actor, assisted by Harry Edwards who handled personnel, promotion and administrative phases of operation.

So ran a report at the end of the second year. No Negro theatre had been organized so well before. The death of the Federal Theatre Project ended the best organized Negro theatre company in history.

Of coordinate importance was the encouragement of Negro playwrights. One critic, writing of Theodore Ward, wrote that the Federal Theatre Project "exactly fulfills the need for which it was created; it has given work and stimulus to a talented youngster who otherwise would have had no job, and if he had had a job, no time to write, and in any case no contact with the theatre. It has given production to a play that would certainly not have been produced commercially." Theodore Ward pays tribute to the Federal Theatre:

> In keeping with its national policy of encouraging the development of the creative talents and abilities of its personnel, it extended to the Negro opportunities such as not even the boldest imagination dared dream previously. At once it supplied an outlet national in scope and scale, while at the same time it guaranteed the security necessary for creative development and work. Unfortunately, this great agency had just begun to assume its real significance in the minds of its Negro members when it was ruthlessly destroyed. ... It was Federal Theatre that proved the open sesame, providing at once a laboratory and the wherewith for creative enterprise. [Although] only a few Negro writers took advantage of Federal Theatre . . . there are those who did seize upon the opportunity to study their craft, and who today demonstrate the skill and proficiency to provide the literature which will serve as a basis for the full flowering of the Negro theatre.

—1940

In Abraham's Bosom, the theatre project of Seattle's Works Progress Administration.

Clarence Winston, Norman Berman and Reo Fitz-
patrick in a Karamu production of Harold Pinter's
The Birthday Party.

Community Ventures

KARAMU
by Arna Bontemps
and Jack Conroy

THE FREE SOUTHERN THEATER:
AN EVALUATION
by Tom Dent

Concert artist and folk singer Raoul Abdul appeared in many Karamu productions. Mr. Abdul frequently returns to Karamu, presenting lieder concerts and his popular program *The Negro Speaks of Rivers*.

At Karamu Theatre, the opening scene of *Cosi Fan Tutte*.

Karamu

by Arna Bontemps and Jack Conroy

THIS IS the story of a good deed shining in a naughty world. When Russell W. Jelliffe was growing up in Mansfield, Ohio, one of the members of the First Congregational Church, which his family attended, was Mrs. Annie Bradford, a Negro woman who occupied a pew directly in front of theirs. To him there was nothing remarkable about Mrs. Bradford's presence there. That much he took for granted. His people had been on the side of freedom for generations. But when the old colored woman died, it was learned that she had provided in her will for the establishment of a library in the church. The books were made available to members of the church, and Russell, to whom books were already beginning to be an important part of life, did not neglect the opportunity to read them.

In those days there was no public library of any sort in the community, but it remained for a Negro member of the church to feel this cultural lack strong enough to do something about it. However, the grateful members soon repaid her thoughtfulness and generosity by hanging a portrait of the late donor near the shelves of books. And the whole experience became one of the sweetest and strongest of the boy's childhood memories. He grew to manhood praising this church member, without reference to her color, because she had been concerned about the intellectual life of her Christian brothers and sisters and had had

the good sense to decide upon books as her contribution toward the improvement of that life.

But another childhood experience left an equally vivid impression on young Jelliffe's mind. He and Boyd Hick, a Negro boy, who happened to be his playmate, presented themselves together for admission to membership in the local Y.M.C.A. When the colored youngster put down his twenty-five-cent fee, the money was refused. When Russell, standing beside his friend, offered his own quarter, it was promptly accepted. The two boys were embarrassed, hurt, confused. No one attempted to explain this incomprehensible act to them.

Both experiences have borne fruit in the adult lives of Russell and Rowena Jelliffe, founders of Cleveland's beloved Karamu House. When these two classmates, who had met as freshmen, became seniors at Oberlin College in 1914, they made up their minds that racial prejudice is "the weakest link in the democratic chain." The next year both of them went to Chicago on scholarships, worked in the slums, at Hull House and other settlements, took masters' degrees, got married, and began casting about for the kind of work into which they could put their hearts.

Rowena Woodham Jelliffe had roots in the Midwest too. Her folks were old Illinois people whose pioneering aim had been to help build a unified nation. Neither they nor she

had thought very much about Negroes one way or another. But a relative of Ernest Hemingway advised the girl's mother to send Rowena to Oberlin, a college to which that branch of the Hemingway family was sentimentally attached. And at Oberlin, where she majored in sociology and psychology, Rowena met Negroes and learned something of their problems.

Without a very definite plan the young couple returned to Cleveland in 1915, at the invitation of the Second Presbyterian Church, and began settlement-house work in a slum neighborhood which was by no means predominantly Negro. They moved into an old frame house that had once been a funeral parlor, made it their home as well as the headquarters of their work, and began a five-year period of experimental study of human personality and the storms and stresses by which it is assailed in a harsh environment. But while they worked and learned, the migration engulfed them.

Thousands of Negroes poured into "the Roaring Third," the community in which the Jelliffes' welfare center was located during those first years. Nearly all of the newcomers were fresh from the South, migrants brought in to work in defense plants and other industrial establishments. And almost immediately the results of bad housing, overcrowding, and inadequate health and recreational facilities began to be noticed: disease and delinquency. With equal swiftness the city as a whole began to mistake effect for cause. The Jelliffes were faced with a problem of analysis and comprehension as well as the responsibility to act in the situation they themselves had elected.

The result was Karamu House and the philosophy which it has come to represent. As the name, a Swahili word, suggests, Karamu thought of itself both as the "center of the community" and a "place of enjoyment." Its "recreational" activities, begun as a side line, became its basic technique. Art, as one observer pointed out, began to wag the welfare. But this was not art with a capital *A*. The Jelliffes observed early in their experience that a certain facility for artistic expression was not at all uncommon among the poor, the lonely, the hurt youngsters who ventured into their center. Indeed, they soon discovered that some of these teenage Negroes, socially repressed and apparently backward, possessed unusual talents. This fact put them on the alert, and they began to note early symptoms of the artistic impulse—careless snatches of song on the playground, pretty flourishes of movement thrown into the games, jigs, struts, and hippety-hops, spontaneous impersonations, casual bits of inspired make-believe, shy attempts to help beautify Karamu's buildings and grounds. This was their lead. They would offer young Negroes an opportunity to liberate themselves, so to speak, through artistic expression. Careers in the arts, fortunately, could be pursued by colored Americans with less opposition than was to be met in most other fields.

Neither of the Jelliffes had special training in any of the arts. They simply worked with the youngsters who came to them and learned as they went along. Their first project in this new area was a children's theater started by Mrs. Jelliffe. The little troupe did so well that older youths and adults began asking for a grown-up company, and soon one was organized. This unit was a lot of fun for the participants from the beginning, but essentially it was just another Little Theater company. Little, if anything, had been added to the stereotype. Then the great Charles Gilpin came to Cleveland to play the title role in Eugene O'Neill's *Emperor Jones*. He attended a performance by the Karamu Players and gave them the suggestion that transformed their group from a carbon copy of every other Little Theater company in the nation to a creative force which has exerted a real influence.

"Look here, you're all wrong," Gilpin said to the group sitting along the apron of the crude stage. "Why don't you take yourselves seriously and really do something? Make this a real Negro theater. You could do it. Look at the material all around you. Learn to see the drama in your own lives, and someday the world will come to see you. If there aren't any plays, get somebody to write them." To show that he was sincere in his criticism, he added, "Here's fifty dollars toward your cause."

This was a blunt and shocking speech, purposely so perhaps, and it came from a disconsolate actor who had suffered his own ups and downs and was even then being criticized for his part in the play which was at last bringing him deserved recognition in the American theater. And the amateurs to whom it was directed were by no means unanimous in approval of the idea. In fact, a serious discussion began after Gilpin left the hall. But after all was said, the actor's suggestion prevailed, and the group decided to make a fresh start along lines which Gilpin had indicated. Their immediate step was to change their name to the Gilpin Players.

Launched on a program of Negro plays, the Karamu group soon discovered that it was *not* following the line of least resistance. Some white people, of course, wanted then—as now—to see the Negro only in ridiculous situations, whether on the stage, screen, or in story. They did not want to be reminded of the essential humanity of colored people, for this throws a burden on the mind and the conscience. Some Negroes resented transcriptions of their lives for very different reasons. They hated to be reminded of their serfdom and their ghetto existence. They especially hated to have these transcriptions exhibited to the world at large, for they feared the world would think Negroes are plantation serfs by choice or that Negroes consent to or approve of the indignities of segregation. The Gilpin

Players had to justify their course in the face of such attitudes. It seemed to them that the right kind of plays—assuming such treatments could be found—would answer everything. The search for scripts became their first enterprise.

The members of the theater group attempted to write plays themselves. Nothing much came of this particular zeal, but their letters to more experienced writers throughout the country did not go unanswered. Their first play was Ridgely Torrence's *Granny Maumee*. Other plays on Negro themes followed. In time the group produced everything written in this field by Torrence and Paul Green and Willis Richardson and Langston Hughes, not to mention works by many less well-known writers.

Meanwhile, they converted an old German saloon into a theater, rebuilding it themselves out of contributed materials, and decorated it with Karamu art work, using an African motif. The research and the creative activity which this involved did worlds of good. It stimulated the art program of Karamu as well as the theater. And it reached a climax when the Gilpin Players raised fifteen hundred dollars, mainly through admissions, toward a fund to purchase specimens of primitive African art to be brought to Karamu House. The African Art Collection has since been given to the Cleveland Museum of Art and to the Cleveland Historical Society. With another three thousand dollars of the company's earnings the Gilpin Players established a scholarship fund at the Cleveland School of Art for Karamu's most promising students. But the important fact was that the Gilpin Players were able to squeeze this kind of money out of their operating budget at all. Charles Gilpin's fifty dollars was the only subsidy they ever received. Thereafter, thanks to his common-sense suggestion, they not only covered all their production expenses but did right by the authors whose plays they used.

When war brought to a temporary halt the activities of the Gilpin Players, the group had already produced one hundred and forty plays, more and more of them having been written especially for a first performance at Karamu. It had given training and experience to more than four hundred actors and stagecrafters. Some of this group had gone on to the professional stage. Many others had found places in colleges and schools and social agencies as teachers and promoters of drama. John Marriott, a Gilpin Players graduate, toured with Tallulah Bankhead in *The Little Foxes*. Frances Williams, another, was in *You Can't Take It With You*. At the same time Edward Tyler, a twenty-year-old baritone, was showing great promise. The Karamu Dancers gave special performances at the 1939 World's Fair in New York, where they were photographed in action by Gjon Mili's speed camera for *Life* magazine. And Langston Hughes, who, as a student at Central High, had come to Karamu to enjoy its facilities while teaching lettering to other youngsters, saw *Mulatto,* one of his plays—first written for the Gilpins—run ten months on Broadway before going on extensive tours. Perhaps these are some of the reasons why the *Theatre Arts Magazine* called the Gilpin Players "the greatest single democratizing force" in their community.

The other art enterprises of Karamu were equally sound, if sometimes less spectacular. Fred Carlo, Elmer Brown, and Zell Ingram were among those who came to the center in short pants. Carlo became the first Negro to make the International Print Show; and Brown, a fugitive from a Mississippi chain gang, became the second. Ingram progressed from puppets to oils and sculpture.

On Karamu's twenty-fifth anniversary the city of Cleveland presented to Russell and Rowena Jelliffe the Charles Eisenman Award, the city's highest civic prize. Dorothy Maynor and Paul Green helped to pay homage to the founders of Karamu over a national broadcast. Said playwright Green: "The Jelliffes are the kind of dreamers who have made America great." And the six hundred Cleveland citizens who came to honor the Jelliffes expressed their approval.

But there were still some Americans who asked, Why an arts program in a settlement house? To them Rowena Jelliffe has replied:

We came upon the Arts Program through a searching for a way by which the Negro could come to feel that his energies headed straight into the main stream of American living. He needed to escape the sense of separateness which is so wasteful to energy and initiative. So much of his living has gone on in the little eddies at the side of the stream. We were looking for a way of challenging and using his best, not his eighth, ninth, or tenth best, but his very best. And it had to be something real enough and challenging enough to make him feel that by use of it he became a participating part of his community.

The field of the arts was the place where prejudice was less of a handicap for the Negro in making his contribution.

The Negro had obvious creative talents, and in the twenties America was just becoming aware of the fact that she hadn't a culture of her own and she decided that she would build one. Obviously, the Negro had much to offer in this structure.

And, too, it was a means of telling his story to America. It is not art for art's sake. It is art as it touches the lives of common people, and becomes a means of telling their sufferings, their joys, their yearnings, their aspirations. We see it as a means of enabling the Negro to tell his story, the truths about his own life. Indeed, we have come, through use of this program, to suspect that art forms may be the only way in which we really tell truths.

His contributions are recognized in this field. He has a sense of bringing something in hand and putting it before his community and saying, "This is mine, I bring this."

And that has become a keynote with us. We come to our community, not with our hand out asking for something, but with a gift in hand.

The Arts Program enables us to be a part of the growing American culture.

Efforts to build and endow a new and greatly expanded Karamu House began when a fire ravaged the original theater in 1939. A nation-wide campaign for a new four-unit plant at East Eighty-ninth Street and Quincy Avenue was undertaken. World War II halted these plans for a time, but a nursery, built in 1945 as a war-emergency child-care center, provided for after-hours youth activities, and in 1947 a temporary arena theater. In 1949 the new Karamu Theater was opened in a building which also provided facilities for other departments. Ten years later long-deferred plans for a Community Service and Music Building reached fulfillment.

When Russell and Rowena Jelliffe retired in 1963, Karamu was operating in a plant that had cost a million and a half dollars. It was debt free and had an endowment of $1,200,000. The annual operating budget was $250,000. Its board consisted of thirty-nine persons, a fair number ... had themselves been products of Karamu's programs. Memberships, about equally divided between the sexes and likewise between children and adults, with a 70–30 ratio of Negroes to whites, had exceeded 4,000. A full-time staff of thirty-four, assisted by eighteen qualified part-time employees, conducted the operation.

On this sad but heart-warming occasion Mrs. Jelliffe reminisced:

> One speaks softly of a thing one loves, and so would I speak of Karamu. We have evolved through the years many programs as a means of reaching our goals. We believe they are good ones. We shall be seeking always to make them better. But I think that, more important to us than our programs, we have evolved a way of life we have found there. We have found a communication between us that bridges differences in background, differences in heritage, differences in social condition, differences in race and religion, to unite us in a concept of man and his function. We have found trust in each other and understanding—and love among us. And this, I think, is Karamu.
>
> We spoke a moment ago of a dream which we, all of us together, have evolved. It has frequently been said of us that Karamu is a dream come true, that the Jelliffes have seen a dream come true. And this is said in all kindness and with a certain tinge of wonder. But I think it must be said that this is not so. Our dream for Karamu, our common dream for Karamu, is not yet come true. Parts of it came to be; fulfillment is there in some degree. But the dream outreaches our achievements; they may outreach our life span. The Karamu dream is fulfilled when every man has the full free right to live out his full potential, undeterred by any other man or group of men.
>
> This night marks the end of our directorship at Karamu, but it marks, too, the beginning of another man's taking into his hands the shuttle for the spinning on the Karamu dream. They are able hands, willing and eager and strong hands, hands you will trust and love.
>
> As we thank you with very full hearts for what you have given to us through a lot of years, we thank you even more for what you will give in future to Olcutt Sanders, our successor.

And Langston Hughes, whose long association with Karamu would make a story in itself, read a poem of tribute he had written for the occasion:

And so the seed
Becomes a flower
And in its hour
Reproduces dreams
And flowers.

And so the root
Becomes a trunk
And then a tree
And seeds of trees
And springtime sap
And summer shade
And autumn leaves
And shape of poems
And dreams—
And more than tree.

—1966

Young playwright Herbert Greggs, a product of Karamu Theatre, is co-author of a musical play, *Ballad of Riverboat Town*, scheduled for Broadway production in 1968.

Larry Barkley and Leonard Parker (bearded) in a Karamu production of *Lost in the Stars*.

The Free Southern Theater: An Evaluation

by Tom Dent

IMAGINE that you are a Negro high school student in Bogalusa, Louisiana. It is late August, a hot, muggy Wednesday night. You are about to watch a play. The play will be performed by the Free Southern Theater, but not tonight from a written script.

The play tonight is about Bogalusa itself. The cast includes not only the members of the FST but some of your classmates, many of whom have participated in protest marches during the summer.

A huge crowd has gathered at the Union Hall despite the heat. It is as if the entire Negro community has come, plus the several CORE workers who have been in town, and others from neighboring towns.

From where you are standing you can see there are as many people outside as inside, even the windows are crowded with eager faces. Outside across the dirt road, the police chief leans against his automobile talking with several of his deputies. The chief is not sure what a play is, but he is present in case any "trouble" develops. Anyway, amidst the excitement no one pays attention to the police. The Deacons for Defense of Equality and Justice are also present. They had escorted the Free Southern Theater without incident from McComb, Mississippi, Monday, and will provide a protective caravan of cars tomorrow morning when the company leaves for New Orleans.

After a brief introduction by Gilbert Moses who explains this will be an improvised play, the scenes begin. The play is about the demonstrations in Bogalusa that summer, about the violence in Bogalusa and the inflexibility of the mayor, his city council and the police in the face of that violence, and about the determination of the Negro citizens to fight back, to fight for their rights, and to take action to insure their safety while protesting for their rights.

The audience responds to the subtleties, humor, truth of every situation as it develops on the makeshift stage. And you too respond though you are not sure this is a great play or that plays should be about something like this. The plays by the Central High School drama club in Bogalusa are certainly not like this. But nevertheless this play is about *your* life, *your* problems, what *you* have been through —and you have heard truths stated tonight which have only been whispered in Bogalusa. And you wished the police chief (who is probably outside wondering what all the shouting, laughter, excitement is about), the mayor, every white person in Bogalusa could be in the Union Hall tonight to see themselves portrayed as they really are.

That such a play did happen in Bogalusa last August to just such a responsive audience is the truest proof of the vitality of the Free Southern Theater.

Several observations can be made from the Bogalusa experience, and the theater's experience after three seasons and two years of existence.

The Free Southern Theater *has* been able to communicate because, first of all, it is theater. Theater has the potential to reach people on several levels: the dramatic, the literary, the visual; through dance, music, costume, ritual—as many forms as the creator can make effective. This has been especially true for FST on tours of small towns like Bogalusa where live theater is new. Last summer FST performed *In White America* in every town. *In White America* is a historically informative, but "speechy" play. Yet audiences could relate to actions, to music, to dialect, to the tone of a scene.

Here is a significant breakthrough toward cultural development of untouched, yet amazingly sophisticated and responsive audiences. For theater, *because* it is such a multi-faceted art, can open the way for other arts to reach these same audiences.

The key to this breakthrough is FST's insistence on not charging admission. Free theater has meant that FST can appear before all classes within the Negro community, all age groups, and those whites who wish to come. Free theater has meant that drama is suddenly more real than "culture," for which Mrs. Beulah Jones must wear her best dress, and from which Mrs. Hattie Jones, who is a domestic, must stay away because she is not "cultured." Free theater means that the kids who may not be able to pay can come. And the kids are the audience and creators of the future.

One valuable function which has developed from FST performances is the addition of clarity to social and cultural issues. The theater received its greatest response last summer from Movement towns like Jackson, Jonesboro and Bogalusa. Art can make possible reflection, evaluation and appreciation of group experience. Certainly plays like *In White America,* Brecht's *The Rifles of Señora Carrar* (a Spanish Civil War play also performed last summer) and the immediate improvisational plays (attempted in Jonesboro, developed in Bogalusa) can throw reflective light on the Movement, help the participants discover what the Movement means or what it should mean. There are other plays which have the same power. There are plays which will come out of our current experience and commitment. An important feature is the discussion of the play between audience and actors after each performance. Sometimes the discussions have been better than the play.

Important, also, is the obvious educational value of performances before audiences which have not associated themselves with the Movement. Or audiences that know nothing of Negro history. At a Catholic school in New Orleans an audience of primarily "Creole" Negroes was exposed to a history of black people in America absolutely foreign to their experience. Several of the teenagers stayed after this performance for the discussion. These youths were completely ignorant of W. E. B. Du Bois, Father Divine—even Booker T. We discussed Du Bois' philosophy of education for Negro youth. The source of Du Bois' conflict with Washington. Who was Father Divine? Marcus Garvey?

All this has fantastic potential for the Negro writer. The Negro writer today as well as yesterday—from Dunbar to LeRoi Jones—writes for a primarily white audience. To say that the Negro writer writes for a white audience does not mean he always writes to *appease* that audience. On the contrary. Today one might say instead that the Negro writer because he lacks a substantial readership among his own people may be forced into bitterness. Forced, because when he writes for a society patterned after and dependent upon the very denial of his humanity it is only natural that he be bitter.

Contrast this increasingly self-defeating situation with that of the Negro jazz musician. The Negro jazz musician creates a music for an audience of and out of the travail, joy, hope of his own people. No matter how inventive his technical development or how suffused in his own vision, he can relate back to something real in people who share his experience and situation. And no matter how commercial he becomes, if he really has something to say he relates to his own audience *first*. This is why Negro jazz musicians dominate American music, and have for some time. Art is not an ivory tower exercise but always, basically, an act of communication. And a subtle, sophisticated, complex creation becomes possible if the creator is assured of the possibility of communication. The first step (for the Negro writer) out of this trap is the development of a responsive audience of his own people.

The irony here is that the Free Southern Theater has received virtually no support from the Negro middle class, financially or otherwise. The support has come from Negroes definitely not middle class, white northern liberals, theater people in northern cities, black and white, and from a handful of people, mostly white, in New Orleans who have involved themselves with the theater since it moved here a year ago.

—1966

Sidney Poitier in
Lilies of the Field.

The Negro Thespian

Abbie Mitchell

The Negro Actor Attempts Legitimate

by Sterling A. Brown

ONE OF the curiosities of the early nineteenth century American stage was the African Company, a group of New York Negroes who in 1821 presented English plays, chiefly Shakespeare, at the African Grove in New York City. Their leader was James Hewlett, who was most famous for his performance of Richard III. The Company was popular and praised by some critics. But there was also much derision from a mob "out for a lark." The Company had to rule that white spectators were to sit in the gallery since they did not know how to behave themselves. Civic authorities frowned on the gathering of so many Negroes and discouraged the plays. The first Negro company, therefore, like almost all of its children, died an early death.

Of the same period was Ira Aldridge, who rose from a carpenter's bench in Maryland to become one of the greatest actors of the early nineteenth century. Like the Negro prizefighters of his time, Aldridge had to go to Europe before his great talents could be recognized. He accompanied the famous Edmund Kean throughout England and the continent. His best liked role was that of Othello to Kean's Iago, but some critics preferred his Shylock. Aldridge played before crowned heads, the King of Prussia conferring upon him the title of chevalier. The French romantics, especially Gautier and Dumas, received him with open arms. Aldridge was well called the "African Roscius"; he was six feet in height with a heavy, well-proportioned frame and a master of the declamatory style of acting. Although the first American Negro to receive international praise in the arts, Ira Aldridge remains more of a "sport" in dramatic history than a representative of the American Negro on the stage.

Nearly a century went by before the Negro actor was accepted on the American stage in legitimate drama. One old trouper, who has had roles in modern plays, recalls the days when a Negro was not allowed to speak a line on the stage, although he might dance or sing a song. The few Negro roles, with one or two exceptions, were played by whites. A relic of that custom is seen in two recent dramas where Eliza in Abbott's adaptation of *Uncle Tom's Cabin,* and the "ingenue" (?) heroine in *Mulatto* were played by white actresses.

Ironically, the first attempts of Negro actors to invade legitimate drama reversed the process. Negroes formed themselves in stock companies to present plays about white characters. In view of the dearth of plays about Negroes—and even those few from the white man's point of view, this should not be surprising. In Harlem two stock companies took over the Lincoln and the Lafayette Theatres.

The Lincoln Stock Company was not so successful as its rival, in spite of Charles Gilpin's membership in the company, but its performance of older Broadway successes was for a time popular to Harlemites. In 1916,

The Theatre Magazine published an article, "A Unique American Playhouse," stating:

> During the past three months, long enough for the success of the undertaking to be firmly established, the Lincoln, catering exclusively to a colored clientele, has housed a stock company composed of Negro players under the direction of Billie Burke, a manager and playwright of long experience. Not merely as an oddity in the history of the stage, but as a factor in broadening the outlook of many hundreds of New York's colored residents the work being accomplished at the New Lincoln merits attention.

Anita Bush, an actress who had played with Williams and Walker, is considered to be one of the moving forces in the development of stock companies among Negroes. Eugene Elmore under whom the Lafayette company was known as the Elite Amusement Corporation was another pioneer. Before long the Elite Amusement Corporation had three stock companies playing at the Lafayette Theatre, at the Howard Theatre in Washington, and in Philadelphia. A. C. Winn, the white director of the Lafayette company, planned a repertory from melodramas and musical comedy to grand opera. This was to be quite an achievement, since most of his actors had been musical comedy and vaudeville stars.

In spite of antagonism that a journalist attributed to Negro social snobs and church folk, the Lafayette Players were well received. *Madame X* was praised as

> the most notable thing in the histrionic art that the race has done since Williams' and Walker's *Abyssinia*, and in theatrical tragedy that the race has done since the days of Ira Aldridge. . . . That these colored stock companies composed for the most part of novice professionals and for the rest of musical comedy vaudevillians could master and portray, week after week, the series of heavy melodramas—with each of which white companies labor throughout seasons—. . . is in itself a great compliment to the latent dramatic talent of the race.

A journalist from Broadway found the company, now known as the Quality Amusement Corporation, thriving after two years.

He was struck by the "cream of colored society," and by the automobiles outside the door, "one of them a limousine." He felt that it was the witchcraft in *Dr. Jekyll and Mr. Hyde* that appealed to the audience, and he was amused at Negroes playing Yankees and Irishmen "with brogues composed equally of Celtic and African accents." But he was surprised at "a theatre of such large dimensions and ornate exterior not devoted to weekly news pictures and flicker vampires." And he praised the seriousness, sincerity and talent of the performers, especially Cleo Desmond, Inez Clough, Clarence Muse, Andrew Bishop, Charles Moore and Tom Brown.

Abbie Mitchell, wife of the Negro musician Will Marion Cook, was singled out for special praise:

> She has had many years experience, having matriculated in the Williams and Walker show and travelled in almost every country in the world, including Scandinavia. Besides English she speaks fluently four languages: French, Italian, German and Hebrew (modern). She used to appear in dramatic playlets at Hammerstein's old Victoria when that theatre was filled with crowds and smoke.

The plays played by this stock company ran the gamut of American subjects, with the striking exception of Negro life. Melodrama was the chief type: *Within the Law, Kick-In, Three Weeks, Damaged Goods, Madame X, Dr. Jekyll and Mr. Hyde, Raffles, Forty-Five Minutes from Broadway* (not in the direction of Harlem, however) were some of these. *The Count of Monte Cristo* was revived. One of the few comedies was *Charley's Aunt*. Comedy was not popular. Negro actors had been known too long as producers of laughter; these actors were intent on producing tears, and gasps and thrills. Dramatic excellence seemed to be in proportion to making your flesh creep.

Toward the end of the life of the Quality Amusement Corporation, Lester Walton, manager of the syndicate, encouraged Negro

playwrights and collected a few "ambitious manuscripts." He also intended to open a school for Negro actors in New York. In the publicity it was called a "little factory to turn out Camilles and Svengalis." A circuit was formed to operate theatres in Chicago, Washington, Pittsburgh, Baltimore, Richmond, Norfolk, Cincinnati, Indianapolis, Louisville and other large cities of the North and South. E. C. Brown, a Negro banker of Philadelphia, headed the syndicate, buying and rebuilding theatres where "race people can be proud and feel at home." But the hopes were unrealized; the venture folded.

The stock companies were really in a blind alley. Confining their attention to melodramas, they were out of the line of dramatic development in America. Their performances revealed that the Negro could perform in the heavy, theatrical manner of Broadway stars. Something of an apprenticeship in acting was given, and yet it is important to note that those who graduated from the Lafayette Players to Broadway or Hollywood—Abbie Mitchell, Edna Thomas, Clarence Muse and Jack Carter—have had to adjust their acting to an entirely different tradition. Negroes were for a time afforded a chance to see legitimate plays. But these were mostly clap-trap, which could not withstand the movies' more exciting rendition of that clap-trap. James Weldon Johnson has praised the stock companies for giving the Negro performer "new freedom and new incentives," proving to be the "exact medium he needed through which to fit himself for the fresh start he was to make." The truth of this is hard to see today. The Negro actor was allowed to do serious roles rather than comic. But the roles were artificial, with no pertinence to his own life. And unfortunately, the Negro audience was led to believe that that which was "foreign," and obviously "play-acting," was the essence of drama; and that that which was "close" was undramatic.

The Negro's groping for the right subject matter was evident in the program of the Ethiopian Art Players, called "the most ambitious attempt Negroes had yet made in the legitimate theatre in New York." This group, organized in Chicago by Raymond O'Neill and Mrs. Sherwood Anderson, presented a jazzed-up version of The Comedy of Errors, Oscar Wilde's Salome and a one-act play of Negro life by Willis Richardson, The Chip Woman's Fortune. Evelyn Preer, one of the outstanding Negro actresses of the time, was praised as Salome. Laura Bowman, Charles Olden and Sidney Kirkpatrick, formerly of the Lafayette Players, likewise received favorable notice.

> Some of the critics said frankly that however well Negroes might play "white" classics like Salome and The Comedy of Errors, it was doubtful if they could be so interesting as they would be in Negro plays, if they could be interesting at all. The Ethiopian Art Players had run up against . . . the paradox which makes it quite seemly for a white person to represent a Negro on the stage, but a violation of some inner code for a Negro to represent a white person.

Alexander Woollcott was one of these critics, saying with point that a Negro Folk Theatre could never expect real recognition until it was able to offer a full program of satisfactory plays of Negro life.

—1940

"Most American performers," James Baldwin says, "seem to find themselves trapped very soon in an 'iron maiden' of mannerisms." He finds this true of Juano Hernandez in Reginald Rose's *Black Monday*. Here, Mr. Hernandez is a hobo in the movie *Hemingway's Adventures of a Young Man*.

James Baldwin on the Negro Actor

by James Baldwin

IT IS A sad fact that I have rarely seen a Negro actor really well used on the American stage or screen, or on television. I am not trying to start an artificial controversy when I say this, for in fact most American performers seem to find themselves trapped very soon in an "iron maiden" of mannerisms.

Somehow, the achieved record falls below the promise. Henry Fonda, for example, is one of the most accomplished actors around, but I find it very difficult to watch him because most of the roles he plays do not seem to me to be worth doing.

Moreover, it would seem to me that his *impulse* as an actor is very truthful; but the roles he plays are not. His physical attributes, and his quality of painful, halting honesty are usually at the mercy of some mediocre playwright's effort to justify the bankruptcy of the American male, e.g., the nebbish with whom he so gallantly struggles in *Two for the Seesaw*.

The point is that one can attend the Broadway theatre, and most of the Off-Broadway theatre all season long without ever being moved, or terrified, or engaged.

The spectacle on the stage does not attempt to recreate our experience—thus helping us to deal with it. The attempt is almost always in the opposite direction: to justify our fantasies, thus locking us within them.

Now, the figure of the Negro is at the very heart of the American confusion. Much of the American confusion, if not most of it, is a direct result of the American effort to avoid dealing with the Negro as a man. The theatre cannot fail to reflect this confusion, with results which are unhealthy for the white actor, and disastrous for the Negro.

The character a white actor is called on to play is usually a wishful fantasy: the person, not as he is, but as he would like to see himself. It need scarcely be said, therefore, that the situations the playwright invents for this person have as their principal intention the support of this fantasy.

The Caine Mutiny Court Martial, A Majority of One, Tea and Sympathy, and *Tall Story* are all utterly untruthful plays. The entire purpose of the prodigies of engineering skill expended on them is to make the false seem true. And this cannot fail, finally, to have a terrible effect on the actor's art, for the depths out of which true inspiration springs are precisely the depths he is forbidden to reach.

I am convinced that this is one of the reasons for the nerve-wracking *busyness* of our stage—"Keep moving, maybe nobody will notice that nothing's happening,"—and the irritating, self-indulgent mannerisms of so many of our actors. In search of a truth which is not in the script, they are reduced to what seem to be psycho-therapeutic exercises.

Listening to actors talk about the means they employ to "justify" this line, or that ac-

tion, is enough to break the heart and set the teeth on edge. Sometimes the actor finds that no amount of skill will "justify" or cover up the hollowness or falsity of what he is called on to do. This is where the director comes in: it would seem that much of his skill involves keeping everything moving at such a clip, and to have so many things happening at once, that the audience will remain, in effect, safely protected from the play.

If this is true for the white actor, it is unimaginably worse for the Negro actor. The characters played by white actors, however untruthful they may essentially be, do depend —indeed, *must* depend—on the accumulation of small, very carefully observed detail. Thus, Chester Morris, playing a thoroughly unreal father, in *Blue Denim,* yet mimics the type so well that it is easy to be misled into believing that you once knew someone like him. But the characters played by Negro actors do not have even this advantage. White people do not know enough about Negro life to know which details to look for, or how to interpret such details as may have been forced on their attention.

To take one of many possible examples: the scene in Reginald Rose's *Black Monday,* in which Juano Hernandez is beaten to death. Hernandez plays a janitor in the Deep South, you will remember, who is opposed to integration. He does not believe—so he informs a marvelously mocking and salty Hilda Simms —in pushing himself in "where he is not wanted." He is also telling this to his twelve-year-old grandson, who is now beginning (somewhat improbably) to wonder if he is as good as white people.

Now, of course, we have all met such janitors and such Negroes. But their tone is very different and their tone betrays what they really feel. However servile they may appear to be, there is always a murderous rage, or a murderous fear, or both, not quite sleeping at the very bottom of their hearts and minds.

The truth is that they do not have any real respect for white people: they despise them and they fear them. They certainly do not trust them. And when such a man confronts his nephew or his grandson, no matter what he says, there cannot fail to be brought alive in him envy and terror and love and hate. He has always hated his condition, even though he feared to change it, even though he may no longer be able to admit it.

If the playwright does not know this, as on the evidence I gather Mr. Rose did not, he cannot draw the character truthfully and the actor who plays him is seriously handicapped.

This shows very painfully in the scene in which Hernandez meets his death. His reaction to the effigy of a hanged Negro, in spite of all Mr. Hernandez's skill, is false. This is not the first time he has seen such an effigy, and if he has been living in that town all his life, it is simply not possible for the white people there to surprise him—at least, they cannot surprise him by being wicked or by being afraid. They have always been that, and he knows that about them, if he knows nothing else. Any Negro, facing, in such a town, three overheated white boys, knows what he is in for.

He can try to outwit, flatter, cajole them, put them at their ease by humiliating himself —though at this point, the spectacle of his humiliation is probably not enough to set them at their ease; or if the chips are really, at last, thank heaven, down, he can resolve to take one of them with him. And even if all the foregoing guesswork is wrong, one thing remains indisputable: once attacked, he would certainly not be trying to get past his attackers in order to go to work. Not on that morning, not in that school, not with death staring at him out of the eyes of three young white men.

All of the training, therefore, all of the skill which Mr. Hernandez has acquired, to say nothing of his talent—for it took a vast amount of talent to bring Lucas, in *Intruder in the Dust,* alive—is here not merely wasted,

which would be bad enough; it is subverted, sabotaged, put at the mercy of a lie; for the well-spring on which the actor must draw, which is his own sense of life, and his own experience, is precisely, here, what Mr. Hernandez cannot use. If he had, it would have torn the scene to pieces, and altered the course of the play. For the play's real intention, after all, is to say something about the integration struggle without saying anything about the root of it.

If you will examine the play carefully, you will find that the only really wicked people in the play are wicked because they are insane. They are covered, therefore, and the crimes of the republic are hidden. If we get rid of all these mad people, the play seems to be saying, "We'll get together and everything will be all right." The realities of economics, sex, politics, and history are thus swept under the rug.

Now the Negro actor, after all, is also a person and was not born two seconds before he enters the casting office. By the time he gets to that office, he has probably been an elevator boy, a cab driver, a dishwasher, a porter, a longshoreman. His blood is already thick with humiliations, and if he has any sense at all, he knows how small are his chances of making it in the theatre. He does a great deal of acting in the casting office, more, probably, than he will ever be allowed to do onstage. And, whatever his training, he is not there to get a role he really wants to play: he is there to get a role which will allow him to be seen.

It is all too likely that he has seen actors inferior to himself in training and talent rise far above him. And now, here he is, once more, facing an essentially ignorant and uncaring white man or woman, who *may* allow him to play a butler or a maid in the show being cast. He dissembles his experience in the office, and he knows that he will probably be lying about it onstage. He also knows why;

it is because nobody wants to know the story. It would upset them. To begin analyzing all of his probable reactions, and the ways in which he reacts against his reactions, would take all of the space of this magazine, and then some. But resentment is compounded by the fact, as a Negro actress once observed to me, that not only does the white world impose the most intolerable conditions on Negro life, they also presume to dictate the mode, manner, terms, and style of one's reactions against these conditions.

Or, as a Negro playwright tells it, explaining how Ketti Frings came to adapt Richard Wright's *Long Dream* for the stage: "She was sitting by this swimming pool, see, and reading this book, and she thought, 'This would make a perfectly *darling* play.'

"So she wrote the first few scenes and called out her Negro butler, chauffeur, and maid, and read it to them and asked, 'Now, isn't that the way you poor, downtrodden, colored people feel about things?' 'Why, yes, Miss Frings,' they answered: and, 'I thought so,' said the playwright—and so we go on. And on and on."

The theatre is perishing for the lack of vitality. Vitality, humanly and artistically speaking, has only one source, and that source is life. Now, the life actually being led on this continent is not the life which we pretend it is. White men are not what they take themselves to be, and Negroes are very different—to say the very least—from the popular image of them.

This image must be cracked, not only if we are to achieve a theatre—for we do not really have a theatre now, only a series of commercial speculations which result in mammoth musicals, and "daring" plays like *Compulsion* and *Inherit the Wind,* which are about as daring as a spayed tom-cat—this image must be cracked if we intend to survive as a nation. The Negro-in-America is increasingly

the central problem in American life, and not merely in social terms, in personal terms as well.

I intend, from time to time, in discussing the theatre, to return to this point, for I think the time has come to begin a bloodless revolution. Only by a more truthful examination of what is really happening here can we realize the real aims of the theatre which are to instruct through terror and pity and delight and love. The only thing we can now do for the "tired business man" is to scare the living daylights out of him.

—1961

Juano Hernandez as the father of
W. C. Handy in the movie *St. Louis Blues*.

The Tattered Queens

by Ruby Dee

WHEN I first learned about the death of Dorothy Dandridge, a tremendous sadness came over me. I'd known her slightly only, really—over the years; our paths had never crossed in work—occasionally socially; but I had seen her, mostly as an actress and remembered with joy her beautiful performance as Carmen in the movie, *Carmen Jones*. I felt I knew her as well as I knew myself . . . What, as a young performer, she aspired to, what she had to settle for—the active search for opportunities, the sporadic success, the long periods of nothing to look forward to, the deliberate pretense of indifference, the deep self-doubt; a major role—then waiting, waiting . . .

She was lucky, for her career as an actress began with a head start as a singer, and between the betweens, she could fill club dates. (How fortunate not to be "Just an actress.")

I wondered if the tragedy of Dorothy was not indeed the tragedy of all Negro actresses.

I worked with an actress once in a huge theatre in the Bronx, in a play—*Arsenic and Old Lace*. I had vaguely known of her. "What style she had," I recall thinking, "what grace." I wondered where she had been trained. There was something about her personality—distinctly royal, profoundly human. She might have played any role from a queen to a peasant, representing any race or country. Her name was Abbie Mitchell. She had worked with some of the leading talents of the early 1900's, she had been acclaimed here, but mostly in Europe, an extraordinary soprano, a *prima donna*. I felt fortunate that our lives had touched. At the time of our meeting I was quite young and coming along well "for a colored girl" at the time. I believe that often young performers lacking a continuity of experience, lacking a knowledge of the history of entertainment, of the tradition and great contribution that our people have made to the theatre, may tend to feel that a whole new world begins with each newcomer. Not so.

Inspired by Abbie Mitchell, I began to read books about and by Negro performers. I am deeply grateful to such people as James Weldon Johnson, Tom Fletcher, and Edith Isaacs for having written on the subject. It was through their books that I began to feel a sense of belonging somewhere as an actress . . . as part of a tradition. I'd almost missed knowing Abbie Mitchell. Where was her scrapbook? Where was there a more complete description of her life? Couldn't my husband, Ossie Davis, write her story as a play? Why didn't I talk to her more, ask her what it is like to reach the top? Is there a top for Negro actresses? Why wasn't she as well known and as frequently employed as the leading white performers of the time? Retired? Why? What would she play next? It was some years later by then. After talking about her, after asking other older performers who "came out of retirement" about her, I finally wrote her asking for an appointment.

Ruby Dee as Katherine in the American Shakespeare Festival Theatre's
1965 production of *The Taming of the Shrew*.

Lena Horne

Dorothy Dandridge

Cicely Tyson

Gloria Foster

Diahann Carroll

Hilda Simms

The letter came back unanswered, unopened. It was marked, "Deceased."

Rose McClendon and the famous walk down those stairs—(even Ethel Barrymore complimented her for it, with kindness that comes only from being white, regularly employed, and nationally recognized)—who was she? Had she worked in more than the half a dozen plays I'd seen referred to? Where was there a record of her accomplishments? I remember tall, sensitive Edna Thomas. Why don't I see her on television sometimes—or Broadway—on or off? Retired now, perhaps; but because she wants to be?

It seems that Negro actresses enjoyed a fuller creative life in the old community theatre: e.g., the all-Negro Lafayette Players. Such actresses as Edna Thomas, Hilda Offley, Evelyn Ellis, and Laura Bowman knew and benefitted from working in stock companies. They had a chance to more fully explore the depths of their talent. They were not primarily restricted to plays about Negroes. One may be extremely talented, *but only constant exposure makes a performer stage-worthy and camera-worthy.* I never heard of a Negro starlet with a seven-year contract, learning the ropes in B movies and studio schools. Quite a few moderately talented white actresses have blossomed into fame and fortune under such attention. What might have happened to Dorothy Dandridge with a seven-year contract? And the security that goes with it?

We actresses are so accustomed to the fact that performers such as Ethel Waters, Lena Horne, Beah Richards, Pauline Myers, Jane White, Hilda Simms, and Claudia McNeil have no part in television, or work regularly in stock, that we stop trying. We hear talk of integration and things getting better, and indeed there are some marvelous integrated commercials, and more Negro actors appearing in incidental parts, and every now and then racially mixed leads, and an occasional all-Negro show, but these are isolated instances, not a trend indicating that things may be somewhat better in an individual sense. Group participation in the creative life of the country is less than ever.

We cannot grow in isolation. The Negro actress is still acting on the fringes, not really a part, only occasionally let in, better off portraying the prostitute, the second—roles written with not enough imagination and truth. We can point to no one of us who has the remotest chance of reaching the prominence of Helen Hayes, Ethel Barrymore, Bette Davis, etc. No one with that kind of economic opportunity either. We dream, we scream, we pretend, we picket. Or like some other of our most gifted—Mildred Joan Smith, Muriel Smith, Marian Douglas—we quit. Will the newer names on the horizon—like Cicely Tyson and Diana Sands and Gloria Foster—escape the paucity of opportunity that always seems to follow occasional spurts of comparative good fortune for "colored stars"?

When we talk or write about ourselves and our place in American society so much is necessarily a lament. But perhaps a look at stark reality may help clarify and make objective our grievances, indicate alternatives to despair through some program of action. I fully realize the cultural poverty that is abroad in the land. Leading white actresses are afflicted by some of the same ills that affect the Negro actress. (Their lowest level of employment is, however, often commensurate with our highest.) There are many more parts written for men than women, white and black. But my concern here is with the Negro actress, who faces double discrimination—that of sex and that of race. What must we do—we Negro actresses—to be saved?

We must, most certainly, make a determined effort to encourage our playwrights—particularly female—to write for all media. There is a kind of autocracy about an enter-

tainer—each one sort of spinning around in a personal orbit, on individual momentum. I maintain that we actresses must concern ourselves more with the fate of each other, and of the younger actresses coming along, by helping to find material and getting it produced, by promoting scholarships for intensive training. We must also see to it that the new theatres springing up over the country include Negro actors as basic and intrinsic parts of their companies. Indeed, the future of the theatre may lie in repertory companies, and on the road.

In the past, musicians—singers and instrumentalists—fared better in relation to their art than we have. They have been for the most part innovators and pace-setters. (Top money and opportunity, however, still go to their white imitators.) Innovators in song, dance, and language. Theirs is a development springing from the soul roots of our people. But that same "soul roots" truth of the lives of our people has yet to be explored in drama. We know best on stage and screen the prostitute. The Negro Maid (as a person rather than a stereotype), the Negro Mother, the Average Woman, and the Middle-Class Woman have for the most part yet to be dealt with in depth.

This holds true of the heroines of our history also. We must ask our playwrights to do better by us. We do have, as a people, an address to life, a cry, a joy, that is particularly ours, that has yet to be fully and unselfconsciously put forward. Women must become producers—pioneering and prospecting among our own for backing. (I am particularly gratified at the work done in this connection by Maria Cole and Juanita Poitier.) We must see to it that our young people consider the very important backstage and off-camera roles as technicians. More

people see films than ever go to the theatre. If one of the purposes of art is to effect change, we must make every effort to become proficient in every phase of film making, working for inclusion in American films at every possible level. The reality is that we are but 10 per cent of a population which is geared to segregate and to discriminate—improving, I believe, but desperately in need of artistic effort to help change the image of the Negro and so effect social change more quickly. As art not only reflects life but also influences it, we must dedicate ourselves to the improvement of life and its truths—about women, about Negroes.

The Negro actress cannot afford to be isolated from this effort. We must not evade the fact that in today's America most Negro "stars" are at best tattered queens, haunted always by an aura of tragedy, failure, and defeat. But we must not be defeated. With a sober look at what is happening with us today, we must make every effort to make things better for those who will come after us.

And I would especially encourage those young women of my race most likely to be overlooked—the very black, the very Africanesque—to study and to work. I believe they have shied away from theatre because their particular kind of beauty has not only not been encouraged, but has been heretofore too often rejected. But how else can a people know its own beauty except that those artists most representative of it come forth and tell it? The fair-skinned, those nearer to Caucasian in appearance and manners, have always fared better in our theatre. But are we not, basically, of African descent? In the better times to come, there will be equal place on our stage and screens for all shades, all types, all colors. We must see to it that this is so.

—1966

As co-chairman of the Committee for the Employment of the Negro Performer, Godfrey Cambridge declared that "Madison Avenue wants to maintain the solemnity and equanimity of the American home. . . . Madison Avenue tells us that *we have to wait till 'the grassroots image' changes* before integrating the shows."

The Negro Actor

by Ray Rogers

NEGROES function quite well as attorneys in a court of law; we see them patrolling a beat and directing traffic in all-white communities; we see them tending the sick; we come upon them more often than not operating elevators; they are virtually everywhere except when we flip on our television sets, or when we attend the theatre and the movies—except when the subject matter pertains to "the problem." For decades, Hollywood consistently managed to integrate its prison sequences with black convicts but never a prison guard.

This means that 13,000 colored card-carrying Actors Equity members in the United States are forced to stand on the sidelines, waiting for the paltry few "black plums" such as *A Raisin in the Sun* and *Porgy and Bess.* If not the "plums," there are the "traditional roles" of maid, butler, African-native-in-loincloth, singer and dancer.

The Negro has been a solid fixture in the American theater since the days of the black Shakespearean actor, Ira Aldridge, more than a hundred years ago. Later on, there were Paul Robeson and Canada Lee, and presently Diahann Carroll and Sidney Poitier—and this is a mere fraction of the Negro talent that exists.

Sometime ago you may have seen the likes of Sidney Chaplin, Oscar Brown, Jr., Charlie Mingus, Max Roach, Ruby Dee, Ossie Davis, and others holding aloft placards which said:

"How to Succeed in Show Business—Be White." "Producers Portray an All-White America—Please Do Not Patronize." The Congress of Racial Equality and the newly formed Committee for the Employment of the Negro Performer sponsored these picket lines jointly.

Mr. Charles Gordone, co-chairman of the Committee for the Employment of the Negro Performer, said that all he hoped to accomplish with these picket lines was a conference with producers. He said, "The Negro is like a lion in the streets because this situation has been allowed to exist for too long."

The moguls of the entertainment industry argue quite seriously that the Negro is a "protest image" and his appearance in a non-Negro theme would confuse the American audience. Madison Avenue backs this up with its mountain of surveys which are supposed to show "the grassroots image of America."

According to co-chairman, actor Godfrey Cambridge, "Madison Avenue wants to maintain the solemnity and equanimity of the American home. The advertising agencies feel that if they attempt to awaken the American people from their semi-comatose state they won't buy more breakfast foods and automobiles when they see a black cop collaring a white villain on their favorite television drama. Madison Avenue tells us that

we have to wait till 'the grassroots image' changes before integrating the shows."

Messrs. Gordone and Cambridge's personal experiences are vivid illustrations of the situation of the Negro actor. Mr. Cambridge is a taxicab driver when he's not appearing anywhere. Not too long ago, while he was appearing in *The Blacks* off-Broadway, he was offered a role in Ossie Davis' *Purlie Victorious.* After it closed recently he returned to *The Blacks* through a prior arrangement—a cycle of "plums" in order to keep "his hand in." Mr. Gordone is a director and a formidable actor. He also appeared in *The Blacks* for a time, then he left to make some revisions on a play that he and his wife were interested in producing. Mr. Gordone can recall, when he was a director, he saw a young white stage manager whom he had hired advanced to the position of director with a television station, a position which Mr. Gordone had applied for earlier.

One Negro actor, P. J. Sidney, led a group of actors in picketing the offices of television producer David Susskind since there were no Negroes in his "portrayal of the American Scene."

Mr. Susskind was properly aroused and invited Mr. Sidney to his offices where a conference was held with a representative of television's "Armstrong Theater," producer Robert Costello. Mr. Sidney promised to withdraw his pickets after he elicited a promise from Messrs. Susskind and Costello that "an earnest effort would be made" to present Negroes consistently with their role in the community. Later Susskind dismissed Sidney's charges as "without merit whatever," but he managed to promise nevertheless to be "more conscientious than before."

Mr. Sidney continued over to the offices of The Theatre Guild where he and the group of actor-pickets made their presence felt. Mr. George Kondolf, a Guild executive, said, "We weren't conscious of the fact that we had not been using Negroes properly, in Mr. Sidney's terms." He added that "the Guild will give the situation greater attention in the future." Armina Marshall, Guild head, cited a long record of Guild productions using Negroes, "going back to *Porgy and Bess,*" then she characterized the charges as a "kind of shock."

Recently the press broke its long silence over this condition. The *New York Times* reported that the new chairman of the State Commission for Human Rights (formerly the State Commission Against Discrimination), George H. Fowler, a Negro, resoundingly criticized the television and movie industry for not presenting a true picture of the Negro on the American scene.

Mr. Fowler said, just days after his appointment by Gov. Nelson Rockefeller, "the Negro image is still being maintained in stereotyped roles that do not show realistically his image as an American citizen. The progress that we have made in this whole field of human relations is not being adequately portrayed by the communications media," Mr. Fowler said. "We don't need to propagandize, but we should not sell ourselves short either. Television," Mr. Fowler concluded, "radio and other communications play an important role in the education of our citizens and the commission is concerned that they properly educate the people."

Some producers have utilized Negro actors in their shows. Others have even gone so far as to publicly scoff at the "protest image" argument of Madison Avenue and have sincerely attempted to integrate their shows. The artistic director of the Drama and Light Opera Companies of the City Center signed an agreement reaffirming its past policy of ensuring the use of Negro actors, dancers and singers in all types of roles. Miss Jean Dalrymple, the director, signed a producers agreement with CORE.

CORE stated that this agreement was "a first major breakthrough." CORE added that the City Center will present an integrated *Fiorello*. When this musical was done on Broadway, Negro performers were excluded —an aspersion upon the memory of New York City's greatest and most popular mayor.

On March 24th, CENP called a mass meeting at the Judson Memorial Church in Greenwich Village. This small community church was packed beyond capacity with musicians, actors, actresses, designers, playwrights, writers, along with representatives of the NAACP and CORE. One young Negro composer who drives a taxi while he awaits his "big opportunity" parked his cab outside the church while he attended the mass meeting.

Before this meeting ended at almost 4 A.M., an eloquent and persuasive resolution was drafted:

> The world moves fast, slow, swift-still, but moves! But our theatrical entrepreneurs remain steadfast in their lonely prehistoric silence, often mumbling phrases that the Negro performer can't play a doctor in an all-white video drama, can't play an elevator operator in the garment district, and walks home when the buses of New York are on strike for it has been verified on the Broadway stage that he doesn't ride subways. They inevitably suggest that he return to the long deathwatch between *Porgy and Bess* and *A Raisin in the Sun*. So be it, that we, as actors, actresses, directors, singers, dancers, other professional and lay people, declare that we have no intention of waiting any longer and hereby resolve with honor, grace and care, to actively and spiritually support the Committee ... in its efforts to effect a qualitative and quantitative change in the practices of hiring Negroes on and off-Broadway and in the television and motion pictures industry by direct action and such methods and techniques which will lead to a positive change based on education, imagination and negotiation with all parties involved.

—1962

The Blacks, in which such performers as Ethel Ayler (above) were featured, ran for over three years Off-Broadway. Some of its actors were able to keep "their hand in" by taking roles in other productions and returning later to star again in *The Blacks*.

Problems Facing Negro Actors

by Woodie King, Jr.

THE PROBLEMS of the Negro actor are not so much the Negro actor's problem as they are the white American problem. When an American Negro actor is faced with playing a character, he must also confront a trio of problems: First, should the character be American in its truest sense? (When American life is most American it is apt to be most theatrical, says Ralph Ellison.) Second, should he be Negro as Negroes really are or Negro as we have led whites to believe we are in order to endure? And third, should the character be American Negro? (The peculiar sensation—double-consciousness—an American, a Negro: W. E. B. Du Bois.) These problems are not easily solved since White America has already told us what the answers are going to be if we intend to act on *its* stage.

An old Negro actor told me he hated LeRoi Jones' two plays *The Slave* and *The Toilet* because they were too filled with protest. His student, a young beginner, agreed with him even to the point of accusing the plays of being vulgar. The strange thing was that the beginner had no idea of the kind of plays or the problems the old actor faced during the Thirties and Forties, no idea of the vast history of his craft. (I will get back to this a little later.) It was a strange conversation— the old actor putting down Jones for protest writing and at the same time telling me:

> Acting in the Thirties had life, vitality . . .
> Federal Theatre . . . Negro *Macbeth* . . .

> *Roll, Sweet Chariot . . . Run, Little Chillun.*
> And the actors! Leigh Whipper, Edna Thomas
> . . . son, you ought a' been there!

BEGINNERS

Interested beginners view bad road companies, inexperienced stock companies and . . . community food digesters. These prospective actors watch plays and actors that say absolutely nothing. The parts the actors play are not worth the time and efforts put into them. Beginners watch plays that do not attempt to recreate our experiences; they watch "cute" white plays because that is all White America wants.

A Negro actor can sometimes be found in these "cute" little comedies—*Anniversary Waltz, Come Blow Your Horn, Enter Laughing, Kiss and Tell,* or something similar. His first lines set the Negro beginner's teeth on edge. The embarrassed prospective actor glances about the white theatre. All the white faces are laughing at the excessive and ridiculous mannerisms the white director has given the Negro actor. If he makes it, the beginner is thinking, this must not happen to him. He must do exactly as the white actors else the audience will laugh at him simply for being a Negro on the stage, too. But the beginner doesn't know that white people, in general, don't know enough about Negro life to know which details to look for, how to absorb the interpretation the Negro actor wants to present.

After reading more plays and "how to act" books, he assumes that he is ready to be Henry Fonda, Marlon Brando, Sidney Poitier, Cary Grant, Sir Laurence Olivier, etc. He scouts until he finds a white theatre group needing a flat painter, carpenter, coffee boy, etc. However, before he can get this job, he must be able to intellectually discuss Sartre, Albee, Pinter, Ionesco, Beckett, Brecht, and Stanislavski.

He can name a hundred white actors, but he can't name five Negro actors. This is a sad fact. Recently, I talked to a young actress who is paying a great deal of money for acting and singing lessons. She had never heard of W. C. Handy or Charlie Parker! And knew absolutely nothing about the history of the Negro theatre. Yet the beginner can tell one everything—after two months with the white group—about the white theatre; he will argue about staging a play, about what a writer means, about the way he would tackle a role if he ever played one.

Finally, the little social group will do a little comedy and the Negro beginner will be given a cute little "buddy" part. And the white audiences will laugh at him exactly as they had done at the plays he had watched that featured professional Negro actors.

The beginner will eventually learn the truth about all the little social groups. He will begin to doubt when white beginners continue to get leading roles, no matter how bad they are, while he paints sets and occasionally is rewarded with a walk-on or a "buddy" part. Or perhaps it will be while reading J. Marriot's massive book on the theatre in which the author warns beginners (whites) against getting *with those little groups and working like a nigger* forever. He learns after about two years of hard labor that Sartre and Beckett are only talk with these little groups. And that they had no intention of using him except as comic relief.

UNIVERSITY THEATRE

The Negro actor enrolls, believing he will appear in the plays because he will be a student paying tuition to learn all phases of the theatre. However, he will not be taught all phases of theatre at a university, least of all acting. Again he is left out because the selections are mostly classics or some other form of archaic theatre that was written when the black man did not figure into the scheme of White America. And we know that the professors who select the plays are white, therefore personal idiosyncrasies enter into the problem. And they keep the Negro actor from the stage. The basic motive is simply resentment towards miscegenation on the American stage in general and the university stage in particular. America doesn't want the Negro actor to be a man on its stage.

And since the basic themes of American plays revolve around sex, the Negro actor's situation is tragic. The student obtains nothing at all. How can he when the acted-out play on stage before an audience is the basic dynamics of such a study? The true understanding of acting comes when the student is involved in acting and producing before a live audience. And the professors prevent this by selecting classics in which the Negro finds difficulty in acting, not to mention the difficulty of being cast.

> I can't use you in this one Mr. ————. It's a Swedish (or Russian, Norwegian, French, etc.) play.

The majority of Negro actors who seek training in university theatre have traces of the southern dialect if they have not assimilated. And the way American education is today, one cannot have any traces of the South in speech. It is an awful but true fact. What, then, if the student actor is cast because of necessity in *Three Sisters, Enemy of the People, Antigone, St. Joan, Major Barbara* . . .? Can he be convincing in such a

dated repertory that was written when he did not figure into the scheme of things?

A drama department must seek "truths" in theatrical works. Many professors keep these "truths" in mind when casting, and very often avoid the Negro actor. The Negro actor cannot bring "truth" (as whites see it) to the classics.

However, a university will—if the National Association for the Advancement of Colored People complains—present *Emperor Jones* or *Othello*. And *maybe* the *Merchant of Venice* after consulting the local synagogue. But a Negro actor cannot look forward to playing a lead character in a university theatre production. After graduating, he knows nothing about acting before an audience.

ITEM: I compared the average ratio of plays a Negro actor appeared in per season to the average number a white actor appeared in per season at Wayne State University in Detroit. I also compared the total number of plays of Negro graduates against white graduates' plays. The ratio was 17–1.

DRAMA SCHOOL

The only place to obtain acting experience is the drama school. The Negro actor either goes to a theatre magazine or obtains information from a friend in the theatre, both stressing how great the instructor is at teaching Mr. Stanislavski's method. The actor finds his past acting experience brushed aside by the teacher. He is immediately tossed into a beginners' class. If he is above average (better than every white actor in the class) he will work with some "name professionals." If not, he will work with a teacher who has no knowledge at all about the Negro, and very little about acting.

The teacher knows that established names are impressive to the new actor. He will occasionally mention the times he worked with Jessie Bonstelle, Poitier, Fiske, Modjeska,

Brando or even Beaumont and Fletcher (not necessarily in this order.) Yet the drama schools, with all their faults, are the only places where a Negro actor can sharpen his craft. This, of course, is because he actually works on a stage with others before a live audience.

Now, after a long and arduous journey, the young Negro aspirant becomes a professional actor. Some use the achievements of the past to guide their future. I said earlier I would get back to this. Now it is fine to be of the present; no one would knock this; but when a performer knows absolutely nothing of the history of his profession, how can he possibly understand the present? The most proficient actors in the business—James Earl Jones, Robert Hooks, Al Freeman, Jr., Diana Sands, Cliff Frazier, Brock Peters, Ivan Dixon, Abby Lincoln, Gloria Foster, Clarence Williams, III, Roscoe Lee Browne—know the past, present, and have ideas of some of the future problems they will encounter.

The photos by Carl Van Vechten and Vandamm of the late Charles Gilpin, Rose McClendon, Canada Lee, Frank Wilson, Jack Carter, Edna Thomas, Abbie Mitchell, and Fredi Washington are the perfect examples of the glory of the past. They were the actors who brought forth to America the famous all-Negro productions of *Macbeth, Porgy, Haiti,* and other exciting plays via the Federal Theatre Project. It grew out of Harlem, and it remains to this day an important contribution to the American stage. I think it is because those actors had a purpose. So many of today's actors lack purpose and direction. How can one grasp for something when there is nothing to grasp? Shout in rage, if not really angry? And, too, one cannot communicate and assimilate at the same time.

ITEM: In the midst of the present racial struggle in this country, our stage ignores it. It treats it as if it doesn't exist.

NEGRO PLAYWRIGHT

The Negro actor's situation can be bettered by (1) joining with Negro writers and (2) building an audience within the Negro community. I think this has been done with great results in Detroit at the Concept-East Theatre and in Harlem with LeRoi Jones' Black Arts Theatre. Both actor and playwright must be willing to experiment with new forms within their respective crafts. If this is done, the small churches and corner store-fronts will be filled with willing ears. And it can be done since there is no one to answer to but each other. It worked in Harlem with the American Negro Theatre; they produced Phillip Yordan's *Anna Lucasta* with great results. It produced worthy plays by Negro writers: Abram Hill's *On Striver's Row,* and early plays by young Ossie Davis. And 20 years later Mr. Davis hit Broadway with his romping comedy, *Purlie Victorious.* Now Ossie Davis is an experienced writer; not one of the typical "library writers" (Clifford Odets) but one who has the background in acting and directing within a Negro community.

And if we do not know yet that a play about Negroes must appeal to Negroes, we should leave the theatre. I do not mean they must love or hate it. But they must *identify* with it.

The playwright must seize new ideas and techniques if the Negro actor is to again be of any importance. He must disregard the argument he received in college—an argument for a standardization which is paradoxically strangling the actor's contribution.

ITEM: The plays of the early Abbey Theatre in Dublin were not considered excellent unless they caused a riot. The theatre, as it is today, without controversy and excitement (save LeRoi Jones), is dead theatre. It is a place to go to and digest dinner.

The Negro playwright should write about what he understands. All around him, he can see what happens when white writers pen Negro "struggle situations." They all fail due to a lack of understanding of the subject.

.   .   .   .

The same thing happened when Baldwin wrote *Blues for Mr. Charlie.* All his white characters were badly drawn; and many thought this would have been impossible for Baldwin to do, since it is he who stresses always that *Negroes know more about whites than whites know of themselves. Negroes have been taking care of their children and kitchens for over 300 years.*

I also think that more Negro novelists should write for the theatre. If plays are to be made from *The Long Dream, The Cool World, Mandingo,* etc., then it should be John O. Killens, Ronald Fair, William Melvin Kelley, Chester Himes or some Negro writer doing the adapting. And even though Baldwin failed with his white characters, his Negro characters are so real and vivid that one is held spellbound by them.

Let me say this in conclusion: If the Negro actor can impose his own values upon the American stage, namely, his past, present, and possible future, he can join with White America in controlling it.

—1966

Young Actor on the Way Up

by Robert Burg

ALMOST everyone in the western hemisphere has heard of Sir Laurence Olivier, the great English actor who has starred in the theater and on motion picture screens. But who, pray tell, is James Earl Jones?

The two names—one so famous, the other practically unknown—came into juxtaposition last year when *Life* magazine ran a review of an Off-Broadway production of *Othello* which featured Jones in the title role. Coincidently, Sir Laurence was playing the same part in a British revival of the ancient play. *Life's* reviewer compared the acting styles of the two men and concluded that Jones more than held his own with his completely individual, completely absorbing portrayal of the Moor of Venice.

In one respect, at least, Sir Laurence was laboring under a handicap which several earlier critics had pointed out: being white, he had to resort to some rather eye-stopping (and, from the critics' point of view, distracting) black-face make-up to more properly assume the role of Othello, who was a Negro. Jones had no such problem—he *is* a Negro.

James Earl Jones is 34 years old, is a little on the heavy side (although he's tall, which compensates for this), and has what many theatergoers and reviewers acknowledge to be a most incredibly striking face, one that is massive and almost biblical in appearance because of the thick, bushy beard that curves around it. Thick black eyebrows top off this imposing combination of facial features and lend to Jones an air of intensity that is just right for the Moor of Venice. He is a bachelor who lives in a messy two-room flat in New York's Lower East Side, and his one interest appears to be acting. Indeed, this young man seems to eat, sleep and live acting and it is possible, just possible, that someday his name may be as well-known as Sir Laurence Olivier's.

At the present, however, Jones is just one of several dozen very talented actors who are little-known in the New York theater world, bobbing about in low-budget productions and waiting to be noticed by top producers. Unlike his struggling colleagues, though, Jones is more than satisfied to be where he is at this particular point in time. In a profession famous for its "stars," this is one man who is seriously pursuing his career by acting and studying, and who professes that he is totally uninterested in the tinsel glamour that accompanies the Hollywood brand of stardom.

A glance at his theatrical record reveals the deliberateness and purpose that mark his budding career; he has had a string of roles which, taken together, comprise a fine apprenticeship in the theater. He has run the gamut from comic roles such as the whimsical cannibal hired to eat the hero's mother-in-law in *The Love Nest,* to more serious portrayals such as the dignified Prince of Morocco in *The Merchant of Venice* and the older brother in *The Cool World,* which played

briefly on Broadway before being made into a film. Yet, despite these and many other parts, Jones is in no hurry to "make a name" for himself. Each week he takes the subway to the Actors Studio to sit in as an observer on study and criticism sessions, and on Monday, his day off from the theater, he is usually in the audience of current plays, looking, analyzing, and even enjoying.

Despite all of this activity and experience, this tall, handsome actor still must face the obvious question of just how far a serious, dedicated Negro can go in the American theater. Below the "star" level of people like Sidney Poitier and Lena Horne and Sammy Davis, Jr., there are dozens, perhaps even a few hundred Negroes in show business who exist in a large gray area where nothing ever seems to happen beyond a hardly noticeable role in an occasional play or film. Is it possible to break out of this area to bigger and better parts?

Jones refuses, however, to view the theater strictly from the viewpoint of being a Negro. "Opportunities for actors in general could be better," he says—and means it.

This is not to say that Jones is completely unaware of the color of his skin. Far from it. There are always little incidents that serve to remind him that he is a Negro. A few years ago, for example, he was playing the part of the bombardier in the motion picture, *Dr. Strangelove*. In the tense, climactic scene in which the American plane is rocked by a Soviet Missile, Jones was being carefully instructed by the director, Stanley Kubrick. Kubrick told him to look upward in fright at the moment of the explosion. "With the camera very low looking up at me," Jones recalls, "I thought to myself, 'Sonofabitch, this guy wants me to roll my eyes.' If it wasn't Kubrick, I would've said, 'Are you trying to get a Stepin Fetchit effect or something?' Actually, I think he almost wanted that effect. He wanted simply to suggest it, to awaken in

the observer's mind the particular image of the Negro in trouble."

An even more subtle complication of his being a Negro as it relates to the theater is that Jones's skin is of a medium shade and his nose is slim and conservative in appearance. Thus, when he comes on stage, the audience—while naturally recognizing him as a Negro—may find itself more readily able to identify with him than with a darker-skinned actor. The writer of a play in which he was understudy to the lead once approached him and told him, "Jimmy, I think that if you were out there the audience might identify better with the character." The actor in the lead, naturally, was several shades darker than Jones.

While he may have his sensitivities about being Negro, there is no question that Jones is proud of what he is. "I don't want to go on stage and eliminate my negritude," he says flatly. "I think there's something so exciting about being what you are, whether it's being seven feet tall or black or blonde, that you shouldn't want to disguise it or pretend it isn't there."

Many white liberals who have applauded the recent trend toward casting Negroes in parts that would normally go to white actors or actresses (such as Ruby Dee playing Cordelia in *King Lear*) will be drawn up short by Jones's attitude toward this development. He does not want to be so "integrated" into a play as to lose his identity as a Negro. Jones definitely wants parts that are meant to be played by Negroes only. He has set up an inflexible condition that an audience must recognize him for what he is—a black man. And then it must accept him this way. He is interested in exploring and developing his blackness and in using it unashamedly in the theater. "I've always wanted to play Mephistopheles and emphasize all of his black aspects," he says.

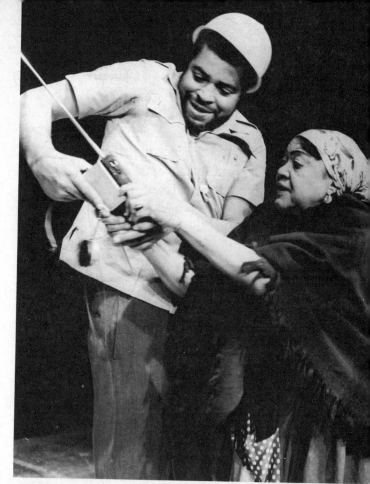

James Earl Jones, as a construction worker in *Bohikee Creek,* with Georgia Burke.

James Earl Jones as the darker brother in the Off-Broadway hit *The Blood Knot* (above and below); J. D. Cannon as the lighter brother, in this imported South African drama of racial conflict within a family.

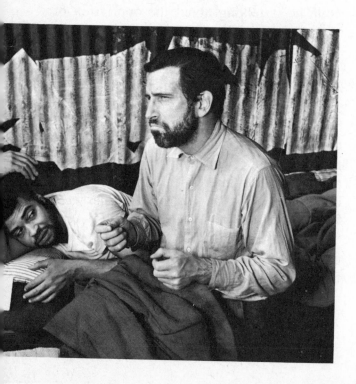

Ellen Holly and Jones as the lovers in Errol John's *Moon on a Rainbow Shawl.*

For all of these conditions and demands on an audience, Jones is resigned—at least for the present—to the fact that it takes theatergoers a few minutes to get used to him as a Negro before it can accept him as a character in the play. "They never really identify," he says. "But they come much closer to it the deeper into the character I get as an actor. I found that people cry watching Othello in the moment of his agony, and at that moment they necessarily have to forget what he is. Even Bull Connor would cry watching Othello, in spite of himself. It's that deep psychic defense that people have that's a hard thing to crack. It keeps them from accepting Negroes in certain capacities."

To illustrate what he means, Jones summons up the story of the time he was sitting in a movie theater watching a newsreel about the Korean War. When a scene flashed on the screen showing American soldiers, both white and black, in action together, a woman sitting nearby Jones suddenly jumped up and said in very shocked tones to her companion, "They don't have Negroes in the front lines!"

One need go no further than the television set to see this kind of mentality in action, Jones believes. He points out that TV commercials are a field that is now opening up to Negro actors—if they are the right shade. "They're trying to do token integration," he asserts. "Take a soap commercial. Let's say it's important for the producers to show a Negro woman using Smith's Soapflakes. Well, it's almost as important not to have her so specifically Negro that anyone couldn't identify with her. You recognize the shade and that's the token."

As a Negro in a profession that makes strenuous physical and mental demands on those who pursue it, Jones has more than once been confronted with the conflict of making a choice of which comes first—civil rights or art. Occasionally he is able to successfully combine one with the other, as when he participated in a taped television program about the three civil rights workers who were murdered in Mississippi not long ago. It was during this taping that he was confronted with yet another manifestation of the same basic dilemma. One of the men in the television studio who had been working with the Student Non-violent Coordinating Committee approached him and tried to talk him into going into the South and working for civil rights there. Jones reluctantly turned him down.

"I think if I went down there," he says, "I would have to devote myself to it totally, and if I did that I don't think I would take the choice that James Forman or Martin Luther King takes. I think I would take the choice of Malcolm X to cope with that situation. There is need for that kind of pressure rather than the moral pressure, because morality is long gone. The more militant black leaders who say that the solution is economics in the North and force in the South are right. I mean for now. Maybe some day morality will be the solution. I don't know."

The curious thing about Jones is that even while he is talking about the oppression of Negroes in America, there is no bitterness in his voice. It is as if he were talking about oppressors he has heard about but never met. Almost in the same breath he will say, "I don't know what Christ was talking about, but he was onto something." His conviction that Malcolm X had the right approach to the race conflict may even be somewhat explained by his interest in the assassinated black nationalist as a dramatic character. "I'd like to perform Malcolm X," he says. "I'd like to explore with an audience and a director and other actors that phenomenon that was called Malcolm X."

This last statement isn't surprising when you understand that Jones looks on the theater as a pressure chamber, where invisible forces froth and boil over. Indeed, it is pos-

sible that for him, as for other dedicated actors, an understanding of life is acquired on the stage in that electric moment when there is that unity of spirit and concentration between actor and audience, in that moment when the spark of life leaps from a script. Jones says that he cannot go onto the stage to pretend to be someone he's not. At the same time, he may often go before an audience and discover in the character something of himself which, until that moment, lay below the threshold of his awareness.

Apart from these abstractions of exploration and discovery, Jones is concerned with the more down-to-earth techniques and tools of his profession. He is a hard worker; for his role in *Othello* he steeped himself in the maze of theories hypothesized by Shakespearean scholars to explain the personality of the dark-skinned general.

Jones has learned that an actor's concentration can be one of his most useful tools. "Gene Frankel [a New York director and drama teacher] taught me that," he says. "Concentration on what you're doing on stage, on your part, is largely responsible for involving your audience. You can even be doing bad work, but if your concentration is strong enough, they'll watch your bad work rather than their dates or the people in the next row. I can sense their involvement when my own involvement in the part is strong enough. If I'm too busy watching to see if I've got them, I don't get them. It's like Zen. It's a yoga of acting: you do it and then you know it. It's a matter of total commitment."

Along with these techniques, Jones has also developed a philosophical attitude toward assessing the value of his own work which other actors might envy. "There are neither successes nor failures," he says. "I think I've committed myself as best I could to everything I've done. If an artist looks at himself objectively, he won't see himself in terms of 'success' or 'failure.' That's usually for somebody else's judgment."

Jones's ambition is to be a great actor, that is, to be able to play a particular role better than anyone else who had the same kind of talents and skills.

In an off-moment once, Jones admitted, "My life is sort of funny in a way. I go around as if the sky could fall in on me at any moment—although so far it hasn't."

Lately he hasn't had much chance to check the sky. He's too busy making a living in the theater.

—1966

Diahann Carroll in *No Strings*.

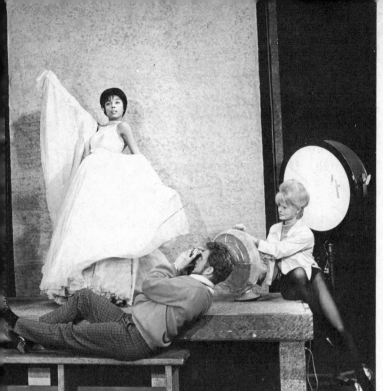

Josephine Premice, Ossie Davis and Lena Horne in *Jamaic*

Tiger Haynes and Carol Burnett do a take-off on Bi Robinson and Shirley Temple in *Fade Out-Fade In*.

Roscoe Lee Browne in *The Old Glory*.

Lou Gossett as the Zulu, with Menasha Skulnik, in *The Zulu and the Zayda*.

Diana Sands was the next-door neighbor in *The Owl and the Pussycat*, a two-character Broadway comedy hit.

Gilbert Price in
The Roar of the Greasepaint, the Smell of the Crowd.

Thelma Oliver in *Cindy*.

Integration on Broadway

by **Lindsay Patterson**

A NUMBER of plays, especially musicals, in the past few years have featured Negro performers in leading or good supporting roles. Diahann Carroll starred in *No Strings,* a successful Broadway musical that was written to suit her talents by Richard Rodgers. Sammy Davis, Jr., had a two-year run in Clifford Odets' *Golden Boy,* which, however, had a primarily Negro cast. Lena Horne's *Jamaica* was the first Broadway show to ever have a million dollar advance sale. Juanita Hall won lasting fame as Bloody Mary in *South Pacific.* Roscoe Lee Browne was the narrator for Edward Albee's *The Ballad of the Sad Café,* and he also starred in Robert Lowell's *The Old Glory.* Lou Gossett has had a number of outstanding roles in Broadway plays, his most successful to date, that of the Zulu in *The Zulu and the Zayda.* Gilbert Price, the only Negro member of *The Roar of the Greasepaint, the Smell of the Crowd,* played the Negro, and was compared to a young Paul Robeson by the critics. Mickey Grant was the Negro member of a company of three in an Off-Broadway production of *Leonard Bernstein's Theatre Songs.* Harry Belafonte secured his place in the entertainers Hall of Fame through his stunning performance in *Three for Tonight.* Thelma Oliver turned in a very professional job in *Sweet Charity* and the Off-Broadway revival of *Cindy,* as did Eartha Kitt in *Archie and Mehitabel* and *Jolly's Progress.* These are only some of the Negroes who have been members of Broadway or Off-Broadway productions by white playwrights in recent years.

—1966

Frederick O'Neal and Rosette
LeNoire in the 1958 movie
version of *Anna Lucasta*.

Peter DeAnda and Evelyn Davis
in Harold Willis' *A Sound of
Silence*, the first Off-Broadway
play by a white author to be
produced by a Negro (Raymond
A. League).

Problems and Prospects

by Frederick O'Neal

FOR A NUMBER of years, Negroes were not allowed to perform on the legitimate stage in America. Negro characters were played by white actors in blackface. Down through the years casting patterns in the various entertainment media have changed to some extent, but not very much.

During the period, roughly between 1910 and 1930, Negro stars such as Bert Williams and others were spotted in white shows as if they were so "super special" that they had to be shown in almost wholly unrelated roles and mostly alone. They were just the darlingest, quaintest, oddest, most interesting, sexiest, most exotic or, in other words, just about the best thing in the show, but not really a part of it. The most common method of handling the Negro actor in the straight play was to cast him exclusively in so-called "Negro roles," which inevitably meant in some servile capacity, such as the maid, butler, cook, etc. Let it be clearly understood here that there is nothing wrong with servant and comedy roles per se; the criticism stems from the characterization, presentation and interpretation of these parts, which until recently took the form of lazy, shuffling characters speaking a dialect that even Negroes had never heard. The *types* of roles played by Negroes are more of a barometer than the number of these roles.

The Negro actor feels that he is grossly discriminated against in the casting of shows in all of the entertainment media. Surely his talents could have been used in many parts in a manner that would not have distorted the artistic concept of the production. Indeed, in many instances, it would have enhanced such values. It would seem that Negroes and Orientals are the only groups whose roles are circumscribed by race. The Irish actor can play a Japanese character; the Jewish actor can play the Indian; German actors play Italian characters, and vice versa, but the Negro actor only has a chance of being cast if the part specifically indicates "Negro."

The imagination of the agent, casting director, play director, playwright or manager, preoccupied with time-worn casting patterns, does not extend beyond the racially designated description in the manuscript. But, these same individuals have no difficulty whatsoever with their imaginations when it comes to the selection of, perhaps, a David Wayne for the part of the Japanese character Sakini in *Teahouse of the August Moon,* or of Jeff Chandler as an American Indian.

Now all of this may sound strange and contradictory when we realize that, by and large, people of the theatre have been opposed to discrimination, segregation and other forms of bigotry and hypocrisy. Actors Equity Association is the union which has jurisdiction over those actors, dancers and singers who work in the legitimate theatre. The Council (its governing body) includes seven Negro

members and one officer among the seventy-two members. For almost twenty years, Equity and the League of New York Theatres (the organization of theatrical producers) have worked in cooperation with other elements inside as well as outside the theatre community to make this area of entertainment free and healthy. The League, Equity, the Dramatists' Guild and other organizations and individuals have, on more than one occasion, joined together to defeat the threat of official censorship. During the dark days of McCarthyism, the Anti-Blacklist Committee in Actors Equity, working with the League, managed to keep the theatre relatively free from political persecution and the principle of guilt by association. As a result of this kind of cooperative effort, the theatre has remained the most free of all entertainment media, while being ever mindful of its collective and individual responsibility and obligation to the public served.

In the mid-1940's, Washington, D.C. was one of the most lucrative stops on the touring theatre circuit, but the management of the National Theatre in that city maintained a policy of racial discrimination. The League and Equity pleaded with the management to drop this vicious and immoral policy, and when this request was refused, these two organizations, together with members of the Dramatists' Guild, decided to refuse bookings in this or any other theatre in Washington until such time as the management could see fit to change this policy. This was in 1948. The National Theatre remained closed for the next five years while touring shows played the Gayety Theatre, a former vaudeville house that had dropped this discriminatory policy. The National was finally remodeled and redecorated under a new management and reopened in 1952, with a welcome to all races and nationalities on a completely non-discriminatory basis.

Inasmuch as Washington was just about the most segregated city in the United States at that time, perhaps it was this collective action that broke the dam of prejudice and bigotry, releasing the first wave of such changes that have taken place in that city since 1952. It was a healthy action that could only terminate in a wholesome result.

Since 1962, by contractual agreement, Equity does not permit its members to work in any theatre where segregation and discrimination are practiced. Inquiries are often made of the union as to the number of Negroes there are among its 14,000 members. Due to the fact that the racial background of members is not indicated in the union's records, no one actually knows. Some say a thousand or more; others maintain that the figure is much lower. Equity's Ethnic Minorities Committee has made an unofficial effort to determine the number of Negro members of the union by inquiry among members, both Negro and white, as to their knowledge of all Negro actors known to them as members of Equity. After examining a number of lists submitted, we found a great deal of duplication. But, from this somewhat unorthodox method, we learned that the figure is around 400. There may be Negro artists who are members of other performing unions, such as: American Guild of Musical Artists, American Federation of Television and Radio Artists, American Guild of Variety Artists and Screen Actors Guild. Actors Equity's jurisdiction is only over those actors, singers and dancers who perform on the legitimate stage in the United States and Canada. Such jurisdiction also includes some industrial shows, a few night club shows, musical theatres, summer stock, etc.

Each year many young Negro and white actor "hopefuls" knock on the doors of producers. They all look forward to a successful career in the theatre. Many inquire as to the chances for such success. Such chances vary somewhat according to the individual,

but on the whole, they are pretty much the same for whites as for Negroes, except that the chances of those of "high visibility" are diminished or complicated by the existence of color.

A great deal of the imagined interest in and fitness for a career in the theatre is occasioned by the very rare freak success of a newcomer to the profession. Such a case is usually accompanied by reams of news stories and in some instances they are stories not really about a newcomer, but about a well-trained and experienced actor or actress being given a publicity buildup and the "newcomer" tag is but a useful gimmick. Unlike many other professions, it is very difficult to establish oneself in the theatre. There are many heartaches, disappointments and frustrations. In some cases, this has led to mental instability.

The American Negro, as a whole, has plumbed more levels of society—economic, religious, political, etc.—than any other comparable group. Such experiences are of particular value to the Negro actor, especially in contemporary drama. Where more restrained portrayals are demanded, however, as in the classics, we have not fared too well. Such style demands dedicated study and effort. Far too many members of the profession (black and white) have aligned themselves with the generally accepted lay opinion that one does not have to study in order to become an actor or actress. Within the last few years that segment of the profession has dwindled considerably and to the point where we now have a fairly large group of competent young actors and actresses who are ready for almost any assignment.

If the Negro actor aspirant will remember all this and also that his chances of success are further complicated by the fact that he is a Negro, then I would suggest he secure a copy of the book *Opportunities in Acting* by Dick Moore, published by Universal Publishing and Distributing Corporation in the "Vocational Guidance Manuals" series. It was written in answer to the many questions asked by those who are seriously considering acting as a career.

The prospects for the Negro actor in search of a career in the theatre are further lessened by the fact that many producers feel the so-called "Negro Show" is not a good financial risk (as theatrical investments go) compared to investments in white shows. They seem to forget about many successful Negro shows which have been produced for years. One could include among them such plays as *Green Pastures, Shuffle Along, Porgy and Bess, Carmen Jones,* and *Emperor Jones. Anna Lucasta* still remains among the all-time record holders for Broadway runs of straight plays. Paul Robeson's *Othello* holds the all-time record for the Broadway run of a Shakespearean play. Even with the bad judgment exercised by some producers in their selection of Negro plays, it is quite possible that an objective survey would indicate that there is a greater proportion of success among these Negro shows based on the total number produced than white shows under similar circumstances.

The availability of stars also plays a great part in the decision of producers. The legitimate stage has not, peculiarly enough, developed many Negro stars. Not one of the current crop of luminaries was developed by the theatre, and yet plays have been shelved for lack of a competent available Negro star of sufficient magnitude to head such productions. This does not mean that Negro actors are not available who could do just as well or possibly better than the desired stars, but the precarious economic position of the commercial theatre does not allow for such experimentation.

In some lay circles, the term "star" has been used rather loosely to the extent it has lost a great deal of its former meaning, except to those producers, theatrical investors and

others who still know and respect the true meaning of the term. Frequently, actors are referred to as having "starred" in this or that play, when in reality the parts played and the billing (if any) given these actors are not even comparable to feature recognition. In the trade, the word "star" is applied to an actor or actress who has reached a stage of artistic development to the extent that they can lend favorable influence to the box-office potential. Once such personalities have attracted a considerable public following, they are in the contractual position to demand that their names, now synonymous with a well desired trade mark, be placed above the title of the play (or directly beneath it in very large letters). True, in many cases, this position is not well earned, but such rewards are not without consideration for commercial values. Opportunities for Negro actors in the legitimate theatre are so few it is seldom, if ever, they can grow steadily to the point where they can reach the star category.

The legitimate theatre has been forced to borrow Negro personalities that have been developed in other media. Many a star has found his original medium more lucrative though, and cannot afford the occasional luxury of doing a play or musical. Top box-office attractions such as Lena Horne and Sammy Davis are not always available, and quite often the roles to be filled are not suited to the particular talents and personalities of this small group. Since the employment of Negro stars usually means the employment of Negro supporting players, whenever a play is shelved or abandoned, it follows that a number of Negro actors have been denied a chance to develop towards the star circle. This box-office draw of such stars as Miss Horne and Mr. Davis was demonstrated in their last appearances on Broadway. Both appeared in plays that did not receive very favorable critical comment, yet Miss Horne's vehicle, *Jamaica,* and Mr. Davis' *Mr. Won-*

derful, had runs of more than a year. Mr. Davis' latest musical, *Golden Boy,* is still running at this writing and playing to full capacity each week with no end in sight, despite not too favorable reviews. Without a doubt, such plays would have closed long since with lesser names. This would be true of shows with white stars as well.

The existence of the "Star System" today is largely due to the desire of the producer to exploit that which he feels creates in the potential theatre-goer a desire to fork over the price of admission. In this respect, he has created what he now terms a "Frankenstein." Essentially, a star's success is related to the star's ability to attract customers to the box-office.

The figures on the employment of Negroes during the past season, 1964–65, as compared to previous seasons are somewhat interesting.

During the above period the total employment of Negro actors on and Off-Broadway dropped considerably from that of the previous season (1963–64). The total number of jobs filled by Negro actors reached a new high during the 1963–64 season. Figures for the last five years are as follows:

	1964–65	1963–64	1962–63	1961–62	1960–61
Jobs Available					
On Bdwy.	74	168	51	123	126
Off-Bdwy.	32	116	26	50	29
Number shows employing Negroes					
On Bdwy.	22	24	21	14	18
Off-Bdwy.	20	27	12	20	9
Number shows with integrated casts					
On Bdwy.	15	16	13	10	8
Off-Bdwy.	11	11	7	11	4

The drop in the total number of jobs available to Negro actors during the season 1964–65, as in certain other past periods, is mainly due to the number of shows produced with predominantly or all-Negro casts. For example, during the 1963–64 season, three

Langston Hughes' *Tambourines to Glory* employed 29 of the 168 Negro actors who took part in the 1963–64 theatre season in New York.

Despite mixed notices from critics, *Golden Boy*, with Sammy Davis, Jr., ran for two years on Broadway and thus was able to keep a number of Negro actors employed.

shows, *Porgy and Bess* (46), *Tambourines to Glory* (29), *Sponomo* (24), accounted for 99 of the total number of 168 employed that years. The works of ten of these writers have same season Off-Broadway, three shows, *Jericho Jim Crow* (20), *Ballad for Bimshire* (26) and *Cabin in the Sky* (18) accounted for all but 52 of the total employed in that area. A total of 67 shows were produced on Broadway last season and 63 during the 1963–64 season.

The most important figures are those under the heading Number of Shows with Integrated Casts. These figures indicate parts played by Negroes that are not designated by the author as so-called "Negro Parts," where race is not thematically necessary to the story and not so directed as to imply racial identification. It will be noted that these figures have held up pretty well and, in fact, increased somewhat.

In addition to the increasing number of Negro artists being used in non-racially designated roles, another encouraging factor is the number of Negro playwrights whose works have been produced in recent years. All of them are not necessarily new playwrights, but with the possible exception of Langston Hughes, they are new to Broadway and Off-Broadway. Such writers as James Baldwin, LeRoi Jones, Lorraine Hansberry (deceased), Louis Peterson, Ann Flagg, Adrienne Kennedy, Errol John, Ossie Davis, William Hairston, Loften Mitchell, Alice Childress, Irving Burgie, Abram Hill and William Branch have been presented to Broadway or Off-Broadway during the past ten or fifteen years. The works of ten of these writers have been produced during the past five years.

Some of these new playwrights might be classified in the "Angry Young Man" category, who sometimes forget that the primary requisite for a good play is its ability to entertain. It must first get and hold the attention of the audience. If this is not done, one might as well be talking to oneself. Surely there is a place in the theatre for ideas, convictions, points of view, but the craftsmanship and technique of playwriting must be employed to express these ideas and convictions in terms of good theatre.

For a number of years the Negro writer seemed to approach his work out of a peculiar psychological or doctrinal fixation. That is, his work takes on a conscious or unconscious protest. It is very difficult for him to develop or summon forth that degree of confidence, self-assurance and inner dignity to approach his work without a certain degree of emotional preoccupation. And, sometimes, that same emotional preoccupation destroys craftsmanship and technique. The result is that the literary work suffers.

Dr. Alain Locke wrote in 1927 as follows: "Propaganda, pro-Negro and anti-Negro, has scotched the dramatic potentialities of the subject (Negro Drama). Especially with the few Negro playwrights has the propaganda motive worked havoc. They have had the dramatic motive deflected at its source. Race drama has appeared to them a matter of race vindication, and pathetically, they have pushed forward their moralistic allegories or melodramatic protests as dramatic correctives and antidotes for race prejudice."

Today, however, the Negro playwright, having become aware of his potential strength in the battle for full citizenship, has been able to overcome a certain amount of this emotional preoccupation. The result is and will be that his work will take on a higher degree of technical perfection and literary value.

In addition to the established and promising Negro playwrights, there is further reason for optimism occasioned by some degree of progress in other areas.

In recent years, one or two stage managers have emerged, such as: Charles Blackwell, formerly of David Merrick Productions and now working with Harry Belafonte; James

Wall, working in a similar capacity in television; Irving Vincent; Maxwell Glanville, currently playing a role in *Golden Boy;* and one or two others.

The work of two Negro directors was seen on Broadway during the past season. Frank Silvera directed *Amen Corner* and also co-produced the play with Mrs. Nat Cole, and Lloyd Richards was represented by the musical *I Had a Ball,* and he will direct another show this season. Other Negro directors who have worked on or Off-Broadway during the past two seasons are Osceola Archer, Ed Cambridge and Vinnette Carroll. Donald McKayle has established himself as one of the top flight choreographers, having served as assistant choreographer for *West Side Story* and *Red Head,* and recently as choreographer for *Golden Boy.* Albert Popwell directed the dances for the revival of *South Pacific* at the New York City Center. Others of this group are Katherine Dunham, Walter Nicks, Talley Beatty and Alvin Ailey.

In addition to Frank Silvera and Mrs. Nat Cole, Irving Burgie, Ellis Haislip and Ossie Davis can be added to the list of Negro producers. This group, as well as the Negro playwrights, can be very instrumental in expanding opportunities for Negroes in the American theatre.

George McClain has worked in several management capacities and is now Assistant Manager of the St. James Theatre. He has served as Company Manager for several large productions on pre-Broadway tours. Dick Campbell was Company Manager for the Langston Hughes show, *Tambourines to Glory,* and for *Ballad for Bimshire*. He is currently working for Crossroads Africa, the project originated by Rev. James Robinson and after which the Peace Corps was patterned.

One of the more successful talent agents is Ernestine McClendon, who holds franchises from all of the major performer unions. Her clients include almost as many white artists as Negroes.

There is a growing use of Negro musicians in the pit orchestras of Broadway shows and, since the desegregation of the New York locals of the Stage Hands Union, Negro craftsmen are working the Broadway theatres. Perry Watkins, veteran Negro scenic designer, has also produced on Broadway. He is currently working with Duke Ellington on his new show.

Civil Rights organizations are beginning to realize that the Negro creative artist, and particularly the playwright and actor, exert the greatest influence in the establishment of the Negro image.

Conferences are currently being held with the NAACP in the hope of establishing an NAACP National Performing Artists Advisory Committee as a permanent department within the national office with a staff person on both the East and West Coasts to pursue on a continuing basis the ultimate objective of complete desegregation of the performing arts.

—1966

HARLEM SUITCASE THEATRE

SECOND SEASON

Sponsored by Lodge 691, In'national Workers Order

317 WEST 125th STREET, New York City

◆ Program for November and December ◆

EVERY SUNDAY NIGHT AT 9 P. M.

From Uncle Tom's Cabin to Em-Fuehrer Jones
A Modern Satire In Five Parts

And

DON'T YOU WANT TO BE FREE?
A Poetic Drama by LANGSTON HUGHES
Directed by HILARY PHILLIPS

:——:

ADMISSION   35 CENTS

Special Prices for Theatre Benefits—Call AL. 4-2321

112

An Afro-American Theatre?

THE NEED FOR AN AFRO-AMERICAN THEATRE
by Langston Hughes

PURLIE TOLD ME!
by Ossie Davis

THE NEED FOR A HARLEM THEATRE
by Jim Williams

THE NEGRO THEATRE AND THE HARLEM COMMUNITY
by Loften Mitchell

Hilda Simms, the original Anna Lucasta.

Eartha Kitt and Harold Scott
in the 1958 movie version of *Anna Lucasta.*

The Need for an Afro-American Theatre

by Langston Hughes

THERE is a very great need for a serious theatre in the Harlem community of New York City—or on the Southside of Chicago, or in Los Angeles—a theatre in which the drama and the folk arts of the Negro people might be presented before the very audiences out of whom this drama and art is born. In these days of hoped for integration, some ask, "Why a Negro theatre?" The answer is two-fold.

The first answer has nothing to do with race, but rather with the state of the American theatre in general, largely centralized on and controlled by the commercialism of Broadway. The high cost of production on Broadway, running into hundreds of thousands of dollars, prevents any sort of art coming into being there that does not have great box office possibilities plus large initial sums of money behind it. These conditions make creative experimentation on Broadway nearly impossible, regardless of race. Such commercial stipulations almost automatically freeze out the art *and the artist* of the Negro community, except for a controlled version of their art such as whites wish to be presented, and a handful of colored Broadway-managed entertainers. It is currently impossible for more than a few Negro actors or singers or dancers to achieve expression in the Broadway theatre, or in Hollywood, or over the radio or in television. If our artists are to live as artists and keep their art alive,

the Negro people themselves must open up avenues of expression for them—and these will in turn be avenues of expression for *all of us*—saying what we would like to see and hear said.

There is a second answer to, "Why a Negro theatre?" That answer is that there is so much abundantly rich material in Negro life in the field of drama, music, and the dance that is still not being used today on the American stage, and there are many talented colored actors, singers, and dancers, who perform most irregularly. We have, too, a number of talented playwrights including Louis Peterson, William Branch, Alice Childress, Charles Sebree, LeRoi Jones, Douglas Turner Ward and Ronald Milner. But we have no theatres of our own in which we may see the plays of the older playwrights in revival, and no stages where the new dramatists may try out their scripts, polish them and learn from the performances. Broadway pays these Negro playwrights very little attention. If their talents are not to "bloom unseen upon the desert air" we ourselves must provide stages for their work. That the largest Negro urban community in the world, Harlem, has not one single serious theatre for its playwrights, actors, singers, musicians, and dancers is a great community deficiency—in fact, an inexcusable deficiency.

Once there was the Lafayette Players and

a stock company at the Old Lincoln Theatre, as well. Once there was the Harlem Suitcase Theatre where *Don't You Want To Be Free?* ran for 135 performances. Once there was the Negro Playwrights Company where Theodore Ward's *Big White Fog* was produced. Finally there was the American Negro Theatre whose *Anna Lucasta* went to Broadway. Out of these groups came some of the best American actors: Charles Gilpin, Canada Lee, Hilda Simms, Earle Hyman, Maxwell Glanville, Hilda Haynes, Earl Jones, Sidney Poitier, Harry Belafonte, and others.

None of these groups exists any longer and our actors are dependent almost entirely upon the whims of Broadway commercial managers for engagements. Because this is so, not only Harlem but all of New York City and the nation is the poorer for lack of opportunity to enjoy more fully the rich talent that Negroes possess—with no showcases, national or local, in which to project it, and no stages on which to act out our dreams. Integration is wonderful, but culture must of necessity begin at home. I propose the creation of a National Afro-American Theatre.

—1965

Langston Hughes and friends.

Purlie Told Me!

by Ossie Davis

NOTHING I had learned from the Baptist Bible, from Howard University, from my long association with Causes, black and white, or from my fifteen years on Broadway, prepared me in any degree for what I was to learn from *Purlie Victorious*—as actor, as author, as Negro, and, as—what I hope some day soon to be—a man!

Had not Purlie come along when he did, and proceeded to shake the living daylight out of me, I would by now have had it made: I would have sidestepped completely the Negro Question (which is, to the best of my knowledge, "When the hell are we gonna be free?!"); I would have safely escaped into the Negro Middle Class, burying my head somewhere between the cadillac and the mink; and would probably have become, by express permission and endorsement of the Great White Father, an Honorary White Man myself. But Purlie came: Purlie saw: Purlie laughed!

In pursuit of Purlie I found more than I had bargained for: the act of writing became my long moment of truth; and it took me five years to adjust my eyesight, to be able to look squarely at the world, and at myself, through Negro-colored glasses. And to decide, on the basis of what I found: it is not enough to be only a Negro in this world . . . one must, and more importantly, also be, a man.

For *Purlie Victorious* is, in essence, the adventures of Negro manhood in search of itself in a world for white folks only. A world

that emasculated me, as it does all Negro men, before I left my mother's breast; and which had taught me to gleefully accept that emasculation as the highest honor America could bestow upon a black man. And in more ways than I thought possible, I had accepted it!

Purlie, in order to get himself put down on paper at all, had to force me to examine myself; to dig deeper and deeper into my own soul, conscious and subconscious, to peel off and rip away layer after layer of sham, hypocrisy, evasion, lies—to rip up by the root the many walls I had erected around the pretense that I was indeed a man—when I knew all along—but had never been before forced to admit even to myself, that, in the context of American Society today, *the term Negro and the term Man must mutually exclude each other!*

Purlie showed me that, whatever I was, I was not a man . . . not yet! that I would never become a man by sacrificing everything I was, merely to become an American. That I would never ease my way into the bosom of American acceptance by pretending, like Jacob, that I was Esau; by pretending that freedom and equality could be practiced between whites and blacks purely on a personal basis; that Negroes could be integrated into American society one at a time; that the doors of opportunity would open wider and wider each day, not only for me, but also for my brothers, as soon as we learned to talk middle-class talk,

dress middle-class dress, behave middle-class behavior, and, literally to "wash ourselves whiter than snow." And above all never to become too clamorously assertive of our rights as Americans, lest it upset those brave and leading souls of other races who know so much better how to conduct our struggles than we do!

Purlie told me I would never find my manhood by asking the white man to define it for me. That I would never become a man until I stopped measuring my black self by white standards—standards set deeply in my own mind, by a racist society, which could almost define itself by its hatred and its fear of me! *And therefore felt impelled to teach me hatred and fear of myself!*

Purlie told me my *manhood* was hidden within my *Negroness,* that I could never find the one without fully, and passionately, embracing the other. That only by turning again homeward, whatever the cost, to my own blackness, to my own people, and to our common experience as Negroes, could I come at last to my manhood—to my *Self!*

Purlie is black laughter, and like all laughter, when it is humane, is liberative. Or intends to be. Based on the simple assumption that segregation is ridiculous, because it makes perfectly wonderful people, black and white, do ridiculous things, Purlie would hold all those "ridiculous things" up to universal scorn, while at the same time maintaining a loving respect for the people, white and black, caught up in this ridiculous nonsense. And when I see people, white and black, sit down side by side and laugh like hell at those ridiculous customs which still serve to keep us artificially separated, then I feel Purlie has done his job. For if men may really laugh together at something disturbing to them both it means that—for the moment—they have overleapt their separateness; and are—for the moment—free to behold the universe, with sorrow or with joy—from the same point of view. Laughter, if it is wise, can lead to many things, even among strangers—not the least of which is that mutual respect for people on which all other relations including the struggle for freedom in this country must ultimately depend.

In the objective sense, the public response to *Purlie,* pro and con, black and white, has been no less educational. The Critics, with one exception, were highly praiseful—some for the wrong reasons. And since these gentlemen usually hold in their hands the decision whether a play will live or die, their enthusiastic reception of Purlie was, in realistic terms indeed, the Kiss of Life. I was disappointed that they did not comment on *Purlie,* good, bad, or indifferent, as *literature;* and more deeply disappointed that most of the white playwrights I had known, with two exceptions—men who were friends and mentors of mine, and whose opinion I still value highly—were silent, and still are. But it is quite possible, and I say this without rancor, that their very talents, and their concepts of what a Negro is, has left them unprepared to understand *Purlie* at all!

The theatre-going public, when it has taken the time to come and see, has usually been both surprised and delighted that comedy—satire in particular—could be such an effective weapon against race prejudice; that a stereotype about Negro life, which would be offensive in the hands of a white writer, might become, in the hands of a Negro writer, a totally unexpected revelation of the true substance of Negro wit and humor.

But *Purlie,* in spite of excellent reviews, and a tremendous word-of-mouth enthusiasm generating from those who have seen it, has never been a big "hit" with the "carriage trade," the "expense-account crowd"; and though we had some early support from theatre parties, it was not enough to really see us through. As a matter of fact, had *Purlie* been forced to rely on the normal avenue of Broad-

Ruby Dee and Ossie Davis in Purlie Victorious.

way patronage we would long ago have sunk and disappeared from sight. But something happened with *Purlie* that was different. And that difference, small as it was in the beginning, has steadily grown, until finally it made all the difference in the world.

Sylvester Leaks and John H. Clarke met Purlie firsthand on opening night, and decided he belonged to the Negro people. That decision made the difference. They went to churches, to lodges, to social clubs, labor unions. They took Purlie directly to the Negro community, and the Negro community got the message. It was, and is, the attendance of *my own people* at the box office that made the difference: it kept Purlie alive. Did this mean that a Negro work, with Negro content, could depend on the Negro community for support, and survive? I believe it did.

Not that *Purlie* is a Negro play only. It is, I hope, much more than that. As Purlie, himself, told me: "Look at the Negro from outside and all you see is oppression. But look at the Negro from the inside, and all you see is resistance to that oppression." Now oppression, and the resistance to oppression, are universal themes. If Purlie speaks at all, he speaks to everybody—black and white. And the white audience still finds its merry way to the Longacre Theatre. But it is no longer always in the majority. Normally a black performer on Broadway will have his wages paid in white money. But for Purlie the situation is reversed. For the first time since I started working in the theatre, *my boss is the Negro People!*

And I choose to believe that this fact has implications for the Negro artist, musician, performer—in his struggle to express himself and survive at the same time—that are revolutionary. For if we can, in fact, create for our own people; work for our own people; belong to our own people; we will no longer be forced into artistic prostitution and self-betrayal in the mad scramble, imposed upon us far too long, to belong to some other people. We can indeed, as long as we *truly* deserve the support of our own, embrace our blackness, and find the stuff of our manhood.

The Negro people, if given a chance, will cherish, defend, and protect its own: *Purlie* is proof of that. If we turn to them ever so little, they will turn to us in full. It is time for us, who call ourselves artists, scholars, and thinkers, to rejoin the people from which we came. We shall then and only then, be free to tell the truth about our people, and that truth shall make us free!

Only then can we begin to take a truly independent position within the confines of American culture, a black position. And from that position, walk, talk, think, fight, and create, like men. Respectful of all, sharing with any, but beholden to none save our own.

For there is hope of a tree, this is Job talking, *if it be cut down, that it will sprout again, and that the tender branch thereof will not cease. Though the root thereof wax old in the earth, and the stock thereof die in the ground; yet through the scent of water it will bud, and bring forth boughs like a plant.*

The profoundest commitment possible to a black creator in this country today—beyond all creeds, crafts, classes and ideologies whatsoever—is to bring before his people the *scent* of freedom. He may rest assured his people will do the rest.

That's what Purlie told me!

—1963

The Need for a Harlem Theatre

by Jim Williams

IN A SPRING issue of *Freedomways* I read a stimulating article by the author-actor Ossie Davis. In "Purlie Told Me!" Davis points out that the white world emasculates him and all Negro men; that the terms Negro and man are mutually exclusive; that we will never be able to define our manhood by asking the white man to define it for us; and that no matter how many white middle class standards we adopt or how mildly we petition for our rights we will never be integrated into American society one at a time.

He also mentions that *Purlie Victorious* was kept alive mainly because of the yeoman work of Sylvester Leaks and John H. Clarke in bringing the Negro people to Broadway. As a result of this salutary and unprecedented experience (Negroes keeping a Negro play going on Broadway), Ossie Davis urged Negro artists, scholars and thinkers to rejoin the people and to turn homeward again. He adds that if we can "create for our own people . . . we will no longer be forced into *artistic prostitution and self-betrayal* in the mad scramble imposed upon us far too long, to belong to some other people" (italics mine). To this I can only add a hearty "Amen!"

Ossie's urgent "turn homeward again" however is a healthy but vague plea unless accompanied by an answer to the questions: Where is home and how do we turn there?

We read many articles on the Negro in the theatre, follow avidly the hearings on dis-crimination conducted by Rep. Adam Powell and his Congressional Committee, and join in spirit the picketing on the part of Negro actors to force their natural inclusion in theatre productions, but nowhere do we read the obvious (to us) conclusion to be drawn from all the foregoing. The only realistic way for theatre workers and buffs to turn home is to build a Negro Community Theatre now! "Only then," to quote Mr. Davis further, "can we begin to take a truly independent position within the confines of American culture, a black position. And from that position, walk, talk, think, fight, and create, like men. Respectful of all, sharing with any, but beholden to none save our own."

We believe fervently in the truth of an oft quoted dictum that "art is not an end in itself, but a means of addressing humanity." But who is humanity—and where is our home?

If we take the Broadway theatre as a guide, then for the most part the Negro people are not a part of humanity, nor do we reside in the U.S.A. If we use the flickering pictures of Hollywood as our image, then the Negro people exist, with the possible exception of Sidney Poitier, solely as servants or ciphers or grotesques—and where is their home? If we believe that the attitude of white Southern politicos and educators reflects our reality, then we are dehumanized tools to be worked and then returned to the shed until called for further use. If we accept the Northern liberal

attitude as expressed in his prayers, platitudes and pleas, then we will remain quarantined for another 100 years in the big city ghettos with all the hopelessly inferior health standards, half-education and demoralizing joblessness attendant hereto.

Television, the infant medium of communication, is playing follow-the-leader despite the so-called twenty-billion-dollar Negro market which consumes enormous chunks of the products beamed at us every day by the advertisers. Book publishers are a little better. They're beginning "to find a Negro writer" and also have begun to have a Negro work on their list each year. Magazines and newspapers have begun to vie with each other for a market hungry with curiosity and a world filled with concern for these "dark citizens" who have been enjoying the "fruits of the free world and the benefits of democracy for so many generations." Oh, what wonders the liberation movement has wrought!

But what of Harlem, the Negro community geographically closest to the Broadway theatre?

EARLIER THEATRE GROUPS

Harlem is the largest black community in the world, where about 400,000 people live, play and die. At one time or another Harlem has been home to over seventeen theatre groups of more or less significance. Some of these come readily to mind—the Lafayette Players, Harlem Suitcase Theatre, The Negro Playwrights, American Negro Theatre, Rose McClendon Players, Federal Theatre and the Committee for the Negro in the Arts, to name but a few. Their careers were all too brief, but they have bequeathed to us a body of experience from which we can draw guidelines. Many reasons have been advanced to explain the failure of these groups to endure: the pervasive influence of Broadway; too much dependence on intellectuals, profes-

sionals and dilettantes who were far removed from the community; admission prices which were too high; assorted coteries or cliques trying to meet their own narrow, short-sighted, selfish needs while ignoring both the needs of the community and their own long term needs as well. We know that all these reasons are valid and can be expanded greatly with strict adherence to truth. While we may disagree as to emphasis, one thing is certain: we are today without a serious cultural center speaking for and in the name of Harlem citizens. As Langston Hughes says, "They done took our blues and gone."

Is it presumptuous to say flatly that home for Negro actors and playwrights is Harlem? Is it presumptuous to add that the Negro actor and creative author can achieve true stature only by addressing themselves directly to their own people? Unfortunately, while having many things in common, man today cannot be addressed as humanity. The differences are many and deep. National differences, class differences, caste differences and ethnic differences are only a part of the welter. The classic anthropologists and ethnologists Boas, Mead, Montagu, Finot, have firmly established the biologic oneness and the potential likenesses of all mankind. It seems to us however that if mankind is ever to achieve the equality of opportunity about which the American founding fathers wrote and spoke so eloquently, we must proceed from a clear recognition of the sociological and psychological differences. Indeed, we American Negro theatre people will fail ourselves and our people by our continued neglect and by our persistent refusal to turn home fully.

Stanislavski, the father of the great Moscow Art Theatre, often told his pupils that the theatre was the most powerful instrument of education for modern man, more powerful than the school or the pulpit could ever be. Even people who are illiterate still enjoy look-

ing at plays, movies, TV, and listening to music. Perhaps this is the reason we have not been able to sustain a theatre tradition, for if there are forces that would deny us our freedom, would they not deny us such a powerful weapon?

Theatre people, like all other sections of the population, can find their correct path only by proceeding from objective facts, from their concrete experiences in life. W. E. B. Du Bois said that the twentieth century was the century of the color question. Well, the twentieth century is still with us and so is the color question. Our decade, the decade of the sixties, serves only to emphasize the correctness of Dr. Du Bois' observation. Spurred by the freedom struggles of the African colonies and their leaders' articulate participation in United Nations debates, encouraged by the 1954 Supreme Court decision making segregated schooling unconstitutional, the Negro people have leaped forward with ever deepening national consciousness.

ROLE OF THE ARTISTS

In a speech delivered at a rally to abolish the House Un-American Activities Committee, Lorraine Hansberry, the author of *A Raisin in the Sun,* urged artists to leave the studios and to participate in protests and rallies, to become committed in the struggles that surround us. As if to answer her "A Challenge to Artists" Al Hibbler, Ray Charles and Dick Gregory hit the headlines with their participation in the Mississippi movement.

We hope that the ranks of the artists who are identifying themselves with the mass movements of our time and people will continue to swell. The formation of a militant national liberation movement is the prime consideration of the decade of the sixties. The civil rights and liberties taken for granted by the population as a whole can no longer remain dead letters to the Negro people.

Every Negro in the United States should become a part in some way of these political and economic struggles for the rights to unsegregated education, to worship wherever we please, to spend our money wherever we please, to vote for candidates of our choice, etc. The mood of our people today is such that they will settle for no less. It is inevitable that this movement soon will take on, in addition, a struggle for jobs, job training and upgrading. With unemployment two and one-half times higher among Negroes, with the introduction of automation by industry making higher skills necessary and the concomitant elimination of the traditional unskilled Negro jobs, we cannot ignore for long the job question nor can the white labor movement continue to rest on its already rusty laurels as fighters for economic rights for Negro workers. According to the 1960 census figures there has been no change since 1950 in the earning gap between white and non-white workers. The Negro wage worker's earnings are three-fifths of the average white worker's and lately even this has been slipping backward.

While the victories are few and by no means far-reaching and the sacrifices great in our sociological struggles, the freedom movement continues unabated. In *Crisis* (March 1963), Carl T. Rowan's article "The Travesty of Integration" (reprinted from *Saturday Evening Post,* Jan. 19, 1963), has this to say: "It bothers me—and it should bother lawyers, judges and all who treasure a society based on justice under law—that in the current school year only 901 of North Carolina's 339,840 Negro school children have secured relief from a practice that, according to our highest tribunal, 'generates a feeling of inferiority . . . that may affect their hearts and minds in a way unlikely ever to be undone.' " And further, "In Texas they may boast about 'the peaceful transition' to 'integration' in Dallas or Houston, but the meaningful thing

to me is that a 'whopping' 2.16% of the Negro children in that state attended integrated schools last year. . . . Alabama, South Carolina and Mississippi have yet to free a single Negro child from this stigma of state-imposed racial isolation." Certainly this is tokenism with a vengeance. The Negro people's answer to this has been simply to step up their struggles, increasing the numbers of demonstrations and increasing the number of lily-white institutions assailed.

One could ask how it is that, in an article which purports to deal with the need for a community theatre, so much time and space is being devoted to politics, economics and sociology. Well, I'm of the school of thought that believes that politics and economics are the basis and foundation of our lives and that art and literature are the superstructure; that the superstructure reflects the base—that the base is specific and concrete. However, once the superstructure comes into being it does not play merely a supine role or remain indifferent to the base. Exactly the opposite obtains; the superstructure plays a vital and dynamic role, aiding and buttressing the old base or helping to destroy an old moribund base in preparation for new conditions and new social forces. No longer can Negro writers and artists continue to rely on spontaneity or simple willy-nilly expediency. The special conditions inherited from the incomplete character of our Civil War have blunted the development of class consciousness and the sharp distinctions of classes among our people. Our struggle to complete the tasks of the second American Revolution (against chattel slavery) takes on an all-class character. This struggle is being led at the moment by the preachers and students of the South and cries out for the active engagement of our creative writers and actors as participants à la Hansberry, Gregory, Hibbler and Charles but also and perhaps more importantly as craftsmen.

Ernest Kaiser, in his article "The Literature of Negro Revolt" (*Freedomways,* Winter 1963), notes that until a year and a half ago there was very little writing in depth on the five-and-a-half-year southern Negro revolt. He also quotes a SCLC *Newsletter* (August 1961) calling attention to the participation of teachers, preachers, and students in the struggles but lamenting the paucity of poems, essays, pamphlets and books appearing from their pens. He encouragingly lists the increase in books, record albums and articles that since have made their appearance. Nowhere, however, has a play made its reluctant debut.

We know that there is a lag between the construction of a foundation and the fashioning of the superstructure, but certainly now is the time to close the gap. It seems to us that it would be naive in the extreme to expect the white people in any sizable numbers, who control the finances of theatre, to allow any honest dramatizations of the lives of Negro people to be placed on the boards at this time. On the contrary, the decisive forces of the power elite seem to be committed to maintaining the status quo at all costs. On the other hand the Negro revolt against the continuing restrictive shackles of second-class citizenship begs for artistic creations in the new image.

How can our creative writers ignore the freedom movements and the police, fire hoses, dogs, bombs, jailings, etc., used to oppose them?

In the qualitative worldwide change represented by the dissolution of classic colonialism and the concomitant national liberation struggles of our own people lies the richest of mines awaiting the creative Negro writers' golden touch. If only our writers will base themselves on the firm foundations being laid down by our people, self-pity and the pathetic tendency to imitate the white middle class intellectuals' sterile absurdities will vanish like fog in the bright sunlight.

Culturally, is it too much to hope that a theatre caucus can be achieved in Harlem from which we can probe the no man's lands of Broadway, Hollywood and Madison Avenue? I think that this paradox conforms to the reality of Negro experience. We are a part of and yet separate from white people in every walk of life. To expect Negro acting and play writing to flourish without a Negro theatre is like asking a farmer to grow vegetables without roots in the soil. You may get the vegetables but, man, they sure will be stunted.

Lionel Abel in "Theatre of Politics and the Negro" (*Nation,* April 27, 1963) says that "the lack of political movements in recent times of the kind we witnessed during the thirties" has been the reason, as he puts it, for the absence of "political plays." He goes on: "However, there have of late been political events that give promise of future effects— political and theatrical. For if there is no labor movement or Socialist movement on the march in this country, there are two new political developments: (1) the peace movement and (2) the movement for Negro liberation. . . . My claim is that the existing movement for Negro liberation has again made political plays possible. . . . What is new in the present situation, as a result of what Negroes have achieved in the North and in the South, is that the individual Negro representing his fellows has become a historical figure."

By contrast, Esther Merle Jackson in "The American Negro and the Image of the Absurd" (*Phylon,* Winter 1962) says," The modern arts, in particular, the art of literature, have dramatized the fact that an ever larger segment of humanity seems to share the kind of existence which has been the lot of the Negro for some three centuries or more. The shape of human suffering defined by Dostoevski, Proust, Gide, Malraux, Mann, Sartre and others mirrors the actual condition of the Negro; his alienation from the larger community, his isolation within abstract walls, his loss of freedom, and his legacy of despair. Although many modern writers trace their vision of the human dilemma to developments in European intellectual history, it is quite clear that one of the perceptions profoundly affecting the modern mind has been the image of the Negro. Indeed, it may be said that he has served as a prototype of that contemporary, philosophic species, the absurd."

Isn't it interesting that though the American Negro may very well be an objective prototype for the absurd, having lived in a world from which he is alien, estranged, unsheltered, threatened, opaque; a world that has been really desolate and bleak for over three hundred years, we have not succumbed subjectively to it nor have we in any numbers embraced the white man's currently popular nihilistic philosophy. Perhaps the reason is that the capitalist world is not ours nor of our making and therefore its dissolution is not of such grave concern to us. On the contrary, if we Negroes are ever going to be able to share in the fruits, real and potential, of mass production, industrial society, it is my belief that the capitalist system will have to be so modified as to be almost unrecognizable.

It is also my belief that our creative people must find another way to create artistically the sinew, sense and soul of the Negro. In an article by John Mason Brown, "What's Right with the Theatre" (*Saturday Review*, May 11, 1963), some of the answers may be found. He said, "Fortunately, there have been exceptions [to the Absurd Playwrights], such as Jean Anouilh, Archibald MacLeish and Robert Bolt, who even in a darkening world have not been embarrassed by a larger vision. They have seen man and seen him plain, and therefore seen him whole, recognizing the strengths that exist within him, side by side with weaknesses. They have not been blind to what Dostoevski called 'the fury and the mire of

human veins.' But, in the interest of the total rather than the fractional truth, they have acknowledged what it is that man can rise to in spite of his mortal frailties.

"Prudery, piety and copybook morality have nothing to do with their attitude toward life as *Becket, J. B.* and *A Man for All Seasons* have proved. Anouilh, MacLeish and Bolt have been as unafraid of evil as they have been prepared to admit virtue. They have sensed that people are what they prove to be in the moments of being most cruelly tested. . . . Their characters have risen to the testing and sought for the reasons that have caused it, rather than submitted to the sheer senselessness of things."

We have cited these examples of the current political, sociological and artistic ferment not to come to any firm conclusions at the moment, but to underscore our deep belief in the need for a Harlem Community Theatre. This Harlem Theatre is not to be viewed as "Little" theatre or institutional theatre but a theatre embracing the highest off-Broadway technical standards; a theatre free to experiment; a theatre free from the stench of commerce; a Negro theatre dedicated to "telling it like it is." By a Negro theatre we do not mean a theatre that will exclude the white world as audience, patrons, technical advisors, teachers or actors, for this would be almost as false and phony as the unreal, commercial, white theatre world. Nor am I concerned at this time with whether the plays that will be performed are expressionistic, realistic, poetic, absurd, political, Freudian or what have you, as long as they do me and do me right.

The theatre I envision needs the active support of every Negro actor, writer and creative person with five minutes to spare from his present work whatever it may be. A Harlem Theatre cannot be looked upon as a contradiction to the understandable ambitions of our theatre workers to emerge on Broadway, Hollywood or TV. If I learned one thing from seeing Jean Genet's black un-merry-go-round, it was that with a fine stage manager such as Ed Cambridge, a play can remain tight though the original cast moves in and out of it like kids seeking a brass ring. Cicely Tyson, Godfrey Cambridge, Helen Martin and many other members of the cast were able to leave *The Blacks* to try more ambitious productions, only to return after the closing of the other plays.

HOME TO HARLEM

I think it's high time we turned all the way home, home to Harlem. Only such an indigenous theatre can take the initiative to distill the essence of our people; can give deeper consciousness to our actors; can give direction to our muted writers. Combining as it does so many arts and crafts, such a theatre can become a small but dynamic voice in the cultural life of our country. With the winds of change blowing up a storm I have deep faith that this theatre would find a healthy direction and in a short time become a jewel in the cultural crown of a new, more rational America.

To continue my temerity just a little further, if one play, *The Blacks,* can run for three years with its song of futility, its message of hopelessness, and cynical nihilism, then certainly a clutch of such fine plays as Loften Mitchell's *A Land Beyond the River,* Langston Hughes' *The Emperor of Haiti,* and William Branch's *In Splendid Error,* if properly housed, cast, directed and promoted, should be able to play in the aggregate for three years to a Negro audience that has never seen them.

In 1958 an attempt was made by twenty actors to establish a Harlem community theatre called Manhattan Art Theatre. Two of them, Godfrey Cambridge and Beah Rich-

ards, appeared in *Purlie Victorious*. Despite many minor differences of opinion it appeared that we might succeed, especially when Langston Hughes gave us his play *The Emperor of Haiti* for our first production. But the then promising Broadway Negro family drama *A Raisin in the Sun* sent out its call and our actors were off and running. Diana Sands, Douglas Turner, Lincoln Kilpatrick, Frances Foster, Louis Gossett, all erstwhile Manhattan Art Theatre members, were to enjoy long runs in the justly successful Lorraine Hansberry play. Abandoned by so many of its creators, Manhattan Art Theatre became a victim of infant mortality. We were able to mount *Emperor* in the fine St. Martin's Episcopal Church Theatre for four weeks and in the Joseph P. Kennedy, Jr., Memorial Community Center Theatre another four weeks. We Manhattan Art Theatre members had pledged ourselves to:

1. Immediately acquire a base of operations (a loft suitable for a small, 199-seat or less, theatre and office).
2. Acquire a number of plays, musicals, etc., to insure the continuity and proper level of work of the group and project.
3. Spell out a constitution which will provide a guide, rules and regulations for the orderly and businesslike conduct of this project.
4. Elect a responsible slate of officers to administer the project.
5. Acquire sufficient funds and the proper type of fund-raising to insure the financing of this project.
6. Form a school and staff same with teachers capable of stimulating the development and growth of the many crafts involved.
7. Acquire the best legal advice possible to insure the protection of our project.
8. Secure the best public relations and publicity possible to guarantee the foregoing.

Let's bring theatre *to* the Negro. When we find the key to open Harlem to a sustained, stable, artistic theatre we will have solved our craft problem of theatrical form and meaningful content, and inevitably some of us will have achieved universality as playwrights and greatness as actors.

We must break through the sound barrier surrounding a Negro people's theatre.

—1963

APOLLO THEATRE

Forty-Second Street
West of Broadway

2

GEORGE WHITE, *Lessee*   **GEORGE F. MORLEY,** *Manager*

<u>FIRE NOTICE:</u> Look around now and choose the nearest exit to your seat. In case of fire, walk (not run) to that exit. Do not try to beat your neighbor to the street.

JOHN J. DORMAN, Fire Commissioner.

WEEK BEGINNING MONDAY EVENING, FEBRUARY 25, 1929
MATINEES WEDNESDAY AND SATURDAY

EDWARD A. BLATT
PRESENTS

"HARLEM"

An Episode of Life in New York's Black Belt

BY WILLIAM JOURDAN RAPP AND WALLACE THURMAN
STAGED BY CHESTER ERSKIN

THE CAST
(AS THEY APPEAR)

ARABELLA WILLIAMS.....................EDNA WISE BARK
GEORGE WILLIAMS.....................CLARENCE TAYLOR
MAZIE WILLIAMS.....................ELISE THOMAS
MA WILLIAMS.....................INEZ CLOUGH
PA WILLIAMS.....................LEW PAYTON
CORDELIA WILLIAMS.....................ISABELL WASHINGTON
BASIL VENERABLE.....................RICHARD LANDERS

PROGRAM CONTINUED ON FOURTH PAGE FOLLOWING

The Negro Theatre and the Harlem Community

by Loften Mitchell

A SCENE in the play, *Star of the Morning,* describes the disbanding of the Williams and Walker Company in 1909. Bert Williams asks Jesse Shipp, the company director: "Jesse, where'll you go?" Jesse answers: "Uptown. 100,000 Negroes in New York now. Lots of them moving to Harlem. I'll go there. Maybe they'll be needing a theatre."

Fifty-three years after Jesse Shipp's statement, Ed Cambridge, the director of *Star of the Morning,* read these lines at an audition. The shoulders of a number of theatre people sagged as the lines left Cambridge's lips. A sharp pain stabbed me. I wished the lines had not been written.

Later that night Gertrude Jeanette, Esther Rolle, Lynn Hamilton, Louis Gossett, Rick Ferrell and Irving Burgie sat in the home of Michael Allen, rector of St. Mark's-in-the Bouwerie, discussing the fact that there was a theatre in Harlem when there were only 100,000 Negroes in the city and not one when the population totalled approximately one and a half million black people. Our trembling fingers spilled coffee into overflowing saucers and onto Priscilla Allen's tablecloth. Ed Cambridge shuddered, banged his cup into the saucer, and growled: "It's a good thing Jesse Shipp didn't go up there this year looking to work in theatre. He'd have been hungry as hell!"

The Harlem to which Jesse Shipp went— like the Harlem of today—was peculiarly a part of this society—this society created by an impoverished, decaying Europe reaching out, searching for a new route to India and finding instead a new Eldorado in the west. The European underprivileged raced to these shores, staked claims, then warred with the red man and with rival European groups. Other Europeans found the rich African continent, enslaved its people, then attempted to justify these atrocities. "The image of Africa," says John Henrik Clarke in his essay, *Reclaiming the Lost African Heritage,* "was deliberately distorted by Europeans who needed a moral justification for the rape, pillage and destruction of African cultural patterns and ways of life."

The image of the African was also distorted in America where a ruling aristocracy sought to break its ties to the old world. Grandiloquent phrases declared equality of all—with the exception of those who were black or those who were white and owned no property. Patrick Henry demanded liberty or death, but he ignored the twenty-three slaves in his possession.

America was, for the African, a strange, hostile land. Everywhere people spoke of freedom, yet he was not free. Everywhere he heard others speak of their glorious ancestry, yet he was told his Africa was a huge jungle, inhabited by cannibals. Sometimes the Negro believed these distortions and saw himself as others saw him—as something sub-human,

deserving a cruel fate. Yet, somehow he dared to dream that some day he would be free.

His dreams were not idle ones. He fought the nation's wars. His hands built the economy. His cultural gifts were either stolen or ignored by white historians who interpreted the nation's history in biased terms. In his essay, *Negritude and Its Relevance to the American Negro Writer,* Samuel Allen describes the Negro's subjection to the cultural imprint of a powerful, dominant majority in an unfriendly land. Mr. Allen tells us that the American Negro group became—if not the only—one of the few black minorities in world history. Despite colonialism, those in Africa had the sheer weight of numbers for allies, plus the realization that the land was rightfully theirs. The West Indian Negro also had the advantage of numerical strength, plus an infrequency of contacts with the ruling group.

The American Negro, however, underwent a physical and spiritual alienation without parallel in modern history. He was overwhelmed militarily and economically, transplanted from his native soil, then subjected not only to a dominant elite, but to what the poet Claude McKay called a cultural hell—a hell created by a powerful, materialistic, brutal frontier society that was uncertain of its own identity, yet seeking to assure itself of status by denying status to its victims.

AFTER THE CIVIL WAR

The slave system crumbled. The Reconstruction Era followed, but this was sabotaged by those who sold the Negro back to his former owners. Jim Crow legislation further oppressed him. The southern slaveholding oligarchy remained unchallenged and now, more than one hundred years later, as the Negro struggles to complete the first American Revolution, it seems remarkable indeed that he ever owned a house, let alone a theatre.

Despite hostility, the Negro was part of the drama long before the United States became a nation. John Leacock's *The Fall of British Tyranny* (1776) described recalcitrant slaves who promised to kill their masters upon attaining freedom. *Yorker's Stratagem* (1795) dealt with a New Yorker's marriage to a West Indian mulatto. Murdock's *The Triumph of Love* (1795) featured the cackling, comic servant, despite the fact that black Crispus Attucks was not comic when he shed the first blood in the American Revolution and black Phoebe Fraunces did not cackle when she saved the life of George Washington.

In the early part of the nineteenth century a group of free New York Negroes, spearheaded by James Hewlett, organized the African Company at Bleecker and Grove Streets. In 1821 this group performed Shakespearean plays before mixed audiences. Disorderly whites forced the management to segregate them and also to lament that whites did not know how to behave at entertainment designed for ladies and gentlemen of color. This theatre, eventually destroyed by white hoodlums, is reported to have influenced the great Ira Aldridge who went abroad where he was acclaimed by European royalty.

ORIGIN OF MINSTREL TRADITION

In the middle of the nineteenth century a number of plays attempted to deal with the Negro as subject matter. J. T. Trowbridge's *Neighbor Jackwood* (1857) and Stowe's *Uncle Tom's Cabin* were notable efforts. Dion Boucicault's *The Octoroon* reflected many of the traditional attitudes towards the Negro— that he was either a happy-go-lucky creature or a person with "unclean blood." The nineteenth century was, however, chiefly the era of the minstrel tradition—*the tradition originally created by slaves to satirize their masters*. White performers copied this pattern, popularized it, and spread the concept of the

shuffling, chicken-stealing Negro to a society willing to embrace any representation of the Negro that denied his humanity. Following the Civil War, Negroes themselves joined the minstrel tradition, blackened their faces and imitated whites imitating them.

The wave of minstrelsy overflowed into the latter part of the nineteenth century. A group of showmen objected to it. Sam T. Jack's *The Creole Show* (1890) broke with the minstrel pattern. Later came *The Octoroons,* then Bob Cole's *A Trip to Coontown* (1898), the first show to be written, directed and produced by Negroes. In 1898 Will Marion Cook and Paul Laurence Dunbar offered *Clorindy, the Origin of the Cakewalk.* Bert Williams, George Walker, Ernest Hogan, Alex Rogers, Jesse Shipp, S. H. Dudley and J. Rosamond Johnson saw to it that the break with minstrelsy was complete. They produced a series of musicals with plot, characterization and meaning.

But, Thomas Dixon's *The Clansman,* later filmed as *The Birth of a Nation,* echoed existing attitudes towards the Negro. Race riots flared. The robber barons built their empires and the Theatrical Trust Syndicate brought the big business concept to the American theatre. This Syndicate controlled the theatre and, because Mrs. Fiske and Sarah Bernhardt incurred their disfavor, the former was compelled to play in second rate theatres and the latter in a tent. The Negro artist found himself unable to get inside the Broadway theatre as performer or patron. Only Bert Williams worked on the Broadway stage. In 1910 the Negro performer had to go to Harlem.

He went because the fabric of theatre life excluded him. Some Negro actors welcomed the exile to Harlem. There they could perform roles previously denied them. They could play love scenes—something that was "taboo" while performing before whites. There, too, they could escape the raging hostility rampant in downtown areas. Many re-

membered too well the 1900 race riot when the mob yelled: "Get Williams and Walker!" Many knew, too, that comedian Ernest Hogan had to lock himself in a theatre overnight to escape from a lynch mob.

Harlem, therefore, offered the new Negro resident a haven from an unfriendly world despite the fact that he often had to fight neighboring whites in hand-to-hand battles. Many classes of Negroes poured into Harlem. Although a large number came from the South, this group had either heard about the theatre or seen Negro touring companies. In America at the turn of the century there existed approximately five thousand theatres as well as tent shows and civic auditoriums. To these came the Williams and Walker Company, Black Patti's Troubadours, and others. The movie industry had not yet challenged the economics of theatre. Despite the rise of the Syndicate, theatre was then a primary form of entertainment. It had not yet become a totally middle class luxury.

The Negro who moved to Harlem, therefore, was receptive to the theatre movement that grew around him. For one thing, he could not go into any other theatre. Had he been able to go, he would have witnessed vapid Cinderella stories unrelated to his daily life. Therefore, he flocked readily to the Crescent Theatre, opened by Eddie Hunter on 135th Street. Lester Walton leased the Lafayette Theatre and later stock companies appeared at the Lincoln and Alhambra Theatres. These groups presented Negro versions of Broadway plays, originals, dance-dramas, classics and musicals. The carriage trade often journeyed uptown to openings. Florenz Ziegfeld bought the finale of *Darktown Follies* for his own production. Another show, *Darkeydom,* saw many of its sketches sold to Broadway producers.

On April 5, 1917, the Negro drama again moved towards downtown circles. Ridgely Torrence's *Three Plays for a Negro Theatre,*

directed by Robert Edmond Jones, opened at the Old Garden Theatre. Charles Gilpin appeared in John Drinkwater's *Abraham Lincoln* and in Eugene O'Neill's *The Emperor Jones* (1920) at the Provincetown Theatre. Later, O'Neill's *All God's Chillun Got Wings* fanned flaming headlines because the play dealt with miscegenation. The Negro theatre artist had returned to the downtown area, doing what he felt whites would pay to see, or performing plays that reflected a white point of view.

The Negro Renaissance flowered. *Shuffle Along, Goat Alley* (1921), *Strut Miss Lizzie* (1922), *The Plantation Revue* (1922), *How Come?* (1923), *Chip Woman's Fortune* (1923), *Chocolate Dandies* (1924), *From Dixie to Broadway* (1924), *Topsy and Eva,* and Paul Robeson in a revival of *The Emperor Jones* (1925) were major downtown offerings during the 1920's. 1925 ushered in the first Negro-written Broadway drama, Garland Anderson's *Appearances.* Also seen were such offerings as *Lucky Sambo, My Magnolias, Deep River, In Abraham's Bosom, Show Boat,* and Wallace Thurman's *Harlem.* Later, too, came *Porgy,* then *The Green Pastures.*

EFFECT OF MOVIES ON THEATRE

Theatrical activity continued in Harlem. Night clubs flourished. This was the period when the Negro was in vogue. Commercialism flooded the community. Stage presentations gave way to vaudeville sketches as the commercial-minded sought to sell to whites what they wanted to see and hear about Negroes. And then the movie industry reared its head. Where there had been approximately five thousand American theatres in 1900, the arrival of talking pictures reduced this amount drastically. By 1940 there were only 200 in the nation. The moving picture replaced the stage and, in addition to the novel form, the prices were considerably cheaper. And many

Negroes frankly sought this type of entertainment because at least it was honest. It did not attempt to represent them in any light.

One of the ventures that suffered as the movies rose to power was the Theatrical Owners and Bookers Association. This group, known as "Toby," was organized, owned and managed by Negroes who controlled a nationwide circuit. Negro performers were assured of continued work.

The depression, the movies and the extended influences of white managers destroyed Toby. Veterans Sidney Easton and Elsworth Wright have declared that Negro actors did not know unemployment until Toby went out of business.

The depression of 1929 temporarily halted the Harlem theatre movement. Negroes appeared in a number of professional shows: *Hot Rhythm, Brown Buddies, Lew Leslie's Blackbirds, Sweet Chariot, Fast and Furious, Swinging the Blues, The House of Connelly, Sugar Hill, Savage Rhythm, Never No More, Bloodstream, Black Souls* and *Blackberries of 1932.* Negroes were in a sober mood during the depression years. Hall Johnson's *Run, Little Chillun,* Langston Hughes' *Mulatto,* John Wexley's *They Shall Not Die* and Paul Peters'-George Sklar's *Stevedore* were serious works. This era ushered in, too, such vehicles as *Four Saints in Three Acts, Mamba's Daughters, Roll Sweet Chariot, Porgy and Bess, The Swing Mikado* and *The Hot Mikado.*

The nineteen-thirties brought professional attempts to the Harlem area. Rose McClendon and Dick Campbell organized the Negro People's Theatre. The Harlem Players, a stock company, presented Negro versions of *Sailor, Beware* and *The Front Page* at the Lafayette Theatre. This group tried to speak to a community that concerned itself with eating regularly, with being dispossessed, and with relatives being lynched in the Southland. The troubles of a sailor and the problems of

a newspaperman hardly interested Harlem. The Harlem Players soon went out of business. Another group, the Harlem Experimental Players, produced Regina Andrews' plays, directed by Harold Jackman. The Harlem Suitcase Theatre presented Langston Hughes' *Don't You Want To Be Free?* and Dick Campbell and Muriel Rahn organized the Rose McClendon Players. Housed at the 124th Street Library auditorium, this group produced George Norford's *Joy Exceeding Glory* and Abram Hill's *On Striver's Row.*

Best known of the uptown groups, however, was the Negro Unit of the Federal Theatre. It presented at the Lafayette such plays as George McEntee's *The Case of Philip Lawrence,* J. Augustus Smith's *Turpentine* (written with Peter Morrell), Frank Wilson's *Walk Together, Chillun,* Rudolph Fisher's *The Conjure Man Dies,* Shaw's *Androcles and the Lion,* William Du Bois' *Haiti* and George Kelly's *The Show Off.* Its most highly acclaimed production was the Orson Welles-John Houseman offering, *Macbeth,* on April 14, 1936. Canada Lee was a member of the cast. This Federal Unit was a solvent, skillful group that attracted theatregoers of all incomes. When an act of Congress ended the Works Progress Administration, it left Harlem without a low-priced professional theatre.

The Negro Playwrights Company, organized towards the end of the nineteen-thirties, attempted to supply the community with professional theatre. Theodore Ward's *Big White Fog,* directed by Powell Lindsay, opened at the Lincoln Theatre and introduced Frank Silvera to New York audiences. Financial difficulties brought this organization to an untimely end.

During the 1940's the Negro was involved on Broadway as well as in Harlem. The Richard Wright-Paul Green play, *Native Son,* starring Canada Lee, and Paul Robeson's *Othello* were significant achievements. *Cabin in the Sky* enjoyed a successful run. In Har-

lem, Abram Hill, Frederick O'Neal, Austin Briggs-Hall, and a number of talented theatre people formed the American Negro Theatre, and housed it in the auditorium of the 135th Street Library. In addition to Hill's two plays, *On Striver's Row* and *Walk Hard,* such worthwhile ventures as Theodore Brown's *Natural Man* and Owen Dodson's *Garden of Time* were shown. But, it was the Abram Hill-Harry Wagstaff Gribble adaptation of *Anna Lucasta* that created a sensation and later moved to Broadway. That sensation also brought the American Negro Theatre into commercial focus—a move not welcomed by the group's founders. Despite its continued efforts to build a community theatre, the group found that, because of its success with *Anna Lucasta,* it was judged in terms of Broadway fare.

With the end of World War II a number of dramatists turned to the post-war adjustment of the Negro. *Deep Are the Roots, Jeb, Strange Fruit* and *On Whitman Avenue* appeared. *St. Louis Woman, Carib Song, Lysistrata, Mr. Peebles and Mr. Hooker, Bal Negre, Beggar's Holiday, Finian's Rainbow, Street Scene, Our Lan',* and *Set My People Free* all involved Negro artists.

American attitudes towards the Negro underwent a change in the post-war world, a change reflected in many avenues of the nation's life. Nationalism roared from colonial lands. American Negroes echoed this roar. Some whites found it easier to accept this roar as the voice of the "New Negro." To some extent this concept alleviated numerous guilt complexes and permitted the ruling group to believe it had only subjugated the "old, non-protesting Negro." What was not faced was the truth that Negroes had been protesting, agitating and fighting for human rights since 1619. But, now, after World War II, sharper lines of communication brought the revolts in Asia and Africa into the lives of Americans. The revolt of sup-

pressed peoples became a reality that had to be met.

A number of barriers relaxed. Negroes now found they could purchase seats to Broadway houses—seats that were not on the aisle. Prior to 1945 only three Broadway houses sold seats to Negroes that were not on the aisle. This practice was based on the belief that whites did not want Negroes climbing over them. The Playwrights Company's declaration of principles in 1945 had much to do with this shift in policy. In addition, the company also declared its members would deal specifically with Negroes in dramatic terms. Interesting examples of the integration of the Negro in "white shows" followed. *Detective Story* (1948) and *The Shrike* (1951–52) featured Negro actors in roles that were not specifically Negroid. Actors Equity Association launched repeated drives, urging the continuation of this pattern. The Greenwich Mews Theatre, a professional Off-Broadway company, followed this pattern in productions of *Widower's Houses, Major Barbara, Time of Storm* and *Monday's Heroes.* Broadway, however, continued to use the Negro actor in specified roles, and in roles the Negro himself did not always find to his liking. *The Member of the Wedding, Lost in the Stars, The Wisteria Trees, The Autumn Garden, The Climate of Eden* and *The Crucible* are plays involving Negroes.

In November, 1950, a group of Negro playwrights met in Harlem with representatives of four community theatre groups: the Harlem Showcase, the Committee for the Negro in the Arts, Ed Cambridge and the "Y" drama group, and the Elks Community Theatre. The American Negro Theatre had disbanded and many of its charter members wandered into the aforementioned groups. At the meeting a Council on the Harlem Theatre was formed. A resolution noted that the use of Negro actors in non-Negro roles offered limited employment to a large group of ac-

tors. In addition, it neither encouraged nor assisted in disseminating the cultural values of the Negro people. The Council noted, too, that the commercial failure of Theodore Ward's *Our Lan'* (1947)—after its initial Off-Broadway success—suggested that the commercial theatre wanted to tolerate the Negro, but it did not want to deal with him in strong, truthful, dramatic terms. The Council members declared that the serious play of Negro life met repeated commercial failure because it was often written from a "white point of view." Generally, plays involving Negroes had a "good" white character helping the black people out of trouble. The obvious implication, the Council noted, was that white theatregoers faced psychological barriers and could not identify with central, sympathetic Negro characters.

The Council urged the representative groups to produce plays by Negro writers and to mutually assist one another in casting, producing and promoting. The target was the Off-Broadway area. A number of Negro-written plays appeared in library basements, in community auditoriums and lodge halls, financed quite often because the group collected money from its members and launched a production. Some of the plays shown were: Harold Holifield's *Cow in the Apartment* and *J. Toth,* this writer's *The Bancroft Dynasty* and *The Cellar,* Gertrude Jeanette's *This Way Forward* and *Bolt from the Blue,* Julian Mayfield's *The Other Foot,* Ossie Davis' *Alice in Wonder* and Alice Childress' *Just a Little Simple.* These plays, written, directed and produced by Negroes, appeared primarily during the 1950–51 period.

In the midst of what Harlemites considered a Renaissance, the Apollo Theatre sponsored two shabby productions of "white" plays with Negro actors: *Detective Story* and *Rain.* Both productions were artistically and commercially unsuccessful. The Apollo's management stated publicly that Harlemites did not

care for serious drama. The Council on the Harlem Theatre issued a statement declaring: "The owner of the Apollo has insulted the Negro people by bringing to this community two inferior pieces with little meaning to our lives. Ridiculous prices were charged and, when we exercised the buyer's right [of withholding patronage] we were accused of lacking taste."

The Apollo management's charge, however, served as a catalytic agent for productions by Negro authors. On October 15, 1951, William Branch's *A Medal for Willie* was presented by the Committee for the Negro in the Arts at the Club Baron on Lenox Avenue. The critics hailed the play which posed in strong dramatic terms the question: should the Negro soldier fight and die abroad or should he take arms against the prejudiced Southland? In September 1952, Ossie Davis' *Alice in Wonder* opened at the Elks Community Theatre and it, too, roared the truth about the Negro's plight in America.

The early nineteen-fifties witnessed another significant event. Large numbers of Negroes moved from Harlem to Long Island, Brooklyn, the Bronx and Westchester. Many theatre workers and playgoers moved, too. Apartment houses became rooming houses, occupied by those who fled the South in terror. There was a shift, too, in methods of producing plays. Community theatres all over the city broke down. The Yiddish Theatre saw an era approaching when it would no longer profit on Second Avenue. Producers were no longer anxious to own theatres, but rather to rent them, produce a play there and let someone else worry about maintaining the property. Those Negroes who had sought so valiantly to build a theatre in the Harlem area now turned towards Broadway and Greenwich Village.

Most of the professional theatre work since that time has been performed in those areas. On September 24, 1953, Louis Peterson's *Take a Giant Step* opened on Broadway. The Charles Sebree-Greer Johnson play, *Mrs. Patterson,* also appeared on Broadway. On October 24, 1954, William Branch's *In Splendid Error* excited audiences at the Greenwich Mews Theatre. In 1955 Alice Childress' satire, *Trouble in Mind,* delighted audiences at the same theatre. Luther James produced an all-Negro version of *Of Mice and Men* in the Greenwich Village area and, on March 29, 1956, Earl Hyman appeared as *Mr. Johnson* on Broadway. Despite Mr. Hyman's remarkable performance, the play failed.

The 1956–57 season brought three Negro-written plays to Off-Broadway stages: Louis Peterson's *Take a Giant Step,* revived at the Jan Hus House, this writer's *A Land Beyond the River* at the Greenwich Mews, and the Langston Hughes-David Martin folk musical, *Simply Heavenly,* at the 84th Street Theatre. These plays should have ended the bromide that Negro audiences do not support theatre. Negro theatregoers were directly responsible for the financial success of these plays.

On March 11, 1959, Lorraine Hansberry's *A Raisin in the Sun* opened on Broadway to acclaim and later won the Critics Circle Award. It enjoyed a long and successful run, then later toured. During the 1961–62 season Errol John's *Moon on a Rainbow Shawl* was shown on the Lower East Side and in May, 1961, Jean Genet's *The Blacks* settled down at the St. Mark's Playhouse for a long run. *Fly Blackbirds,* a revue, won critical acclaim Off-Broadway while the Ossie Davis satire, *Purlie Victorious,* was hailed by Broadway theatregoers during the 1961–62 season.

In reviewing this brief—and, of necessity, superficial—survey, it seems amazing that Negro theatre workers have managed such a considerable output. It should be remembered that many of the ventures discussed here were written, directed and produced under harrowing circumstances. The artists gen-

erally worked full time at other jobs. They had no well-to-do relatives who could maintain them. They performed at night while working or struggling during the day to pay their rents. And, too, these plays were supported by people whose incomes were, at most, uncertain.

Whether it is possible to build a Harlem community theatre in an era when community theatres are almost non-existent remains a tantalizing question. However, people like Maxwell Glanville, Jay Brooks and other tireless workers continue their efforts in Harlem. They fight eternally rising costs, the omnipotence of Broadway, cheap movie and television fare and a changing community.

For the theatre worker outside Harlem, we can only foresee an occasional successful production. One cannot resist noting, however, that the produced plays will be written by whites dealing with the strings attached to an interracial love affair or some other area of Negro life receptive to white audiences. We may even have the Birmingham story brought to the stage, but it will probably be written by a white author who will deal with the problem of a "good" white caught in the throes of an uprising. Theatre in America remains a middle class luxury wherein the playwright speaks, cajoles, seduces, and lies to an expense-account audience. Until it becomes once again an art form willing to attract all people, we see no change in the type of play being produced.

Yet, a courageous producer has before him a rich opportunity. Negro playwrights are numerous and they wait eagerly for a producer who has not been "brainwashed." One of the most needed theatre workers at present is the Negro producer. He could utilize the rich dramatic history of these times, the wonderful artists and the splendid audiences that can be attracted if the theatre speaks to them in terms of the truth of their daily lives.

—1963

Vinnette Carroll and Robert Earl Jones in *Moon on a Rainbow Shawl*.

Gershwin's Folly

PORGY AND BESS—A FOLK OPERA?
by Hall Johnson

First Production of the **Tenth** *Subscription Season*

THE THEATRE GUILD *presents*

PORGY

A FOLK PLAY

By

DOROTHY *and* DUBOSE HEYWARD

The production directed by ROUBEN MAMOULIAN

Settings by CLEON THROCKMORTON

CHARACTERS
(in the order of appearance)

Maria, keeper of the cookshop	Georgette Harvey
Jake, captain of the fishing fleet	Wesley Hill
Lily	Dorothy Paul
Mingo	Richard Huey
Annie	Ella Madison
Sporting Life	Percy Verwayne
Serena, Robbin's wife	Rose MacClendon
Robbins, a young stevedore	Lloyd Gray
Jim, a stevedore	Peter Clark
Clara, Jake's wife	Marie Young
Peter, the honeyman	Hayes Pryor
Porgy, a crippled beggar	Frank Wilson
Crown, a stevedore	Jack Carter
Crown's Bess	Evelyn Ellis
A Detective	Stanley de Wolfe

Porgy and Bess—A Folk Opera?

WHEN IT was first announced that an operatic version of *Porgy* was in preparation, I had grave misgivings about it. From my previous knowledge of the original novel and the subsequent dramatic version, I was unable to believe that a musical setting could add anything to the value of the story—that, in fact, it could not do anything but weaken and sentimentalize it. Here was a play, it seemed, which simply did not "invite" music other than, maybe, a few incidental tunes for atmosphere. Nor was I reassured by the names of those to be connected with the production. It is one thing to approach a task with good intentions. But the best of intentions can never take the place of adequate preparation and seasoned experience in the particular requirements of that task. And it seemed to me that a job of such a special nature made very special requirements. To begin with, there was the question of opera as a musical form; there was the question of Negro music, the behavior of Negroes in general and of Porgy and Bess in particular; and then there was Mr. Gershwin, who was to make an artistic unity of all these ingredients. This would be a stiff test, even for a specialist, and I was not optimistic. However, I wanted to be able to like it and I did want it to be, at least, a good show.

After having sat and stood through four performances of *Porgy and Bess,* I am now certain that I do like it and that it is a good show. I like it because I have always admired Gershwin's music and this opera, whatever its faults, contains some very good Gershwin. Nobody should have expected it to be a perfect Negro opera. That would have been miraculous. In fact, it is only as good as it seems to be because of the intelligent pliability of the large Negro cast. While obviously working under strict direction, they still are able to infuse enough of their own natural racial qualities into the proceedings to invest them with a convincing semblance of plausibility. This is true even in the musical and dramatic moments most alien to the real Negro *genre*. If these singing actors had been as inexperienced as the composer, *Porgy and Bess* might have turned out to be as stiff and artificial in performance as it is on paper. Fortunately for all concerned, this is not the case. And I think it is a good show for no other reason than that it presents these capable people in an interesting and varied entertainment.

For *Porgy and Bess* is *interesting,* in its faults as well as in its virtues. And it is *varied,* oh, so varied! Now, even the freest conception of opera (grand-, folk- or any other kind) must respect some sort of form, since it is the musical embodiment of a story and a story without form is aesthetically unthinkable. Hence, while extreme interest is the one desirable quality, this interest is absolutely dependent upon the logical development of

Todd Duncan, the original Porgy of *Porgy and Bess*. Anne Brown was Bess.

William Warfield is probably the best-known stage Porgy. He has performed the role more than two hundred times, here and on a tour of Europe sponsored by the State Department.

The Crap Game.

Leontyne Price is one of the outstanding actresses who have played Bess. She toured abroad in this role for the State Department in 1952, with William Warfield as Porgy.

Another Bess has been Joyce Bryant. Jimmy Randolph played Crown.

the chosen form. Extreme variety, therefore, whether in the material or in its treatment, is valuable only to the degree in which it can subserve the general interest. This requires it to be so subtly blended into the form that there are no seams nor wrinkles; otherwise the interest is broken up and dispersed. Successfully handled, the variety-element in an opera should be noticeable only in retrospect —after the performance is all over. The performance in progress must give the impression of *one* experience, seen and felt through its own necessary and illuminating ramifications.

From a purely technical angle, the chief fault in Mr. Gershwin's opera is inexpert craftsmanship in the manipulation of the variety-element. We are confronted with a series of musical episodes which, even if they do not belong together, could be made to appear as if they do by a better handling of the musical connecting tissue. Without necessarily using the *leit-motif* system, there could and should be more consistent thematic development in the orchestral interludes which join these episodes. When the responsibility of bridging the gap is left to conversational *recitativo,* our composer is even less successful. The speeches are set to musical lines which hamper their intelligibility by the use of misplaced accents and unnatural inflections. The Mendelssohn of *Elijah* or the Strauss of *Salomé* would be excellent schoolmasters for Mr. Gershwin in this subject of *recitativo.* Even better, for his current needs, would be a perusal of the freer verse-lines of any of the Negro spirituals, wherein the significance of every word is immeasurably heightened by its tonal investiture. These things are of paramount importance in opera, the most artificial of musical forms. By the very act of constantly singing, the actor is denied any serious attempt at dramatic realism, so it is the music which must be the authoritative story-teller. The orchestra must govern and define the changes of mood, the

recitativo must be more eloquent than the spoken word and the solo and ensemble numbers must grow naturally out of the ebb and flow of the story as told in the music. One life must animate the whole. So, while *Porgy and Bess* may be delightful as a musical show, it is a bit disconcerting as opera.

Now, what should be the requisites for writing good Negro opera—or a good opera *about* Negroes—which is an altogether different affair? Both must be a musical recounting of a good story of Negro life dominated by Negro thought. If the operatic technique is sound, no matter what the musical idiom, the result can be a good opera about Negroes. A good Negro opera, however, must be not only good opera but must be written in an authentic Negro musical language and sung and acted in a characteristic Negro style. Perhaps it is Mr. Gershwin's fault if he has not written a good opera, but he can hardly be blamed if he has not quite satisfied our notion of what a good Negro opera should be. This would require more time and application than any composer not a specialist in this line could be expected to put into it. The informing spirit of Negro music is not to be caught and understood merely by listening to the tunes and Mr. Gershwin's much-publicized visits to Charleston for local color do not amount even to a matriculation in the preparatory school that he needed for his work. Nothing can be more misleading, especially to an alien musician, than a *few* visits to Negro revivals and funerals. Here one encounters the "outside" at its most external. The obvious sights and sounds are only the foam which has no meaning without the beer. And here let it be said that it is not the color nor the aloofness of the white investigator which keeps him on the outside. It is the powerful tang and thrill of the "foam" which excites him prematurely and makes him rush away too soon—to write books and music on a subject of which he has not even begun to

scratch the surface. It is to be regretted that the whites who have remained longer and learned more seem to count no serious musicians among their number.

Mr. Gershwin has at his command, however, a certain Negroid flavor which has lent piquancy to some of his earlier compositions and which shows up to occasional advantage in his opera. But, while we agree that a composition in a definite racial vein must not necessarily reek in every single measure with that particular style, still, we feel that, in a work of the proportions of *Porgy and Bess,* there should be more than just an occasional flavor. I am, doubtless, discrediting many places where Mr. Gershwin himself is sure he has caught the "color." That is to be expected and can be easily accounted for. But there is, in his approach to Negro music, another flaw, much more serious because more elementary, which should be noticed first.

One basic quality exists in genuine Negro music which even the fairly musical layman must have recognized long ago. That is the quality of utter simplicity—in theme and in style. It is only in the singing of large groups of Negroes that a contrapuntal or harmonic complexity may occasionally seem to be present, and this illusion is due to the simple approach of the individual singers. Each sings his part as he feels it. The result is musical because each contrapuntal part keeps constantly in mind the announced theme; it sounds complicated because the rapt creator of each part is not bothering himself at all about the elaborate improvisation his neighbor may be preferring at the same moment. But the fundamental idea of simplicity is still active, following the law that simple people reacting to elementary situations will express themselves simply and directly. Mr. Gershwin must be aware of this law. Still, in the heavy, involved treatment of his thematic material, he suggests sophisticated intricacies of attitude which could not possibly be native to

the minds of the people who make up his story.

If this is a matter of deliberate choice on Mr. Gershwin's part, we will still try to accept him on his own grounds. After all, he is an individual artist, as free to write about Negroes in his own way as any other composer to write about anything else. The only thing a really creative artist can be expected to give us is an expression of *his own* reaction to a given stimulus. We are not compelled to agree with it or even to like it. It is not to be considered as just another photograph of *our* old estimates snap-shotted by a new photographer. True, we should expect Mr. Gershwin to have a more intimate contact with his subject than the European composers who have attempted Negro idioms. But, if he has and does not care to profit by it, we still must accept his contribution as the sum total of what he really feels. What we are to consider then is not a Negro opera by Gershwin, but Gershwin's idea of what a Negro opera should be. The fact that it is advertised under the broader sub-title, *American Folk Opera,* does not disguise the specific direction of his attempt.

Now, if we accept Mr. Gershwin's point of view, it becomes much easier for us to understand and forgive many things. We may even begin to enjoy the French Creole quality of Clara's lullaby and the Russian cathedral suggestions in the wake scene with Serena's beautiful lament in three-four rhythm which should, by all means, have been in four-four. We can also see why the normal exigencies of good musicianship should occasionally have to give way before the necessity (?) of speaking a Broadway language on Broadway. Thus, Porgy's song, "I Got Plenty of Nothin'," besides lacking every true racial quality, gets punctuated (or punctured), by a series of sudden off-tone shouts in the manner of the cheaper Escamillos about to enter the bull ring—a style no Negro singer ever uses. And the inimitable Sportin' Life, who can moan so

naturally and persuasively to Bess—"Dere's a Boat Leavin' Soon for New York," is required in the picnic scene to try to sing "It Ain't Necessarily So." The first song becomes, through the art of John Bubbles, a real Negro gem. The second-named song is so un-Negroid, in thought and in structure, that even Bubbles cannot save it. Without the least shadow of a dramatic pretext, poor Sportin' Life, otherwise a well-drawn character, is pulled out of focus to sing to his merry friends *at a picnic* this would-be-sophisticated sort of song with verses compounded of flippant wisecracks on Biblical characters. Now, we can believe that a boastful bully like Crown, in the excitement of a dreadful hurricane, might stalk fearlessly among his panic-stricken brethren and jeer at their prayers to a God who, for that moment, at least, seems to have nothing but scorn for everything weak. It is not easy, however, to believe that Sportin' Life (a genuine product of Catfish Row, for all his smart talk about New York), could be so entirely liberated from that superstitious awe of Divinity which even the most depraved Southern Negro never quite loses. His immorality is fleshly, not cerebral. In a white revue and sung by the proper type of comedian, this song would be actually clever and amusing. Here, in the wrong place and in the wrong hands, it can only suggest a pathetic Gilbert and Sullivan vainly trying to go slumming in a very smudgy coat of burnt-cork.

These are a few of the instances where Mr. Gershwin's music has missed a Negro feeling. At other times he has succeeded in catching a real racial strain. For example, the opening measures of the love-duet between Porgy and Bess have a delightful Negroid flavor which is already familiar to the composer and his admirers. And later in the opera, when Bess is trying to resist the ferocious blandishments of Crown on the island, she sings a few pages of such vibrant beauty, so replete with the tragedy of the minor spirituals, that most of what follows is made to sound a little more false by reason of the absolute rightness of this episode.

So much for the music of *Porgy and Bess.* But no matter what it may present now in point of authenticity or spuriousness, we may be sure that it would have been certain of better results if the staging had been more sympathetic. Of what good could be the truest Negro operatic idiom if it is to be coupled, as in this case, with a stage-direction which affronts every sensibility of the Negro temperament? Will the time ever come when a colored performer on a Broadway stage can be subtle, quiet or even silent—just for a moment, and still be interesting? Must the light revues always be hot, fast and *loud,* and the serious (?) pieces always profane, hysterical and *louder? Always loudness! Always anything* makes for monotony and Negroes can *truthfully* be everything *but* monotonous. On the contrary, the faculty of rapid and complete change of mood has always been their principal artistic charm as well as their surest social salvation. Why does Clara have to *scream* the lullaby to her baby in the middle of the noisome courtyard of Catfish Row where only a drunk could sleep? Why does Porgy have to *bawl out* his contentment, his new-found, inward happiness—like a young and fiery captain of Hussars brandishing his sword before his men about to rush into battle? This inexcusably incorrect treatment falsifies and weakens the effect of the only two quiet and introspective songs in the whole piece. And why, *in opera,* spoil two songs in order to keep a stageful of people in turbulent motion—and for no other reason?

Again, we may pretend not to notice that Bess lags a little behind on the island for the sole purpose of being intercepted by Crown, and we can easily imagine that the watchful Maria, who passes just a few feet ahead, has just turned a sudden corner to keep from hearing and seeing the whole occurrence.

Also by now we are fully and painfully aware that in all Negro group-scenes on Broadway there must be much swaying of bodies and brandishing of arms with SHADOW EFFECTS —though this has not always been so stiffly stylized as in the present Russian Pictorial Edition. But we do think that the end of Serena's death-chant for her lost husband is sufficiently moving in itself and does not gain anything by her deliberate approach to the "baby spotlight" for a bigger and better shadow. In opera, shouldn't the song be more important than the shadow? There are already shadows enough and to spare.

Later, when Serena's room is being used by the crowd as a shelter from the hurricane and the combined effort of everybody present is centered for interminable minutes on keeping the door closed, we fail to see why the door *has* to be left open at the end of the scene. Of course, it did let the lightning flash in on the howling crowd. Result—more shadows and more *loudness!* But these shadows were distinctly anti-climactic after the better shadows of the wake scene, and the howling was all wrong *for once.* One does not have to know the simpler Negroes very long to learn how absolutely quiet they can be indoors during a storm. Some even crawl between mattresses. And that door would have been CLOSED! The second-hand lightning effect did not justify the sacrifice of a more veracious direction. Indeed, a sudden bang, a sudden hush and a "black-out" would have been better theatre.

So, taken in all, Mr. Gershwin has had several serious handicaps in trying to write his Negro opera: (1) the lack of story-telling qualities in the music, due to faulty operatic technique; (2) too little first-hand knowledge of his character-types and their real music; (3) the necessity (?) of perverting that little to satisfy Broadway tastes; (4) the colossal handicap of a direction which flounders uncertainly between alternating periods of *tableaux-vivants,* Russian ballet, conven-

tional opera and slapstick vaudeville. (One wished for the tipsy comedian to come out and have fun with the "animated" rocking-chairs. His presence was so thoroughly implied.)

Considering the many and diverse burdens American Folk Opera has had to struggle up under, *Porgy and Bess* has turned out surprisingly well. Manufactured and presented by such a brilliant array of names and performed with such faithful earnestness by such a clever cast, it affords quite adequate fare for the average uncritical audience without too much interest either in opera or in Negroes. This audience admires Gershwin (as I do) for his nice tunes, whether they appear singly, in rows or in clusters—like a bunch of grapes. At the moment, it also admires the Broadway Negro style because it does not know the real, and its intelligence is not yet insulted when Negro folk-material is mis-stated in foreign terms.

There are, at least, two signs of progress. Producers and audiences alike have admitted: (1) the value of Negro dramatic and musical material and (2) the folly of offering it with any other than Negro performers. The next step forward will be the insistence upon *authenticity of style.* But the first two admissions were the hard-won results of forced comparisons and the next step will be achieved only when the public has been made to see and like Negro material presented as its creators understand and feel it. Which places a definite responsibility upon all theatre-loving Negroes as well as upon every person, of whatever race, who loves and welcomes new expressions of beauty in the theatrical arts. The answer is simple and unavoidable.

There must be born a genuine Negro theatre in which superior training in theatrical technique must be the wise and willing servant of superior familiarity with the new material. Heretofore the reverse has always been

Bess: "I loves you Porgy, don't let him take me. . . ."

Porgy: "Tell me the truth, where is she, where is my gal, where is my Bess!

Porgy: "Oh, Lord, I'm on my way. I'm on my way to the Heavenly Land."

Crown slays his victim.

Diahann Carroll as Clara.

Sporting Life: "I got plenty of nothin' an' nothin's plenty for me . . ."

true. Capable Negro actors, no matter how deeply immersed in the folk-ways and folk-talk of their own people, have been made to take incorrect direction from clever theatre men who knew everything about everybody but Negroes—or, at best, had only the old spurious stage-imitations as models. And so the circle goes round and round.

Artistically, we darker Americans are in a most peculiar situation with regard to what we have to give the world. In our several hundred years of enforced isolation in this country we have had plenty of time and plenty of reason to sing each other songs and tell each other tales. These songs and stories have a hidden depth of meaning as well as a simple and sincere external beauty. But the same wall which forced them into existence has closed in tight upon their *meaning* and allows only their *beauty* to escape through the chinks. So that our folk-culture is like the growth of some hardy, yet exotic, shrub, whose fragrance never fails to delight discriminating nostrils even when there is no interest in the depths of its roots. But when the leaves are gathered by strange hands they soon wither, and when cuttings are transplanted into strange soil, they have but a short and sickly life. Only those who sowed the seed may know the secret at the root.

In other words, the folk-lore of the American Negro is not a frayed rag of a culture torn off by immigrants from the mother-garment in the old country and kept intact in the new by journals and periodic meetings. No matter what land saw the projection of its primal germ, its fecundation, growth and maturity occurred here and *here it must have its say*. If a thing of such beauty had come into being on some remote portion of the globe, women's clubs all over America would be paying lecturers to tell them all about it and enterprising

Broadway managers would be importing samples. But the externals of it have been lying around underfoot for generations and, by long familiarity with these externals, those who would make casual use of them are persuaded that what they see is all there is.

Peasants of other countries, on coming to America, quickly (and voluntarily) lose their individual folk-qualities in the effort to become Americans. They are encouraged in this process by every American institution. So that, in the theatre, no matter what the theme of the play, who produces it or who listens to it, it is an American play for an American audience. The Negro seems to melt into this theatrical pot only in direct proportion to the ignorance of the critic or the wilfulness of the director. The essential temper of his *true* folk-culture is so unique that it must be weakened if it is to be assimilated. In this state it is undervalued, like some common chemical which we use daily for humble purposes without suspecting its greater possibilities. Suddenly, an obscure scientist, who has been studying its properties for years, announces that it is a sure cure for a certain baffling disease. There is a period of surprise and skepticism. Then he proves the truth of his claim and there follows a period of gratitude for a new blessing.

It is possible, and not improbable, that an injection of genuine Negro folk-culture may be good for the anemia of the American theatre. If so, who will prove it? Only we who sowed the seed can know the full and potent secret of the flower. The fact that others try to master it and fail (while we are making up our minds what to do with it) should not fill us with resentment, but with pride and fresh determination. With the greatest patience and the best of intentions, all they can ever grasp is—a handful of leaves.

—1936

Perspectives

HISTORY AND THEATER
by Martin Duberman

THAT BOY LeROI
by Langston Hughes

EVERY NEGRO IN HIS PLACE
by William Talbot

In the play *In White America* Gloria Foster portrays the
15-year-old girl who tried to enter Central High School
in Little Rock. Michael O'Sullivan is the sympathetic white
man: "She just sat there, her head down. Tears were
streaming down her cheeks. I don't know what made me
put my arm around her, saying, 'Don't let them see you cry.'
Maybe she reminded me of my 15-year-old daughter."

Gloria Foster, Moses Gunn and Claudette Nevins in
Martin Duberman's *In White America*.

History and Theater

by Martin Duberman

Come, sit down, every mother's son, and re-hearse your parts.—Shakespeare, *A Midsummer Night's Dream*

I SUSPECT there are many besides myself who feel that historians are not communicating as well as they could, and that dramatists are not communicating as much as they might. It is the argument of this essay that the deficiencies of history and theater might be lessened if each would pay some attention to the virtues of the other.

First, however, I should make clear an underlying assumption: I believe the past has something to say to us. This may seem a truism, but an opposite view can be, and has been, cogently argued—the argument, if not the cogency, summed up in Henry Ford's statement, "History is all bunk." It is not my purpose to enter here in detail into the long-standing debate on whether history is or is not relevant to contemporary needs, can or cannot be objectively reconstructed, will or will not reflect the temporary bias of the historian and his culture. For the moment, I want only to make explicit my own premise that a knowledge of past experience can provide valuable guidelines, though not blueprints, for acting in the present. Those who do not share this assumption will hardly be concerned with the argument based upon it; there can be no wish to increase our awareness of the past if one holds that the past has

no present meaning. And in the same way, those who believe that the theater is already rich enough in ideas and perspectives will have little patience with my further argument that its range needs amplification.

But to begin with history. Professional historians do, of course, worry about the shortcomings of their craft, but their dominant concern is with the difficulty of reconstructing past events "objectively." Handicapped both by the paucity of evidence and by the distortions in it which their own preconceptions introduce, historians have fits of self-doubt as to whether they are re-creating the past or merely projecting onto it their own, and their society's, transient needs. Yet few historians are concerned with shortcomings of another sort: whether their findings have much meaning for modern man. Too often today the academic historian seems to think his job is over once he has wrestled with the problems inherent in assembling data. He is, he would say, a scholar, not a policy adviser or a communications expert; it is up to others to draw and transmit the relevance of his findings.

Not only is the historian himself likely to be indifferent to the contemporary significance of his research, but suspicious of others who emphasize it; they are thought to be "propagandists." It is right, of course, to be on guard against any attempt to distort past evidence in the service of some present need.

Yet such vigilance must be discriminating; a distinction should be made between reading contemporary meaning *into* the evidence, which is reprehensible, and reading it *from* the evidence, which is not. To do the latter is only to make explicit those conclusions already suggested by the data. The overt attempt to read "lessons" from history can, of course, be treacherous, but no worthwhile goal should be abandoned because it is difficult to attain. The effort to extract from the past something of use for our own experience is all that saves historical study from antiquarianism, the accumulation of detail for its own sake. If the past cannot be used—however conditionally—as a guide for the present, then its study is difficult to justify, at least to serious men. Historical writing becomes esthetics, the arrangement of past events in "pleasing" patterns, which, of course, can carry values of their own—except that historians have never been very good at esthetics. In asking them instead actively to search for "lessons," it should be stressed that no necessary threat is posed to historical objectivity. We would not ask historians to distort their findings, but to evaluate them, to be as eager to serve the living as the dead.

Assuming, then, that the past has some relevance for us, and that it is among a historian's proper functions—my own feeling is that it should be his preeminent function—to search for that relevance, it then becomes necessary to question the effectiveness with which such relevance (when found) is communicated. Since the invention of the printing press, the record of the past has been largely transmitted through the written word, and writing, a rational way of ordering and clarifying experience, makes an essentially intellectual appeal. Not always, of course, at the expense of the emotions: where the wish and skill are present, the writer can do much to evoke and engage our feelings. But the arousal of feelings is generally frowned on by the historian; emotion is thought to be an enemy rather than an adjunct of mind. Not surprisingly, therefore, historians have shown little regard for those literary skills best calculated to engage emotions. The majority of historians today eschew "lively" writing as a means of communication in much the same constricting way that they eschew relevance as its end. "Style" is thought to be an impediment to analysis, a frivolous sugar-coating repellent to those tough-minded heroes of the mind who prefer their ideas "straight."

Even were the historian more sensitive to the evocative potential of the written word, in immediacy he still could not rival the spoken word, which benefits from the direct confrontation of personality. In its beginnings, of course, the historical record *was* transmitted orally; in that sense, history began as theater. While no sensible person would advocate a return to this tradition, we may still wish to recapture something of its emotional impact. If we could bring the spoken word's immediacy and emotion to the presentation of history, a new richness of response, a new measure of involvement with the past, would be possible.

Almost all combinations of history and theater have been made by dramatists, with the result—as in Shakespeare's *Richard II* or John Osborne's *Luther*—that historical episodes have been used, shaped, and embellished for imaginative purposes. The past event becomes the occasion for a statement not in itself strictly historical. This is in accord with a writer's usual procedure; he transposes the raw material of experience, he makes it his own and, if he has sufficient insight and artistry, everyone's.

But the imaginative reworking of historical data is fundamentally inimical to what the professionals regard as "proper" history. The historian knows that his personality influences his interpretations, but this is not the same, he would say, as advocating such influence; a

virtue should not be made of necessity. Control and restriction of interaction between the subjective historian and his "objective" materials is essential. This intellectual fastidiousness may severely limit the opportunity for speculation, but it also minimizes the risk of contaminating the data. The professionals, in short, prefer to emphasize information rather than informing.

Yet the contrast between the historian's "objective" presentation of the past and, say, the novelist's subjective reworking of it, is overdrawn. It describes the historian's intention more than his result, for in a real sense he too necessarily indulges in imaginative combinations of fact and opinion. Historical writing is never merely litmus paper, recording an exact facsimile of past events, but always consists to some degree of one man's idiosyncratic interaction with the data. It may be, too, that if the historian is ever to make widely relevant statements, he will have to become more consciously and extensively the philosopher *commenting* upon historical materials.

But if the contrast between the writing of history and fiction has been overdrawn, it is nevertheless a contrast the historian cherishes. He would protest being asked to play philosopher speculating on human ends, or psychologist investigating human needs, or novelist describing human conditions. He defines the role of a historian as simply one of collecting and recording what survives of past experience, *not* commenting upon it. Given this self-image, he objects especially to the "distortions" which a writer like John Osborne makes in the historical record when converting it for the stage. This, the historian would say, is adding immediacy and emotion to the past at the sacrifice of accuracy and intellectual subtlety.

An historian myself, I am sympathetic to these professional scruples even while not being fully convinced by them. Despite the

risks, it seems to me worth searching for valid ways to combine history and theater, and not only to enrich historical presentation, but also to revitalize theatrical statement. For the benefits of a union between history and drama would not by any means be all on one side. If theater, with its ample skill in communication, could increase the immediacy of past experience, history, with its ample material on human behavior, could broaden the range of theatrical testimony. And there are grounds for believing that the theater's present range is badly in need of amplification.

The current mode of dramatic writing has been variously called the theater of the absurd, the theater of revolt, the theater of despair. The ugly, the empty, the irrational, the mechanical, the brutal, the apathetic—these are the dominant themes of contemporary theater. And they may well be the dominant themes of contemporary life. Perhaps today's playwrights, whose personal lives, we are told, have often been so melancholy, overdo the importance of these themes, confusing their own sorrows with the world's decline. But if the modern playwright has overdrawn the disintegrative aspects of modern life, it is not by much, judging from what we see around us. And the evidence of our senses is corroborated by the evidence of science. The portrayal of human behavior in the theater of the absurd closely resembles the description provided by sociologists, psychologists, and anthropologists. Man, these behavioral scientists tell us, *is* a creature who flees reality, who prefers comfortable deceptions to hard truths, whose yearning for approval drives him to think and act as his society dictates, whose libidinous instincts can propel him into brutal, selfish, destructive behavior. Thus the behavioral view of man seems to support the current theatrical view of man. If, therefore, we take the function of drama to be the accurate reflecting of contemporary life, the state of our current theater must be judged

satisfactory. Or, if unsatisfactory, only because our playwrights have not described the modern predicament with sufficient skill; the failure, according to this canon, would be one of execution, not intent.

It is possible to suggest, though, that the intent as well is too restricted. There is no inherent reason why drama need be limited to describing what *is*; it could also become concerned with what *might be*. One function of the theater should obviously be to reflect the actuality of life, but another might be to change it. Instead, by presenting man largely as brute, child or fool, the current theater fortifies and perpetuates those qualities. If men are told that they are at the mercy of impulse and irrationality, they become more likely to behave accordingly. Like it or not, the theater, partaking as it does of self-fulfilling prophecy, is a social force, though at present an inadvertent and negative one. Man's destructive qualities are real enough and must be faced. But other qualities—or at least potentials—are real as well, and they too should be brought to attention. At present they are not. Theater audiences see little to counteract the view that self-deception, hysteria, and savagery are synonyms for human nature.

Once again, the perspective of behavioral science is useful. Just as its findings validate the theater of the absurd, so they also support the need to supplement it. Psychologists and sociologists have made abundantly clear the immense plasticity and enormous adaptive power of human beings; if social demands and emphases are shifted, human action shifts accordingly. Thus, if we would not today celebrate man's innate goodness, we should be equally ready to recognize that nothing predetermines him to be cruel, vacuous, and selfish. As Berelson and Steiner point out in *Human Behavior,* man's "evil comes from frustration, not from inherent nature . . . he seeks acceptance . . . more than he seeks political power or economic riches, and he can

even control his strongest instincts, the libidinous side of his nature, to this end." Man is not only a social creature, but also a social product. If challenged to do so, he is capable of using reason and will to develop integrative, and control destructive, impulses. Why should not the theater put such a challenge to him? Why could it not help to alter the destructive behavioral patterns it now merely describes? There is no inherent reason why drama cannot be an agency of amelioration as well as a voice of despair.

We need not be sentimental about all this and emblazon Victorian mottoes like SHINE IN USE on our playbills. I am certainly not suggesting that the theater of absurdity be supplemented by some crude theater of "positive thinking." I am suggesting only that since integrative experiences exist in our lives, they should also have some representation in our theater. Though despair and disintegration may well characterize the dominant mood today, they do not tell the whole story either of our present condition, or, more significantly still, of our potential one. The theater, by making room for a demonstration of other aspects of human nature, could help to see that the current mood of disintegration does not become the permanent one.

One way (though certainly not the only one) of demonstrating man's potential for a wide variety of experiences and behavior is to put more history on the stage, either in fictional or documentary form. Both approaches have their drawbacks. Those characterizing fiction (à la Osborne) have already been discussed; my own experience with the documentary approach may serve to illustrate the special problems of that form.

In wanting to tell the story of being black "in white America" with maximum impact, I thought it worth trying to combine the evocative power of the spoken word with the confirming power of historical fact. Yet I did not wish to sacrifice historical accuracy in the

process. And so I tried staging the raw material of history itself rather than a fictionalized version of it. The two modes of procedure, of course, are not entirely different—as I argued earlier. Using historical documents—letters, news reports, diaries, and the like—does not guarantee objectivity; it would be naive to think that in selecting, abridging, cutting, and juxtaposing the materials of history, I was not also transmuting them. The past does not speak for itself, and the ordering intelligence that renders it, necessarily injects some degree of idiosyncrasy. The advantage of the documentary approach (if one is primarily interested in historical accuracy) is that it does at least minimize subjectivity and restrict invention. Its disadvantage (if one is primarily interested in making statements about experience) is that it circumscribes reflection and generalization. Instead of confining myself, for example, to the actual words John Brown spoke at his trial, I might have invented words to represent what I guessed to be his thoughts and feelings during his speech. In not doing so, I suspect that what I gained in accuracy I lost in insight. Truth of fact has less durable relevance than truth of feeling, for a fact is rooted in a particular context, whereas a feeling, being universal, can cross time.

There are, then, inherent difficulties in putting history on the stage: fictionalization can caricature the past, documentation can straitjacket it. Yet both techniques seem worth experimenting with, for history and theater, though the union be flawed, can contribute much to each other.

The great virtue of history, one the theater stands in need of, is that it counteracts present-mindedness—the belief that what *is* has always been and must always be. To have historical perspective is to become aware of the range of human adaptability and purpose. Thus the ancient world (and the eighteenth-century Enlightenment) saw man as a crea-

ture capable of using reason to perceive and follow "virtue"; the Christian view saw man capable of love as well as sin; the Renaissance believed that man's energy and will were sufficient to control both his personal destiny and his social environment.

Such views, of course, were philosophical models of what men could be, not necessarily what they were. But the dominant outlook of any period reflects actual as well as ideal behavior, for men build their self-images out of their experience as well as their aspirations. At any period, to be sure, ideal behavior is only approximated. Enlightenment France may have believed in the possibility—and necessity—of a rational life, but it was hardly free of sophistry and corruption; moderns have neither invented nor discovered man's capacity for the irrational and the vicious. But in other eras such qualities were not considered sufficient descriptions of human nature or insurmountable barriers to human aspiration; men could, they were told, resist their destructive impulses, could lead more than merely instinctive lives.

No doubt most of us today proceed on similar asumptions in daily life. But the assumptions get less formal recognition than they once did. We are not encouraged—in our culture generally, in our theater particularly—to recognize that human nature is malleable, capable of many forms and many goals. We are not encouraged to see that "absurdity" is only a partially true description of the way we live, and even more, that it tells us little of how we *might* live.

It is not the responsibility of the Albees or the Becketts to show us what we might be; their responsibility is to their own, not to all possible, visions. But for those concerned with the future as well as the present, something more in our theater wants saying. To recognize that human beings are curious, do strive, will reason, can love, is to wish for a theater that might express and encourage this

kind of human potential—precisely because that potential is scarcely visible today. We need the theater of the absurd to dramatize our weaknesses and failings, but we also need theater which might indicate our potential strengths and possible successes.

Putting history on the stage is hardly a cure-all. Not only does the technique, as I have argued, hold intrinsic difficulties, but it is true as well that historical theater would not necessarily be a theater of "affirmation"; undoubtedly much in man's past experience would underscore, rather than counteract, present pessimism. My only point is that the totality of past experience does include more than despair and defeat; there *is* material in history which chronicles achievement and possibility. Such evidence is around us today as well, of course, but we seem unable to use it; it may be a case of not being able to see the forest for the trees. This is exactly why an historical context may be needed if the "positive" aspects of human experience are to become accessible.

Merging the competencies of history and drama, therefore, could help to diminish the parochialism of both. Currently, historical study is fixated on past patterns and the theater on present ones; neither is sufficiently concerned with the future. If the variety of past experience could be communicated with an immediacy drawn from the theatrical idiom, both history and drama might become vehicles for change rather than only the recorders, respectively, of past and present attitudes. In being more fully exposed to the *diversity* of past human behavior, we might come to see that men (even if only *sometimes*) can give purpose and structure to their lives; can use the tensions of existence creatively, or at the worst, accept them with dignity; can, without sacrificing self-interest, treat others with respect and compassion. Such an awareness could be a useful corrective to the current penchant for underestimating ourselves, which, after all, is but one way of excusing and indulging our defeats.

—1964

That Boy LeRoi

by Langston Hughes

IT IS THE fashion for young authors of Negro plays nowadays to make their heroes all villains of the darkest hue, or crazy, living in crazy houses. The whites are for the most part villains or neurotics, too, so I gather that contemporary Negro playwrights do not like anybody any more—neither their stage characters, their audiences, their mothers, nor themselves. For poetry in the theater, some of them substitute bad language, obscenities of the foulest sort, and basic filth which seemingly is intended to evoke the sickest of reactions in an audience.

Certainly, "times do change," as the saying goes. I remember a quarter of a century ago when a few scattered damns in the theater were considered most advanced. When the word *God* was coupled with *damn* in Broadway's *What Price Glory?* it caused consternation. But in this Year of our Lord, 1965, four-letter words are flung across the footlights with impunity. A few seasons ago, such words might have been taken as adding a bit of spice to the dramatic cake. But nowadays bad words are in danger of becoming the whole cake. Why Lenny Bruce should go to jail alone while playwrights and actors from Broadway to Off-Broadway are having a field day with graffiti, I do not know. Since many novelists and playwrights, white and Negro, nowadays make no bones about printing the unprintable and speaking the unspeakable (insofar as good taste, decency and good manners go), why, in nightclubs, where the risqué has long been acceptable, should Lenny Bruce be shackled, muzzled and put behind bars? Did Mr. Bruce invent some new bad words?

In a talk I made in Paris concerning American Negro poetry, I said that I am glad Negro poets are doing everything other American poets are doing, and that their styles range from Harlemese to Villagese, from the conventional to the beatnik, from Pulitzer Prize winning Gwendolyn Brooks to Obie Award winner LeRoi Jones. Mr. Jones is currently the white-haired black boy of American poetry. Talented in other forms of writing as well, particularly theater, Mr. Jones might become America's new Eugene O'Neill—provided he does not knock himself out with pure manure. His current offering, *The Toilet,* is full of verbal excrement.

I remember that much vaunted realism of David Belasco in my youth. None of the Belasco productions I saw on Broadway can hold a candle to *The Toilet,* scenic or acting-wise. The set for *The Toilet* consists largely of a series of urinals, and the first thing the first actor does when he comes onstage is to use one. All the facilities of a high school toilet are used by the other performers, too, at various times. The bold and brilliant bunch of young Negro actors look as if they all come directly from Shirley Clark's roughneck film, *The Cool World,* whose leading

man now plays, as if to the manner born, the leading role in *The Toilet*. So realistic is both acting and direction in this play that the leading white boy, beaten to his knees by a gang of Negroes, drools spittle upon the stage as he tries to rise. The triumphant black boys end up sticking the white student's head into a urinal. What all this does for race relations (as if it mattered at this late date) I do not know.

Both *The Toilet* and *The Slave* may be taken as serious exercises in masochism and sadism, full of bloody kicks, and better than *The Brig* for thrills. Certainly the whites at the St. Mark's Playhouse are well beaten up in both plays before the evening ends. In *The Slave,* Al Freeman, Jr., as a black nationalist violently opposed to white liberals, slaps, kicks, punches, shoots and physically does in all the whites on stage. At one point in the proceedings, he pointed his pistol dead at Nat Hentoff in the first row of the auditorium. Long ago, the bully boy of Southern folklore, Stackolee, used to boast, "I'm the baddest Negro God's got." But Stackolee grew up in the good old days before the era of James Baldwin and LeRoi Jones, so Stackolee never laid eyes on Al Freeman, Jr., in a New York theater. I think that Stackolee, as a Negro of the old school, although of the sporting world, might be horrified, especially at the language used before ladies.

Therefore, for the sake of today's sensitive Negroes and battered white liberals, I would like to offer the producers at St. Mark's Playhouse a suggestion—double cast both plays, and alternate performances racially. Every other night let all the present Negro characters be played by white actors, and vice versa. Four times a week I would like to see *white* school boys in *The Toilet* beating up a *colored* boy and sticking his head into a urinal. In *The Slave* let a bullying *white* man kick, curse, browbeat and shoot a nice liberal *black* professor and his wife in their suburban living room. To reverse the complexions on stage every other night by alternating casts would make for very intriguing theatrical evenings. Black would then be white—and white, black —which alternately would cancel out each other—since some critics (like the able Michael Smith in *The Village Voice*) claim that LeRoi Jones may not really be writing about color at all, but instead is concerned with no group "smaller than mankind." God help us all!

—1965

LeRoi Jones' *The Toilet*, the most provocative Off-Broadway play of the 1965 season.

The Slave, on the same bill as *The Toilet*, was dramatically less successful. Many critics thought *The Slave* pointed out fundamental weaknesses in Jones' technique as a playwright.

Every Negro in His Place

The Scene on and off Broadway

by William Talbot

AT THE moment of this writing a New York producer of thirty-odd years experience, deeply involved in several forthcoming productions, sits in his modern office-with-patio, staring at the walls; while his son, a graduate student in political science at Yale, sits in a Florida jail with several whites and Negroes, including the mother of the governor of the State of Massachusetts. The art to which this producer has devoted his life seems to have failed where the sciences—social and political—have succeeded. Suddenly it seems that art is impotent, that it pales in importance at the critical moments of human history. And this producer is now brought forcefully to face the same moral dilemma that has only vaguely troubled most of us: what has the profession of the theatre done for the Negro?

To the regret of many, the truth is that the theatre does not lend itself to action, but to contemplation; it is not in the nature of the theatre arts that they do the field work of the social sciences. In spite of this, however, the theatre can point to some extraordinary achievements, commencing with *Uncle Tom's Cabin*, the very play that triggered the Negroes' emancipation; so it cannot be said to have been always impotent in the course of human history. The achievements are sparse,

however; and occasions such as this, when we might think we are standing idly by while others stand in for us in a noble cause, are the very times when we should take stock. The theatre has probably been more often delinquent than not. It seems to have disparaged the Negro more often than it has raised him to eminence. But I venture to say that hereafter the theatre—and through it, the other dramatic media—will be the subtlest and most powerful influence in dignifying the American Negro.

It is a big jump, but one we must take, from *Uncle Tom's Cabin* and *The Octoroon* to the memorable Pulitzer Prize plays by Paul Green and Marc Connelly, *In Abraham's Bosom* and *The Green Pastures*; and thence, through the agitprop plays of John Howard Lawson and his contemporaries of the depression era, to World War II. In the thirty-four years of the modern theatre since then, forty-odd plays about or related to Negro subjects have been produced in New York. A number of them we can dismiss immediately because they originated or were set abroad—*Lost in the Stars, House of Flowers, Jamaica, Kwamina, A Taste of Honey* (the cohabitation of a Negro boy and a white girl), and *Sponono*, which opened during the week of this writing.

John McCurry tries to gain admittance to a Southern
hospital for the injured Bessie Smith.

Harold Scott as the Negro orderly in Edward Albee's
The Death of Bessie Smith.

Jean Genet's *The Blacks*.

Ellen Holly (top) and Cynthia Belgrave in
Adrienne Kennedy's *Funnyhouse of a Negro*.

Until quite recently, American plays have followed mainly one of two lines: that of protest, and that of degradation. Protest plays have depicted the Negro as a victim of prejudice. He is compromised by immoral white women in *Native Son* and *Respectful Prostitute*. He is driven to tragedy when he forgets his place and ventures into the community of whites in *On Whitman Avenue,* or into a rapport with a white girl in *Deep Are the Roots.* And he will bleed to death because no white doctor will touch his colored skin in *The Death of Bessie Smith.* The protest plays, surprisingly, have been preponderantly written by white authors. On the other hand, the play of Negro life, the type that stems from *The Green Pastures,* has been composed with considerable help from Negro artisans; and, sad to say, it is this type of play that has most contributed, however inadvertently, to the denigration of the Negro on the American scene. Though there may be a good guy here or there, it is both the economic and moral squalor of Negro life that we remember in *Cabin in the Sky, Porgy and Bess*, Ketti Frings' *The Long Dream* (a five-performance adaptation of Richard Wright's novel; 1960), and Errol John's *Moon on a Rainbow Shawl* (a moderate Off-Broadway success in the spring of 1962). Frings and John wrote their plays in the dark with the light on. For the Negro drama took a momentous turn back in September, 1953, and neither the play of protest nor that of Negro life may ever be the same again.

In 1953, Louis Peterson was a young writer who knew what it was like to be a Negro growing up with white boys: it was all stick-ball, ice cream and camaraderie; until one day he found that the boys were more interested in girls than in games, and that there was no longer any room for him in their lives: a Negro boy ultimately has to find girls and friends of his own. *Take a Giant Step,* the story of this boy's coming of age

and of his emergence into a hostile adult world, was touched with gentle humor and poignancy. It was followed in 1959 by Lorraine Hansberry's superb drama of Negro life, *A Raisin in the Sun.* There is some protest in it, to be sure, for the family does summon up its dignity when all else is gone, and move into the forbidden white neighborhood. But primarily this is a story of Negro life, of decent folk, their family relationships, their hopes and dreams; and especially of the invincible determination of the young truck-driver to pass on, just as his brick-layer father had passed on to him, a better life to his son. Just a bit each generation, the play seems to say, and we'll have a dignified family. This was a play to make a white person proud to share the same humanity as the Negro.

It is significant that the new wave of plays of Negro life are also by Negro authors; and those of protest, also by white authors. Michael Shurtleff's *Call Me by My Rightful Name* had a good run Off-Broadway in 1961, won a Drama Desk Award and may have set the pattern of protest plays for many years to come. It is the story of a liberal, nonconformist student who shares his room with a Phi Beta Kappa Negro, to show that he practices his beliefs and to prove that he is without prejudice. Later, however, when he learns that his rich girl friend had once been his roommate's mistress, he reverts. "When the chips are down," his father remarks, "you scream 'nigger' like everybody else." The play does not club you over the head; but at the same time you cannot leave the theatre without the torturing thought that *in extremis* you too might not be able to overlook the color of another person's skin.

Just two months later—and twenty years too late—Edward Albee presented his protest play, *The Death of Bessie Smith,* an Off-Broadway one-acter about a famous jazz singer who dies following an automobile ac-

cident because she is denied admission to a white hospital. It is so vulgar and so vulgarized that the theme itself is besmirched. Hardin Lemay's *Look at Any Man,* produced this season in the ANTA Matinee Series, is really a sardonic copy of *Call Me by My Rightful Name:* the husband-and-wife biographers of a Negro youth do not really have the regard that they profess for him.

What has superseded both types of Negro plays is a profoundly new kind that was inaugurated in May, 1961, by Genet's *The Blacks,* and that has carried through *Purlie Victorious,* of September of the same year, and *Funnyhouse of a Negro,* a one-acter that opened in January, 1964, under the aegis of Richard Barr, Clinton Wilder, and Edward Albee. This type of play is characterized by masks and fantasies, by irony and satire, by preposterous exaggerations, and by the continuing conflict of black and white. *Purlie Victorious,* by actor Ossie Davis, is comic as well, a marvelous parody on old Southern clichés (Colonel: "Are you trying to get nonviolent with me, boy?"), and yet immensely human (Woman: "Oh, child, being colored can be a lot of fun when they ain't nobody looking").

Adrienne Kennedy's *Funnyhouse of a Negro,* on the other hand, is dead serious. Because of its subconscious rationale, I found it hardly more satisfying than *The Blacks.* But the trio who brought us *Who's Afraid of Virginia Woolf?* is responsible for it; a lot of critics liked it; and so it will be set down here for the record. A Negro woman awakens in a phantasmagoric West Side roominghouse, and is immediately visited, in her populous imagination, by The Duchess of Hapsburg, Queen Victoria, Patrice Lumumba and Jesus Christ. The stage is set in this manner: all eight roles are played by Negroes; all the phantasms have whitened faces in the "dreams"; and all wear white except Lumumba and herself, who are in black. The woman

is a poet with a Jewish poet as her lover. Her father was very black, her mother light. She wants to be whiter, to have white friends, dine at white tables and be rid of kinky hair. We are given three stories about her father: that she killed him for giving her the strain of the jungle; that he committed suicide when Lumumba was killed; and that neither previous story is true, but that he is now living with a white whore. Her mother wanted her to be Jesus, and to "go back to Africa and Genesis and save the race." And Jesus responds: "My father is a black man." Speeches are repeated verbatim, over and over, in roundelay. At the final curtain, in silhouette, the woman is seen hanged. It will be a long, long time before the Negro theatre sees anything quite so cynical.

In May, 1964, *The Blacks* will complete its third year. It is so well known that I need not labor through a recapitulation of it here. Inasmuch as Genet's premise at the outset is, "We shall make communication impossible," it would be very nearly ridiculous to try. For my part, I have usually found him, in the mode of modern art, less conscious than sub- or pre-conscious; obscure, if not arcane; more romantic than rational; and more offensive than cordial. And I am constantly amazed at the number of He's who go to him to get slapped. But there is no gainsaying that *The Blacks* is a new departure in Negro theatre, and a hope for something good.

Lastly we come to a superb theatrical piece, the praises of which I'll be glad to sing forever. It is a history, and history in its ultimate form: a documentary of the Negro in the United States, from the days of the slave trade to the days of Little Rock, arranged from the actual records by Professor Martin B. Duberman, and entitled *In White America.* It consists of vignettes enacted on platforms by four men and two women, half of them Negro and half white. The topics, in historical progression, include slavery, the Civil

War, the Emancipation Proclamation ("The first day the Negro could be said to have a country"), education, Booker T. Washington, the Ku Klux Klan and Father Divine. Do not for an instant, however, think that *In White America* is a loaded lecture; it is admirably fair. Indeed, the most moving of many very exciting moments comes when a Southern senator rises in Congress to defend lynching in a masterpiece of emotionalism.

If these are the patterns of plays about Negroes, what of the Negroes themselves in the theatre? Will their roles change? Positively, but not overnight. First, there is a new postwar generation of Negro authors coming along who have genuine talent. Add to the Lorraine Hansberrys and the Ossie Davises the names of Adrienne Kennedy, Ann Flagg, and James Baldwin, and you've got a running start. Baldwin is currently writing a play. Ann Flagg has not been previously mentioned, but in 1963 her play won the Annual National Collegiate Playwriting Contest and was subsequently televised by CBS. Miss Flagg is typical: no one knew—no one cared—that she was a Negro. I would suspect that Junius Edwards, whose excellent *If We Must Die* was published by Doubleday in 1963, is also a Negro. There are surely many more than we know of.

The situation of the Negro director and actor is also changing. Lloyd Richards, who has heretofore been directing Negro plays, will stage a Broadway musical for Joseph Kipness in November. There are already a dozen top-notch Negro actors, including Sidney Poitier, Claudia McNeil, Cicely Tyson, James Earl Jones, Roscoe Browne, and Earle Hyman. And their ranks will grow; not only because they will have more and better roles from better writers, but also because of a change in casting procedures. If you will recall, it has only been since the war that Marian Anderson has been invited to sing with Metropolitan Opera Company; and that as late as 1946 Canada Lee, in order to obtain a genuine acting role, donned white-face to act in *The Duchess of Malfi*.

Negro performers are steadily increasing in number, even as the number of new American plays is declining. This has come about because of changes in casting, and in the long run this I think will be the most significant contribution of the theatre to the Negro. Soon it will not be surprising to you to see many more Negroes on the stage than previously, though generally in nondescript roles. Then gradually you will see the effect of this in other media. One night, for instance, you will be watching, say, "That Was the Week That Was," and as the camera goes from one performer to another you will be surprised to see a Negro who wasn't there last week. (Leland Hayward, the producer of the show, is really at heart a theatre producer.) This is all to the good. Soon the surprise will wear off, and you will accept it as customary. And that is really all the dignity and all the opportunity the Negro needs: he belongs; he is not out of place among us.

—1964

Originally from Trinidad, Geoffrey Holder is best known for his highly gifted interpretations of the West Indian dance.

Like Geoffrey Holder, Percival Borde was born in Trinidad and is a specialist in the cultural heritage of the peoples of the Caribbean. For more than ten years, he has been investigating the influences of the dances of Africa in the West Indies. He is married to Pearl Primus.

Dance

ONE OF OUR NATIONAL TREASURES
by Arthur Todd

Katherine Dunham exhibits the "Dunham Technique," which has immeasurably shaped the course of modern American dance.

Carmen de Lavallade has distinguished herself as a soloist with the Ballet Theatre and the John Butler company at Spoleto's Festival of the Two Worlds. She has also appeared in Metropolitan Opera productions.

Pearl Primus, an outstanding dancer and choreographer, has based much of her work on her scholarly research in the field of African dance.

Arthur Mitchell, a principal dancer with the New York City Ballet, is the first Negro "star" in ballet. Of his performance as Puck in *A Midsummer Night's Dream,* Walter Terry of the *New York Times* wrote, "It is one of the truly great comedy portrayals of our day."

One of Our National Treasures

by Arthur Todd

CHECK OFF a list of some of America's most noteworthy creative dancers and choreographers and you find names like Katherine Dunham, Pearl Primus, Talley Beatty, Janet Collins, Alvin Ailey, Carmen de Lavallade, Mary Hinkson, Matt Turney, Donald Mc-Kayle, John Jones, Louis Johnson and Arthur Mitchell. First and foremost, of course, it is their art which has placed them in such major positions in the United States dance scene to-day. The fact that they also happen to be Negro as well matters not a bit to their Caucasian brothers and sisters in the Northern states or across the world, where they have won a continuingly wider following and acceptance during the past two decades. Martha Graham, of all choreographers, stated this belief most eloquently when she recently said, "I'm not interested in race, creed, color or nationality. I'm only interested in talent. I've said this over all the world on my tours and I *mean* it."

This rise of American Negro dance has not, however, burgeoned overnight, although it commenced some two decades ago in the concert field, when Katherine Dunham and her company sky-rocketed into the Windsor Theatre, in New York, from Chicago, in 1940, and made an indelible stamp on the dance world. In addition, Miss Dunham opened the doors that made possible the rapid upswing of this dance for the present generation in America. Actually, however, the roots and basis of American Negro dance may be traced as far back as 1610, when the first shipment of slaves from Africa arrived at Jamestown Bay.

Important to dance, . . . is the fact that these people brought with them all the rich art heritage of Africa. Included in this was their tradition and background of ring shouts and ritual dances . . . done for a religious reason, because almost every aspect of their lives—birth, puberty, mating, fertility and death—was related to dance. Interestingly enough, too, their ancestral memory of elaborate and intricate steps caused them to stamp these out in a 4/4 or 2/2 rhythm.

Up until the time of the Civil War, the American Negro had but three methods of escape and peace from his bitter days of slavery. These were his newly found Christian religion, his spirituals and his dances. The spirituals, of course, have gone down in the annals of truly American music and are known around the globe. As Pearl Primus has described them, "The spirituals were the fighting songs of a people enslaved. . . ."

The Slave Laws of 1740 prohibited "the beating of drums, blowing horns or the like which might on occasion be used to arouse slaves to insurrectionary activity." Therefore, these people handily and inventively adapted instruments that were more readily available. These included the banjo, bone clappers and heel and toe beats with their feet. All of these

were incorporated into the daily songs of work and play and, sometimes, were taken directly into church services, where hands clapped, bodies swayed and feet tapped in rhythm to the spirituals. As Martha Graham expresses it, "The Negro dance was towards freedom, often Dionysiac in its abandon and the raw splendor of its rhythm."

At the same time . . . the American Negro was also open to the inspiration of the then popular folk-dances he saw around him. Therefore, it is more than likely that such folk-dances as "The Tennessee Double Shuffle," "The Louisiana Heel and Toe," "The Virginia Breakdown" and "The Alabama Kick-Up" contained the first fusions of Negro and Caucasian folk-dance and, as Katherine Dunham points out, "These early Negro dances stemmed from the South. After the Civil War, the Negro dance development was transferred from the plantation to the minstrel show."

As early as 1781, a troupe of Negro entertainers, under the aegis of Louis Tabrey, gave public performances in New Orleans. Then, too, there was William Henry Lane, who became known as "Juba" to theatre-goers of the 1840's. He achieved a place and fame during his short career that was equal to that of any American white dancer. What is more, it is now believed that William Henry Lane was the Negro dancer described so vividly in Charles Dickens' American Journals. The first completely all-Negro minstrel show appeared at the Bowery Amphitheatre in New York in 1843, with the title "Virginia Minstrels." The Negro minstrel show, which was as popular in America in the last half of the nineteenth century as were pantomimes in England, was really an outgrowth of the primitive African tradition of hand-clapping and circle dances. The entertainers were seated in a semicircular line of chairs on-stage. Here, in transition, the dance ringleader became the interlocutor, or master of ceremonies. The chorus sang for the

dancers, as they first had in Africa, while the rest of the group clapped their hands or shook tambourines, and everyone in the company was given an opportunity for a solo bit of some sort. Their songs included such choices as "Turkey in the Straw," "Oh, Susannah" and "Negro Capetown Hornpipe." The dancing to these melodies was influenced by the Negro's interpretation and was instilled with syncopation, off-beats and contrapuntal harmony and was danced as an obbligato with toe and heel. Contrariwise, the taps and shuffling were improvised into a new melodic form that was accompanied by the banjo. This became a distinctive beat that later swept the world of the twentieth century under the name of jazz.

There were over seventy minstrel shows touring across America from 1843 to 1912, and of these the most famous were the companies of Primrose and Dockstader and E. P. Christy. Another, one of the most successful all-Negro companies, was organized in 1865 by Charles Hicks and was called the Georgia Minstrels. Others were Richards' and Pringle's Minstrels and the McCabe and Young Minstrels. It was the basic format of these minstrel shows that set the pattern for what we know today as the American musical comedy. However, this was not until the coming of Bert A. Williams and George W. Walker, who began appearing at Koster and Bial's Theatre, singing such Afro-American songs as "My Dahomian Queen," "My Castle on the Nile" and "My Zula Babe," in 1896—1898, and introducing the cakewalk, which swept America like a prairie fire. In this dance, couples "walked" against each other in a competition that led each team to outdo the one before with higher kicks, faster steps, leaps and turns that were more spectacular and intricate. The winning couple, determined by audience applause, was awarded the "cake." This dance, like the later Charleston, swept the ballrooms of the nation, too. Another musical, *The South before the*

War, which opened in 1892, was important for two reasons. First, it provided many examples of authentic plantation dances. Secondly, it marked the first New York appearance of a young Negro tap dancer of great promise. His name was Bill Robinson.

In 1903, Bert Williams and George Walker appeared at the Shaftesbury Theatre in *In Dahomey* to only moderate success until they were invited to appear in a Command Performance at Buckingham Palace in a birthday celebration held in honor of the young Prince of Wales. From that point on, their company was the rage of London.

In America before the First World War, jazz and blues songs swept up from New Orleans. This music was both Negro inspired and composed by such notables as W. C. Handy, Ford Dabney, Will Marion Cook and James Reese Europe. This was the music Negroes danced to both off-stage and on, and it was more often "on" during the first three decades of this century. This was the time of lovely Florence Mills, of whom St. John Ervine said, "She is by far the most artistic person London has had the good fortune to see, something unequaled by any American playing here in the past decade." He wrote this when she was appearing in *From Dover to Dixie*. She returned to London in *Blackbirds* in late 1926, when, according to reports in the Press at that time, this Negro musical was seen by the Prince of Wales sixteen times.

During the 1920's the only arena for Negro dancers was the Broadway stage, night-clubs and vaudeville. In the Broadway theatre, however, there were many musicals and revues that took noteworthy steps forward. These included *Shuffle Along, Runnin' Wild, Rang Tang, Dixie to Broadway* (played in England as *From Dover to Dixie*), *The Plantation Revue* and a series of *Blackbirds*. Florence Mills had her first important role in *Shuffle Along*, then went on to stardom dancing in *The Plantation Revue, Dixie to Broad-*

way and the first *Blackbirds* in 1926. Meanwhile, Josephine Baker made her major Broadway appearance in *Chocolate Dandies* before departing for Europe where she has since had her greatest success. Then, in 1928, Bill Robinson appeared on Broadway in *Blackbirds of 1928*, where he began establishing his legend as the greatest tap dancer of the twentieth century.

Angna Enters once claimed that Bill Robinson was the greatest dancer in America. When one was in his audience, it certainly was difficult to dispute her statement because he won over his audience with his infectious ebullience and great natural warmth before he took his first step. When I first saw him in 1934, his style was meticulous and his dancing, including the famous "stair dance," in which he tapped up and down a small flight of steps, was executed in complete physical relaxation. This "stair dance," indeed, became one of his trade marks, as did the nickname, "Bojangles." (Fred Astaire paid homage to this master in a dance in one of his films that was simply called "Bojangles of Harlem.") During the 1930's and 1940's, Bill Robinson appeared in fourteen films, that have served to preserve his legend, as well as in an hilarious "swing" version of *The Mikado* called *The Hot Mikado*. Though his dances were always in the popular idiom, his technique and artistry made him the greatest tap dancer of our time.

Quite the opposite contribution was made to American Negro dance by Asadata Dafora, particularly in his stirring African opera, *Kykunkor*, the first serious work in the field. Produced in 1934, after a long period of research of the African arts, Dafora's stunning work showed the relationship and base between African and American Negro dance. Its plot dealt mainly with birth, puberty and marriage rites, and I remember a stage full of witch doctors, warriors, chieftains and hunters. There were throbbing drums and vivid costumes, and large and free dance

patterns that made much use of the fluid torso. Some of the choreography employed only the most simple walking steps while other sections called for a precise and exacting virtuosity. Looking back on this work now, more than a quarter of a century later, one realizes that it was a landmark and that it opened the doors and enabled others to recognize their rich heritage.

One other event of 1934 was also of more than passing interest in the theatre. This was the Gertrude Stein–Virgil Thompson *Four Saints in Three Acts,* with an all-Negro cast. Its choreographer was a talented young Englishman, Frederick Ashton, who was brought to America especially for this project. He created a form of stylized movement that was completely appropriate to this sung-danced opera that provided a true feeling of lyric theatre.

Then, in 1935, came George Gershwin's monumental *Porgy and Bess,* which is now acknowledged as the first American folk opera. Although it did not make much use of dance, John W. Bubbles made a noteworthy Sportin' Life as he sang and danced the insinuating "It Ain't Necessarily So." However, in the 1942 revival, which, overall, had a much greater public success than the original, Avon Long took over the role of Sportin' Life and made it his own. He danced with lightness, litheness and literally slid around the stage. As in the later *Beggar's Holiday,* he had superb timing, an impeccable style and a fantastic sense of rhythm.

During the late 1930's in Chicago a very young dancer of uncommon ability was also beginning to delve into the roots of American Negro dance. Her name was Katherine Dunham and when the Rosenwald Foundation awarded her a fellowship she went off to the West Indies to study native dancing in Haiti, Jamaica, Martinique and Trinidad. She came back with voluminous notes and became a guest choreographer for the Chicago Federal Theatre. Then, in 1940, she brought her own company to the Windsor Theatre, in New York, introducing native dance forms from the United States and the Caribbean. Her innate sense of theatre and music, the glorious costumes and the wonderful dancers in her company, as well as her own choreography and dancing, put Negro dancing on the map once and for all, and her work has since had enormous influence. (A young dancer in her company, then in his teen-age years, was Talley Beatty, who has since become one of the outstanding dancer-choreographers in his field.)

Later that same year Katherine Dunham and her dancers captured Broadway as well in the delightful musical *Cabin in the Sky.* She then appeared in such motion pictures as *Star Spangled Rhythm, Carnival of Rhythm* and *Stormy Weather.* In between, she kept her company and school going and appeared with them in *Carib Song, Bal Nègre* and *Caribbean Rhapsody.* Katherine Dunham and her dancers have appeared throughout Europe, the United States and South America, and equaled their success in any of these areas in the triumphant appearances in London. That Dunham is one of our great cultural ambassadors goes without saying. Interestingly enough, neither she nor her company have ever been subsidized as have other American groups. Strangely, too, her tremendous value as a cultural bond between nations has been overlooked by the President's Special International Program for Cultural Presentations, which is administered in conjunction with the American National Theatre and Academy and the Department of State. However, she is now working in her new studio in Haiti on the formation of a fresh company that will doubtless emerge to charm and delight us again.

The only other dancer of major importance to come to fame in the 1940's was Pearl Primus, a graduate of Hunter College, who studied briefly with Doris Humphrey, Charles Weidman and Martha Graham. After her

This fight scene, choreographed by Donald McKayle for the musical *Golden Boy,* was considered by dance critics to be one of the finest ballet sequences ever to be on Broadway.

John Jones, a member of Lincoln Center's outstanding Robert Joffrey Ballet.

Eleo Pomare, the most exciting Negro modern dancer since Alvin Ailey, aims "to break away from confining stereotypes of Negro and Primitive Dance."

The most acclaimed modern dance group in the world is the Martha Graham troupe; and since its inception in the early 1930's, Miss Graham (extreme right) has employed dancers only on the basis of talent. Pictured above is Clive Thompson, a principal dancer with the Graham troupe in *Legend of Judith*.

Clive Thompson in Martha Graham's *Circe*.

Matt Turney in Martha Graham's *Seraphic Dialogue*.

Mary Hinkson in Martha Graham's *Part Real — Part Dream*.

Mary Hinkson (left rear) and Matt Turney (right front), with members of the Graham company, in *"Embattled Garden."*

research into the rich Negro heritage, she set off by giving a stunning series of serious African and Negro American dances at the most unlikely of places, Café Society Downtown, a then smart and popular nightclub. Word quickly spread about her talents through the grapevine of studios and dancers in New York, and soon she was playing to cheering capacity audiences nightly. This led to her first engagement at the Y.M.-Y.W.H.A. and from then onwards her success was assured after rave notices from the major critics. Pearl Primus has never been a purely decorative or entertaining dancer. That is not what she seeks, despite the fact that she scored a major success on Broadway in 1947 as the leading dancer in a revival of *Show Boat*. Rather, she is serious, earnest, intelligent, a noteworthy choreographer and a superb dancer. What interests her most are the earlier spirituals of her own race, contemporary subject matter (her *Strange Fruit*, the dance about the aftermath of a lynching, is an eloquent solo) and dance rituals based directly on her active research in Africa. President William V. S. Tubman of Liberia was directly responsible for inviting Pearl Primus to Africa in 1959 to become director of the African Performing Arts Centre in Monrovia. In this, which is the major assignment of her career, she is responsible for the collection and preservation of authentic folk material, teaching, training dancers and a company to be presented professionally in and outside of Africa. When this company emerges, it will unquestionably be one of the major performing units of the world. It is indeed pleasant to anticipate this and to realize that it will be because of the joint collaboration of an American dancer and an African republic.

After the arrival upon the dance scene of Katherine Dunham and Pearl Primus, it was not long before Broadway choreographers began incorporating and integrating Negro dancers in musicals. Jerome Robbins did this

in 1944 in *On the Town*, Helen Tamiris did likewise in *Inside U.S.A.* and *Show Boat*, and so did Michael Kidd in *Finian's Rainbow* in 1947. Eugene Loring, creator of *Billy the Kid*, staged some marvelous dance routines for the all-Negro version of *Carmen*, with new lyrics and book by Oscar Hammerstein, II, which was retitled for Broadway *Carmen Jones*. Moreover, Valerie Bettis as choreographer used a mixed cast of dancers in *Beggar's Holiday* (1946), in which Avon Long almost danced away with the show. Anna Sokolow used an integrated cast for the dance scenes in the striking musicalization of *Street Scene*.

Going back a bit, it is only fair to interpolate the fact that Helen Tamiris used Negro spirituals as the basis for a series of danced solos that were titled *Negro Spirituals*. Martha Graham, likewise, admits to the influence of the Negro minstrel show in her *American Document*, first danced in 1938, that was complete down to the use of an interlocutor, end men and a walk-around.

While the outstanding choreographers in the modern dance field—Doris Humphrey, Charles Weidman and Martha Graham—never were concerned with the race, creed or color of their dancers, credit must be given, too, to Lester Horton, the late West Coast teacher and choreographer, who brought to fruition four of today's major dancers. The first to arrive in New York, back in 1949, was the exquisite and beautiful Janet Collins, who moved like a dream and was aeriality personified. Miss Collins was a featured dancer in Hanya Holm's *Out of This World* and also the leading dancer in the Metropolitan Opera Company's production of *Aida*.

Carmen de Lavallade, who is now in the front rank of American dancers, is a cousin of Janet Collins, and also stemmed from the Lester Horton studio. She has danced on television, in the New York City Opera, and is one of the soloists most in demand as a guest star with virtually every modern dance com-

pany that gives a concert today. Indeed, she has been called the most beautiful dancer in America—physically and technically—by one of the greatest British ballet teachers now in residence in the United States.

James Truitte, another graduate of the Horton school, has made noteworthy appearances in the East, since moving here permanently, and is, perhaps, the finest teacher of the Lester Horton method, a method that is just now being understood in New York as one that prepares a dancer's body with a technique which appears to be as valuable as that of Humphrey, Weidman, Holm or Graham.

Alvin Ailey, the fourth Horton disciple, made his initial impact on Broadway as the leading dancer in two Broadway musicals, *House of Flowers* and *Jamaica*. After saving all of his earnings possible from these two musicals, he sank the entire amount in presenting his own company in a memorable first concert at the Y.M.-Y.W.H.A. This was followed by a second concert which included a new work, *Revelations,* danced to Negro spirituals, that is one of the most beautifully constructed and moving works in the repertory of any company at the present. During the past year, Mr. Ailey has been a leading actor in the off-Broadway play, *Call Me by My Rightful Name,* and has also been studying singing and acting as well as teaching every day. His newest work, *Roots of the Blues,* composed for himself and Carmen de Lavallade, gained ovations at the Boston Arts Festival and, again, later during the summer, at the Jacob's Pillow Dance Festival. Mr. Ailey has mastered all the technique and virtuosity one could wish. He moves with a personal magnificence that is breathtaking and, for many, is the greatest male dancer in his field today.

Talley Beatty, whose beginnings were with Katherine Dunham, is another dancer-choreographer with enormous creative talent and a phenomenal technique. This was as apparent in one of his wonderfully controlled earlier solos, *Mourner's Bench,* as it now is, to an even greater degree, in two of his large works for his company, *The Road of the Phoebe Snow* and *Come Get the Beauty of It While It's Hot*. Recently, he also staged all of the movement passages in the New York production of Genet's *The Blacks*.

Louis Johnson, who studied at the School of American Ballet and appeared in Jerome Robbins' *Ballade* for the New York City Ballet, is another young dancer who has formed his own company after first appearing on Broadway in the revival of *Four Saints in Three Acts, My Darlin' Aida, House of Flowers* and *Damn Yankees*. His ballet *Lament* was a highlight on one of the programs of the New York Ballet Club's Annual Choreographers' Nights, and, since, he has divided his time touring with his company and appearing on television shows. In addition, there is Arthur Mitchell, of the New York City Ballet, who can be a remarkable dancer when he is properly cast. He has shown us that a Negro can achieve a pure classical style. In Balanchine's *Agon* and Robbins' *Interplay* he is brilliant.

No survey of the current scene would be complete without mention of two dancers who have been members of the Martha Graham Dance Company for the past ten years. They are Mary Hinkson and Matt Turney, both graduates of the University of Wisconsin. Since joining the company, both have appeared in every one of Miss Graham's New York seasons as well as upon the European, Oriental and Israeli tours and in the film *A Dancer's World*. Mary Hinkson has also danced with the New York City Opera for three seasons, toured the United States with Harry Belafonte, and appeared in George Balanchine's *The Figure in the Carpet*. Matt Turney has also made a name for herself in concert appearances with Robert Cohan, a former member of the Graham company.

Alvin Ailey, a product of the Lester Horton Dance Theatre in Los Angeles, has been called in America and abroad the "greatest" modern male dancer. After Horton's death, Ailey served as choreographer and artistic director of the company for several seasons before moving to New York.

Members of the Alvin Ailey Dance Theatre performing *Blues Suite*.

The Alvin Ailey Dance Company performs *Revelations*, a suite of dances based on Negro spirituals.

The processional from Alvin Ailey's *Revelations*.

Many white choreographers have been influenced directly or indirectly by the rise of Negro dance in America. Peter Gennaro, an important new choreographer, who staged the dances for *Fiorello* and *The Unsinkable Molly Brown,* originally studied with Katherine Dunham. Similarly, it is fairly easy to find influences of Negro timing and movement in some of the works of Michael Kidd, Jerome Robbins and Jack Cole.

A younger generation of Negro dancers, now moving forward, has worked in a considerably broader channel of dance, for example John Jones, who toured Europe again this year in Jerome Robbins' *Ballets: U.S.A.* As Alvin Ailey points out, "We have been subject to all the influences that have been right for us. We have used the influences of Katherine Dunham, Pearl Primus, Martha Graham, José Limon and the classical ballet. However, we've all gone about this in a different way. As far as choreography is concerned, we can do contemporary dances as well as anyone."

This autumn, Donald McKayle, who created a wonderful dance work, *Games,* a short while ago, is choreographer for *Kicks and Co.,* an integrated musical headed for Broadway. And Agnes de Mille is staging the dances and musical numbers for *Kwamina,* the new musical with an African locale. Obviously, Negro dance will be a major factor in the Broadway musical theatre this year and it will, indeed, be a great advance over such earlier musicals as *Shuffle Along,*

The Plantation Revue and *Blackbirds.* However, as Katherine Dunham points out, "I think that we will have to admit that with all of the progress that is being made, the field is still proportionately limited, and the young Negro dancer or aspirant has not too much to look forward to. The exceptions sound fine but they are still exceptions. And they are not being absorbed at a great rate by other companies." This is perfectly true, but it is always heartening to remember Ted Shawn's statement, "The Negro has enriched the American dance in every way—ethnic, modern and ballet. They have, of course, an extraordinary gift of rhythm, dramatic movement, joyousness, humour, and altogether are racially endowed with dance gifts which place them equal to the Russians, the Spaniards and the Japanese." All of these qualities are becoming apparent in some of the young dancers of the next generation such as Minnie Marshall of the Alvin Ailey Company, Mabel Robinson, Dudley Williams and William Louther. Unfortunately, this article is chiefly concerned with American Negro dancing and cannot deal equally with such notable dancers from the Caribbean as Jean Leon Destiné, Geoffrey Holder, Percival Borde, Edward Thomas or Clive Thompson. They have a background fully as rich and talent just as evident to offer to the world of dance.

It will be fascinating to observe how the West Indian settlers in the British Isles [will] enrich the dance forms . . . and we shall look forward to seeing the results.

—1962

Films

THE NEGRO IN AMERICAN FILMS
by Carlton Moss

THE COMING OF THE SOUND FILM
by Peter Noble

Sidney Poitier in Lilies of the Field

Sidney Poitier is the first Negro actor ever to reach stardom in Hollywood. When he accepted the Academy Award as Best Actor of 1963 for his performance in *Lilies of the Field*, he stated quietly that "it had been a long journey to this moment." It truly had, and Poitier could look back with pride at many of the roles he had played, almost all of which were unstereotyped. Only one other Negro, Hattie McDaniel, has won an Academy Award, and it was for Best Supporting Actress in *Gone With The Wind*. However, there had been objections from segments of the Negro community over her acceptance of the award for her "Mammy" role. Miss McDaniel was further criticized for generally playing maid parts; she answered her critics by saying that it was better to play a maid than be one.

The Negro in American Films

by Carlton Moss

EVERY week five and a half million colored Americans go to the movies. Their total admissions are a small dent in the gross "take" from one hundred million weekly moviegoers. But not so small that the motion picture industry is indifferent to it. In a way it can be said this concern for the "colored market" is due to the struggle going on between rival movie companies for the largest possible market.

But, equally important in these days of struggle for liberation by the colored peoples of the world, the movie makers look toward the colored audience with an eye set on winning it in a struggle to maintain the status quo. This status quo has given the men who own the motion picture industry—or American Investment as it is popularly called—a substantial profit since the inception of the business.

No one will challenge the fact that American movies have been and are one of the most powerful media of social expression the world has ever known. There is no part of the globe that has not been influenced by the ideas, standards of taste, and information disseminated in American motion pictures.

What better time than now for the molders of public opinion in the United States to show the world that colored Americans are judges, school teachers, brave soldiers, songwriters, home owners, and that they are integrated into prosperous American life like any other person who lives on these shores.

But to what extent are Negro Americans integrated into the motion picture industry itself? To begin with it might be helpful to glance at the history of colored people in American movies.

* * * * * *

Significantly Negroes appeared in the first creative films ever made. In the very first film to exploit the medium as an art the plot concerned a situation in which a group of colored characters were the center of interest. The film, made in France in 1902, told this tale:

> An omnibus drawn by an extraordinary mechanical horse is driven by four Negroes. The horse kicks and upsets the Negroes, who falling are changed into white clowns. They begin slapping each other's faces and by the blows become black again. Kicking each other they become white once more. Suddenly they are all merged into one gigantic Negro, and when he refuses to pay his carfare, the conductor sets fire to the omnibus, and the Negro bursts into a thousand pieces.

But it was the American motion picture that set the pattern for the handling of Negroes on the screen. The presence of colored people in American life, their second-class status, often defined by local law, national customs and community mores, was a source of comedy for the early American motion picture producers. However, Negroes themselves did not appear on the screen in actual-

ity. The characters, supposedly portraying colored people, were played by white actors who smeared their faces with black grease-paint.

In 1905, just one year before W. E. B. Du Bois called the founding conference of the Niagara Movement (forerunner of the National Association for the Advancement of Colored People), the movie makers released a film which set the precedent for the treatment of colored people in films. That was to stand for more than fifty years. A short film, *The Wooing and Wedding of a Coon,* showed a colored man and his bride as stupid and immoral. The producers described it as a "genuine Ethiopian comedy."

In 1907, one year after the founding of the Niagara Movement, the movie producers gave America its second film on the "place of colored people" in white America. It was as if the film were made to answer Dr. Du Bois' Niagara proclamation that Negro Americans would not accept less than their full manhood rights—for the film dealt with social relations between colored and white people. Released under the title *The Masher* it told this story:

> *A lady-killer is unsuccessful in his wooing with every woman with whom he tries to flirt. Finally he becomes successful with a lady wearing a veil, who quickly responds to this flirtation. However, when the lady-killer makes further advances and lifts the lady's veil, he discovers to his consternation that the lady of his choice is colored. Horrified, the lady-killer runs away as fast as his legs can carry him.*

Once the industry was established, the pattern for the handling of Negroes settled into two categories—films in which colored people were the butt-end of crude and insulting jokes, and films in which colored people were portrayed as devoted slaves who "knew their place."

In 1914, Bert Williams tried to break the boycott against employing colored artists by producing his own films. The attempt met with disastrous results. His first film was badly received by white audiences and even

resulted in a "race" riot in Brooklyn, New York. Elsewhere it met an undercover boycott.

* * * * * *

Shortly after the unsuccessful attempt by Bert Williams to give Negro people a voice in the film industry, another gifted artist, D. W. Griffith, used his unusual motion picture craftsmanship to state the case of American racists. In a motion picture, originally called *The Clansman* after a novel which painted the racist Ku Klux Klan of the 1870's as a band of knights, Griffith fashioned a skillfully told sentimental story that projected a thesis which called for a United States in which colored people would be separated from white people—with white people as rulers.

Immediately following the release of the film, it was re-titled *The Birth of a Nation.* Significantly, Woodrow Wilson, the President of the United States, welcomed the Griffith movie to the White House. This was the first film ever to be so honored. The President, who had consistently turned a deaf ear to the pleas of colored Americans for federal protection against the wave of lynching then sweeping the country, is said to have remarked, after seeing *The Birth of a Nation* —"It is like writing history with lightning."

But, despite White House acceptance of *The Birth of a Nation,* the film aroused a storm of protest throughout the Northern states. Colored and white people united in attacking the picture because of its extreme bias and many historical inaccuracies. Race riots broke out in Boston and other "abolitionist" cities.

Several states refused to issue a license for the exhibition of *The Birth of a Nation.* Many prominent people spoke bitterly, and often, against the showing of the film. Oswald Garrison Villard, grandson of William Lloyd Garrison, the famed anti-slavery crusader, condemned it as "a deliberate attempt to humiliate ten million American citizens." New

York City's distinguished Rabbi Stephen Wise declared it was "an intolerable insult to the Negro people" and Charles W. Eliot, president of Harvard University, charged the movie "with a tendency to perversion of white ideals."

Unquestionably, *The Birth of a Nation* proved the power of the screen to mold and shape opinion. Can it be challenged that the film's justification of the Ku Klux Klan was at least one factor which enabled the Klan to enter upon its period of greatest expansion—reaching a total membership of more than five million by 1924. Nevertheless, Griffith and the film industry were not completely insensitive to the protest against the film. In an obvious attempt to atone for the harm he had done to the colored people he included a scene in a subsequent picture which showed a white soldier kissing his wounded colored comrade.

Simultaneously, the industry, called upon to use the power of its medium to rally the total population around the slogan "Make the World Safe for Democracy," relaxed its policy toward Negroes. The most significant change, in the period following the First World War, was the introduction of colored actors to play the roles that hitherto had been played by white men and women using black make-up. The concept of the characters didn't change except in their relationship to the story. Heretofore, colored characters had been a central part of the short film stories. Now that films were greater in length, colored characters were relegated to incidental parts of the story.

Again it remained for D. W. Griffith to set the tone for the handling of Negro actors in motion pictures. Once more he seemed bent on avenging the defeat of his rebel father's army—for again he demonstrated how a director steeped in anti-Negro prejudice can influence his audience.

Here for the first time film-goers were given the cowardly black man whose hair turns white when he meets danger in any form. He is afraid of the dark, of thunderstorms, of firearms, of animals, of police and above all—of white folks. This contemptible comic relief character "stole" the show in Griffith's *One Exciting Night,* released in 1922. Although the character was played by a white man, with black greasepaint on his face, every colored actor who applied for work, following the release of this film, was expected to imitate the frightened, weak-kneed, stupid creature created by D. W. Griffith.

During this period, Negroes again tried to produce their own films. This second attempt found an audience in theatres catering exclusively to Negro patronage—theatres which had opened since Bert Williams' earlier experiment.

But it was too late in the history of the motion picture industry for anyone to make films for so limited a market. At best, there were some four hundred to five hundred "colored" theatres of a total of more than fifteen thousand motion picture houses throughout the United States. Basic economics intervened. The colored producer, making films for the handful of "colored" theatres, had to make them on a very limited budget. Further, he had to compete with the white producers—because not enough "colored" films were made to keep the "colored houses" open every week in the year.

Even more important was the handicap of experience and technique. From the very inception of motion pictures no colored man or woman was hired to work in any of the technical departments of the industry.

* * * * * *

The Negro producer, operating with extremely limited funds and the barest necessities of equipment, found that all the facilities for making and processing films were in the

hands of the white producers. With no experienced colored technicians available, he had to hire such white personnel as were available to him—the most inefficient, least skilled and inexperienced in the industry, whom he could only equip with the cheapest and most inadequate production facilities. As though these handicaps were not sufficient, the colored producer found himself running counter to what his very own organizations were fighting, namely, an end to Jim Crow. For the white theatres would not buy his product, and his films were, of necessity, limited only to Jim Crow houses. To add insult to injury, the content of his films had to conform to what the status quo approved, for any film which portrayed Negro Americans in any context of militancy would have been challenged by the police and other arms of government.

The status of colored Americans during the years in which the motion picture industry was being organized made it impossible for them to control the real estate and laboratories which are the very basis of the business. True, there were a few Negro Americans who might have had the money to open a nickelodeon, but the hurdles in their path were insurmountable. Further, the kind of social and business contact which would have brought Negro aspirants into the laboratories and equipment manufacturing services were completely closed to all but whites. The only phase of the industry which was open to colored people was that of the performing artist —and even here, as we have shown, he had to stand aside and let white people "imitate" him for the first thirty years. When he finally achieved the role, he was expected to insult himself and his own people.

Today, the motion picture business represents a capital investment of $2,966,000,000. In 1962 its approximate world-wide gross income was $3,000,000,000. The investment in theatres is $2,700,000,000. It employs 25,400 production workers, a personnel of 10,000 for distribution and a staff of 150,000 for exhibition. Its total yearly payroll is $580,000,000. And to this day, the participation of colored Americans is basically still that of the paying audience.

Despite the advances in the trade union movement, in Fair Employment Practices, and the general awakening in the United States to the treatment of colored people, only a handful of Negro Americans can earn a living in the industry—and they are employed only in front of the cameras. All of the business and technical opportunities of the industry are to this day barred to Negroes. True, the industry has shifted its method of production and slashed the number of its personnel. Nevertheless, it hires new writers, directors, composers and set designers constantly. Occasionally, a Negro writer is employed to work on the script for a "colored picture"—even then the Negro writer is teamed with a white writer, which is not necessarily objectionable—however, once the "colored picture" is completed the Negro writer is never heard from again. The Negro public relations man gets the same treatment. He, too, is occasionally hired to work on a film that the producer believes should be of interest to colored theatregoers.

Employment opportunities for Negroes are just as limited in the non-theatrical motion picture industry. In 1962, this branch of film-making spent in excess of $389,000,000 on sales, educational, industrial, religious, military and institutional films. Negro participation in these films amounted to a half-dozen acting roles in a limited number of race relation films produced by makers of religious motion pictures.

* * * * * *

But the future of the Negro in films is not as bleak as these facts suggest. For there are other facts which if grappled with can lead to a new day for the Negro people in American films.

First, the myth that "white audiences are not interested in seeing Negroes on the screen" has long since been exploded. The box office returns as listed in the film magazine, *Box Office Barometer,* clearly show that films featuring Negro actors and actresses *do* make money. The *Box Office Annual* for 1961 credits *A Raisin in the Sun* with a rating of 144 which is 44 points above the hundred points used by *Box Office Magazine* to indicate that a motion picture is making money. *Paris Blues* starring Paul Newman, Sidney Poitier, Diahann Carroll and Joanne Woodward is also listed among the 1961 money-makers. It had a rating of 163.

Granted films featuring Negro artists have not yet made millions in profits, as the producers would have the public believe a "colored interest" film must make if the industry is to continue making them. In proportion to what it actually costs to make the specific film, they don't lose money. Unless, of course, the film is wrapped in bandanas. Further, investigation shows that none of the "colored interest" films play all the theatres available to the producer. Many exhibitors refuse to play "colored films" on the grounds that they would attract too many colored people to the theatre.

Another film that shows the potential of motion pictures featuring Negro talent is the Brazilian-made movie *Black Orpheus.* This film succeeded on its own. It did not have the advantage of a guaranteed release or the budget for a high-powered advertising campaign. Nevertheless, it found theatres and has been attracting audiences since its release in the United States more than three years ago. The success of *Black Orpheus* shows that it is possible to find an audience for films featuring Negro artists without going through the giant motion picture distributing companies. Heretofore, as we have shown, the Negro producer was faced with the problem of a very limited number of small theatres in

which he could show his production. The experience of *Black Orpheus* certainly indicates there is a profitable market in the United States for an imaginatively made independent film.

In addition to this market a new foreign outlet is opening up. This market has already captured the attention of the giants of American movies. Under the guidance of Eric Johnston, president of the Motion Picture Producers Association, a group called American Motion Picture Export Company has been organized. According to their press release, "The purpose of the new company is to open up distribution of the American films on a sound basis in the new nations of Africa and to bring the best American products to wide audiences in Africa. It will create the basis for the construction of modern theatres. I am convinced that by bringing up-to-date film distribution to Africa the Africans, themselves, will be given opportunities to participate in new businesses thus stimulated." This organization has already taken steps to open offices in Lagos, Nigeria and Accra, Ghana.

Irrespective of what Mr. Eric Johnston and company think they are going to do in Africa, it is apparent that the new nations of Africa have no intention of giving up control of their resources. Neither is it probable that they would refuse to book a film because they would be afraid it would attract too many "colored people."

* * * * * *

The second point of interest is the availability of skilled film craftsmen. Mainly through University Cinema Schools a number of Negroes have had the opportunity to learn how to make motion pictures. A few of these have found free-lance work which has given them the opportunity to gain film-making experience. In addition, the unity between Negro and white has now developed to the point that makes it possible to get some of the most skilled and experienced craftsmen in the in-

Behind the Scenes

A recent innovation for Negroes in Hollywood is their employment in the routine production end of movie making. Ron Threatt (left) and Don Davis (lower right) are both in the art department of a major studio and prepare layouts, an essential pre-production step.

Quincy Jones, the well-known band leader and record company executive, has had four movie assignments composing both soundtrack and songs for multi-million-dollar films (*Walk, Don't Run, Mirage, The Pawnbroker* and *The Slender Thread*).

Negro clerical workers are still a rarity in Hollywood executive offices, and one of the few is Elaine Cox, secretary to a top Universal Pictures executive.

Wendell Franklin, shown with Shirley MacLaine on the set of *Gambit*, assists in the actual filming of movies.

One of the first Negroes to work behind the scenes in Hollywood was Phil Moore, who assisted in writing scores for musicals and coaching actresses in singing roles. At MGM, he conducted the first interracial studio orchestra.

dustry to work with colored producers who would want to make films of quality and content. Incidentally, the making of such films in this context would provide an opportunity for the training and developing of real skills among colored aspirants. The combination of a potential market and the availability of production talent paves the way for a new day in film making.

But the making of such a film calls for a pioneer—a pioneer in the tradition of the Negro men and women who founded our press and historical publications. There is no place for such a producer in Hollywood. The very nature of Hollywood production methods makes it impossible for a Negro producer to make an independent film. Hollywood films, in the main, are financed by banks, the same banks that provide funds for the real estate interests, Southern farming and industry, Northern and Western ghettos, and all other facets of American investment that thrive on Jim Crow and gradualism. If the Negro producer is to make an independent film he must turn his back on Hollywood and draw on the experience of the film makers who have defied the industry and made successful motion pictures. An example of a successful film made outside of the industry is the recent production *David and Lisa*. The producers (an inspired husband and wife) solicited investments of fifty to a hundred dollars until they had a total budget of $200,000. On this . . . they produced a film devoid of the glamorous trappings and

waste of Hollywood, yet sensitive in its story, and imaginative in its execution. So effective is *David and Lisa* that it has won film prizes and is generally considered one of the finest films produced in 1962. With such attention it can hardly fail to make money for its investors and appeal to an extremely wide audience.

In 1964, another "shoestring" production, *One Potato, Two Potato,* was highly praised by judges and reviewers at the Cannes Film Festival, although it was not an official entry. Directed by Larry Peerce, son of the opera star Jan Peerce, it was produced by Sam Weston of television, and "shot" in Ohio. Its story does not linger on the fringe of life as the Negro-American knows it, but deals with one of his problems in depth. The film's further outstanding success at a second film festival —this time in Karlovy Vary where, again, it was not an official entry— made its showing at a Broadway theatre a profitable undertaking. Here, again, it repeated its success with public and critics alike.

David and Lisa and *One Potato, Two Potato* do not show a trend, for they stand alone among the hundreds of motion pictures produced every year.

But they do show that there is no reason why a Negro producer cannot emulate these outstanding achievements. Certainly enough material of a tremendously inspirational nature exists within the heart of the Negro community.

—1964

Dorothy Dandridge and Harry Belafonte in *Island in the Sun*.

Ella Fitzgerald in *Pete Kelley's Blues*.

Woody Strode in *The Ten Commandments*.

Juanita Hall in *South Pacific*.

Louis Armstrong in *Satchmo the Great*.

Sidney Poitier in *The Defiant Ones*.

Sammy Davis, Jr., in *Anna Lucasta*.

Chico Hamilton in *Jazz on a Summer's Day*.

James Edwards in *Home of the Brave*.

Sammy Davis, Jr. in *Ocean's Eleven.*

Harry Belafonte in his own company's production
of *Odds Against Tomorrow.*

Lena Horne in *Meet Me in Las Vegas.*

Dorothy Dandridge and Alex Cressan in *Tamango*.

Rafer Johnson in *The Fiercest Heart*.

Ruby Dee in *A Raisin in the Sun*.

Sidney Poitier in *Paris Blues*.

Ray Charles in *Blues for Lovers*.

Mahalia Jackson in *The Best Man*.

Roscoe Lee Browne in *Black Like Me*.

Thelma Oliver in *The Pawnbroker*.

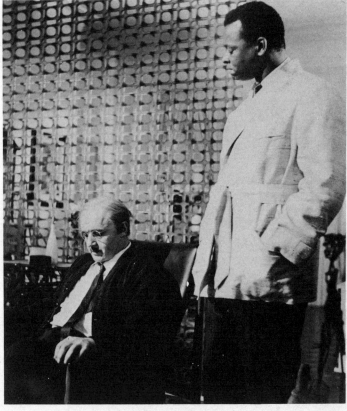

Brock Peters in *The Pawnbroker*.

Eartha Kitt in *Synannon*.

Jimmy Brown in *Rio Conchos*.

Sidney Poitier in *The Bedford Incident*.

Leonard Parker, Helen Williams and Ivan Dixon in *Nothing but a Man*.

Sidney Poitier in *The Slender Thread*.

Mark Clay in *Beau Geste*.

Johnny Nash in *Take a Giant Step*.

Sammy Davis, Jr., and Ossie Davis in *A Man Called Adam*.

The Coming of the Sound Film

by Peter Noble

ON AUGUST 6th, 1926, at the Warner Theatre in New York, a new era was born—the sound film was pioneered by the Warner Brothers. Since 1900 many inventors, including Thomas Edison and Lee De Forest, had been experimenting with recorded sound, and as early as 1923 Phonofilms, the first sound-on-film system, invented by De Forest, had been introduced into cinemas as a novelty interlude. But in 1926, the Warners' program of seven short vocal and musical subjects and their feature, *Don Juan,* with John Barrymore, demonstrated that a miracle had arrived—music and song could be heard on the screen. Immediately Warner Brothers' Vitaphone productions was established, and the Broadway singing star Al Jolson was signed to appear in their first feature film using the new system. This was *The Jazz Singer,* in which Jolson's songs were to be recorded, though no attempt was to be made yet to record actual dialogue.

When this film was shown in 1927 it made history, for as Jolson crossed the screen to sing his song the microphone picked up an ad lib line, "Say Ma, listen to this," and the packed first night audience roared their approval. Talking films had come to stay. In *The Jazz Singer,* and later in *The Singing Fool,* Al Jolson, famous on the stage for many years for his black-face singing and Negro impersonations, sang such songs as "Mammy" with his face smeared in the tradi-

tional burnt cork. The Negro had arrived in talking pictures—as a black-face comedian! This may be considered ironically significant since the Negro actor's film career for a number of years followed in the same tradition: white men in black-face, or colored men in inane black masks—on the screen it amounted to the same thing.

During the early 1930's all-colored stage productions such as *Blackbirds* and *Porgy,* produced in New York and elsewhere, had spot-lighted the Negro's capabilities as a song and dance performer. Hollywood, which had enthusiastically entered the era of the talking film and was recklessly signing up all available musical comedy talent, was quick to realise the commercial potentialities of Negro entertainers, with a consequence that in many early "all talking, all singing, all dancing epics," numbers of Negro singers, dancers and jazz musicians imported from the New York stage and night clubs were featured prominently. Such names as Stepin Fetchit, Hazel Jones, Snowball, and later Ethel Waters, Nina Mae McKinney and Sleep 'n' Eat came to the fore, bringing with them a recurrence of the popular myth that the American Negro was a happy, laughing, dancing imbecile, with permanently rolling eyes and widespread, empty grin. In films too numerous to mention actors like Fetchit demeaned themselves, bringing Negro dignity to its lowest common denominator. "Stepin Fetchit has dawdled

and shuffled through identical performances in a number of Hollywood films as if he were bent on demonstrating the descent of the Negro from a lower order of the animal kingdom." So wrote film critic Robert Stebbins in *New Theatre* in 1935. It is recorded that this actor made (and subsequently lost) a great fortune playing stupid "darkies" and, not unnaturally, other Negro actors followed suit.

HEARTS IN DIXIE

By 1929 no film had succeeded in giving any real indication of the Negro's immense acting ability. The first of Hollywood's all-colored films, *Hearts in Dixie,* directed by Paul Sloane for Fox, promised much, but we were given no new slant on Negro life and thought, just the same old hackneyed routine. The story was so slight as to be almost non-existent, but apparently we were to be compensated for this by a succession of endless musical numbers, spirituals, prayer meetings, cotton-picking and the like. The film could have been a turning-point for colored players, and was produced with a great blare of publicity. It was eagerly awaited by Negroes everywhere, but unfortunately did not succeed in living up to its promise. Nevertheless it takes its place in this brief history, since it was the pioneer all-Negro film made in Hollywood. And, in *Opportunity,* April, 1929, film critic Robert Benchley gave it as his opinion that this film demonstrated that "in the Negro the sound picture had found its ideal protagonist." Was he right?

Once again we had the Southern plantation in "dear old Dixie," a place obviously beloved more by Hollywood than by Negroes themselves. Again we were introduced to the faithful black plantation workers, toiling hard in the cotton fields all day, and relaxing at night by singing, dancing and generally making merry under the benevolent eye of the white master, always held in such affec-

tion by his black servants. Stepin Fetchit typifies the lazy, good-for-nothing but good-natured slave, unwilling to work yet forgiven for his back-slidings and errant ways. The boss "playfully" kicks him in the rear, and Fetchit responds with a broad grin and a sly wink to the audience. Here is the typical screen "darkie," a picture distorted out of all serious reality. Black clown Fetchit follows in the Uncle Tom tradition: he is a "good nigger," he is lazy and shiftless, yet "all right at heart," and—most important of all—*he knows his place.* Paul Sloane's film contained no theme of any real significance; he remained in the well-worked groove, he avoided controversy, perhaps did not admit that any existed. To sum up: *Hearts in Dixie* was an ambitious, probably well-meaning pioneer effort, chiefly known as the film responsible for bringing to the screen that gifted and wholly delightful actor Clarence Muse, who has stayed in Hollywood since that time. His charming performance, fine dignity, grand voice and noble bearing more than compensated for the appearance of Stepin Fetchit in one of his more nauseating "lazy but lovable vagabond" parts.

Discerning critic Henry Dobb wrote pungently of this film in *Close Up*: "Superficially we might have advanced since the mountebankery of Griffith's *One Exciting Night,* though Stepin Fetchit's roles in *The Ghost Talks* and *Hearts in Dixie* are directly in the traditions of the vaudeville stage and the black-face comics. The Negro, in short, for all his humanity, is still behind the bars of the cage, a cage flooded with the glare of publicity and intoned with 'the haunting strains of Negro spirituals.' It is obvious from *Hearts in Dixie* that director Paul Sloane has not yet emerged from that state of mind which conceives of the Negro film as leaning towards open-necked shirts, bandana hats and the melodic charms of 'Old Black Joe'

and 'The Lonesome Road.' The tragedy is not the tragedy in the film, but the tragedy of the film; the tragedy of these untainted folk strutting their stuff to the required pattern, playing their parts as the white man likes to believe they do. The Negro and all his colored brothers are not museum specimens. Nor are they mountebanks. If they are blessed with a more than human power of music and speech, of rhythm and colour, then they have it over us mere whites. But if *Hearts in Dixie* is a specimen of colored expression under the aegis of Hollywood let us next time hand the whole process over to the Negroes themselves."

HALLELUJAH

At all events *Hearts in Dixie* almost started one of the well-known Hollywood cycles, for soon after its production was announced Metro-Goldwyn-Mayer assigned King Vidor to direct *Hallelujah* which, to quote a 1929 publicity blurb—"will be the ace of the all-Negro talking pictures." If it was hoped that a director as intelligent as Vidor, and Negro actors like Daniel Haynes and Nina Mae McKinney, would make *Hallelujah* memorable, then expectations were short-lived. The slight story, of a country boy who temporarily succumbs to the wiles of a bad woman, probably seemed at first to possess some dramatic power; and Daniel Haynes as the boy gave a performance which was extremely moving in its simplicity and sincerity. But the central theme became swamped, inevitably perhaps, by the forty or so singing sequences of folk songs, spirituals, baptism wails, work songs and blues. *Hallelujah,* written by novelist Wanda Tuchock, was, however, an interesting film, and certain parts of it indicated the undeniable power of the director. But how much King Vidor was influenced by Hollywood's attitude to Negroes generally, and how much the film was altered in the cutting room are

questions which must forever remain unanswered. Suffice to say that, in spite of all its promise, M.G.M.'s "all-Negro epic" made only a minor contribution to the Negro struggle for recognition on the screen.

The scene of *Hallelujah* was laid in the cotton fields of the South, and in some of the mean dives of a Southern state, and was concerned with the eternal struggle between good and evil, as symbolised naively by the religious, God-fearing Negro and a loose, sophisticated colored woman of the town. Effective character drawing was swamped by a great deal of preaching, shouting, baptizing, soul-saving, dancing, gambling, love-making, continual singing of spirituals and happy work songs. A general "hot" time was had by all, in the accustomed tradition of the "good-for-nothing black man." Writers in the Negro press considered, however, that *Hallelujah* was something of a step forward in the struggle for Negro expression on the screen, and even such severe critics as W. E. B. Du Bois admitted that it was beautifully staged under severe limitations and possessed common-sense and real life without the exaggerated farce and usual horse-play. But, as usual, opinion was divided, and certain Negro film critics referred to "King Vidor's filthy hands reeking with prejudice," and to the film's "insulting niggerisms." Sections of the white press seemed to find the characterizations quite *amusing.* As the critic of the *New York Times* remarked: "The audience was especially amused by the baptism scene with a host of white-clad Hallelujah-rousing blacks standing on the side of the water ready to go through the baptism but evidently fearful of the ducking!" Lawrence Reddick observes: "*Hallelujah* was significant in that it gave Negro actors important roles and did not exhibit the crude insults which disturb Negro patrons; however, it did not advance very far beyond the usual stereotypes and, as every-

one could see, being all-Negro it was by that token a Jim Crow film."

Lewis Jacobs went even further. "In undertaking *Hallelujah*, King Vidor also said he was primarily interested in showing the Southern Negro as he is," he wrote, and went on: "The deed fell short of the intent. The film turned out to be a melodramatic piece replete with all the conventionalities of the white man's conception of the spiritual-singing, crap-shooting Negro. But whatever its sociological faults, and it had many, its technique reflected a thinking director."

Hallelujah received, on the whole, a favorable press, since at the time it was produced it was considered by Bohemians and so-called intellectuals as "the fashionable thing" to be pro-Negro. (In New York this cult reached fantastic proportions for a period and has been described in a number of books, including Carl Van Vechten's famous novel *Nigger Heaven*.) But in all the reviews which praised the movie one could determine the basic deficiencies of the narrow outlook which characterized film critics and audiences at that time. Here is a typical review from *Theatre and Film Illustrated*, February, 1930: "From the very first shot of the cotton fields, where the colored workers are heard singing at their work, the atmosphere of *Hallelujah* takes hold of one and one lives amongst and understands the people King Vidor is depicting. It can well be described as a song of the American Negro, in which are skillfully blended humor, pathos, sentiment, fervent religious emotions and equally fervent passion. The film is imbued with the revivalist spirit which, as it were, demonstrates the characters and films the main motif against which is played the drama of a Negro's love and emotions. It is instinct with an irresistible childishness which is at once transparently sincere and wholly moving."

And again: "King Vidor shows us the fanatical expressions of grief in which Ne-

groes indulge. All through this sequence there is rhythm and music just as there is when they are rejoicing in the cotton fields; only the theme is changed. Zeke becomes a revivalist preacher and gives addresses which admit the humor and allusion that are so essential to the make up of his kind." And the reviewer finishes by saying, "Rarely has the spirit of the Negro people been so finely portrayed as in this picture."

Although one may admit King Vidor's sincerity, and recognize his inspired direction of the crowd scenes and of the revivalist meeting sequences, one is forced to the conclusion that his film continued the hackneyed tradition, and showed the Negro as a simple, often stupid, religious, superstitious creature. "The picture of Negro life presented by *Hallelujah* as it finally appeared was still romantic, still shadowed by traditional clichés of Negro character and action"; so wrote Edith Isaacs in *Theatre Arts*, August, 1942. The author went to see the film again, when it was shown in London by the New London Film Society in 1946, and realized once more that the creatures on the screen were not really human beings. They were merely black dolts dancing at the end of a string held by King Vidor, a white man with no real insight into the mind of the Negro or knowledge of his aspirations and ambitions. As film critic Robert Herring wrote some fifteen years ago: "Both *Hallelujah* and *Hearts in Dixie* perpetuate the 'way down South in the land of cotton' idea, which by now ought really to be forgotten."

And as Paul Robeson commented, in *Film Weekly*, September 1, 1933: "The box office insistence that the Negro shall figure always as a clown has spoiled the two Negro films which have been made in Hollywood, *Hallelujah* and *Hearts in Dixie*. In *Hallelujah* they took the Negro and his church services and made them funny. America may have found it amusing, but to English audi-

ences the burlesquing of religious matters appeared sheer blasphemy."

In *Close Up,* August, 1929, the editor, Kenneth Macpherson, had some interesting things to say on the subject. Here is an extract: "Now take the Negro film and decide whether you think international cinema is going to mean a thing when a white man directs, no matter how charmingly, blacks so that they must always seem to be direfully dependent on white man's wisdom. For all the coal-black hearts in Dixie must beat to please—meekly Uncle Tom, pleasant, thankful, serf beats. Confronted with an instability (his own) which he calls a race problem, the white man is always going to portray the Negro as he likes to see him; no matter how benevolently. Benevolence, indeed, is the danger. Apart from being the most tricky and unkind form of human selfishness, it is often more than humbugged and always less than seeing, and does to sugar-coat much that is not, so to speak, edible."

But some critics found things in Vidor's film to praise. For example, Helen Fletcher, film critic of the *Sunday Graphic* and *Time and Tide,* wrote recently: "I found myself unusually excited by this Negro film. It has a curious hypnotic quality. Other films stress Negro insouciance and charm; King Vidor's film stresses Negro intensity and even agony. Above all the film treats Negroes with equality; it seems to me a film which does not date but which is as shaking to smugness now as it was in 1929."

Between 1929 and 1933 certain anti-Negro productions, like R.K.O. Radio's *Prestige* and *Secret Service,* became popular with cinema audiences, and drove the stereotype conception deeper into the public mind. *Prestige,* directed by Charles R. Rogers in 1932, was laid in a French penal colony. The theme of the film was the eternal superiority of the whites over the black prisoners, and the

"prestige" of the title referred, in fact, to the prestige of the white man. An example from the script serves to indicate the film's message.

" 'Back you swine!' Verlaine cried fiercely. The blacks drew back; the prestige of the white race was being revived."

Clarence Muse, nevertheless, gave an excellent study of the faithful friend and servant of Captain Verlaine, the French officer, played by Adolphe Menjou, and managed to off-set some of the film's many reactionary sequences. A production like *Secret Service,* directed by J. Walter Ruben in 1932, was typical of the kind of Civil War film popularized by Hollywood in the 1930's. The hero, Richard Dix, is a gallant Southern gentleman in the Confederate Army, while Gavin Gordon, inescapably villainous, played (inevitably) an officer in the Federal Army. Just as inevitably, Shirley Grey as a Northern beauty, forsook her creed to follow her Southern lover. *Secret Service* was not, perhaps in itself, an important film, but it serves as an example of the type of Hollywood motion picture so often met with, in which the hero is always a gentlemanly Southerner, usually surrounded by faithful Uncle Tom retainers, while the Yankees are always drawn in the most unfavorable light.

Musical productions such as *Gold Diggers of Broadway, Stand Up and Cheer, Fox Movietone Follies* and others, continued to feature outstanding Negro personalities from the Broadway stage, and night-club singers like Ethel Waters, Mamie Smith and Nina Mae McKinney. But although most filmgoers were agreed that the Negro seemed to possess enormous filmic potentialities, Hollywood failed to do much about this. When colored people were used in films they were cast in the familiar groove, or alternatively an attempt was made to camouflage their color. Thus, actress Hazel Jones played a beautiful

Burmese siren in the Walter Huston film *West of Singapore,* while Etta Moten danced and sang in R.K.O. Radio's *Flying Down to Rio,* as a dusky *South American.*

By 1931 Harry Alan Potamkin felt obliged to declare: "The Hollywood sound film is bringing the Negro in with a sort of Eastman Johnson–Stephen Foster–Kentucky Jubilee *genre,* or with the Octavus Roy Cohen–Hugh Wiley crowd satisfiers, where the Negro is still the nigger-clown, shrewd sometimes and butt always." He was right. Hollywood had failed; and it was thus left to two idealistic men in New York to make the first really important movie giving a Negro a role he could, as it were, get his teeth into. The film was *The Emperor Jones,* from the play by Eugene O'Neill, and the actor was Paul Robeson.

THE EMPEROR JONES

O'Neill had concerned himself with Negro themes in several of his plays, including the above, *All God's Chillun Got Wings* and *The Dreamy Kid.* He was among the few American playwrights who foresaw the rapidly growing part the Negro would play in the American scene, and he is included in that small but important band of white dramatists who have written soberly and sincerely about Negroes. Two young men of the theatre, John Krimsky and Gifford Cochran, planned to make a series of films of O'Neill's plays and for their first independent effort they decided to produce *The Emperor Jones* in a small New York film studio. They chose for the leading part thirty-five year old actor and singer Paul Robeson, who had previously made a great success on the stage as Brutus Jones, both in New York and London.

Robeson, like many other colored actors and actresses, found his work appreciated more in England and on the Continent than it had been in the United States, and up to 1933 he had practically made his home in London. He returned to New York (after having made his first screen appearance in an English silent film called *Borderline*), making his debut in sound films by playing one of his favorite stage roles. To say that his screen performance as Jones was a *tour de force* is perhaps an understatement. The film itself was not entirely satisfactory, but Robeson's work showed that he had reached maturity as an actor, and was potentially one of the greatest screen personalities. *The Emperor Jones* was remarkable in that it gave to a Negro actor a leading part in a film also featuring white actors, something never previously experienced (a possible exception being the case of James B. Lowe who played Uncle Tom in a silent version of *Uncle Tom's Cabin*). To have a black man playing the star part in a film in which the white actors were of lesser importance was indeed something of a filmic revolution. Indeed it was enough of a social revolution to make the film a financial failure! Distribution difficulties were encountered, especially in the Southern states, and *The Emperor Jones* was seen only by a relatively small number of people, although it was warmly received by the critics. Nevertheless Krimsky and Cochran abandoned their project of making *All God's Chillun Got Wings* and other O'Neill plays, and so far as is known neither has produced a film since. Their names, however, will be remembered with gratitude by the millions of filmgoers who have since enjoyed the work of Robeson on the screen. It was their foresight and courage in starring a Negro actor, at a time when Hollywood was doing its best to kill all attempts by colored actors and actresses to bring real characterization to their meager roles, which started Paul Robeson on a brilliant film career. *The Emperor Jones* also gave encouragement to many independent Negro producers, who thereafter began to make their own films to be shown mainly to Negro audiences.

This O'Neill film was praised by most critics in the U.S.A. and Europe as one of the outstanding films of the year, with such notable exceptions as Robert Stebbins, who wrote in *New Theatre,* July, 1935: "*The Emperor Jones* maintained unbroken the chain of white chauvinism forged in the carbon-arc lights of the Hollywood studios. Paul Robeson is presented as a vainglorious braggart, a murderer, a tin-foil Napoleon who imposes upon and exploits heartlessly members of his own race. And when finally they rise against him his false front falls away. He is revealed for what he is, and by extension, what all Negroes are supposed to be, creatures who stand trembling in a murky land of shadow, peopled with the ghosts that rise up out of the swamps and jungles of the primitive mind."

Critics of the Negro newspapers were divided; some believed that it was a significant gesture that a white man could be presented on the screen as the "lackey" of the Negro Brutus Jones, and as his intellectual and social inferior. Others, however, emphasized the scenes where Robeson was shown as a humble and servile Pullman porter, and afterwards as a convict in a chain gang. These sequences, asserted some critics, put Robeson in an unsympathetic light, and the final scene, when Brutus Jones is grovelling in superstititous fear in the jungle, was cited as a negation of all the film's good points (in that it indicated that a Negro servant who rose to fame as a black emperor would ultimately achieve only death and disgrace). There were many such criticisms, and even Robeson himself was not completely satisfied with the results of what must, however, be reckoned as a worthwhile and distinctly revolutionary venture. (It is interesting to note that in a review of this film appearing in the magazine *Film Art,* Summer, 1934, the word "nigger" appears twice, surely an indication of the derogatory attitude of some reviewers at that time to a dignified Negro personality, an attitude which persists in many quarters even today.) However, the film followed O'Neill's play religiously, and attacks on it for the above reasons constituted, in effect, an attack on the play itself (and were to a degree justified). Nevertheless, *The Emperor Jones* was a landmark in Negro films, and is still considered among the most original motion pictures of the past decade.

An early talking film which had given a fine part to a colored man was *Arrowsmith,* directed by John Ford, in 1932, in which Ronald Colman played a doctor and scientist and an excellent Negro actor, Clarence Brooks, played the part of a dignified doctor, who stood side by side with Arrowsmith in his experiments in the West Indian jungle and his struggles and triumphs in the cause of science. *Arrowsmith* was hailed everywhere as the best example of fair and tolerant film treatment of a Negro since the arrival of sound films, but it was, unfortunately, swamped by a mass of Hollywood efforts in which Negro characters behaved like half-wits. In films such as *The Ghost Talks, Judge Priest, The Littlest Rebel* and *In Old Kentucky,* the colored people were treated like animals, and behaved like them. Stepin Fetchit, for instance, was much to blame for popularizing a characterization which was to incur the bitter hatred of all intelligent Negroes. As servants or as tap dancers he, and other colored performers, grinned and gaped their way through both major and minor Hollywood productions, demolishing all the good work done by fine Negro stage players on Broadway and elsewhere. To most filmgoers Robeson was yet to come, Rex Ingram was unknown and the word "Negro" was inextricably interwoven in the minds of audiences with "Stepin Fetchit."

There were, of course, a number of early Hollywood musicals which starred well-

known black-face comedians from the American vaudeville stage and radio. Among these were *Why Bring That Up?* and *Two Black Crows in the A.E.F.,* both featuring Moran and Mack, and *Check and Double Check,* in which Amos and Andy, the famous radio act, were starred. These "nigger minstrel" movies were not, however, a great success, and in the past fifteen years there have been few pictures of this type made by Hollywood, exceptions being *Hypnotized* with Moran and Mack, *The Phantom President,* in which George M. Cohan performed an obnoxious black-face act, and certain of Al Jolson's films.

IMITATION OF LIFE

In 1934 Universal produced a film of Fannie Hurst's novel *Imitation of Life* (reissued in 1946), in which Louise Beavers appeared as the self-effacing, faithful, kind-hearted epitome of the worst type of "mammy" role. A widespread and bitter controversy arose on the showing of this production and Fannie Hurst and Sterling Brown, film critic of the magazine *Opportunity,* became involved in a clash of opinion concerning the effect of the film upon world audiences. Miss Hurst indignantly gave it as her opinion that Negroes should express "a little more gratitude" for the fact that she had featured them and their problems in her novel and screenplay. But Brown continued to attack the film, pointing out that the Negro character followed too closely so many others in a long line of stupid subservience. As an example, he drew attention to sequences of the film in which Louise Beavers tells her white mistress (Claudette Colbert) that she does not want to take her share of the profits from their joint pancake business, preferring to remain on the premises and to serve her white ma'am with true Negro dog-like devotion. All she desired, it seemed, was to be able to serve her mistress well, and "to have a big funeral

with white horses" when she died. And in spite of the part being played with great charm by Louise Beavers, who excels in this type of role, it was obvious that this study of abject servility was a reflection of the worst elements of Negro and white relations in American society.

As William Harrison pointed out in *Sight and Sound,* Spring, 1939, "Professor Brown of Howard University recorded his objection to a line uttered by a character in the film, played by Ned Sparks, who referring to the Negro cook's refusal to take a share in the profits, made the remark, 'Once a pancake, always a pancake,' for he held that this particular line, in its context, was a slur cast upon the Negro race. In rebuttal Miss Hurst countered that all her Negro characters were serious and so afforded scope for Negro actors and actresses wider than that previously enjoyed by them. She felt that Negroes owed her a debt of gratitude for this service, but her statement aroused even further resentment from a notoriously sensitive people, as her knowledge of the nuance of inter-racial relations in the United States was not equal to her sympathy. Yet," added Harrison, "the Negro spokesman had to realize that without financial resources for large-scale production the Negro community is dependent, and will be so for a long time, upon the Hollywood industry."

Imitation of Life was also important in that, in the sub-plot, attention was drawn to the Negro cook's mulatto daughter, a girl who could easily pass for white because of her extremely light skin. (This delicate subject has never been dealt with by Hollywood since that time.) Fredi Washington, a fine and sensitive New York stage actress, played this role with great intelligence, and brought sympathy, understanding and attention to what was originally quite a minor character in the film. As *Literary Digest,* December 8, 1934, remarked about this: "The real

story, the narrative which is merely hinted at, never really contemplated, is that of the beautiful and rebellious daughter of the loyal Negro friend. She is light-skinned, sensitive, tempestuous; and grows bitterly indignant when she sees that the white girl with whom she has been reared is getting all the fine things of life while she is subjected to humiliation and unhappiness. Obviously she is the most interesting person in the cast. Her drama is the most poignant, but the producers not only confine her to a minor and carefully handled sub-plot, but appear to regard her with distaste. They appear to be fond of her mother, because she is of the meek type of old-fashioned Negro that, as they say, 'knows his place,' but the daughter is too bitter and lacking in resignation for them."

To return to Fetchit, Snowball, Sleep 'n' Eat, Louise Beavers, and the others, it is safe to say that all the films featuring such actors as these showed the black man in a contemptible light. Fetchit portrayed the lazy, ignorant, good-for-nothing colored servant in dozens of films, including *Swing High, Stand Up and Cheer, Carolina,* and others, and the American public lapped it up. In fact, so successful was his contemptible impersonation of this type of part that Fox Studios signed him to a fat contract, so that his long line of biased characterizations might be continued in films like *David Harum, Helldorado, The Country Chairman* and similar productions. It is not suggested that the studio deliberately "wrote in" anti-Negro parts in their films, but since Fetchit's popularity with mass movie audiences was founded upon these unfair portrayals, Hollywood, notorious for its system of type casting, continued to allot him similar roles, especially in films dealing with the Southern states.

To an extent his position was taken over in the middle thirties by veteran dancer and actor Bill Robinson who, while remaining a pleasant and ingenuous figure, nevertheless began to portray a series of "Fetchit" characterizations after he had appeared with some success as Shirley Temple's good-natured servant in the Fox film *The Little Colonel* in 1935. Thenceforth Robinson danced and "mugged" his way through a number of "faithful servant" parts in such productions as *The Littlest Rebel, Steamboat Round the Bend, In Old Kentucky, Rebecca of Sunnybrook Farm* and *Road Demon.* In each of these he was the same genial underling, quite charming, but contributing very little towards the encouraging of a more realistic attitude of world filmgoers to the thirteen million black Americans. Only once did he play a dignified role with distinction, and that was in the Fox film *One Mile from Heaven,* produced in 1937 (and in which, incidentally, the beautiful Fredi Washington gave another extremely moving performance). It is not a condemnation of Bill Robinson that he was rarely seen in a part which reflected beneficially on the Negro race. Rather has it been the fault of the producers themselves, who never allow sympathetic colored *characters* to find their way into pictures. Thus Robinson shares the same dilemma of all Negro players: either they appear in subservient parts and endow them with what sympathy they can, or else they boycott Hollywood altogether and try to earn a living in stage and radio productions. The difficulties and disadvantages of the latter course are fairly obvious. Most Negro actors feel that it is a step forward to play a speaking part in a film, providing it is not too maliciously overdrawn; and this attitude is partially justified. The history of Negro film actors has shown that whereas twenty years ago colored players were never given parts of even minor importance, today some dozens of Negroes appear regularly on the screen. And, of course, some colored actors and actresses, like Paul Robeson, Eddie "Rochester" Ander-

son, Rex Ingram and Lena Horne, have become extremely popular "names" at the box office. This then must be considered something of a forward move. Obviously the next step is for those actors who have become important box office names to refuse roles which reflect even by implication a derogatory attitude to colored people generally.

SO RED THE ROSE

In 1935 King Vidor, director of *Hallelujah* five years previously, directed the film version of Stark Young's best-selling anti-Negro novel of the old South, *So Red the Rose*, with Margaret Sullavan, Walter Connolly, Randolph Scott, Daniel Haynes and Clarence Muse. Like *The Birth of a Nation*, the film was concerned with the Civil War period in American history, and like Griffith's film it was a libellous presentation of the social conditions of the Southern slaves, picturing their revolt against their owners as based only upon laziness, greed and hysteria. Negro leaders were shown as opportunists, misleading a simple-minded people who were happy enough to be left in their lowly place in American society, and, in fact, were obstinately devoted to their white masters. This film was a colossal travesty in every possible way.

Paramount issued a number of publicity stories in connection with the making of the film. One such hand-out read: "Sociological experiments are by no means the purpose of film-making and the few daring souls who have invaded this most controversial of all fields have met with disastrous failures. Yet there is a tendency in 1935 to depart somewhat from the standardized forms of screen literature and to liberalize this media to conform to modern tolerance and thought."

This was a subtle and cynical method of drawing the sting of those liberal organizations which the studio knew would immediately attack the finished film for its misrepresentation of Negro efforts towards their own emancipation. The producers were already preening themselves for *having* colored actors in their film; this, seemingly, being their method of conforming to "modern tolerance and thought" (see above). In the same publicity release the studio stated: "There has been a marked decrease in that form of intolerance which specialises in the drawing of color lines and your colored performer of merit now shares marquee distinction with the whites." How true was this, then and now? The Negro actor's salary is a great deal lower than the white actor's in the same category. Whether he is a small part or featured player he is discriminated against on the set and in the finished picture; his photograph never appears in a newspaper advertisement of the film, nor are publicity photographs of colored artists distributed to the Press. So much for Paramount's assertion.

To refer again to the general line of studio publicity: "King Vidor holds the opinion that the colored race is the most difficult of all people to handle as a group in the making of motion pictures. *Fundamentally living only for the joy they get out of life* (author's italics) they are inclined to laugh at serious things and this native comedy is sometimes difficult to overcome when sheer drama is necessary."

Let us take a look at another publicity paragraph: "King Vidor took this day's work most seriously. He outlined his story to his colored group and made some of them cry through a somewhat maudlin presentation of the evils which their ancestors were *supposed to have suffered* (author's italics). This had the effect of putting them in the proper mood and the rapid change from happiness to sullen anger was accomplished without delay."

This then was the line taken by the publicity department before the screening of *So Red the Rose*. Now for the film itself. It

tells the story of an old Southern family during the Civil War, whose treatment of its slaves is humane and understanding (at least from the white point of view). There is no reference to the deep feelings of bitterness due to the splitting-up of Negro families, the starvation of the slaves and general ill-treatment of the black workers which took place during the Civil War itself, treatment which became more vicious as the military situation worsened for the South. In Stark Young's film there is no apparent reason given for the revolt of the slaves on the plantation, except that Cato, a trouble-making slave, played by Clarence Muse, causes unrest by holding before his fellows a high colored picture of a life of greed, luxury and happiness, which should rightfully be theirs. And when the crazed Negroes, ugly with hate, turn against the gentle hand that has fed them for so many years, the audience is encouraged to feel only resentment at their efforts to become free. When William the faithful butler, in true Uncle Tom tradition (played by that good Negro actor Daniel Haynes), tells the coachman to unhitch the horses, the man replies, "I've unhitched horses for the last time. Let the white folks unhitch their own horses. I'se gonna be free." And with an hysterical shout he runs towards the slave quarters in a frenzy of ecstasy and excitement, shouting "Free, free for true. I'se gonna be free." He arrives at the spot in the plantation where the slaves are gathered in rebellion, hatred and malignity transforming their faces. Cato, the ringleader, now shown as a brutal hate-crazed slave, is haranguing the mob:

"You been slaves long enough, ain't yer?" he cries.

"Yes, that's right," comes the answer.

"You want what belongs to you, don't yer?"

"Yes, ain't it true?"

"Thass right!"

"Are yer gonna take what belongs to yer?"

"Yes! Yes! We sho' is!"

"Or wait until somebody else eats it up."

"No! No! No, we ain't."

"All this is yours! Go and get it!"

Following this the slaves rush hither and thither, greedily stealing pigs, chickens and horses, screaming and shouting "I got mine! I got mine!" And Cato declares: "Before long we'll all be sitting in the golden chairs in the big house. It all belongs to us now! We're the kings! No more ploughing, no more chopping cotton, no more planting, jest sittin' in the sun!" Then the slaves work themselves up into a veritable frenzy, the while stealing and plundering and generally making merry on the plantation. "Lincoln has given us de land!" they cry, "no more work for us!"

But in the old Southern homestead sits the mistress of the house, a proud daughter of the Confederacy (Margaret Sullavan). She is worried in case the sound of the rebellion should reach to the manor house, where her father, the traditional Southern colonel, is dying. The girl knows that his heart will break if he realizes that his devoted servants and slaves have turned upon him; so with a heart-warming simplicity she strides fearlessly into the slave quarters, and breaks up the rebellion by slapping one of the ringleaders in the face, and shaming the rest of the rioters with a reminder that they are all her dear, dear friends and they must continue to be "good" for the sake of her dying father. Confronted by the brave little woman whom they have loved since she was a child, the slaves break down and cry, chanting hymns and following her to the manor. And when their beloved colonel finally dies peacefully the slaves disperse quietly, and go about their work on the plantation. The revolt is crushed; white supremacy, kindness and courage have won the day!

Many critics attacked the film. As Arthur Draper pointed out in an article, entitled "Uncle Tom, Will You Never Die?" in *New*

Theatre, January, 1936, "If *So Red the Rose* succeeds at the box office in the South it will be at the cost once again of provoking even sharper racial lines than exist in these states at the present time, of provoking an even greater hatred by the whites for the Negroes, of breaking the solidarity between workers of all races that is today beginning to change the Old South of infamous reputation into a New South built on workers' pride."

The movie had a fair success due mainly to the performance of Margaret Sullavan, but was heavily critized by the Negro press and by liberal organizations everywhere. Daniel Haynes was so hurt and disgusted with the finished film that he returned to New York and refused to appear in movies again unless he had the right to approve the theme, and then only if the part gave him an opportunity to show his race in a sympathetic light. He bitterly regretted the contribution he had made to race hatred in this film, and to my knowledge, like Charles Gilpin, he never went back to Hollywood.

THE GREEN PASTURES

Since the time of *Hearts in Dixie* and *Hallelujah,* Hollywood had fought shy of making all-Negro movies. But in 1936 Warner Brothers decided to film the successful long-running *The Green Pastures* by Marc Connelly, with a well-known Broadway actor, Rex Ingram, as De Lawd. The play purported to be "a delightful and daring portrayal of Negro religion." As a publicity hand-out read: "The stories of childhood live again in the naive beliefs of these colored Christians. Humor, courage, love and forgiveness are inter-woven in this moving panorama of primitive life. Biblical incidents are transmuted into a living faith which plays on the humanity of God. One of the most original features is the symbolizing of a religious development as God learning from

experience." For censorship reasons Hollywood had never extensively tackled religious subjects, but Warners decided that *The Green Pastures* was a play which deserved to be seen by a wider audience, and asked author Marc Connelly to co-direct the film (with William Keighley) in order to ensure that the sincerity of the original conception would not be lost in the film treatment.

The film of *The Green Pastures* was in the form of a flashback, with a prologue and an epilogue set in a Sunday School for colored children. The preacher is reading from an early chapter, and endeavors to transpose explanations for the benefit of his pupils. The film then dissolves into a kind of juvenile Negro idea of Heaven in which the Lord (beautifully played by Rex Ingram) is shown as a kindly Negro parson. The story concerns itself with the creating of the world, from the Garden of Eden, to the murder of Abel and finally to the incident of Noah and the Ark. It is simple but effective. Felix Barker wrote of it in *World Film News,* September, 1936, as follows: "Rex Ingram's every feature is of purity and benign goodness. The measure of beauty which the film brings to the public consciousness ought certainly to outweigh ordinary rule and precedent."

But in the opinion of some critics, *The Green Pastures,* adapted from Roark Bradford's sketches of Southern life, *Ole Man Adam and His Chillun,* offered little that was new. Though delightfully written, with a nice sense of humor and some original touches, Connelly's play nevertheless did very little to enhance the status of colored people in the public mind, and, for that matter, neither did the film. Well-intentioned, it merely gave filmgoers once more the happy, religious, hymn-singing black man, whose idea of Heaven seems to consist mainly of long white nightgowns, hymn-shouting and fish-fries. In fact, "quaint" was the word

most used by reviewers to describe the acting of the all-colored cast, although every critic was insistent that Rex Ingram, who gave a dignified and moving portrayal, deserved to be rewarded with important roles in further films. Eddie Anderson's Noah and Ernest Whitman's Pharaoh were other outstanding studies which received critical praise in a well-acted film. Like *Hearts in Dixie* and *Hallelujah, The Green Pastures* served to point once more to the high quality of much Negro talent in the field of filmic interpretation. As William Harrison asserted in *Sight and Sound,* Spring, 1939: "It is universally recognized that the Negro possesses considerable and unusual histrionic ability." He went on to say, "This talent has imperfectly revealed itself in the cinema. The reason for this deficiency in utilizing an admitted reservoir of talent must be sought in the fact that the roles usually assigned to Negro actors have had only two stops: farce and pathos."

Ingram's performance in *The Green Pastures* managed in many ways to depart from the above, and his work, in particular, brought to the screen a new conception of Negro dignity, of the kind indicated previously by the acting of Paul Robeson, Fredi Washington, Daniel Haynes and some others. The film was generally well received. The critic of *Time* wrote: "One of the principal dangers of the cinema was that Heaven would either be improved beyond any Southern pickaninny's dreams, or else that the artfulness of its simplicity might seem condescending. The producers have avoided both these pitfalls. Heaven has been improved, but only slightly. God is still a shabby Negro preacher, calm, elderly and not too competent. He has notions what to do about the earth, but the notions do not often work, and he is still puzzling when the picture ends." Some interesting examples of the diversity of other critical opinion are given below:—

"Nothing will induce me to argue about whether this picture is what is called 'commercial' or not. But with my last breath I will defend its beauty, its sincerity, its nobility, and its piety. If you are interested to see a film that unquestionably has these fine qualities, then see *The Green Pastures.* Lack of commercial success of such a film could only be a criticism of the public, not of the picture. It is beside the point to discuss 'acting' and 'production' of such a picture. Thanks to the nature of the colored people, I can believe that the players lived their parts in a spirit of reverence. To suggest blasphemy . . . is to deny divine ubiquity . . .."
Stephen Watts, *The Sunday Express.*

"If this film is allowed, the Divine Judgment cannot but fall upon this country."
Rev. F. L. Langton.

"The picture is too blasphemous and shocking to contemplate!"
Admiral Sir George King-Hall.

Lawrence Reddick gives as his opinion that Hollywood turned a rather majestic and dignified play into a light and, for the most part, ridiculous travesty; and sections of the Negro press were inclined to agree with him. Nevertheless the film constituted a landmark in Negro progress on the screen. It gave roles of importance to some well-known Broadway players who remained in the film city thereafter, actors such as Clinton Rosemond, Oscar Polk, Ernest Whitman, Eddie Anderson and others, many of them coming to screen prominence within the next few years. The film further revealed the potentialities of movies exclusively Negro, while pointing out the deficiencies in the unrealistic attitude which leads Hollywood to make them. However well-intentioned, they inevitably line themselves up on the Jim Crow side of the fence.

There are two schools of thought on this subject, both vigorously asserting their points of view and both carrying a measure of justification. This difference of opinion has been present since the colored artist first appeared in Hollywood. On one side there are those who assert that a Negro playing *any* part on the screen is better than no Negroes on the screen at all, and on the other side those who believe the Negro should appear only in films which show his correct relationship to a white community and not in fairy-tales, fantasies or films treating the subject lightly and unrealistically. Ultimately it would seem that the intelligent cinemagoer very naturally condemns all films which show the Negro in an unsympathetic light, while still applauding any production, all-Negro or otherwise, which gives a colored actor an opportunity to show his talent, and to play his part towards wider recognition of the Negro's role both in the film and in society.

An example of the strong division of opinion is indicated in the following comments: "Because of the Negro movie many a prejudiced white who would not accept a Negro unless as a servant will be compelled to admit that at least he can be something else; many an indifferent white will be beguiled into a positive attitude of friendliness; many a Negro will have his race consciousness and self-respect stimulated. In short, the Negro movie actor is a means of getting acquainted with Negroes." So wrote Geraldyn Dismond some ten years ago in *Close Up.* But as Robert Stebbins replied, in *New Theatre,* "It would be difficult to hit upon another such example as Dismond's of wishful prophecy so precisely unfulfilled!"

MERVYN LE ROY AND FRITZ LANG

Mervyn Le Roy, a Hollywood director whose best work was done during his long and successful association with Warner Brothers, demonstrates in his films a keen sense of sympathy with the Negro. One remembers his treatment of the Negro prisoner, played by Everett Brown, in that superb movie, *I Am a Fugitive From a Chain Gang,* dealing with Southern labor camps and produced in 1932. The Negro is shown in the early part of the film as one of Paul Muni's comrades. He reveals a good brain, a friendly nature and a clear philosophy. It is hinted that, like Muni, he also came into the chain gang as a result of circumstances almost amounting to a Southern states' "frame up." Le Roy's sympathetic handling of the Negro role reached its climax in the scene where Muni, rebelling at the injustices of the labor camp system and realizing that the bigoted Southern wardens will see that he never gets his long-promised reprieve, decides to make his escape. He is helped by his black friend, who with his great strength, patience and selfless bravery aids Muni to make a getaway by breaking his chains with his sledge-hammer. The feeling which remained after seeing *I Am a Fugitive* was that the Negro is an ordinary human being, capable of great friendship, loyalty and courage.

One of the most effective attacks on the old American custom of lynching and therefore, by implication, an anti-discrimination movie, was Fritz Lang's magnificent film, *Fury,* made for M.G.M. in 1936, with Spencer Tracy and Sylvia Sidney. It was indeed significant that Lang, a foreigner, should choose for the subject of his first American film a story about mob violence, one of the most striking and least savory aspects of the U.S.A. The details of the lynching in this film made it of unbearable horror, of a kind only equalled by the more recent *Strange Incident,* directed by William A. Wellman. There was no Negro character in *Fury,* but it was one of the most moving appeals for greater tolerance ever made in Hollywood and a really great motion picture. I do not think Lang has directed a better American

film than *Fury,* one of the landmarks of motion picture progress.

Warner Brothers made a film called *Black Legion* in the middle 1930's, which starred Humphrey Bogart and was an excellently produced attack on the Ku Klux Klan. Depicting how in the U.S.A. an ordinary worker with progressive views could be threatened, beaten and even murdered by anti-Jew, anti-Negro, anti-foreigner Fascist organisations such as the Klan, it was an intelligent and timely effort which lined up with such other notable Warners' productions as *I Am a Fugitive, They Won't Forget* (and *In This Our Life* which came a few years later). *Black Legion* was a forthright critical examination of that dreaded terrorist organization, the New Ku Klux Klan, which flourished in the Middle West between 1935 and 1937. It was, in effect, an indictment of the notorious Ku Klux Klan of the earlier period, that murderous group of fanatics glorified by Griffith in *The Birth of a Nation,* and reveals American brutality, stupidity and hypocrisy masquerading under the cloak of patriotism. A courageous production, extremely progressive in treatment and implication, it was, not unnaturally, widely boycotted by exhibitors in the Southern states.

THEY WON'T FORGET

Mervyn Le Roy again showed his deep interest in the color problem of the South in his memorable film *They Won't Forget,* which he directed for Warners in 1937. Adapted from Ward Greene's powerful novel *Death in the Deep South,* it was, broadly speaking, an indictment of Southern intolerance. Greene's book is the story of the rape and murder of a young girl in a Southern town, and the arrest of a new schoolteacher who, being a Northerner, has previously incurred disapproval from his fellow citizens in this prejudiced and bigoted little township

of the Old South. Quickly the law gets to work in condemning the Northerner without evidence, and when a famous liberal lawyer arrives from New York to defend the schoolteacher the issue soon becomes not so much the Law versus the Accused as the North versus the South. As Mervyn Le Roy stresses again and again in this grim and moving film —they won't forget! Of it, *Cinema Arts,* July, 1937, said: "Warners have tackled a sociological problem regardless of possible hostile reaction from sectional audiences" (meaning the South).

And not for a long time has there been such a sane filmic assessment of Southern values. The picture attempts to portray with clarity, understatement, and no degree of bitterness, the continued existence below the Mason-Dixon line (in the 1930's at least) of a spiritual revival of the worst elements in Southern tradition. Symptomatic of this revival is the flaring up of an added ferocity in the treatment by the whites of their Negro fellow-citizens. Le Roy shows how every year, on the anniversary of the end of the Civil War, the bitterness of the white townsfolk towards their former slaves evinces itself in a number of outbreaks, not the least of which is a renewal of mob hooliganism, as well as major and minor persecutions—and occasional lynching. More vividly than any other Hollywood film, *They Won't Forget* points to the tragedy of some backward Southern communities, still living in their feudal past, still refusing to acknowledge that the Civil War brought with it a revolution in the American scene. It takes its place alongside the significant social documents of the screen.

Giving many acting opportunities to such first-rate players as Claude Rains, Allyn Joslyn, Gloria Dickson and Edward Norris, the film also saw a memorable performance from that fine actor Clinton Rosemond, who played the colored janitor. Naturally, being

black, and having worked near the scene of the crime, this quiet, kindly and harmless old menial is suspected of the murder and, in a particularly brutal scene, is third-degreed by some semi-Fascist Southern police officers. The Negro is blackjacked, brutally beaten and finally thrown back into his cell, with clothes torn and head bleeding. His poignant cry, "I didn't do it. So help me. I didn't do it," as he lies moaning in his cell, will remain long in the memory of those who saw the film. Inevitably the drama ends in a lynching, though in this case the victim is the white Northerner.

In her book *America at the Movies,* Margaret Farrand Thorp writes: *"They Won't Forget,* which concerned a Southern town's lynching of a schoolteacher suspected of murder chiefly because he was a Northerner, could not be shown in theatres below Washington. The director, Mervyn Le Roy, was, the report goes, surprised; he did not expect the South to take it personally. The North, on the other hand, has so forgotten the emotions of the War Between the States that a New England audience is no more insulted by the sight of Yankee troops burning a Mississippi mansion (*So Red the Rose, Gone With the Wind*) than by the spectacle of the hordes at the gates of Peking."

The film was indeed attacked bitterly by the Southern states, but critics in all parts of the world acclaimed it as a great American film. Howard Barnes wrote in the New York *Herald Tribune*: *"They Won't Forget* takes its place naturally with *Fury* and *Black Legion* as one of Hollywood's infrequent but exciting excursions into the more sinister expressions of our social system. In my opinion it is finer than either of them. The film is much more than the screen record of a specific mob murder. There is a dispassionate perspective in the script and in Mr. Le Roy's consummate direction that makes this a universal and abiding arraignment of intolerance

and crowd fury." Richard Kerr described *They Won't Forget* as "a truly great picture." In Britain, too, the film received high praise. Basil Wright, in *World Film News,* December, 1937, stated: *"They Won't Forget* is a savage, terrible, horrifying, cynical and unequivocal exposé of the backwardness and degeneration of the small-time towns of the Southern states, which have, with their lynchings and their Scottsboro Trials, made American justice stink to Heaven."

They Won't Forget occupies an honored position in the annals of serious movie-making. It reflects great credit on Mervyn Le Roy and Warner Brothers, a studio which has never hesitated to make films on controversial themes. For that praiseworthy pre-war series of hard-hitting motion pictures which began with *I Am a Fugitive* and ended with *Confessions of a Nazi Spy* in 1939, Warner Brothers deserves a permanent place in the Honor Roll of the Hollywood industry.

GONE WITH THE WIND

And so we come to *Gone With the Wind.* Like Griffith's historic film, it dealt with the South, the Civil War and the efforts of the Negro to free himself from slavery, and, as Lawrence Reddick remarks, these films possess interesting similarities. Both were extraordinary from an artistic and technical point of view, both were heralded with almost fantastic publicity, both were remarkably long (*Gone With the Wind* lasted nearly four hours) and both were huge financial successes. Nevertheless it could be seen that the American film itself and film audiences generally had grown up considerably. No longer was it possible, as Griffith had done, to lay stress upon inflammatory appeal. Director Victor Fleming concentrated instead on the characters of Scarlett O'Hara and Rhett Butler, the "romantic leads," and his attitude to the black characters in the film

was notable for its subtlety. Whether this was the subtlety of unconscious discrimination or that of a fully conscious desire to follow, a little more carefully, in the footsteps of Griffith, one cannot say. At any rate many critics felt that where Griffith's film ended Fleming's film began.

The novel is probably well-known to most people. Apart from its rather florid central theme, it succeeds in eradicating from the mind of the reader any liberal consciousness which may have resulted from knowing that the Northern states won a victory over intolerance when they achieved the larger political and military victory in the Civil War. The film succeeded admirably in continuing the popular Southern myth that the South had in fact won an ideological war, that, indeed, although the Negroes had been set free they still remained inescapably fettered as historic inferiors to the white race, socially, politically and economically. *Gone With the Wind* marked a high point in the Hollywood move to show that so far as the Negro was concerned United States opinion had reverted to the "Southern Mammy and Uncle Tom tradition." Hollywood's apparent obsession with films on Southern themes, especially films which "put the Negro in his place," cannot always have been a mere accident. Surely it is not unreasonable to suggest that those who make these films possess pre-conceived notions on this subject, with the result that literally millions of filmgoers are yearly doped with a subtle—and sometimes extremely unsubtle—form of harmful propaganda. As an indication that I do not underestimate the potential audience of an anti-Negro film, I should like to point out that by 1944 David O. Selznick, the producer of *Gone With the Wind,* estimated that nearly sixty-four *million* people in the United States and Canada had seen his film! Add to that the audiences in the United Kingdom, the British Empire and in other parts of the world and you have

a startling indication of the very real menace of a film which propagates anti-social ideas and around which is wrapped the pill of "starstudded entertainment."

During the making of *Gone With the Wind,* the National Association for the Advancement of Colored People (N.A.A.C.P.) instituted a vigorous fight to have some of the most offensive scenes eliminated or, at least, softened; as a result, the film, when finally shown, was not by any means as vicious as the novel. And bodies like the National Negro Congress, the Negro magazine *Opportunity,* other Negro newspapers, and certain left and liberal political groups, continued to denounce the film in the press.

Negro leaders, lecturers, educationists, public figures, artists, actors, and many others condemned the film, and some trade unions supported moves to picket cinemas where *Gone With the Wind* was showing. Their combined efforts, however, to have it banned or to have the offending passages removed were not successful. Nevertheless, such was the interest aroused by mass demonstrations against this famous film that it served to educate the public to a further awareness, firstly of the fact that there *were* anti-Negro elements in certain Hollywood films, and secondly of the dangerous power of the movie for developing reactionary social attitudes. For, as Lawrence Reddick says, "The net effect of such a film on the public mind can only be guessed."

Walter White, Secretary of the N.A.A.C.P., stated, "Whatever sentiment there was in the South for Federal anti-lynch law evaporated during the *Gone With the Wind* vogue." And, in his pamphlet examining race relations in motion pictures, Reddick records that at least one Southern child who had seen the film is reported to have told his Negro nursemaid that she would still be a slave and his daddy would not have to pay her if it had not been for the Yankees!

Ethel Waters, Eddie "Rochester" Anderson and Paul Robeson in *Tales of Manhattan*.

Ethel Waters in *Cabin in the Sky*.

William Warfield, as Joe, in *Show Boat*.

Hattie McDaniel in *The Little Colonel*.

Bill Robinson in *The Littlest Rebel*.

Paul Robeson and Nina Mae McKinney in *Sanders Of The River*.

Hattie McDaniel was given an Academy Award for the best acting of the year in a supporting role for her work in *Gone With the Wind*. This was the first time that a Negro had ever received such an award from the Academy of Motion Picture Arts and Sciences, but the fact that she was given an "Oscar" for her work as a stereotyped "Mammy" in this highly controversial film caused a great deal of further dissension. Indeed many Negroes felt that Miss McDaniel should have refused to take the award as a protest against her part.

To sum up: *Gone With the Wind* convinced millions of Southerners that the war had been for them an ideological victory, and that the place for the black man was in the lowest stratum of society. It stirred up further feeling against the "damned Yankees"; and as a prime example of how a moving picture can incite intense racial hatred, Victor Fleming's film of the Margaret Mitchell novel lines up worthily alongside Griffith's film of *The Clansman*.

—1948

Radio and Television

THE WASTE LANDS
by Lindsay Patterson

Sammy Davis, Jr.

The Waste Lands

by Lindsay Patterson

Radio (in its heyday) and television reach more people daily than any other entertainment media, and have been just as guilty in perpetuating stereotypes of the Negro as Hollywood. On radio, the chief offender had been "Amos 'n' Andy," one of white America's favorite shows since its inception on a local Chicago radio station as "Sam 'n' Henry" nearly a half century ago. When television came along, "Amos 'n' Andy" successfully made the transition, lost little of its devoted audience and threatened to match its long radio stand until various pressure groups were instrumental in having the show "retired" from the home screens.

Radio, like television, used most Negro performers as guest artists. Billie Holiday was one of the first and few Negroes to perform regularly on a coast-to-coast network show as a band vocalist. Thelma Carpenter was employed purely as a singer on the "Eddie Cantor Show" for a time. Singing groups, however, were the most prevalent, especially in the forties, when trios and quartets were in vogue. One of the most popular was the King Cole Trio, which frequently appeared on the "Frank Sinatra" and "Supper Club" shows. The Charioteers, perhaps the best known quartet in the mid-forties, were featured for three years on Bing Crosby's "Kraft Music Hall." One of the all time great quartets, the Inkspots, were never regular members of any program, but were much sought after guests for many shows. An unusual team of singers were the Four Vagabonds, who at their height were featured on nine shows weekly. This group also did commercials, a rarity which virtually no other Negroes were allowed for a national audience. Though the big bands were still thriving in the forties, not one Negro band had a regular berth on a radio show. Duke Ellington and Count Basie were everyone's favorites, but the most they could hope for were occasional guest spots on a variety show.

Many of the high-rated comedy shows featured at least one Negro performer who was pertinent to the action of the program and contributed in large measure to its success. One such was the "Jack Benny Show" with Eddie "Rochester" Anderson as Benny's valet. Butterfly McQueen, who received more criticism than Hattie McDaniel for playing maid roles in Hollywood, once walked out of rehearsal for a "Jack Benny Show," protesting the language of the maid role she had contracted to play. Later, Miss McQueen was featured in a non-stereotyped role on the "Danny Kaye Show," as president of his one-woman fan club. A show that drew much displeasure from Negroes was "The Great Gildersleeve," featuring Lillian Randolph as Birdie. Miss Randolph also played the part of Madam Queen on the "Amos 'n' Andy Show."

In the late forties it became increasingly

clear that television was around to stay, and many of the staple radio shows moved to television. "Amos 'n' Andy," of course, made the transformation, virtually intact, with an all Negro cast. On radio, the two main characters were played by its creators in blackface before a studio audience. For television, Tim Moore landed the role of the Kingfish, the main protagonist of the show, and Ernestine Wade continued to play his wife, Sapphire.

Ed Sullivan's "Toast of the Town," was one of the earliest variety shows on television, and Sullivan, who has long been a champion of Negro rights used an abundance of Negro performers. When Southern stations balked, Sullivan steadfastly refused to alter his policy or limit the number of Negro guests, insisting upon his right to use as many talented performers as he wished, regardless of color. Milton Berle, known for several years as "Mr. Television," was another TV star who employed Negroes regularly on his show. Arthur Godfrey presented a mixed quartet, the Mariners as his "family of friends" without much adverse reaction from Southern viewers. Perry Como was another star who employed Negro artists regularly on his show.

Finally, television did take the big step and presented a Negro performer with a show of his own. The "Nat 'King' Cole Show," though popular in rating, did not attract a sponsor and was dropped after a year on the air. Cole was offered an inferior time spot by the network but refused, though praising NBC for its courage and condemning Madison Avenue for its failure to obtain a national sponsor. Oddly enough, a show that obtained a national sponsor was a dramatic series, "I Spy," co-starring Bill Cosby. It is a show that has steadily built up a devoted audience in its two

seasons on the air. Cosby has won two Emmy Awards as Best Actor in a running series. The third Negro to be given an all-network show was Sammy Davis, Jr., but unfortunately Davis had other commitments when his show premiered, and when he did take over the reins, the rating had slumped to such a low point that he was unable to regain his initial audience.

It is still a sad fact that television, like radio, employs the bulk of Negro performers as guest artists on variety shows. Seldom does a top Negro performer have his own special as do white stars. Groups like the Supremes, stellar attractions like Lena Horne, Eartha Kitt, Nancy Wilson and James Brown can only depend upon a few infrequent guest spots. White performers who reach the pinnacle in show business are eagerly offered network series or at least hour specials of their own. Lena Horne, called the "greatest" nightclub performer in the world, has had to go to England to make specials, as has Eartha Kitt.

Few Negroes work in the technical end of television or in any executive capacities. Harry Belafonte, who has had several award-winning specials, has been the only Negro producer.

Television's record has certainly been far better than radio's. In radio's heyday, there were no Ivan Dixons or Cicely Tysons in a continuing dramatic series as supporting players. No Nipsey Russells sharing hosting duties with a white m.c., or Leslie Uggams as on Mitch Miller's show. Television integration is far from complete, and sometimes, after viewing the late, late movies it is difficult to ascertain whether or not television is seriously working toward that aim.

—1967

Billie Holiday was one of the first of the few Negro singers to perform regularly on a coast-to-coast radio network show as a band vocalist (with Artie Shaw).

Tim Moore was the Kingfish on the "Amos 'n' Andy Show" on TV.

Ethel Waters has starred in "Beulah," a favorite radio show in the forties, which made the transition to television.

Nipsey Russell (top left) was co-host of the "Les Crane Show" on television for a season, marking the first time a Negro was regularly employed as a master of ceremonies on a nationally televised program. Increasingly, Negroes are being used on television as newsmen. Bob Teague (top right), with WNBC in New York, has his own local news program. Max Goode (bottom) is with ABC news.

The Supremes, the most popular female singing trio to emerge in the sixties, are much sought after as guests for variety shows.

Leslie Uggams gained fame on the "Sing Along with Mitch" show. In 1967, she made her Broadway debut as star of the musical *Hallelujah, Baby!*

Barbara Alston was the lead dancer on "The Sammy Davis, Jr., Show." She also appeared regularly on "Hullabaloo."

Bill Cosby is the first Negro to be starred in a weekly dramatic series, in "I Spy," an adventure-comedy show of international intrigue. Co-star Robert Culp plays a tennis star and Cosby travels as his trainer. Most of the program's episodes occur in foreign capitals. (Above) Cosby with Rafaella Carra and Enzo Cerusico in an episode titled "Sophia." (Bottom left) Cosby confers with his executive producer, Sheldon Leonard, before filming a scene on a Rome, Italy, street. (Bottom right) Cosby in Venice.

In 1966, Cosby was awarded a television Emmy as the best actor in a continuing dramatic series. (Top left) Cosby assumes his guise as a trainer. (Top right) With co-star Robert Culp, and Diana Hyland. (Bottom) The two stars reveal their identity to Rome policemen.

Donald McKayle (second from right) has choreographed many shows on television. Here, he appears in *Amahl and the Night Visitors*, an annual Christmas special on NBC television for which he also did the choreography.

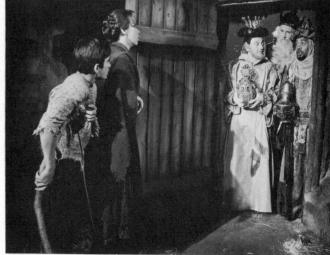

Willis Patterson plays one of the Three Kings in *Amahl*.

Frequent guest appearances on the "Tonight Show," revived the career of John Bubbles, who was the original Sporting Life in *Porgy and Bess*. Bubbles' initial fame came in the twenties, when he was half of the comedy-dance team of Buck and Bubbles.

Harry Belafonte (above) has been the only Negro TV producer. His "Strollin' Twenties" and "100 Years of Laughter" were high points of the 1966 and 1967 seasons.

Top musical groups like Duke Ellington and his orchestra (above) and the Ramsey Lewis Trio (below) receive most of their television exposure from appearances on variety shows.

EAST END THEATER

THEATER 1964

Richard Barr   Clinton Wilder   Edward Albee

presents

ADRIENNE KENNEDY'S

FUNNYHOUSE OF A NEGRO

with

BILLIE ALLEN   ELLEN HOLLY

CYNTHIA BELGRAVE   LESLIE RIVERS

NORMAN BUSH   RUTH VOLNER

LEONARD FREY   GUS WILLIAMS

Directed by
MICHAEL KAHN

Settings and Lighting by   *Costumes by*
WILLIAM RITMAN   **WILLA KIM**

SHOWCARD   January 7 & January 14

New Frontiers

FUNNYHOUSE OF A NEGRO
by Adrienne Kennedy

INTRODUCTION

America has always complained about its scarcity of talented young writers. This is especially true of the theatre, where critics, after each Broadway season, faithfully perform a post-mortem, then predict the certain death of all theatre for lack of significant contributors. *But alas! All hope is not lost.* Miraculously, there is one shining light, a glimmer of hope, as it were, that the critics skeptically pluck from their drama bag as they direly ponder whether he is the fair-haired boy who will save the day. He appears, not in the conventional mold, but with a new, atomic approach to the old verities. It is not quite understood just what he attempts to communicate; there is no patience with the bizarre, and so their voices dissolve into a mixed chorus of befuddlements, hostilities and disappointments—through which is sometimes heard a faint echo of praise.

It is a condition under which the most talented writer could be crushed, for there is almost never any constructive encouragement, only a blanket dismissal. If the writer is not yet a full-blown playwright, he is chided for having wasted their time. It goes without saying that if any talented young white writer of the unconventional finds it rough going, the talented young Negro of similar bent finds it impossible. Critics, to date, have not attempted to interpret the Negro writer's experimentation. When the Negro writer probes the depths of human emotions and behavior in an unconventional way, he is more than suspect—he is accused outright of self-hatred.

Two of our most talented young playwrights—LeRoi Jones and Adrienne Kennedy—have been thus accused. When Jones' *The Toilet* and *The Slave* appeared, one critic headlined his review "Several Thousand Dirty Words," and in tones of hysterical horror dismissed Jones. Another critic, however, did probe beneath the surface and came to some significant conclusions (though not failing to point out the author's faults and weaknesses), proclaiming Jones a much needed force in America's "anemic" theatre.

Indeed, the work of both Jones and Miss Kennedy has met with greater appreciation in Europe than here. Miss Kennedy has found great favor in England, where her play *Funnyhouse of a Negro* was televised and subsequently had several showings. This play is about to be made into a feature-length movie in England. Jones' play *Dutchman,* which has just been filmed in England, has, as its entire setting, a New York subway car. New York City officials refused the use of subway facilities to Jones' independent producers, although Hollywood companies have been given carte blanche on city property.

What is to happen to our two most talented young playwrights? Will they be forced into exile, as many of our talented novelists have been?

Everyone knows the theatre is a risky way to live. White authors who have not had even the modicum of success that Jones and Miss Kennedy have had are offered movie, television and radio assignments that keep them eating between plays. Gloria Foster, a young Negro actress of enormous talent, received one of the best personal reviews for her performance in *In White America* that any actress could hope for. No offers of any kind, from Broadway to Hollywood, were forthcoming. A young white playwright that I know had a moderate Off-Broadway success; his phone has not stopped ringing. Last year, a well-known Hollywood director with whom I discussed the employment of Negro screen writers asked for a list of names. The writers have yet to be approached.

If I seem to dwell on the writer, it is not because I favor him above all other practitioners in the theatre; it is because I think the Negro's viewpoints have been too long suppressed—and who better than the playwright to air them. There are twenty-two million Negroes in this country, and each, I suspect, has a different view of life. Many, I'm sure, share mundane views similar to those of their white counterparts. But I'm also sure that there are a good dozen who have that special viewpoint that we all should share, and it is time America became acquainted with them.

Lindsay Patterson

FUNNYHOUSE OF A NEGRO

A One-Act Play

BY ADRIENNE KENNEDY

Funnyhouse of a Negro by Adrienne Kennedy became a controversial play when it opened at the Cricket Theatre in New York on January 18, 1964. Some reviewers did not understand the play, but all hailed Miss Kennedy as a new and exciting playwright. Funnyhouse is scheduled for movie production in England with Diana Sands in the lead role.

CHARACTERS

SARAH, Negro
DUCHESS OF HAPSBURG, One of Herselves
QUEEN VICTORIA, One of Herselves
PATRICE LUMUMBA, One of Herselves
JESUS, One of Herselves
THE MOTHER
LANDLADY, Funnylady
RAYMOND, Funnyman

BEGINNING: *Before the closed curtain a woman dressed in a white nightgown walks across the stage carrying before her a bald head. She moves as one in a trance and is mumbling something inaudible to herself. She appears faceless, wearing a yellow whitish mask over her face, with no apparent eyes. Her hair is wild, straight and black and falls to her waist. As she moves, holding her hands before her, she gives the effect of one in a dream. She crosses the stage from right to left. Before she has barely vanished, the curtain opens. It is a white satin curtain of a cheap material and a ghastly white, a material that brings to mind the interior of a cheap casket; parts of it are frayed and it looks as if it has been gnawed by rats.*

THE SCENE: *Two women are sitting in what appears to be a queen's chamber. It is set in the middle of the stage in a strong white light, while the rest of the stage is in strong unnatural blackness. The quality of the white light is unreal and ugly. The monumental bed resembling an ebony tomb, a low dark chandelier with candles and wine-colored walls. Flying about are great black ravens. Queen Victoria is standing before her bed, holding a small mirror in her hand. On the white pillow of her bed is a dark indistinguishable object. The Duchess of Hapsburg is standing at the foot of her bed. Her back is to us as is the Queen's. Throughout the entire scene they do not move. Both women are dressed in royal gowns of white, a*

white similar to the white of the curtain, the material cheap satin. Their head-pieces are white and of a net that falls over their faces. From beneath both their headpieces springs a headful of wild kinky hair. Although in this scene we do not see their faces, they look exactly alike and will wear masks or be made up to appear a whitish yellow. It is an alabaster face, the skin drawn tightly over the high cheekbones, great dark eyes that seem gouged out of the head, a high forehead, a full red mouth and a head of frizzy hair. If the characters do not wear a mask, the face must be highly powdered and possess a hard expressionless quality and a stillness as in the fact of death.

We hear a knocking.

VICTORIA (*listening to the knocking*). It is my father. He is arriving again for the night.

The DUCHESS *makes no reply.*

He comes through the jungle to find me. He never tires of his journey.

DUCHESS. How dare he enter the castle, he who is the darkest of them all, the darkest one. My mother looked like a white woman, hair as straight as any white woman's. And at least I am yellow, but he is black, the blackest one of them all. I hoped he was dead. Yet he still comes through the jungle to find me.

The knocking is louder.

VICTORIA. He never tires of the journey, does he, Duchess?

Looking at herself in the mirror.

DUCHESS. How dare him enter the castle of Queen Victoria Regina, Monarch of England. It is because of him that my mother died. The wild black beast put his hands on her. She died.

VICTORIA. Why does he keep returning? He keeps returning forever, coming back ever and keeps coming back forever. He is my father.

DUCHESS. He is a black Negro.

VICTORIA. He is my father. I am tied to the black Negro. He came when I was a child

in the south, before I was born he haunted my conception, diseased my birth.

DUCHESS. Killed my mother.

VICTORIA. My mother was the light. She was the lightest one. She looked like a white woman.

DUCHESS. We are tied to him unless, of course, he should die.

VICTORIA. But he is dead.

DUCHESS. And he keeps returning.

The knocking is louder, blackout. Onto the stage from the left comes the figure in the white nightgown carrying the bald head. This time we hear her speak.

MOTHER. Black man, black man, I never should have let a black man put his hands on me. The wild black beast raped me and now my skull is shining.

She disappears to the right. Now the light is focused on a single white square wall that is to the left of the stage that is suspended and stands alone, of about five feet in dimension and width. It stands with the narrow part facing the audience. A character steps through. She is a faceless dark character with a hangman's rope about her neck and red blood on the part that would be her face. She is the Negro. On first glance she might be a young person but at a closer look the impression of an ancient character is given. The most noticeable aspect of her looks is her wild kinky hair, part of which is missing. It is a ragged head with a patch of hair missing from the crown which the Negro carries in her hand. She is dressed in black. She steps slowly through the wall, stands still before it and begins her monologue.

NEGRO. Part of the time I live with Raymond, part of the time with God, Prince Charlies and Albert Saxe Coburg. I live in my room. It is a small room on the top floor of a brownstone in the West Nineties in New York, a room filled with my dark old volumes, a narrow bed and on the wall old photographs, castles and monarchs of England. It is also Victoria's chamber, Queen Victoria Regina's. Partly because it is consumed by a gigantic plaster statue of Queen Victoria, who is my idol, and

partly for other reasons; three steps that I contrived out of boards lead to the statue which I have placed opposite the door as I enter the room. It is a sitting figure, a replica of one in London, and a thing of astonishing whiteness. I found it in a dusty shop on Morningside Heights. Raymond says it is a thing of terror, possessing the quality of nightmares, suggesting large and probable deaths. And of course he is right. When I am the Duchess of Hapsburg, I sit opposite Victoria in my headpiece and we talk. The other times I wear the dress of a student, dark clothes and dark stockings. Victoria always wants me to tell her of whiteness. She wants me to tell her of a royal world where everything and everyone is white and there are no unfortunate black ones. For as we of royal blood know, black is evil and has been from the beginning. Even before my mother's hair started to fall out. Before she was raped by a wild black beast. Black was evil.

When I am not the Duchess of Hapsburg I am myself. As for myself, I long to become even a more pallid Negro than I am now, pallid like Negroes on the covers of American Negro magazines; soulless, educated and irreligious. I want to possess no moral value, particularly value as to my being. I want not to be. I ask nothing except anonymity.

I am an English major, as my mother was when she went to school in Atlanta. My father majored in social work. I am graduated from a city college and have occasional work in libraries, but mostly spend my days preoccupied with the placement and geometric position of words on paper. I write poetry, filling white page after white page with imitations of Edith Sitwell. It is my dream to live in rooms with European antiques and my Queen Victoria, photographs of Roman ruins, walls of books, a piano, oriental carpets, and to eat my meals on a white glass table. I will visit my friends' apartments which will contain books, photographs of Roman ruins, pianos and oriental carpets. My friends will be white. I need them as an embankment to keep me from reflecting too much upon the fact that I am a Negro. For, like all educated Negroes—out of life

and death essential—I find it necessary to maintain a stark fortress against recognition of myself. My white friends like myself will be shrewd, intellectual and anxious for death. Anyone's death. I will mistrust them, as I do myself. But if I had not wavered in my opinion of myself then my hair would never have fallen out. And if my hair hadn't fallen out, I wouldn't have bludgeoned my father's head with an ebony mask.

In appearance I am good-looking in a boring way; no glaring Negroid features, medium nose, medium mouth and pale yellow skin. My one defect is that I have a head of frizzy hair, unmistakably Negro kinky hair; and it is indisguisable. I would like to lie and say I love Raymond. But I do not. He is a poet and is Jewish. He is very interested in Negroes.

The Negro stands by the wall and throughout her following speech, the following characters come through the wall, disappearing off into the varying directions in the darkened night of the stage — DUCHESS, QUEEN VICTORIA, JESUS, PATRICE LUMUMBA. JESUS *is a hunchback, yellow-skinned dwarf, dressed in white rags and sandals.* PATRICE LUMUMBA *is a black man. His head appears to be split in two with blood and tissue in eyes. He carries an ebony mask.*

The characters are myself: the Duchess of Hapsburg, Queen Victoria Regina, Jesus, Patrice Lumumba. The rooms are my rooms; a Hapsburg chamber, a chamber in a Victorian castle, the hotel where I killed my father, the jungle. These are the places myselves exist in. I know no places. That is I cannot believe in places. To believe in places is to know hope and to know the emotion of hope is to know beauty. It links us across a horizon and connects us to the world. I find there are no places, only my funnyhouse. Streets are rooms, cities are rooms, eternal rooms. I try to create a space for myself in cities. New York, the midwest, a southern town but it becomes a lie. I try to give myselves a logical relationship but that too is a lie. For relationships was one of my last religions. I clung

loyally to the lie of relationships, again and again seeking to establish a connection between my characters. Jesus is Victoria's son. Mother loved my father before her hair fell out. A loving relationship exists between myself and Jesus but they are lies. You will assume I am trifling with you, teasing your intellect, dealing in subtleties, denying connection then suddenly at a point reveal a startling heartbreaking connection. You are wrong. For the days are past when there are places and characters with connections with themes as in stories you pick up on the shelves of public libraries.

Too, there is no theme. No statements. I might borrow a statement, struggle to fabricate a theme, borrow one from my contemporaries, renew one from the master, hawkishly scan other stories searching for statements, consider the theme then deceive myself that I held such a statement within me, refusing to accept the fact that a statement has to come from an ordered force. I might try to join horizontal elements such as dots on a horizontal line, or create a centrifugal force, or create causes and effects so that they would equal a quantity but it would be a lie. For the statement is the characters and the characters are myself.

> *Blackout—then to the right front of the stage comes the white light. It goes to a suspended stairway. At the foot of it stands the* LANDLADY. *She is a tall, thin woman dressed in a black hat with red and appears to be talking to someone in a suggested open doorway in a corridor of a rooming house. She laughs like a mad character in a funnyhouse throughout her speech.*

LANDLADY (*looking up the stairway*). Ever since her father hung himself in a Harlem hotel when Patrice Lumumba was murdered, she hides in her room. Each night she repeats; he keeps returning. How dare he enter the castle walls, he who is the darkest of them all, the darkest one. My mother looked like a white woman, hair as straight as any white woman's. And I am yellow but he, he is black, the blackest one of them all. I hoped he was dead. Yet still he comes through the jungle.

I tell her: Sarah, honey, the man hung himself. It's not your blame. But, no, she stares at me: No, Mrs. Conrad, he did not hang himself, that is only the way they understand it, they do, but the truth is that I bludgeoned his head with an ebony skull that he carries about with him. Wherever he goes, he carries out black masks and heads.

She's suffering so till her hair has fallen out. But then she did always hide herself in that room with the walls of books and her statues. I always did know she thought she was somebody else, a Queen or something, somebody else.

> *Blackout.* FUNNYMAN'S *place. The next scene is enacted with the* DUCHESS *and* RAYMOND. RAYMOND'S *place is suggested as being above the* NEGRO'S *room, and is etched in with a prop of blinds and a bed ... behind the blinds are mirrors and when the blinds are opened and closed by* RAYMOND, *this is revealed.* RAYMOND *turns out to be the* FUNNYMAN *of the funnyhouse. He is tall, white and ghostly thin and dressed in a black shirt and black trousers in attire suggesting an artist. Throughout his dialogue he laughs. The* DUCHESS *is partially disrobed and it is implied from their attitudes of physical intimacy—he is standing and she is sitting before him clinging to his leg. During the scene,* RAYMOND *keeps opening and closing the blinds. His face has black sores on it and he is wearing a black hat. Throughout the scene he strikes her as in affection when he speaks to her.*

DUCHESS (*carrying a red paper bag*). My father is arriving, and what am I to do?

> RAYMOND *walks about the place opening the blinds and laughing.*

FUNNYMAN. He is arriving from Africa, is he not?

DUCHESS. Yes, yes, he is arriving from Africa.

FUNNYMAN. I always knew your father was African.

DUCHESS. He is an African who lives in the jungle. He is an African who has always lived in the jungle. Yes, he is a nigger who is an African, who is a missionary teacher

and is now dedicating his life to the erection of a Christian mission in the middle of the jungle. He is a black man.

FUNNYMAN. He is a black man who shot himself when they murdered Patrice Lumumba.

DUCHESS (*goes on wildly*). Yes, my father is a black man who went to Africa years ago as a missionary teacher, got mixed up in politics, was reviled and is now devoting his foolish life to the erection of a Christian mission in the middle of the jungle in one of those newly freed countries. Hide me.

> *Clinging to his knees.*

Hide me here so the nigger will not find me.

FUNNYMAN (*laughing*). Your father is in the jungle dedicating his life to the erection of a Christian mission.

DUCHESS. Hide me here so the jungle will not find me. Hide me.

FUNNYMAN. Isn't it cruel of you?

DUCHESS. Hide me from the jungle.

FUNNYMAN. Isn't it cruel?

DUCHESS. No, no.

FUNNYMAN. Isn't it cruel of you?

DUCHESS. No.

> *She screams and opens her red paper bag and draws from it her fallen hair. It is a great mass of dark wild. She holds it up to him. He appears not to understand. He stares at it.*

It is my hair.

> *He continues to stare at her.*

When I awakened this morning it had fallen out, not all of it but a mass from the crown of my head that lay on the center of my pillow. I rose and in the greyish winter morning light of my room I stood staring at my hair, dazed by my sleeplessness, still shaken by nightmares of my mother. Was it true, yes, it was my hair. In the mirror I saw that, although my hair remained on both sides, clearly on the crown and at my temples my scalp was bare.

> *She removes her black crown and shows him the top of her head.*

RAYMOND (FUNNYMAN) (*staring at her*). Why would your hair fall out? Is it because

you are cruel? How could a black father haunt you so?

DUCHESS. He haunted my very conception. He was a black wild beast who raped my mother.

RAYMOND (FUNNYMAN). He is a black Negro.

> *Laughing.*

DUCHESS. Ever since I can remember he's been a nigger pose of agony. He is the wilderness. He speaks niggerly, grovelling about wanting to touch me with his black hand.

FUNNYMAN. How tormented and cruel you are.

DUCHESS (*as if not comprehending*). Yes, yes, the man's dark, very dark skinned. He is the darkest, my father is the darkest, my mother is the lightest. I am between. But my father is the darkest. My father is a nigger who drives me to misery. Any time spent with him evolves itself into suffering. He is a black man and the wilderness.

FUNNYMAN. How tormented and cruel you are.

DUCHESS. He is a nigger.

FUNNYMAN. And your mother, where is she?

DUCHESS. She is in the asylum. In the asylum bald. Her father was a white man. And she is the asylum.

> *He takes her in his arms. She responds wildly.*

> *Blackout. Knocking is heard, it continues, then somewhere near the center of the stage a figure appears in the darkness, a large dark faceless man carrying a mask in his hand.*

HE SPEAKS. It begins with the disaster of my hair. I awaken. My hair has fallen out, not all of it, but a mass from the crown of my head that lies on the center of my white pillow. I arise and in the greyish winter morning light of my room I stand staring at my hair, dazed by sleeplessness, still shaken by nightmares of my mother. Is it true? Yes. It is my hair. In the mirror I see that although my hair remains on both sides, clearly on the crown and at my temples my scalp is bare. And in my sleep I had been visited by my bald crazy

mother who comes to me crying, calling me to her bedside. She lies on the bed watching the strands of her own hair fall out. Her hair fell out after she married and she spent her days lying on the bed watching the strands fall from her scalp, covering the bedspread until she was bald and admitted to the hospital. Black man, black man, my mother says I never should have let a black man put his hands on me. She comes to me, her bald skull shining. Black diseases, Sarah, she says. Black diseases. I run. She follows me, her bald skull shining. That is the beginning.

Several women with white nightgowns on, waistlength black hair, all identical, emerge from the sides of the stage and run into the darkness, toward him shouting—black man, black man. They are carrying bald heads. Blackout.

Queen's Chamber: Her hair is in a small pile on the bed and in a small pile on the floor, several other small piles of hair are scattered about her and her white gown is covered with fallen out hair.

QUEEN VICTORIA *acts out the following scene: She awakens (in pantomime) and discovers her hair has fallen. It is on her pillow. She arises and stands at the side of the bed with her back toward us staring at her hair. She opens the red paper bag that she is carrying and takes out her hair, attempting to place it back on her head (for unlike Victoria, she does not wear her headpiece now). Suddenly the women in white gowns come carrying their skulls before them screaming.*

The unidentified MAN *returns out of the darkness and speaks. He carries the mask.*

MAN. I am a nigger of two generations. I am Patrice Lumumba.

PATRICE LUMUMBA. I am a nigger of two generations. I am the black shadow that haunted my mother's conception. I belong to the generation born at the turn of the century and the generation born before the depression. At present I reside in New York City in a brownstone in the West Nineties. I am an English major at a city college. My nigger father majored in so-

cial work, so did my mother. I am a student and have occasional work in libraries. But mostly I spend my vile days preoccupied with the placement and geometric position of words on paper. I write poetry filling white page after white page with imitations of Sitwell. It is my vile dream to live in rooms with European antiques and my statues of Queen Victoria, photographs of Roman ruins, pianos and oriental carpets. My friends will be white. I need them as an embankment to keep me from reflecting too much upon the fact that I am Patrice Lumumba who haunted my mother's conception. They are necessary for me to maintain recognition against myself. My white friends, like myself, will be shrewd intellectuals and anxious for death. Anyone's death. I will despise them as I do myself. For if I did not despise myself then my hair would not have fallen and if my hair had not fallen then I would not have bludgeoned my father's face with the ebony mask.

Then another wall is dropped, larger than the first one was. This one is near the front of the stage facing thus.
Throughout the following monologue the characters DUCHESS, VICTORIA *and* JESUS *go back and forth. As they go in their backs are to us but the* NEGRO *faces us speaking.*

NEGRO. I always dreamed of a day when my mother would smile at me. My father— his mother wanted him to be Christ. From the beginning in the lamp of their dark room she said—I want you to be Jesus, to walk in Genesis and save the race. You must return to Africa, find revelation in the midst of golden savannas, nim and white frankopenny trees, white stallions roaming under a blue sky, you must walk with a white dove and heal the race, heal the misery, take us off the cross . . . at dawn he watched her rise, kill a hen for him to eat at breakfast, then go to work, down at the big house till dusk, till she died.

His father told him the race was no damn good. He hated his father and adores his mother. His mother didn't want him to marry my mother and sent a dead chicken to the wedding. I *don't* want you marrying

that child, she wrote, she's not good enough for you, I want you to go to Africa. When they first married they lived in New York.

Then they went to Africa where my mother fell out of love with my father. She didn't want him to save the black race and spent her days combing her hair. She would not let him touch her in their wedding bed and called him black. He is black of skin with dark eyes and a great dark square brow. Then in Africa he started to drink and came home drunk one night and raped my mother. The child from the union is me. I clung to my mother. Long after she went to the asylum I wove long dreams of her beauty, her straight hair and fair skin and gray eyes, so identical to mine. How it anguished him. I turned from him, nailing him to the cross, he said, dragging him through grass and nailing him on a cross until he bled. He pleaded with me to help him find Genesis, search for Genesis in the minds of golden savannas, nim and white frankopenny trees and white stallions roaming under a blue sky, help him search for the white dove; he wanted the black man to make a pure statement, he wanted the black man to rise from colonialism. But I sat in the room with my mother, sat by her bedside and helped her comb her straight black hair and wove long dreams of her beauty. She had long since begun to curse the place and spoke of herself trapped in blackness. She preferred the company of night owls. Only at night did she rise, walking in the garden among the trees with the owls. When I spoke to her she saw I was a black man's child and she preferred speaking to owls. Nights my father came from his school in the village struggling to embrace me. But I fled and hid under my mother's bed while she screamed of remorse. Her hair was falling badly and after a while we had to return to this country.

He tried to hang himself once. After my mother went to the asylum he had hallucinations, his mother threw a dead chicken at him, his father laughed and said the race was no damn good, my mother appeared in her nightgown screaming she had trapped herself in blackness. No white doves flew. He had left Africa and was again in New York. We lived in Harlem and no white doves flew. Sarah, Sarah, he would say to me, the soldiers are coming and a cross they are placing high on a tree and are dragging me through the grass and nailing me upon the cross. My blood is gushing. I wanted to live in Genesis in the midst of golden savannas, nim and white frankopenny trees and white stallions roaming under a blue sky. I wanted to walk with a white dove. I wanted to be a Christian. Now I am Judas, I betrayed my mother. I sent your mother to the asylum. I created a yellow child who hates me. And he tried to hang himself in a Harlem hotel.

Blackout. A bald head is dropped on a string. We hear laughing.

DUCHESS'S *place: The next scene is done in the Duchess of Hapsburg's place which is a chandelier ballroom with snow falling, a black and white marble floor, a bench decorated with white flowers, all of this can be made of obviously fake materials as they would be in a funnyhouse. The* DUCHESS *is wearing a white dress and as in the previous scene a white headpiece with her kinky hair springing out from under it. In the scene are the* DUCHESS *and* JESUS. JESUS *enters the room which is at first dark, then suddenly brilliant, he starts to cry out at the* DUCHESS *who is seated on a bench under the chandelier, and pulls his hair from the red paper bag holding it up for the* DUCHESS *to see.*

JESUS. My hair!

The DUCHESS *does not speak,* JESUS *again screams.*

My hair.

Holding the hair up, waiting for a reaction from the DUCHESS.

DUCHESS (*as if oblivious*). I have something I must show you.

She goes quickly to shutters and darkens the room, returning standing before JESUS. *She then slowly removes her headpiece and from under it takes a mass of her hair.*

When I awakened I found it fallen out, not all of it but a mass that lay on my white pillow. I could see, although my hair hung

down at the sides, clearly on my white scalp it was missing.

Her baldness is identical to JESUS'S.

A blackout. Then the light comes back up. They are both sitting on the bench examining each other's hair, running it through their fingers, then slowly the DUCHESS *disappears behind the shutters and returns with a long red comb. She sits on the bench next to* JESUS *and starts to comb her remaining hair over her baldness. (This is done slowly.)* JESUS *then takes the comb and proceeds to do the same to the* DUCHESS *of* HAPS-BURG'S *hair. After they finish they place the* DUCHESS'S *headpiece back on and we can see the strands of their hair falling to the floor.* JESUS *then lies down across the bench while the* DUCHESS *walks back and forth, the knocking does not cease.*

They speak in unison as the DUCHESS *walks and* JESUS *lies on the bench in the falling snow, staring at the ceiling.*

DUCHESS and JESUS (*their hair is falling more now, they are both hideous*). My father isn't going to let us alone.

Knocking.

Our father isn't going to let us alone, our father is the darkest of us all, my mother was the fairest, I am in between, but my father is the darkest of them all. He is a black man. Our father is the darkest of them all. He is a black man. My father is a dead man.

Then they suddenly look up at each other and scream, the lights go to their heads and we see that they are totally bald.

There is a knocking. Lights go to the stairs and the LANDLADY.

LANDLADY. He wrote to her saying he loved her and asked for forgiveness. He begged her to take him off the cross. (He had dreamed she would.) Stop them for tormenting him, the one with the chicken and his cursing father. Her mother's hair fell out, the races' hair fell out because he left Africa, he said. He had tried to save them. She must embrace him. He said his existence depended on her embrace. He wrote her from Africa where he is creating his

Christian center in the jungle and that is why he came here. I know that he wanted her to return there with him and not desert the race. He came to see her once before he tried to hang himself, appearing in the corridor of my apartment. I had let him in. I found him sitting on a bench in the hallway. He put out his hand to her, tried to take her in his arms, crying out—Forgiveness, Sarah, Is it that you will never forgive me for being black. I know you were a child of torment. But forgiveness. That was before his breakdown. Then, he wrote her and repeated that his mother hoped he would be Christ but he failed. He had married his mother because he could not resist the light. Yet, his mother from the beginning in the kerosene lamp of their dark rooms in Georgia said—I want you to be Jesus, to walk in Genesis and save the race, return to Africa, find revelation in the black. He went away.

But Easter morning, she got to feeling badly and went into Harlem to see him; the streets were filled with vendors selling lilies. He had checked out of that hotel. When she arrived back at my brownstone he was there, dressed badly, rather drunk. I had let him in again. He sat on a bench in the dark hallway, put out his hand to her, trying to take her in his arms, crying out—Forgiveness, Sarah. Forgiveness for my being black, Sarah. I know you are a child of torment. I know on dark winter afternoons you sat alone, weaving stories of your mother's beauty. But, Sarah, answer me, don't turn away, Sarah. Forgive my blackness. She would not answer. He put out his hand to her. She ran past him on the stairs, left him there with his hands out to me, repeating his past, saying his mother hoped he would be Christ. From the beginning in the kerosene lamp of their dark room, she said—Wally, I want you to be Jesus, to walk in Genesis and save the race. You must return to Africa, Wally, find revelation in the midst of golden savannas, nim and white frankopenny trees and white stallions roaming under a blue sky. Wally, you must find the white dove and heal the pain of the race, heal the misery of the black man, Wally, take us off the cross, Wally. In the kerosene light

she stared at him anguished from her old Negro face . . . but she ran past him leaving him. And now he is dead, she says, now he is dead. He left Africa and now Patrice Lumumba is dead.

The next scene is enacted back in the DUCHESS *of* HAPSBURG'S *place.* JESUS *is still in the* DUCHESS'S *chamber, apparently he has fallen asleep and we see him awakening with the* DUCHESS *by his side, and then sitting as in a trance. He rises terrified and speaks.*

JESUS (*He is awakening*). Through my apocalypses and my raging sermons I have tried so to escape him, through God Almighty I have tried to escape being black.

He then appears to rouse himself from his thoughts and calls.

Duchess, Duchess.

He looks about for her, there is no answer. He gets up slowly, walks back into the darkness and there we see that she is hanging on the chandelier, her bald head suddenly drops to the floor and she falls upon JESUS. *He screams.*

I am going to Africa and kill this black man named Patrice Lumumba. Why? Because all my life I believed my Holy Father to be God, but now I know that my father is a black man. I have no fear for whatever I do I will do in the name of God, I will do in the name of Albert Saxe Godburg, in the name of Victoria, Queen Victoria Regina, the monarch of England, I will.

Blackout.

Next scene. In the jungle, red run, flying things, wild black grass. The effect of the jungle is that it, unlike the other scenes, is over the entire scene. In time this is the longest scene in the play and is played the slowest as the slow, almost standstill, stages of a dream. By lighting the desired effect would be—suddenly the jungle has overgrown the chambers and all the other places with a violence and a dark brightness, a grim yellowness.

JESUS *is the first to appear in the center of the jungle darkness. Unlike in previous scenes, he has a nimbus above his head. As they each successively appear, they all too have nimbuses atop their heads in a manner to suggest that they are saviours.*

JESUS. I always believed my father to be God.

Suddenly they all appear in various parts of the jungle. PATRICE LUMUMBA, *the* DUCHESS, VICTORIA, *wandering about speaking at once. Their speeches are mixed and repeated by one another.*

He never tires of the journey, he who is the darkest one, the darkest one of them all. My mother looked like a white woman, hair as straight as any white woman's. I am yellow but he is black, the darkest one of us all. How I hoped he was dead, yet he never tired of the journey. It was because of him that my mother died because she let a black man put his hands on her. Why does he keep returning? He keeps returning forever, keeps returning and returning and he is my father. He is a black Negro. They told me my father was God but my father is black. He is my father. I am tied to a black Negro. He returned when I lived in the south back in the twenties, when I was a child, he returned. Before I was born at the turn of the century, he haunted my conception, diseased my birth . . . killed my mother. He killed the light. My mother was the lightest one. I am bound to him unless, of course, he should die.

But he is dead.

And he keeps returning. Then he is not dead.

Then he is not dead.

Yes, he is dead, but dead he comes knocking at my door.

This is repeated several times, finally reaching a loud pitch and then all rushing about the grass. They stop and stand perfectly still. All speaking tensely at various times in a chant.

I see him. The black ugly thing is sitting in his hallway, surrounded by his ebony masks, surrounded by the blackness of himself. My mother comes into the room. He is there with his hand out to me, groveling, saying—Forgiveness, Sarah, is it that you will never forgive me for being black.

Forgiveness, Sarah. I know you are a nigger of torment.

Why? Christ would not rape anyone.

You will never forgive me for being black.

Wild beast. Why did you rape my mother?

Black beast, Christ would not rape anyone.

He is in grief from that black anguished face of his. Then at once the room will grow bright and my mother will come toward me smiling while I stand before his face and bludgeon him with an ebony head.

Forgiveness, Sarah, I know you are a nigger of torment.

SILENCE—VICTORY: *Then they suddenly begin to laugh and shout as though they are in. They continue for some minutes running about laughing and shouting.*

Blackout.

Another wall drops. There is a white plaster of QUEEN VICTORIA *which represents the* NEGRO'S *room in the brownstone, the room appears near the staircases highly lit and small. The main prop is the statue but a bed could be suggested. The figure of* VICTORIA *is a sitting figure, one of astonishing repulsive whiteness, possessing the quality of nightmares and terror. Sarah's room could be further suggested by dusty volumes of books and old yellowed walls. The* NEGRO SARAH *is standing perfectly still, we hear the knocking, the lights come on quickly, her father's black figures with bludgeoned hands rush upon her, the lights black and we see her hanging in the room.*

Lights come on the laughing LANDLADY. *At the same time remain on the hanging figure of the* NEGRO.

LANDLADY. The poor bitch has hung herself.
FUNNYMAN RAYMOND *appears from his room at the commotion.*

LANDLADY. The poor bitch has hung herself.

RAYMOND (*observing her hanging figure*). She was a funny little liar.

LANDLADY (*informing him*). Her father hung himself in a Harlem hotel when Patrice Lumumba died.

RAYMOND. She was a funny little liar.

LANDLADY. Her father hung himself in a Harlem hotel when Patrice Lumumba died.

RAYMOND. Her father never hung himself in a Harlem hotel when Patrice Lumumba was murdered.

I know the man. He is a doctor, married to a white whore. He lives in the city in a room with European antiques, photographs of Roman ruins, walls of books and oriental carpets. Her father is a nigger who eats his meals on a white glass table.

CURTAIN

Biographies

ABDUL, RAOUL ("The Negro Playwright on Broadway"), received his early training in the theatre at the Cleveland Playhouse and Karamu Theatre. He is a graduate of the Vienna (Austria) Academy of Music and Dramatic Arts, and has served as drama critic for the *Cleveland Call Post,* the *New York Age* and the *Associated Negro Press.*

ANDERSON, GARLAND ("How I Became a Playwright"), is the author of the first full-length drama by a Negro to be produced on Broadway. He wrote the play *Appearances* while a bellhop in a San Francisco hotel; this play ran for 23 performances on Broadway and subsequently had two revivals in New York and a production in London.

BALDWIN, JAMES ("James Baldwin on the Negro Actor"), is the author of *The Fire Next Time* and *Another Country,* and is perhaps the most successful Negro writer to date.

BONTEMPS, ARNA ("Karamu"), is a former librarian of Fisk University and is a prolific author. He is now public relations director at Fisk, from which he has taken a leave of absence to be a guest professor at the University of Chicago for the 1966–67 academic year.

BRADLEY, GERALD ("Goodbye, Mister Bones"), is a staff writer for publications of the Gulf Oil Corporation. He worked as a reporter, copy editor and theatrical press agent after receiving a Master of Fine Arts degree in drama at the Carnegie Institute of Technology, where he both wrote plays and acted in them.

BROWN, STERLING A. ("The Federal Theatre" and "The Negro Actor Attempts Legitimate"), is a professor of English at Howard University. He is the author of numerous books and articles on the Negro in literature and on the stage. He is co-editor of *Negro Caravan.*

BURG, ROBERT ("Young Actor on the Way Up"), is a young New York free-lance writer.

CHILDRESS, ALICE ("A Woman Playwright Speaks Her Mind"), is primarily a playwright (*Trouble in Mind; Just a Little Simple*), but began her career as an actress. She has won a number of fellowships and awards for her plays.

CONROY, JACK ("Karamu"), is an editor of the *New Standard Encyclopedia* and is also a literary critic and folklorist. He is co-author with Arna Bontemps of *Any Place but Here.* His first novel, *The Disinherited,* has just been reissued.

COOK, WILL MARION ("Clorindy, the Origin of the Cakewalk"), though author of many popular songs and musicals, was also a serious composer and musician, having attended Oberlin College and studied the violin under Joachim in Berlin. He was also a pupil of Anton Dvorak.

CUNEY-HARE, MAUD ("Musical Comedy"), was a pianist, lecturer and writer. She graduated from the New England Conservatory of Music and was one of the first persons to write extensively on the history of the Negro in music. Her best-known work is *Negro Musicians and Their Music.*

DAVIS, OSSIE ("Purlie Told Me!"), is a distinguished actor and author, having written for both Broadway and Off-Broadway.

DEE, RUBY ("The Tattered Queens"), is one of the fiinest actresses in America today. Miss Dee has played a variety of roles from classical to avant-garde, winning acclaim every time. She is the wife of Ossie Davis.

DENT, TOM ("The Free Southern Theater"), a native of New Orleans, is a free-lance writer and one of the founders of *Umbra.* He is also a guiding force behind the Free Southern Theater.

DUBERMAN, MARTIN ("History and Theater"), is author of *In White America.* Mr. Duberman is a distinguished critic who contributes regularly to the leading literary magazines. He is an associate professor of English at Princeton University.

FAUSET, JESSIE ("The Gift of Laughter"), was born in Philadelphia and educated at Cornell University and the Sorbonne. She taught French and Latin at Dunbar High School in Washington, D.C., and for many years was literary critic of *Crisis* magazine.

GREGORY, MONTGOMERY ("The Drama of Negro Life"), a Harvard graduate and a professor of English at Howard University, was organizer and director of the Howard Players from 1919 to 1924.

HUGHES, LANGSTON ("The Need for an Afro-American Theatre" and "That Boy LeRoi"), the dean of Negro writers, has published some forty books, including two autobiographies, *The Big Sea* and *I Wonder as I Wander.*

JOHNSON, HALL ("Porgy and Bess—A Folk Opera?"), is one of the nation's outstanding choir directors, and an arranger of spirituals. He is the organizer of the Hall Johnson Choir, which provided the music for both the stage and movie versions of *The Green Pastures.*

KENNEDY, ADRIENNE (*Funnyhouse of a Negro*), born in Pittsburgh in 1931, grew up in Cleveland, Ohio. She attended Ohio State University. Since she was 20, she has written constantly. She joined Edward Albee's workshop in 1962, and became a member of Actor's Studio. Her play *Funnyhouse of a Negro* is being made into a film in Britain.

KING, WOODIE, JR. ("Problems Facing Negro Actors"), is a playwright, actor and director. He is one of the founders of the Concept-East Theatre. In addition to his theatrical chores, he is director of the Cultural Arts Program of Mobilization for Youth in New York.

LOCKE, ALAIN ("The Negro and the American Stage"), graduated from Harvard and was a Rhodes Scholar. A professor of philosophy at Howard University, he was also the author of many articles on the theatre and on the Negro in literature.

MITCHELL, LOFTEN ("The Negro Theatre and the Harlem Community"), is a playwright who is best known for his much acclaimed *Land Beyond the River.*

MORRISON, ALLAN ("One Hundred Years of Negro Entertainment"), since 1949 has been New York editor of *Ebony* magazine and is also editorial bureau chief for the Johnson Publishing Company.

MOSS, CARLTON ("The Negro in American Films"), a writer of documentary films, has authored documentaries on the lives of Frederick Douglass and George Washington Carver.

NOBLE, PETER ("The Coming of the Sound Film"), an Englishman, is author of *The Negro in Films.* He has written and lectured widely on the problem of racial intolerance. He is also author of *The Cinema and the Negro (1905–1948).*

O'NEAL, FREDERICK ("Problems and Prospects"), is the president of Actors Equity and a distinguished actor. He is a founder of the Negro Theatre (1940).

RICHARDSON, WILLIS (*The Chip Woman's Fortune*), was the first Negro to have a play produced on Broadway. A native of North Carolina, he was educated in the public schools of Washington, D.C., where he worked in government service for many years. He is now retired.

ROGERS, RAY ("The Negro Actor"), is director of public relations for HARYOU (Harlem Youth Opportunities Unlimited) and a frequent contributor to *Freedomways.*

TALBOT, WILLIAM ("Every Negro in His Place"), is editor of the New York, Hollywood and Toronto offices of Samuel French, Inc. He has taught playwriting at Columbia University and serves as treasurer of the New York Drama Desk. He lectures widely on the theatre.

TODD, ARTHUR ("One of Our National Treasures"), is an associate editor of *Dance Observer* and the American correspondent for *Dance and Dancers,* London.

TURNER, DARWIN T. ("The Negro Dramatist's Image of the Universe, 1920–1960"), a Phi Beta Kappa graduate of the University of Cincinnati, received his Ph.D. in English from the University of Chicago. He is chairman of the English Department at North Carolina A. and T. College.

WILLIAMS, JIM ("The Need for a Harlem Theatre"), is an actor who has appeared in *Land Beyond the River* and *Othello.* Mr. Williams also writes poetry.

PATTERSON, LINDSAY (Editor of this Anthology), is a native of Louisiana and was educated in Virginia. He began his writing career as a special feature writer for the Army Information Service in Heidelberg, Germany, contributing articles to *Stars and Stripes, Army Times* and German national newspapers. He has been book review editor and feature writer for the Associated Negro Press, and has contributed to such publications as the *Saturday Review.* In 1965, he received a fellowship to the MacDowell Colony, Peterboro, New Hampshire, to continue work on a first novel, *Pierian Spring.*

Bibliography

BLUM, DANIEL. *A Pictorial History of the American Theatre: 100 Years—1860–1960*. Philadelphia, 1960.

BOND, FREDERICK W. *The Negro and the Drama*. Washington, 1940.

BONTEMPS, ARNA, and CONROY, JACK. *Any Place but Here*. New York, 1966.

BUTCHER, MARGARET JUST. *The Negro in American Culture*. New York, 1957.

CLARK, JOHN HENRIK (ed.). *Harlem U.S.A.* New York, 1964.

CUNEY-HARE, MAUD. *Negro Musicians and Their Music*. Washington, 1936.

DUBERMAN, MARTIN B. *In White America*. New York, 1964.

FERGUSSON, FRANCIS. *Idea of a Theatre*. Princeton, N.J., 1949.

FLETCHER, TOM. *100 Years of the Negro in Show Business*. New York, 1954.

GILDER, ROSAMOND (ed.). *Theatre Arts Anthology*. New York, 1950.

GOGET, EDMOND MACADOO. *Revolution in American Drama*. New York, 1947.

GORELIK, MORDECAI. *New Theatres for Old*. New York, 1940.

HASSNER, JOHN. *Human Relations in the Theatre*. New York, 1949.

HOYT, HARLOWE RANDALL. *Town Hall Tonight*. New York, 1955.

HUGHES, GLENN. *A History of the American Theatre, 1700–1950*. New York, 1951.

HUGHES, LANGSTON, and MELTZER, MILTON. *Black Magic: A Pictorial History of the Negro in American Entertainment*. Englewood Cliffs, N.J., 1967.

HUTTON, LAURENCE. *Curiosities of the American Stage*. New York, 1891.

ISAACS, EDITH J. R. *The Negro in the American Theatre*. New York, 1947.

——— (ed.). *Theatre Essays on the Arts of the Theatre*. Boston, 1927.

JEROME, V. J. *The Negro in Hollywood Films*. New York, 1950.

JOHNSON, JAMES WELDON. *Black Manhattan*. New York, 1930.

KENNETT, BART. *Colored Actors' Union Theatrical Guide*. Washington, 1920.

KRUTCH, JOSEPH W. *American Drama since 1918*. New York, 1939.

LEWIS, ALLAN. *American Plays and Playwrights of the Contemporary Theatre*. New York, 1965.

Life of Jim Crow, by Jim Crow. Philadelphia, 1837.

LOCKE, ALAIN (ed.). *The New Negro: An Interpretation*. New York, 1925.

MANTLE, BURNS (ed.). *The Best Plays of 1940–41*. New York, 1941.

MITCHELL, LOFTEN. *Black Drama: The Story of the American Negro in the Theatre*. New York, 1967.

MOODY, RICHARD. *America Takes the Stage, 1750–1900*. Bloomington, Ind., 1955.

NOBLE, PETER. *The Negro in Films*. London, 1948.

REYNOLDS, HARRY. *Minstrel Memories: The Story of Burnt Cork Minstrelsy in Great Britain from 1837–1927*. London, 1928.

ROWE, KENNETH THORPE. *A Theater in Your Head*. New York, 1960.

TAUBMAN, HOWARD. *The Making of the American Theatre*. New York, 1967.

The Schomburg Collection of the New York Public Library contains primary source material on the following plays:

Cabin in the Sky; Call Me by My Rightful Name; Carib Song; Carmen Jones; Cindy; Clandestine on the Morning Line; Cool World; Deep Are the Roots; Duchess of Malfi; Dutchman; Emperor Jones; Fast and Furious; Finian's Rainbow; Fly Blackbird; Four Saints in Three Acts; Free and Easy; Funnyhouse of a Negro; Golden Boy; Green Pastures; Haiti; Happy Ending; Harlem; House of Flowers; In Abraham's Bosom; In Splendid Error; In White America; Jamaica; Jericho–Jim Crow; Jolly's Progress; Just a Little Simple; Kwamina; Land Beyond the River; Living Premise; Long Dream; Lost in the

Stars; Macbeth; Mamba's Daughters; Mandingo; Medal for Willie; Member of the Wedding; Memphis Bound; Mikado (Hot and *Swing); Mr. Johnson; Mr. Wonderful; Mrs. Patterson; Moon on a Rainbow Shawl; Mulatto; Nat Turner; Native Son; No Strings; Octoroon; On Strivers' Row; On Whitman Avenue; Othello; Our Lan'; Owl and the Pussycat; Porgy; Purlie Victorious; Raisin in the Sun; Roll, Sweet Chariot; Run, Little Chillun; St. Louis Woman; Set My People Free; Shakespeare in Harlem; Shinbone Alley; Sign in Sidney Brustein's Window; Simply Heavenly; Slave; Slow Dance on the Killing Ground; Sojourner Truth; Sound of Silence; Stevedore; Strange Fruit; Street Scene; Sweet Chariot; Take a Giant Step; Tambourines to Glory; Taste of Honey; They Shall Not Die; Three for Tonight; Tiger, Tiger, Burning Bright; Toilet; Trouble in Mind; Trumpets of the Lord; Turpentine; Uncle Tom's Cabin; Valmouth; Waiting for Godot; Walk in Darkness.*

The New York Public Library Theatre Collection at the Lincoln Center has primary source material on the following plays and personalities:

Abyssinia; Anna Lucasta; Appearances; Big White Fog; Conjure Man Dies; Deep Are the Roots; Green Pastures; Harlem; In Dahomey; Louisiana; Lulu Belle; Meek Mose; Member of the Wedding; Mulatto; Native Son; Octoroons; Porgy; Run, Little Chillun; Shuffle Along; Strange Fruit; Strut Miss Lizzie; Uncle Tom's Cabin.

Cook, Will Marion; Cole, Bob; Connelly, Marc; Hughes, Langston; Kitt, Eartha; Muse, Clarence; Peterson, Louis; Richardson, Willis; Vandamm, Florence; Williams, Bert; Wilson, Frank.

Picture Credits

The author is grateful to the following for their aid in the search for unusual and interesting photographs with which to illustrate the text:

KEY: T: Top; B: Bottom; L: Left; R: Right; C: Center

ABC–TV: 272B; 273T; 273BL

ADLER, HARRY, AGENCY: 272TL

ALEXANDER, WILLARD, INC.: 234BL

AILEY, ALVIN: 225T; 225B

ALDENE: 49

ANDREWS, BERT: 80; 84; 140; 151B; 271T

BROWN, JIM: 110T

CHICAGO HISTORICAL SOCIETY: 8

COLE, BERNARD: 6, 20, 35

COLUMBIA PICTURES: 64TL; 64TR; 64BL; 64BR; 132BR; 189T; 194TL; 194TR; 194B; 195T; 195BL; 195BR; 212T

CONTINENTAL DISTRIBUTING: 243T

CRICKMAY, ANTHONY–London: 224B; 220B

DALMAN, JAN–Amsterdam: 219BR

DOMINIC–Paris: 224TL

EMBASSY PICTURES: 246B

FEHL, FRED: 189BR

FRIEDMAN-ABELES: 132BL; 147BR; 150TL; 150TR; 150CL; 150CR; 150BL; 150BR; 184; 198T; 198B

GOODKIND, LARNEY: 41TR; 189BL; 264BR

GROSSMAN, HENRY: 63BL

HOLMES, MARTHA: 58BL; 157T

HUROK ATTRACTIONS: 214TL

INGRAM, CALVIN J.: 110B

JEFFRY, MISS ALIX: 63TR; 63BR; 208TL; 208TR; 208BR

KIER, HENRY: 162T; 246T

LANDAU COMPANY: 243BL; 243BR

LIBRARY OF CONGRESS: 10; 26TL; 26TR; 41TL; 122

MERCURY ARTISTS: 214TR

METRO-GOLDWYN-MAYER: 240R

MITCHELL, JACK: 219BL

NAACP: 224TR

NATIONAL ARCHIVES RECORD GROUPS: 107B

NBC–TV: 273BR; 274T; 274BL; 274BR; 275TL; 275TR; 275B; 276T; 276BR; 277TR; 277B

NEW YORK CITY BALLET COMPANY: 214BR

NEW YORK COURIER: 79T; 147BL; 152B; 166; 244TL

NEW YORK PUBLIC LIBRARY–SCHOMBURG COLLECTION: 2; 12; 88; 100T; 176

OSTERTAG, BARNA: 58BR

PARAMOUNT PICTURES: 130; 237BR; 245BL

PETERICH, GERDA: 214BL; 222

PRIMUS–BORDE STUDIO: 212B

STEWART, CHARLES: 235B

SWOPE, MARTHA: 139

TWENTIETH CENTURY–FOX: 126; 237T; 238TL; 241BL; 244TR; 264T

UNIVERSAL PICTURES: 234T; 235TL; 235TR; 235BR; 245BR

UNITED ARTISTS: 152T; 162; 238TR; 238B; 239T; 239BR; 240BL; 242T; 242BR

WARNER BROTHERS: 240TL

WILLARD, AVERY: 70T; 70BR; 147TR

WILMER, VALERIE: 164

WPA FEDERAL THEATRE PHOTOS: 100B

YEARWOOD, LLOYD: 206L; 206R

Index

Figures in *italic* type refer to picture pages.